English / Japanese
英語 / 日本語

THE OXFORD
Picture
Dictionary

NORMA SHAPIRO AND JAYME ADELSON-GOLDSTEIN

Translated by Techno-Graphics & Translations, Inc.

Oxford University Press

Oxford University Press
198 Madison Avenue, New York, NY 10016 USA
Great Clarendon Street, Oxford OX2 6DP England

Oxford New York
Athens Auckland Bangkok Bogotá Buenos Aires
Cape Town Chennai Dar es Salaam Delhi
Florence Hong Kong Istanbul Karachi Kolkata
Kuala Lumpur Madrid Melbourne Mexico City
Mumbai Nairobi Paris São Paulo Shanghai
Singapore Taipei Tokyo Toronto Warsaw

And associated companies in
Berlin Ibadan

OXFORD is a trademark of Oxford University Press.

Library of Congress Cataloging-in-Publication Data

Shapiro, Norma.
      The Oxford picture dictionary : English/Japanese
Norma Shapiro and Jayme Adelson-Goldstein; translation
by Techno-Graphics and Translations, Inc.
            p.   cm.
      Includes bibliographical references and index.
      ISBN 0-19-435190-4
      1. Picture dictionaries, Japanese.   2. Picture dictionaries,
English.   3. English language — Dictionaries—Japanese.
      4. Japanese language — Dictionaries—English.
      I. Adelson-Goldstein, Jayme.   II. Title.
PL676.S53   1998   98-10946
495.6'321—dc21

No unauthorized photocopying.

Translation reviewed by Cambridge Resources
Editorial Manager: Susan Lanzano
Senior Editor: Eliza Jensen
Production Editor: Tyrone Prescod
Art Director: Lynn Luchetti
Senior Designer: Susan P. Brorein
Art Buyer: Tracy A. Hammond
Cover Design Production: Brett Sonnenschein
Production Manager: Abram Hall
Production Controller: Georgiann Baran
Production Services by: Techno-Graphics and Translations, Inc.
Cover design by Silver Editions

Printing (last digit): 10 9 8 7 6 5 4

Printed in China

Illustrations by: David Aikins, Doug Archer, Craig Attebery,
Garin Baker, Sally Bensusen, Eliot Bergman, Mark Bischel, Dan
Brown / Artworks NY, Roy Douglas Buchman, George Burgos /
Larry Dodge, Carl Cassler, Mary Chandler, Robert Crawford, Jim
DeLapine, Judy Francis, Graphic Chart and Map Co., Dale
Gustafson, Biruta Akerbergs Hansen, Marcia Hartsock, C.M.I.,
David Hildebrand, The Ivy League of Artists, Inc. / Judy
Degraffenreid, The Ivy League of Artists, Inc. / Tom Powers, The
Ivy League of Artists, Inc. / John Rice, Pam Johnson, Ed
Kurtzman, Narda Lebo, Scott A. MacNeill / MACNEILL &
MACINTOSH, Andy Lendway / Deborah Wolfe Ltd., Jeffrey
Mangiat, Suzanne Mogensen, Mohammad Mansoor, Tom
Newsom, Melodye Benson Rosales, Stacey Schuett, Rob
Schuster, James Seward, Larry Taugher, Bill Thomson, Anna
Veltfort, Nina Wallace, Wendy Wassink-Ackison, Michael
Wepplo, Don Wieland
Thanks to Mike Mikos for his preliminary architectural sketches
of several pieces.

References
Boyer, Paul S., Clifford E. Clark, Jr., Joseph F. Kett, Thomas L.
Purvis, Harvard Sitkoff, Nancy Woloch *The Enduring Vision: A
History of the American People*, Lexington, Massachusetts:
D.C. Heath and Co., 1990.

Grun, Bernard, *The Timetables of History: A Horizontal Linkage
of People and Events,* (based on Werner Stein's Kulturfahrplan)
New York: A Touchstone Book, Simon and Schuster, 1946,
1963, 1975, 1979.

Statistical Abstract of the United States: 1996, 116th Edition,
Washington, DC: US Bureau of the Census, 1996.

The World Book Encyclopedia, Chicago: World Book Inc., a
Scott Fetzer Co., 1988 Edition.

Toff, Nancy, Editor-in-Chief, *The People of North America*
(Series), New York: Chelsea House Publishers, Main Line
Books, 1988.

Trager, James, *The People's Chronology, A Year-by-Year Record
of Human Events from Prehistory to the Present,* New York:
Henry Holt Reference Book, 1992.

Acknowledgments

The publisher and authors would like to thank the following people for reviewing the manuscript and/or participating in focus groups as the book was being developed:

Ana Maria Aguilera, Lubie Alatriste, Ann Albarelli, Margaret Albers, Sherry Allen, Fiona Armstrong, Ted Auerbach, Steve Austen, Jean Barlow, Sally Bates, Sharon Batson, Myra Baum, Mary Beauparlant, Gretchen Bitterlin, Margrajean Bonilla, Mike Bostwick, Shirley Brod, Lihn Brown, Trish Brys-Overeem, Lynn Bundy, Chris Bunn, Carol Carvel, Leslie Crucil, Robert Denheim, Joshua Denk, Kay Devonshire, Thomas Dougherty, Gudrun Draper, Sara Eisen, Lynda Elkins, Ed Ende, Michele Epstein, Beth Fatemi, Andra R. Fawcett, Alice Fiedler, Harriet Fisher, James Fitzgerald, Mary Fitzsimmons, Scott Ford, Barbara Gaines, Elizabeth Garcia Grenados, Maria T. Gerdes, Penny Giacalone, Elliott Glazer, Jill Gluck de la Llata, Javier Gomez, Pura Gonzales, Carole Goodman, Joyce Grabowski, Maggie Grennan, Joanie Griffin, Sally Hansen, Fotini Haritos, Alice Hartley, Fernando Herrera, Ann Hillborn, Mary Hopkins, Lori Howard, Leann Howard, Pamela Howard, Rebecca Hubner, Jan Jarrell, Vicki Johnson, Michele Kagan, Nanette Kafka, Gena Katsaros, Evelyn Kay, Greg Keech, Cliff Ker, Gwen Kerner-Mayer, Marilou Kessler, Patty King, Linda Kiperman, Joyce Klapp, Susan Knutson, Sandy Kobrine, Marinna Kolaitis, Donna Korol, Lorraine Krampe, Karen Kuser, Andrea Lang, Nancy Lebow, Tay Lesley, Gale Lichter, Sandie Linn, Rosario Lorenzano, Louise Louie, Cheryl Lucas, Ronna Magy, Juanita Maltese, Mary Marquardsen, Carmen Marques Rivera, Susan McDowell, Alma McGee, Jerry McLeroy, Kevin McLure, Joan Meier, Patsy Mills, Judy Montague, Vicki Moore, Eneida Morales, Glenn Nadelbach, Elizabeth Neblett, Kathleen Newton, Yvonne Nishio, Afra Nobay, Rosa Elena Ochoa, Jean Owensby, Jim Park, John Perkins, Jane Pers, Laura Peskin, Maria Pick, Percy Pleasant, Selma Porter, Kathy Quinones, Susan Ritter, Martha Robledo, Maureen Rooney, Jean Rose, David Ross, Julietta Ruppert, Lorraine Ruston, Susan Ryan, Frederico Salas, Leslie Salmon, Jim Sandifer, Linda Sasser, Lisa Schreiber, Mary Segovia, Abe Shames, Debra Shaw, Stephanie Shipp, Pat Singh, Mary Sklavos, Donna Stark, Claire Cocoran Stehling, Lynn Sweeden, Joy Tesh, Sue Thompson, Christine Tierney, Laura Topete, Carmen Villanueva, Laura Webber, Renée Weiss, Beth Winningham, Cindy Wislofsky, Judy Wood, Paula Yerman.

A special thanks to Marna Shulberg and the students of the Saticoy Branch of Van Nuys Community Adult School.

We would also like to thank the following individuals and organizations who provided their expertise:

Carl Abato, Alan Goldman, Dr. Larry Falk, Caroll Gray, Henry Haskell, Susan Haskell, Los Angeles Fire Department, Malcolm Loeb, Barbara Lozano, Lorne Dubin, United Farm Workers.

Authors' Acknowledgments

Throughout our careers as English language teachers, we have found inspiration in many places—in the classroom with our remarkable students, at schools, conferences, and workshops with our fellow teachers, and with our colleagues at the ESL Teacher Institute. We are grateful to be part of this international community.

We would like to sincerely thank and acknowledge Eliza Jensen, the project's Senior Editor. Without Eliza, this book would not have been possible. Her indomitable spirit, commitment to clarity, and unwavering advocacy allowed us to realize the book we envisioned.

Creating this dictionary was a collaborative effort and it has been our privilege to work with an exceptionally talented group of individuals who, along with Eliza Jensen, make up the Oxford Picture Dictionary team. We deeply appreciate the contributions of the following people:

Lynn Luchetti, Art Director, whose aesthetic sense and sensibility guided the art direction of this book,

Susan Brorein, Senior Designer, who carefully considered the design of each and every page,

Klaus Jekeli, Production Editor, who pored over both manuscript and art to ensure consistency and accuracy, and

Tracy Hammond, Art Buyer, who skillfully managed thousands of pieces of art and reference material.

We also want to thank Susan Mazer, the talented artist who was by our side for the initial problem-solving and Mary Chandler who also lent her expertise to the project.

We have learned much working with Marjorie Fuchs, Lori Howard, and Renée Weiss, authors of the dictionary's ancillary materials. We thank them for their on-going contributions to the dictionary program.

We must make special mention of Susan Lanzano, Editorial Manager, whose invaluable advice, insights, and queries were an integral part of the writing process.

This book is dedicated to my husband, Neil Reichline, who has encouraged me to take the road less traveled, and to my sons, Eli and Alex, who have allowed me to sit at their baseball games with my yellow notepad. —NS

This book is lovingly dedicated to my husband, Gary and my daughter, Emily Rose, both of whom hugged me tight and let me work into the night. —JAG

A Letter to the Teacher

Welcome to The Oxford Picture Dictionary.

This comprehensive vocabulary resource provides you and your students with over 3,700 words, each defined by engaging art and presented in a meaningful context. *The Oxford Picture Dictionary* enables your students to learn and use English in all aspects of their daily lives. The 140 key topics cover home and family, the workplace, the community, health care, and academic studies. The topics are organized into 12 thematic units that are based on the curriculum of beginning and low-intermediate level English language coursework. The word lists of the dictionary include both single word entries and verb phrases. Many of the prepositions and adjectives are presented in phrases as well, demonstrating the natural use of words in conjunction with one another.

The Oxford Picture Dictionary uses a variety of visual formats, each suited to the topic being represented. Where appropriate, word lists are categorized and pages are divided into sections, allowing you to focus your students' attention on one aspect of a topic at a time.

Within the word lists:

- nouns, adjectives, prepositions, and adverbs are numbered,

- verbs are bolded and identified by letters, and

- targeted prepositions and adjectives within phrases are bolded.

The dictionary includes a variety of exercises and self-access tools that will guide your students toward accurate and fluent use of the new words.

- Exercises at the bottom of the pages provide vocabulary development through pattern practice, application of the new language to other topics, and personalization questions.

- An alphabetical index assists students in locating all words and topics in the dictionary.

- A phonetic listing for each word in the index and a pronunciation guide give students the key to accurate pronunciation.

- A verb index of all the verbs presented in the dictionary provides students with information on the present, past, and past participle forms of the verbs.

The Oxford Picture Dictionary is the core of *The Oxford Picture Dictionary Program* which includes a *Dictionary Cassette,* a *Teacher's Book* and its companion *Focused Listening Cassette, Beginning* and *Intermediate Workbooks, Classic Classroom Activities* (a photocopiable activity book), *Overhead Transparencies,* and *Read All About It 1* and *2.* Bilingual editions of *The Oxford Picture Dictionary* are available in Spanish, Chinese, Vietnamese, and many other languages.

TEACHING THE VOCABULARY

Your students' needs and your own teaching philosophy will dictate how you use *The Oxford Picture Dictionary* with your students. The following general guidelines, however, may help you adapt the dictionary's pages to your particular course and students. (For topic-specific, step-by-step guidelines and activities for presenting and practicing the vocabulary on each dictionary page see the *Oxford Picture Dictionary Teacher's Book.*)

Preview the topic

A good way to begin any lesson is to talk with students to determine what they already know about the topic. Some different ways to do this are:

- Ask general questions related to the topic;

- Have students brainstorm a list of words they know from the topic; or

- Ask questions about the picture(s) on the page.

Present the vocabulary

Once you've discovered which words your students already know, you are ready to focus on presenting the words they need. Introducing 10–15 new words in a lesson allows students to really learn the new words. On pages where the word lists are longer, and students are unfamiliar with many of the words, you may wish to introduce the words by categories or sections, or simply choose the words you want in the lesson.

Here are four different presentation techniques. The techniques you choose will depend on the topic being studied and the level of your students.

- Say each new word and describe or define it within the context of the picture.

- Demonstrate verbs or verb sequences for the students, and have volunteers demonstrate the actions as you say them.

- Use Total Physical Response commands to build comprehension of the vocabulary: *Put the pencil on your book. Put it on your notebook. Put it on your desk.*

- Ask a series of questions to build comprehension and give students an opportunity to say the new words:

▶ Begin with *yes/no* questions. *Is #16 chalk?* (yes)

▶ Progress to *or* questions. *Is #16 chalk or a marker?* (chalk)

▶ Finally ask *Wh* questions.

What can I use to write on this paper? (a marker/ Use a marker.)

Check comprehension

Before moving on to the practice stage, it is helpful to be sure all students understand the target vocabulary. There are many different things you can do to check students' understanding. Here are two activities to try:

• Tell students to open their books and point to the items they hear you say. Call out target vocabulary at random as you walk around the room checking to see if students are pointing to the correct pictures.

• Make true/false statements about the target vocabulary. Have students hold up two fingers for true, three fingers for false. *You can write with a marker.* [two fingers] *You raise your notebook to talk to the teacher.* [three fingers]

Take a moment to review any words with which students are having difficulty before beginning the practice activities.

Practice the vocabulary

Guided practice activities give your students an opportunity to use the new vocabulary in meaningful communication. The exercises at the bottom of the pages are one source of guided practice activities.

• **Talk about...** This activity gives students an opportunity to practice the target vocabulary through sentence substitutions with meaningful topics.

e.g. **Talk about your feelings.**

I feel <u>happy</u> when I see my friends.

• **Practice...** This activity gives students practice using the vocabulary within common conversational functions such as making introductions, ordering food, making requests, etc.

e.g. **Practice asking for things in the dining room.**

Please pass <u>the platter</u>.

May I have <u>the creamer</u>?

Could I have <u>a fork</u>, please?

• **Use the new language.** This activity asks students to brainstorm words within various categories, or may

ask them to apply what they have learned to another topic in the dictionary. For example, on *Colors*, page 12, students are asked to look at *Clothing I*, pages 64–65, and name the colors of the clothing they see.

• **Share your answers.** These questions provide students with an opportunity to expand their use of the target vocabulary in personalized discussion. Students can ask and answer these questions in whole class discussions, pair or group work, or they can write the answers as journal entries.

Further guided and communicative practice can be found in the *Oxford Picture Dictionary Teacher's Book* and in *Classic Classroom Activities*. The *Oxford Picture Dictionary Beginning* and *Intermediate Workbooks* and *Read All About It 1 and 2* provide your students with controlled and communicative reading and writing practice.

We encourage you to adapt the materials to suit the needs of your classes, and we welcome your comments and ideas. Write to us at:

Oxford University Press
ESL Department
198 Madison Avenue
New York, NY 10016

Jayme Adelson-Goldstein

Norma Shapiro

A Letter to the Student

Dear Student of English,

Welcome to *The Oxford Picture Dictionary*. The more than 3,700 words in this book will help you as you study English.

Each page in this dictionary teaches about a specific topic. The topics are grouped together in units. All pages in a unit have the same color and symbol. For example, each page in the Food unit has this symbol:

On each page you will see pictures and words. The pictures have numbers or letters that match the numbers or letters in the word lists. Verbs (action words) are identified by letters and all other words are identified by numbers.

How to find words in this book

- Use the Table of Contents, pages ix–xi.
  Look up the general topic you want to learn about.

- Use the Index, pages 173–205.
  Look up individual words in alphabetical (A–Z) order.

- Go topic by topic.
  Look through the book until you find something that interests you.

How to use the Index

When you look for a word in the index this is what you will see:

the word   the number (or letter) in the word list

apples [ăp/əlz] **50**–4

the pronunciation   the page number

If the word is on one of the maps, pages 122–125, you will find it in the Geographical Index on pages 206–208.

How to use the Verb Guide

When you want to know the past form of a verb or its past participle form, look up the verb in the verb guide. The regular verbs and their spelling changes are listed on pages 170–171. The simple form, past form, and past participle form of irregular verbs are listed on page 172.

Workbooks

There are two workbooks to help you practice the new words:
The Oxford Picture Dictionary Beginning and *Intermediate Workbooks*.

As authors and teachers we both know how difficult English can be (and we're native speakers!). When we wrote this book, we asked teachers and students from the U.S. and other countries for their help and ideas. We hope their ideas and ours will help you. Please write to us with your comments or questions at:

Oxford University Press
ESL Department
198 Madison Avenue
New York, NY 10016

We wish you success!

Jayme Adelson-Goldstein   *Norma Shapiro*

学生の皆さんに

英語を学習されている学生の皆さん、

The Oxford Picture Dictionary の世界にようこそ。本書には、皆さんの英語学習に役立つ 3,700 語を超す単語が収録されています。

本辞典の各ページでは、それぞれ特定のトピックをとり上げています。トピックはユニット単位にまとめられ、同一ユニット内のページには、すべて同じ色で同じデザインのシンボルが付いています。たとえば、「食べ物」ユニットの各ページには、次のシンボルが付いています。

また、各ページには挿し絵と語句が載っています。挿し絵には数字またはアルファベットが付いており、語句のリストにある数字ないしアルファベットに対応しています。動詞（動作を表わす語）にはアルファベットが付いており、その他の語句には数字が付いて区別されています。

本書での語句の捜し方

* 目次 (ix～xiページ) を使用。
  学ぼうとする一般的なトピックを調べます。

* 索引 (173～205ページ) を使用。
  アルファベット順 (A～Z) で個々の単語を調べます。

* トピックごとに見る。
  ページを順に繰って行き、興味のあるものを探します。

索引の使い方

索引で単語を探す際には、次のようなものを見ることになります。

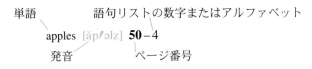

単語が 122～125 ページの地図のいずれかにある場合は、206～208 ページの地理索引を使用します。

動詞表の使い方

動詞の過去形または過去分詞形を知りたいときには、動詞表でその動詞を見つけます。規則動詞とその語形変化は、170～171 ページに載っています。不規則動詞の原形、過去形、過去分詞形は 172 ページです。

ワークブック

次のような 2 冊のワークブックもあり、新しい単語の練習に役立ちます。
The Oxford Picture Dictionary Beginning と Intermediate Workbooks です。

私共は、著者として、教師として、またネイティブスピーカーとして、英語がいかに難しいかを分かっています。この本を執筆する際には、米国内および諸外国からの教師や学生の方々の助言とアイデアを募りました。これらの方々や私共のアイデアが、お役に立てることを願っております。コメントないしご質問は以下の住所までお送りください。

Oxford University Press
ESL Department
198 Madison Avenue
New York, NY 10016

ご成功をお祈りします。

Jayme Adelson-Goldstein   *Norma Shapiro*

Contents 目次

1. Everyday Language 日常用語

A Classroom 教室	2–3
Personal Information 自己紹介	4
School 学校	5
Studying 学習	6–7
Everyday Conversation 日常会話	8
The Telephone 電話	9
Weather 天気	10
Describing Things 物の描写	11
Colors 色	12
Prepositions 前置詞	13
Numbers and Measurements 数字と度量法	14–15
Time 時間	16–17
The Calendar カレンダー	18–19
Money 通貨	20
Shopping 買物	21

2. People 人々

Age and Physical Description 年齢、体の特徴	22
Describing Hair 髪型の特徴	23
Family 家族	24–25
Daily Routines 日常生活	26–27
Life Events 一生の中の出来事	28–29
Feelings 感情	30–31
A Graduation 卒業	32–33

3. Housing 住宅

Places to Live 住居	34
Finding a Home 家を見つける	35
Apartments アパート	36–37
A House 家	38
A Yard 庭	39
A Kitchen 台所	40
A Dining Area 食堂	41
A Living Room 居間	42
A Bathroom トイレ、風呂場	43
A Bedroom 寝室	44
A Children's Bedroom 子供部屋	45
Housework 家事	46
Cleaning Supplies 掃除、洗濯の用具	47
Household Problems and Repairs 家の修理	48–49

4. Food 食べ物

Fruit 果物	50
Vegetables 野菜	51
Meat and Poultry 肉類	52
Deli and Seafood お惣菜と魚介類	53
The Market スーパー	54–55
Containers and Packaged Foods 容器とパッケージ食品	56
Weights and Measures 重さと計量	57
Food Preparation 料理	58
Kitchen Utensils 台所用品	59

Contents 目次

Fast Food　ファーストフード　60
A Coffee Shop Menu　喫茶店のメニュー　61
A Restaurant　レストラン　62–63

5. Clothing 衣類

Clothing I　衣類 I　64–65
Clothing II　衣類 II　66
Clothing III　衣類 III　67
Shoes and Accessories　靴とアクセサリー　68–69
Describing Clothes　衣服の説明　70–71
Doing the Laundry　洗濯をする　72
Sewing and Alterations　裁縫とサイズ直し　73

6. Health 健康

The Body　体　74–75
Personal Hygiene　みだしなみ　76–77
Symptoms and Injuries　症状とけが　78
Illnesses and Medical Conditions　疾患と症状　79
Health Care　ヘルスケア　80–81
Medical Emergencies　救急の病状　82
First Aid　応急手当　83
Clinics　診療所　84
Medical and Dental Exams　体と歯の診断　85
A Hospital　病院　86–87

7. Community 地域社会

City Streets　街　88–89
An Intersection　交差点　90–91
A Mall　ショッピングモール　92–93
A Childcare Center　託児所　94–95
U.S. Mail　米国郵便　96
A Bank　銀行　97
A Library　図書館　98
The Legal System　法律　99
Crime　犯罪　100
Public Safety　公共の安全　101
Emergencies and Natural Disasters　緊急事態と自然災害　102–103

8. Transportation 交通

Public Transportation　公共の交通機関　104
Prepositions of Motion　動作の前置詞　105
Cars and Trucks　車とトラック　106
Directions and Traffic Signs　方向と交通標識　107
Parts of a Car and Car Maintenance　車の部品とメンテナンス　108–109
An Airport　空港　110
A Plane Trip　空の旅　111

9. Areas of Study 学習科目

Types of Schools　学校の種類　112
English Composition　英作文　113
U.S. History　アメリカ史　114–115

U.S. Government and Citizenship　アメリカ政府と市民権　116
Geography　地理　117
Mathematics　数学　118
Science　科学　119
Music　音楽　120
More School Subjects　その他の科目　121
North America and Central America　北アメリカと中央アメリカ　122–123
The World　世界　124–125
Energy and the Environment　エネルギーと環境　126
The Universe　宇宙　127

10. Plants and Animals　植物と動物

Trees and Plants　樹木と植物　128
Flowers　花　129
Marine Life, Amphibians, and Reptiles　海の生物、両生類、は虫類　130–131
Birds, Insects, and Arachnids　鳥、昆虫、蛛形類　132
Domestic Animals and Rodents　家畜とげっ歯動物　133
Mammals　哺乳類　134–135

11. Work　仕事

Jobs and Occupations, A–H　仕事と職業、A〜H　136–137
Jobs and Occupations, H–W　仕事と職業、H〜W　138–139
Job Skills　技能　140
Job Search　求職　141
An Office　オフィス　142–143
Computers　コンピューター　144
A Hotel　ホテル　145
A Factory　工場　146
Job Safety　職場の安全対策　147
Farming and Ranching　農耕と牧畜　148
Construction　建設工事　149
Tools and Building Supplies　道具と建築用材　150–151

12. Recreation　レクリエーション

Places to Go　遊びに行く場所　152
The Park and Playground　公園と運動場　153
Outdoor Recreation　戸外のレクリエーション　154
The Beach　海岸　155
Sports Verbs　スポーツ関連の動詞　156–157
Team Sports　団体競技　158
Individual Sports　個人競技　159
Winter Sports and Water Sports　ウィンタースポーツとウォーター
　　スポーツ　160
Sports Equipment　スポーツ用品　161
Hobbies and Games　趣味とゲーム　162–163
Electronics and Photography　電化製品と写真　164–165
Entertainment　娯楽　166–167
Holidays　祝祭日　168
A Party　パーティー　169
Verb Guide　動詞表　170
Index　索引（英語）　173
Geographical Index　地理索引　206
Japanese Index　索引（日本語）　209

A Classroom 教室

1. chalkboard
黒板

2. screen
スクリーン

3. student
学生

4. overhead projector
OHP

5. teacher
先生

6. desk
机

7. chair / seat
いす

A. Raise your hand.
手をあげる

B. Talk to the teacher.
先生と話す

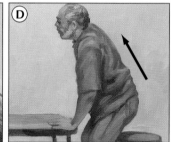

C. Listen to a cassette.
テープを聞く

D. Stand up.
立つ

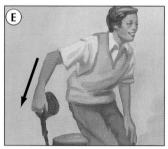

E. Sit down. / Take a seat.
座る / 席につく

F. Point to the picture.
絵を指す

G. Write on the board.
黒板に書く

H. Erase the board.
黒板を消す

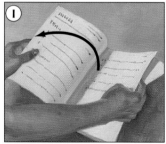

I. Open your book.
本を開く

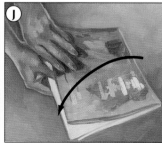

J. Close your book.
本を閉じる

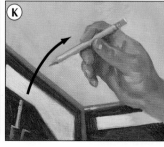

K. Take out your pencil.
鉛筆をとり出す

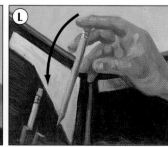

L. Put away your pencil.
鉛筆をしまう

8. bookcase 本だな	**10.** clock 時計	**12.** map 地図	**14.** bulletin board 掲示板
9. globe 地球儀	**11.** cassette player カセットプレーヤー	**13.** pencil sharpener 鉛筆削り	**15.** computer コンピューター

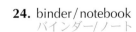

16. chalk チョーク	**20.** pencil 鉛筆	**24.** binder/notebook バインダー/ノート	**28.** dictionary 辞書
17. chalkboard eraser 黒板消し	**21.** pencil eraser 消しゴム	**25.** notebook paper ルーズリーフ	**29.** picture dictionary 絵辞典
18. pen ペン	**22.** textbook 教科書	**26.** spiral notebook らせんノート	**30.** the alphabet アルファベット
19. marker マジック（ペン）	**23.** workbook ワークブック	**27.** ruler 定規	**31.** numbers 数字

Use the new language.

1. Name three things you can open.

2. Name three things you can put away.

3. Name three things you can write with.

Share your answers.

1. Do you like to raise your hand?

2. Do you ever listen to cassettes in class?

3. Do you ever write on the board?

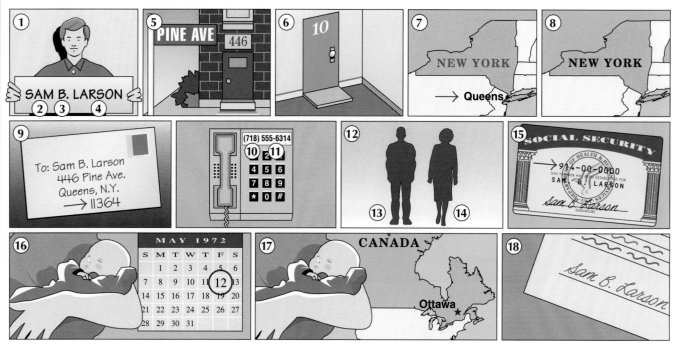

School Registration Form　学校登録用の用紙

1. name _____
氏名　　**2.** first name　　　　**3.** middle initial　　　　　　**4.** last name
　　　　　名　　　　　　　　　　ミドルネーム　　　　　　　　　　姓

5. address _____　　**6.** apt. # * _____
住所　　　　　　　　　　　　　　　　　　　　　アパート番号

7. city _____　　**8.** state _____　　**9.** ZIP code _____
市　　　　　　　　　　　　　　　　県　　　　　　　　　　　　郵便番号

(　　　)　　　　　　　　　　　　　　　　　　　　　　　　　　　　_　　_
10. area code　**11.** telephone number　　**12.** sex: **13.** ☐ male　　**15.** Social Security number
市外局番　　　電話番号　　　　　　　　性別　　　　男　　　　　　社会保障番号
　　　　　　　　　　　　　　　　　　　　　　　14. ☐ female
　　　　　　　　　　　　　　　　　　　　　　　　　　　女

16. date of birth _____　　**17.** place of birth _____
生年月日　　　　(month)　(date)　(year)　　出生地
　　　　　　　　(月)　　(日)　　(年)
　　　　　　　　　　　　　　　　　　　　　　18. signature _____
　　　　　　　　　　　　　　　　　　　　　　署名

* apt. # = apartment number

A. **Spell** your name.
名前をつづる

B. **Fill out** a form.
用紙に記入する

C. **Print** your name.
名前を活字体で書く

D. **Sign** your name.
サインする

Talk about yourself.

My first name is <u>Sam</u>.
My last name is spelled <u>L-A-R-S-O-N</u>.
I come from <u>Ottawa</u>.

Share your answers.

1. Do you like your first name?
2. Is your last name from your mother? father? husband?
3. What is your middle name?

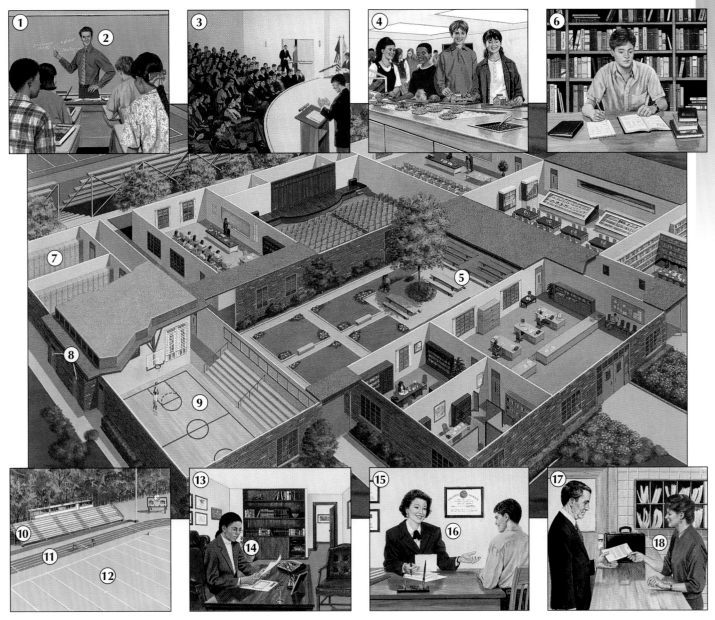

1. classroom 教室	**7.** lockers ロッカー	**13.** principal's office 校長室
2. teacher 教師 / 先生	**8.** rest rooms 手洗い	**14.** principal 校長
3. auditorium 講堂	**9.** gym 体育館	**15.** counselor's office カウンセラー室
4. cafeteria 食堂 / カフェテリア	**10.** bleachers 屋外観覧席	**16.** counselor カウンセラー
5. lunch benches ベンチ	**11.** track トラック	**17.** main office 事務室
6. library 図書館	**12.** field フィールド / 競技場	**18.** clerk 職員

More vocabulary

instructor: teacher

coach: gym teacher

administrator: principal or other school supervisor

Share your answers.

1. Do you ever talk to the principal of your school?

2. Is there a place for you to eat at your school?

3. Does your school look the same as or different from the one in the picture?

Dictionary work 辞書を使う

A. Look up a word.
言葉を調べる

B. Read the word.
言葉を読む

C. Say the word.
言葉を言う

D. Repeat the word.
言葉をくりかえす

E. Spell the word.
言葉をつづる

F. Copy the word.
言葉を書き写す

Work with a partner 二人で学習する

G. Ask a question.
質問する

H. Answer a question.
質問に答える

I. Share a book.
本を一緒に使う

J. Help your partner.
パートナーを手伝う

Work in a group グループで学習する

K. Brainstorm a list.
アイデアを次々と出し合
いリストにする

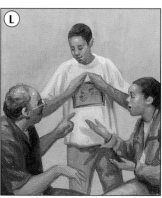

L. Discuss the list.
リストについて話し合う

M. Draw a picture.
絵を描く

N. Dictate a sentence.
文を書き取り用に口述
する

Class work　教室で学ぶ

O. Pass out the papers.
用紙を配る

P. Talk with each other.
お互いに話し合う

Q. Collect the papers.
用紙を集める

Follow directions　指示に従う

R. Fill in the blank.
空欄を埋める

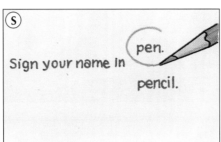

S. Circle the answer.
答えを丸で囲む

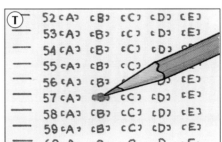

T. Mark the answer sheet.
解答用紙の答えに印を付ける

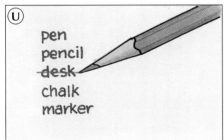

U. Cross out the word.
文字を線で消す

V. Underline the word.
言葉に下線を引く

W. Put the words **in order.**
言葉を正しい順に並べる

X. Match the items.
合う項目を選ぶ

Y. Check your work.
答えを確認する

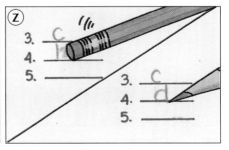

Z. Correct the mistake.
間違いを正す

Share your answers.

1. Do you like to work in groups?

2. Do you like to share books?

3. Do you like to answer questions?

4. Is it easy for you to talk with your classmates?

5. Do you always check your work?

6. Do you cross out your mistakes or erase them?

A. greet someone
あいさつをする

B. begin a conversation
会話を始める

C. end the conversation
会話を終える

D. introduce yourself
自己紹介する

E. make sure you **understand**
聞いたことを確認する

F. introduce your friend
友達を紹介する

G. compliment your friend
友達をほめる

H. thank your friend
友達にお礼を言う

I. apologize
あやまる

Practice introductions.

Hi, I'm <u>Sam Jones</u> and this is my friend, <u>Pat Green</u>.

Nice to meet you. I'm <u>Tomas Garcia</u>.

Practice giving compliments.

That's a great <u>sweater</u>, <u>Tomas</u>.

Thanks <u>Pat</u>. I like your <u>shoes</u>.

Look at **Clothing I,** pages **64–65** for more ideas.

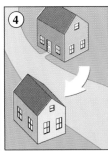

1. telephone/phone
電話

2. receiver
受話器

3. cord
電話線

4. local call
市内通話

5. long-distance call
長距離電話

6. international call
国際電話

7. operator
交換手

8. directory assistance (411)
電話番号案内 (411)

9. emergency service (911)
緊急サービス (911)

10. phone card
テレフォンカード

11. pay phone
公衆電話

12. cordless phone
コードレス電話

13. cellular phone
携帯電話

14. answering machine
留守番電話

15. telephone book
電話帳

16. pager
ポケットベル

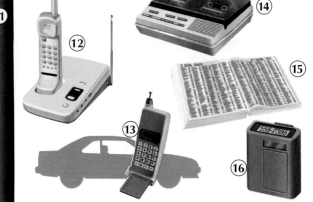

Using a pay phone　公衆電話の使用

A. **Pick up** the receiver.
受話器を取る

B. **Listen** for the dial tone.
発信音を聞く

C. **Deposit** coins.
硬貨を入れる

D. **Dial** the number.
ダイヤルを回す

E. **Leave** a message.
伝言を残す

F. **Hang up** the receiver.
電話を切る

More vocabulary

When you get a person or place that you didn't want to call, we say you have the **wrong number.**

Share your answers.

1. What kinds of calls do you make?

2. How much does it cost to call your country?

3. Do you like to talk on the telephone?

Weather 天気

Temperature
気温

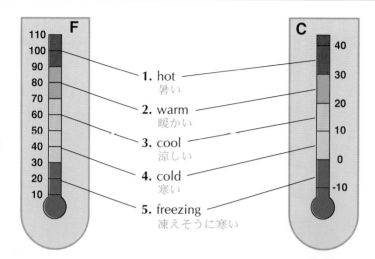

Degrees Fahrenheit

Degrees Celsius

1. hot
   暑い
2. warm
   暖かい
3. cool
   涼しい
4. cold
   寒い
5. freezing
   凍えそうに寒い

6. sunny/clear
   晴れ

7. cloudy
   曇り

8. raining
   雨

9. snowing
   雪

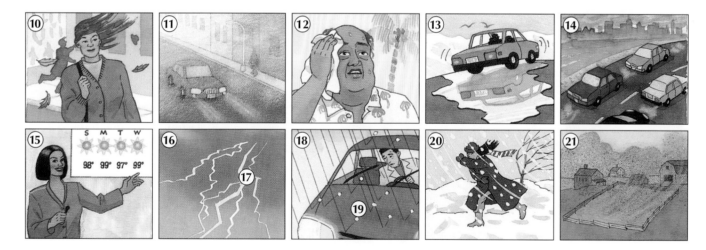

10. windy
    風がある
11. foggy
    霧が出ている
12. humid
    蒸し暑い

13. icy
    氷が張っている
14. smoggy
    スモッグが出ている
15. heat wave
    熱波

16. thunderstorm
    雷をともなった嵐
17. lightning
    稲光り
18. hailstorm
    雹の大降り

19. hail
    雹
20. snowstorm
    吹雪
21. dust storm
    砂塵あらし

Language note: *it is, there is*

For **1–14** we use,   *It's cloudy.*

For **15–21** we use,   *There's a heat wave.*

    There's lightning.

Talk about the weather.

Today it's hot. It's 98 degrees.

Yesterday it was warm. It was 85 degrees.

1. **little** hand
   小さい手
2. **big** hand
   大きい手

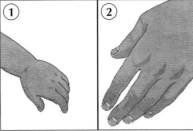

3. **fast** driver
   速く運転する人
4. **slow** driver
   ゆっくり運転する人

5. **hard** chair
   固い椅子
6. **soft** chair
   柔らかい椅子

7. **thick** book/
   fat book
   厚い本
8. **thin** book
   薄い本

9. **full** glass
   いっぱい入ったコップ
10. **empty** glass
    空のコップ

11. **noisy** children/
    loud children
    騒がしい子供
12. **quiet** children
    静かな子供

13. **heavy** box
    重い箱
14. **light** box
    軽い箱

15. **neat** closet
    整理された押し入れ
16. **messy** closet
    散らかった
    押し入れ

17. **good** dog
    良い犬
18. **bad** dog
    悪い犬

19. **expensive** ring
    高い指輪
20. **cheap** ring
    安い指輪

21. **beautiful** view
    美しい眺め
22. **ugly** view
    不快な眺め

23. **easy** problem
    簡単な問題
24. **difficult** problem/
    hard problem
    難しい問題

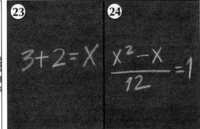

Use the new language.

1. Name three things that are thick.
2. Name three things that are soft.
3. Name three things that are heavy.

Share your answers.

1. Are you a slow driver or a fast driver?
2. Do you have a neat closet or a messy closet?
3. Do you like loud or quiet parties?

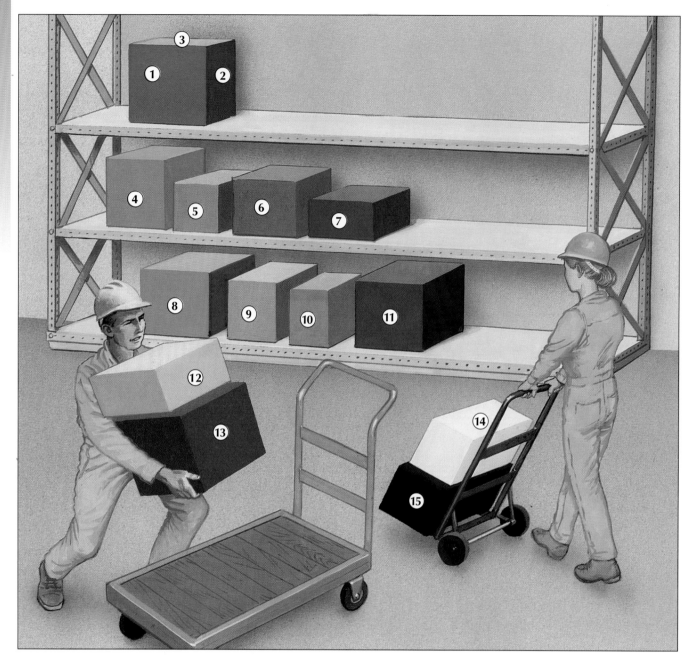

1. blue 青色	**6.** orange オレンジ色	**11.** brown 茶色
2. dark blue 紺色	**7.** purple 紫色	**12.** yellow 黄色
3. light blue 水色	**8.** green 緑色	**13.** red 赤色
4. turquoise 青緑色	**9.** beige ベージュ	**14.** white 白色
5. gray 灰色	**10.** pink ピンク	**15.** black 黒色

Use the new language.

Look at **Clothing I,** pages **64–65.**

Name the colors of the clothing you see.

That's <u>a dark blue suit</u>.

Share your answers.

1. What colors are you wearing today?

2. What colors do you like?

3. Is there a color you don't like? What is it?

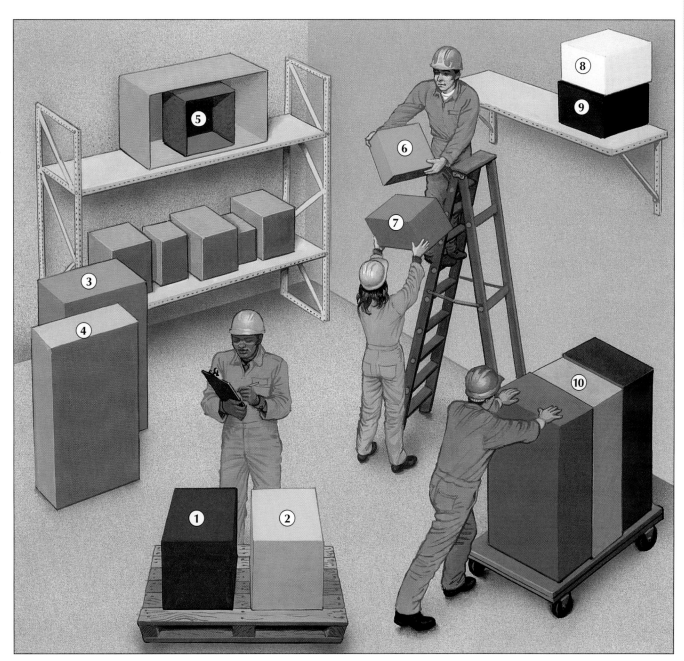

1. The red box is **next to** the yellow box, **on the left.**
   赤色の箱は黄色の箱の**左側**にあります

2. The yellow box is **next to** the red box, **on the right.**
   黄色の箱は赤色の箱の**右側**にあります

3. The turquoise box is **behind** the gray box.
   青緑色の箱は灰色の箱の**後ろ**にあります

4. The gray box is **in front of** the turquoise box.
   灰色の箱は青緑色の箱の**前**にあります

5. The dark blue box is **in** the beige box.
   紺色の箱はベージュの箱の**中**にあります

6. The green box is **above** the orange box.
   緑色の箱はオレンジ色の箱の**上**にあります

7. The orange box is **below** the green box.
   オレンジ色の箱は緑色の箱の**下**にあります

8. The white box is **on** the black box.
   白色の箱は黒色の箱の**上**にあります

9. The black box is **under** the white box.
   黒色の箱は白色の箱の**下**にあります

10. The pink box is **between** the purple box and the brown box.
    ピンクの箱は紫色の箱と茶色の箱の**間**にあります

More vocabulary

near: in the same area
*The white box is **near** the black box.*

far from: not near
*The red box is **far from** the black box.*

HOME **1** **8**

VISITOR **2** **2**

SAN DIEGO
235 miles

Cardinals 数字

0 zero
零/ゼロ
	11 eleven
	十一
		21 twenty-one
		二十一
			101
			   one hundred one
			   百一

1 one
一
	12 twelve
	十二
		22 twenty-two
		二十二
			1,000
			   one thousand
			   千

2 two
二
	13 thirteen
	十三
		30 thirty
		三十
			1,001
			   one thousand one
			   千一

3 three
三
	14 fourteen
	十四
		40 forty
		四十
			10,000
			   ten thousand
			   一万

4 four
四
	15 fifteen
	十五
		50 fifty
		五十
			100,000
			   one hundred thousand
			   十万

5 five
五
	16 sixteen
	十六
		60 sixty
		六十
			1,000,000
			   one million
			   百万

6 six
六
	17 seventeen
	十七
		70 seventy
		七十
			1,000,000,000
			   one billion
			   十億

7 seven 七	18 eighteen 十八	80 eighty 八十	
8 eight 八	19 nineteen 十九	90 ninety 九十	
9 nine 九	20 twenty 二十	100 one hundred 百	
10 ten 十			

Ordinals 順番

FINISH

1st first 一番	8th eighth 八番	15th fifteenth 十五番
2nd second 二番	9th ninth 九番	16th sixteenth 十六番
3rd third 三番	10th tenth 十番	17th seventeenth 十七番
4th fourth 四番	11th eleventh 十一番	18th eighteenth 十八番
5th fifth 五番	12th twelfth 十二番	19th nineteenth 十九番
6th sixth 六番	13th thirteenth 十三番	20th twentieth 二十番
7th seventh 七番	14th fourteenth 十四番	

Roman numerals ローマ数字

I	= 1	VII	= 7	XXX	= 30
II	= 2	VIII	= 8	XL	= 40
III	= 3	IX	= 9	L	= 50
IV	= 4	X	= 10	C	= 100
V	= 5	XV	= 15	D	= 500
VI	= 6	XX	= 20	M	= 1,000

Fractions　分数

1. 1/8　one-eighth
8分の1

2. 1/4　one-fourth
4分の1

3. 1/3　one-third
3分の1

4. 1/2　one-half
2分の1 / 半分

5. 3/4　three-fourths
4分の3

6. 1　whole
全部

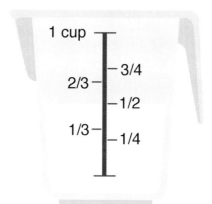

1 cup
- 3/4
2/3 -
- 1/2
1/3 -
- 1/4

Percents　パーセント

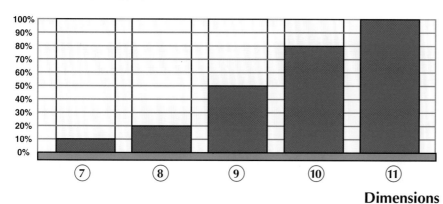

⑦　⑧　⑨　⑩　⑪

7. 10%　ten percent
10%　10パーセント

8. 20%　twenty percent
20%　20パーセント

9. 50%　fifty percent
50%　50パーセント

10. 80%　eighty percent
80%　80パーセント

11. 100%　one hundred percent
100%　100パーセント

Measurement　度量法

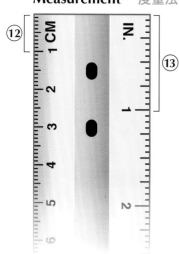

12. centimeter [cm]
センチ

13. inch [in.]
インチ

Equivalencies　等量

```
1 inch  = 2.54 centimeters
1 yard  =  .91 meters
1 mile  = 1.6 kilometers

12 inches    = 1 foot
3 feet       = 1 yard
1,760 yards  = 1 mile
```

Dimensions　寸法

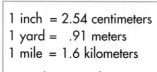

14. height
高さ

15. depth
奥行き/深さ

16. length
長さ

17. width
幅

More vocabulary

measure: to find the size or amount of something

count: to find the total number of something

Share your answers.

1. How many students are in class today?

2. Who was the first person in class today?

3. How far is it from your home to your school?

Time 時間

1. second
秒

2. minute
分

3. hour
時間

A.M.

4. 1:00
one o'clock
1時

5. 1:05
one-oh-five
1時5分
five after one
1時5分

6. 1:10
one-ten
1時10分
ten after one
1時10分

P.M.

7. 1:15
one-fifteen
1時15分
a quarter after one
1時15分

8. 1:20
one-twenty
1時20分
twenty after one
1時20分

9. 1:25
one twenty-five
1時25分
twenty-five after one
1時25分

10. 1:30
one-thirty
1時30分
half past one
1時30分

11. 1:35
one thirty-five
1時35分
twenty-five to two
2時25分前

12. 1:40
one-forty
1時40分
twenty to two
2時20分前

13. 1:45
one forty-five
1時45分
a quarter to two
2時15分前

14. 1:50
one-fifty
1時50分
ten to two
2時10分前

15. 1:55
one fifty-five
1時55分
five to two
2時5分前

Talk about the time.

What time is it? It's 10:00 a.m.

What time do you wake up on weekdays? At 6:30 a.m.

What time do you wake up on weekends? At 9:30 a.m.

Share your answers.

1. How many hours a day do you study English?

2. You are meeting friends at 1:00. How long will you wait for them if they are late?

16

16. morning
朝

17. noon
正午

18. afternoon
午後

19. evening
夕方

20. night
夜

21. midnight
真夜中

22. early
早い

23. late
遅い

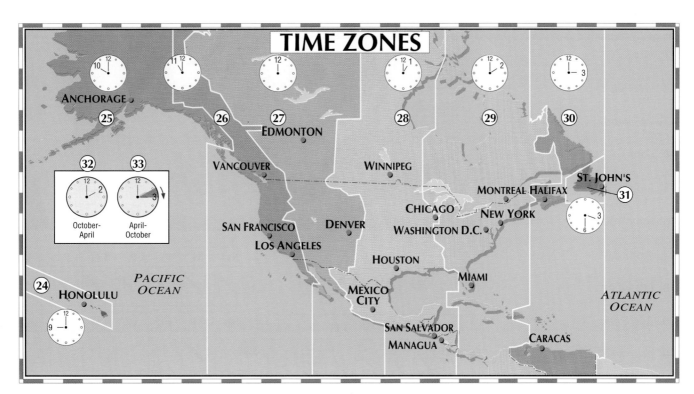

TIME ZONES

24. Hawaii-Aleutian time
ハワイ・アリューシャン
時間

25. Alaska time
アラスカ時間

26. Pacific time
太平洋時間

27. mountain time
山地時間

28. central time
中央時間

29. eastern time
東部時間

30. Atlantic time
大西洋時間

31. Newfoundland time
ニューファウンドランド
時間

32. standard time
標準時

33. daylight saving time
夏時間

More vocabulary

on time: not early and not late

*He's **on time**.*

Share your answers.

1. When do you watch television? study?
do housework?

2. Do you come to class on time? early? late?

Days of the week
曜日

1. Sunday
日曜日

2. Monday
月曜日

3. Tuesday
火曜日

4. Wednesday
水曜日

5. Thursday
木曜日

6. Friday
金曜日

7. Saturday
土曜日

8. year
年

9. month
月

10. day
日

11. week
週

12. weekdays
平日

13. weekend
週末

14. date
日付

15. today
今日

16. tomorrow
明日

17. yesterday
昨日

18. last week
先週

19. this week
今週

20. next week
来週

21. every day
毎日

22. once a week
週1度

23. twice a week
週2度

24. three times a week
週3度

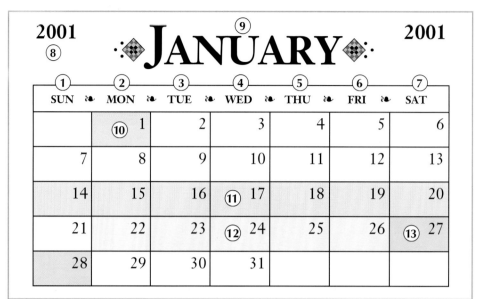

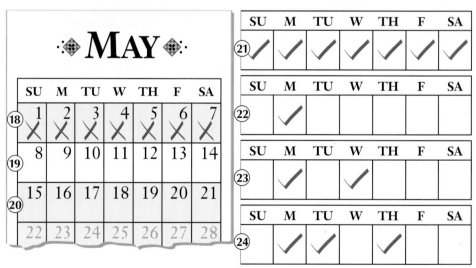

Talk about the calendar.

What's today's date? It's <u>March 10th</u>.

What day is it? It's <u>Tuesday</u>.

What day was yesterday? It was <u>Monday</u>.

Share your answers.

1. How often do you come to school?

2. How long have you been in this school?

2001

JAN ㉕
SUN	MON	TUE	WED	THU	FRI	SAT
	1	2	3	4	5	6
7	8	9	10	11	12	13
14	15	16	17	18	19	20
21	22	23	24	25	26	27
28	29	30	31			

FEB ㉖
SUN	MON	TUE	WED	THU	FRI	SAT
				1	2	3
4	5	6	7	8	9	10
11	12	13	14	15	16	17
18	19	20	21	22	23	24
25	26	27	28			

MAR ㉗
SUN	MON	TUE	WED	THU	FRI	SAT
				1	2	3
4	5	6	7	8	9	10
11	12	13	14	15	16	17
18	19	20	21	22	23	24
25	26	27	28	29	30	31

APR ㉘
SUN	MON	TUE	WED	THU	FRI	SAT
1	2	3	4	5	6	7
8	9	10	11	12	13	14
15	16	17	18	19	20	21
22	23	24	25	26	27	28
29	30					

MAY ㉙
SUN	MON	TUE	WED	THU	FRI	SAT
		1	2	3	4	5
6	7	8	9	10	11	12
13	14	15	16	17	18	19
20	21	22	23	24	25	26
27	28	29	30	31		

JUN ㉚
SUN	MON	TUE	WED	THU	FRI	SAT
					1	2
3	4	5	6	7	8	9
10	11	12	13	14	15	16
17	18	19	20	21	22	23
24	25	26	27	28	29	30

JUL ㉛
SUN	MON	TUE	WED	THU	FRI	SAT
1	2	3	4	5	6	7
8	9	10	11	12	13	14
15	16	17	18	19	20	21
22	23	24	25	26	27	28
29	30	31				

AUG ㉜
SUN	MON	TUE	WED	THU	FRI	SAT
			1	2	3	4
5	6	7	8	9	10	11
12	13	14	15	16	17	18
19	20	21	22	23	24	25
26	27	28	29	30	31	

SEP ㉝
SUN	MON	TUE	WED	THU	FRI	SAT
						1
2	3	4	5	6	7	8
9	10	11	12	13	14	15
16	17	18	19	20	21	22
23/30	24	25	26	27	28	29

OCT ㉞
SUN	MON	TUE	WED	THU	FRI	SAT
	1	2	3	4	5	6
7	8	9	10	11	12	13
14	15	16	17	18	19	20
21	22	23	24	25	26	27
28	29	30	31			

NOV ㉟
SUN	MON	TUE	WED	THU	FRI	SAT
				1	2	3
4	5	6	7	8	9	10
11	12	13	14	15	16	17
18	19	20	21	22	23	24
25	26	27	28	29	30	

DEC ㊱
SUN	MON	TUE	WED	THU	FRI	SAT
						1
2	3	4	5	6	7	8
9	10	11	12	13	14	15
16	17	18	19	20	21	22
23/30	24/31	25	26	27	28	29

MARCH 21 / JUNE 21 / SEPT. 21 / DEC. 21

㊲ ㊳ ㊴ ㊵

JUNE 5 — TIM!

㊶

MARCH 2 — ANNIVERSARY

㊷

JULY 4 — INDEPENDENCE DAY / STATE BANK / CLOSED—JULY 4

㊸

APRIL 4 — EASTER SUNDAY

㊹

MAY 17 — DOCTOR 4:30

㊺

AUGUST

㊻

Months of the year
十二か月

25. January
1月

26. February
2月

27. March
3月

28. April
4月

29. May
5月

30. June
6月

31. July
7月

32. August
8月

33. September
9月

34. October
10月

35. November
11月

36. December
12月

Seasons
四季

37. spring
春

38. summer
夏

39. fall
秋

40. winter
冬

41. birthday
誕生日

42. anniversary
記念日

43. legal holiday
祝日

44. religious holiday
祭日

45. appointment
約束/予約

46. vacation
休暇

Use the new language.

Look at the **ordinal numbers** on page **14.**

Use ordinal numbers to say the date.

It's June 5th. It's the fifth.

Talk about your birthday.

My birthday is in the winter.

My birthday is in January.

My birthday is on January twenty-sixth.

Coins 硬貨

1. $.01 = 1¢
a penny/1 cent
ペニー/1セント

2. $.05 = 5¢
a nickel/5 cents
ニッケル/5セント

3. $.10 = 10¢
a dime/10 cents
ダイム/10セント

4. $.25 = 25¢
a quarter/25 cents
クオーター/25セント

5. $.50 = 50¢
a half dollar
50セント

6. $1.00
a silver dollar
1ドル銀貨

Bills 紙幣

7. $1.00
a dollar
1ドル

8. $5.00
five dollars
5ドル

9. $10.00
ten dollars
10ドル

10. $20.00
twenty dollars
20ドル

11. $50.00
fifty dollars
50ドル

12. $100.00
one hundred dollars
100ドル

Ways to pay 支払方法

13. cash
現金

14. personal check
個人用小切手

15. credit card
クレジットカード

16. money order
為替

17. traveler's check
旅行者小切手/トラベラーズチェック

More vocabulary

borrow: to get money from someone and return it later

lend: to give money to someone and get it back later

pay back: to return the money that you borrowed

Other ways to talk about money:

a dollar bill or *a one*

a five-dollar bill or *a five*

a ten-dollar bill or *a ten*

a twenty-dollar bill or *a twenty*

A. shop for 〜の買物をする	**E. keep** 保持する	**2.** regular price 定価	**6.** price/cost 値段
B. sell 売る	**F. return** 返品する	**3.** sale price セール価格	**7.** sales tax 売上税
C. pay for/**buy** 〜の代金を払う/買う	**G. exchange** 取り替える	**4.** bar code バーコード	**8.** total 合計
D. give 贈る	**1.** price tag 値札	**5.** receipt 領収書/レシート	**9.** change おつり

More vocabulary

When you use a credit card to shop, you get a **bill** in the mail. Bills list, in writing, the items you bought and the total you have to pay.

Share your answers.

1. Name three things you pay for every month.
2. Name one thing you will buy this week.
3. Where do you like to shop?

1. children
   子供
2. baby
   赤ん坊
3. toddler
   幼児
4. 6-year-old boy
   6才の少年
5. 10-year-old girl
   10才の少女
6. teenagers
   10代の少年少女
7. 13-year-old boy
   13歳の少年
8. 19-year-old girl
   19歳の少女
9. adults
   大人
10. woman
    女性
11. man
    男性
12. senior citizen
    老人

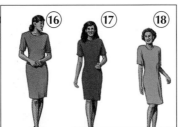
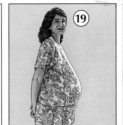

13. young
    若い
14. middle-aged
    中年の
15. elderly
    年をとった
16. tall
    背が高い
17. average height
    平均身長
18. short
    背が低い
19. pregnant
    妊娠している
20. heavyset
    太っている
21. average weight
    平均体重
22. thin/slim
    細い/やせた
23. attractive
    すてきな
24. cute
    かわいい
25. physically challenged
    身体障害者
26. sight impaired/blind
    視覚障害のある/目が見えない
27. hearing impaired/deaf
    難聴の/耳が聞こえない

Talk about yourself and your teacher.

I am <u>young</u>, <u>average height</u>, and <u>average weight</u>.

My teacher is <u>a middle-aged</u>, <u>tall</u>, <u>thin</u> man.

Use the new language.

Turn to **Hobbies and Games**, pages **162–163**.

Describe each person on the page.

He's <u>a heavyset</u>, <u>short</u>, <u>senior citizen</u>.

22

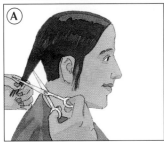
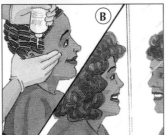

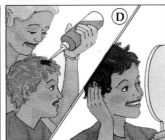

1. short hair
短髪

2. shoulder-length hair
肩までの髪

3. long hair
長髪

4. part
髪を分ける

5. mustache
口髭

6. beard
顎髭

7. sideburns
もみあげ

8. bangs
前髪

9. straight hair
直毛

10. wavy hair
ウエーブしている髪

11. curly hair
巻毛

12. bald
はげ

13. gray hair
白髪

14. red hair
赤毛

15. black hair
黒髪

16. blond hair
金髪

17. brown hair
茶色髪

18. brush
ブラシ

19. scissors
はさみ

20. blow dryer
ドライヤー

21. rollers
カーラー

22. comb
クシ

A. **cut** hair
髪を切る

B. **perm** hair
パーマをかける

C. **set** hair
髪をセットする

D. **color** hair/**dye** hair
髪を染める

More vocabulary

hair stylist: a person who cuts, sets, and perms hair

hair salon: the place where a hair stylist works

Talk about your hair.

My hair is <u>long</u>, <u>straight</u>, and <u>brown</u>.

I have <u>long</u>, <u>straight</u>, <u>brown</u> hair.

When I was a child my hair was <u>short</u>, <u>curly</u>, and <u>blond</u>.

Tom Lee's Family

1. grandparents
祖父母

Min — Lu

2. grandmother
祖母

3. grandfather
祖父

4. parents
両親

Rose — Chang

Helen — Daniel

5. mother
母

6. father
父

10. aunt
伯母／叔母

11. uncle
伯父／叔父

Tom

Lily — Alex

Emily

8. sister
姉／妹

9. brother
兄／弟

12. cousin
いとこ

7. (Min and Lu's)
grandson
(Min と Lu の) 孫

Berta — Mario

Ana Garcia's Family

13. mother-in-law
義母

14. father-in-law
義父

Ana

Marta — Carlos

Tito

20. (Tito's) wife
(Tito の) 妻

15. sister-in-law
義理の姉妹

16. brother-in-law
義理の兄弟

19. husband
夫

Alice — Eddie

Sara — Felix

17. niece
姪

18. nephew
甥

21. daughter
娘

22. son
息子

More vocabulary

Lily and Emily are Min and Lu's **granddaughters**.

Daniel is Min and Lu's **son-in-law**.

Ana is Berta and Mario's **daughter-in-law**.

Share your answers.

1. How many brothers and sisters do you have?

2. What number son or daughter are you?

3. Do you have any children?

Lisa Smith's Family

23. married
結婚

Carol   Dan

Lisa

24. divorced
離婚

25. single mother
女の片親

26. single father
男 の片親

Rick   Carol

27. remarried
再婚

Dan   Sue

Rick   Carol

28. stepfather
義父

David

Mary

29. half brother
異母(父)兄弟

30. half sister
異母(父)兄弟

Lisa

Dan   Sue

31. stepmother
義母

Kim   Bill

32. stepsister
義理の姉妹

33. stepbrother
義理の兄弟

More vocabulary

Carol is Dan's **former wife**.

Sue is Dan's **wife**.

Dan is Carol's **former husband**.

Rick is Carol's **husband**.

Lisa is the **stepdaughter** of both Rick and Sue.

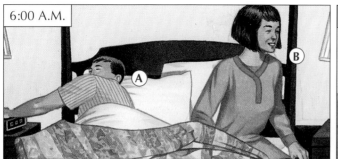

6:00 A.M.

Ⓐ Ⓑ

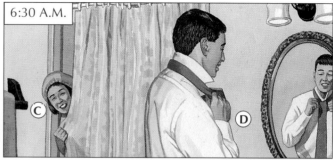

6:30 A.M.

Ⓒ Ⓓ

7:00 A.M.

Ⓔ Ⓕ

7:30 A.M.

Ⓖ

8:00 A.M.

Ⓗ Ⓘ

10:00 A.M.

Ⓙ Ⓚ

4:30 P.M.

Ⓛ

5:00 P.M.

CLOSED

Ⓜ

A. wake up
目を覚ます

B. get up
起きる

C. take a shower
シャワーを浴びる

D. get dressed
服を着る

E. eat breakfast
朝食を食べる

F. make lunch
お弁当を作る

G. take the children to school
子供を学校に連れていく

H. take the bus to school
バスに乗って学校に行く

I. drive to work / **go** to work
車で通勤する / 通勤する

J. be in school
学校で

K. work
働く

L. go to the market
スーパーに行く

M. leave work
会社を出る

Grammar point: 3rd person singular

For **he** and **she**, we add **-s** or **-es** to the verb.

He/She wakes up.

He/She watches TV.

These verbs are different (irregular):

be   *He/She **is** in school at 10:00 a.m.*

have   *He/She **has** dinner at 6:30 p.m.*

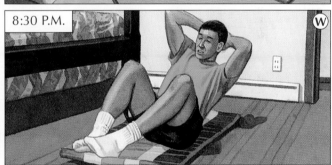

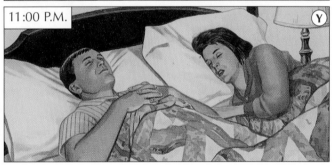

N. **clean** the house
家の掃除をする

O. **pick up** the children
子供を迎えに行く

P. **cook** dinner
夕食を作る

Q. **come** home / **get** home
家に帰る

R. **have** dinner
夕食を食べる

S. **watch** TV
テレビを見る

T. **do** homework
宿題をする

U. **relax**
くつろぐ

V. **read** the paper
新聞を読む

W. **exercise**
運動する

X. **go** to bed
寝る

Y. **go** to sleep
眠る

Talk about your daily routine.

I take a shower in the morning.

I go to school in the evening.

I go to bed at 11 o'clock.

Share your answers.

1. Who makes dinner in your family?

2. Who goes to the market?

3. Who goes to work?

A. be born
生まれる

B. start school
入学する

C. immigrate
移住する

D. graduate
卒業する

E. learn to drive
車の運転を習う

F. join the army
軍隊に入る

G. get a job
就職する

H. become a citizen
市民権を得る

I. rent an apartment
アパートを借りる

J. go to college
大学に行く

K. fall in love
恋をする

L. get married
結婚する

Grammar point: past tense

start		immigrate	
learn		graduate	
join	+ed	move	+d
rent		retire	
travel		die	

These verbs are different (irregular):

be	— was	have	— had
get	— got	buy	— bought
become	— became		
go	— went		
fall	— fell		

28

1960

1967

M. have a baby
子供が生まれる

N. travel
旅行する

1971

1971

O. buy a house
家を買う

P. move
引っ越しする

1985

1997

Q. have a grandchild
孫が生まれる

R. die
死ぬ

1. birth certificate
出生証明書

2. diploma
卒業証明書

3. Resident Alien card
永住権カード

4. driver's license
運転免許証

5. Social Security card
社会保障番号証

6. Certificate of Naturalization
市民権獲得証明書

7. college degree
大学卒業証書

8. marriage license
結婚証明書

9. passport
パスポート

More vocabulary

When a husband dies, his wife becomes a **widow**.

When a wife dies, her husband becomes a **widower**.

When older people stop working, we say they **retire**.

Talk about yourself.

I was born in 1968.

I learned to drive in 1987.

I immigrated in 1990.

1. hot
   暑い

2. thirsty
   のどが渇いた

3. sleepy
   眠い

4. cold
   寒い

5. hungry
   お腹がすいた

6. full
   お腹がいっぱい

7. comfortable
   気持ちがいい

8. uncomfortable
   不快な

9. disgusted
   いやな

10. calm
    落ち着いた

11. nervous
    緊張して

12. in pain
    痛い

13. worried
    心配して

14. sick
    気分が悪い

15. well
    気分が良い

16. relieved
    安心して

17. hurt
    傷ついた

18. lonely
    寂しい

19. in love
    恋をして

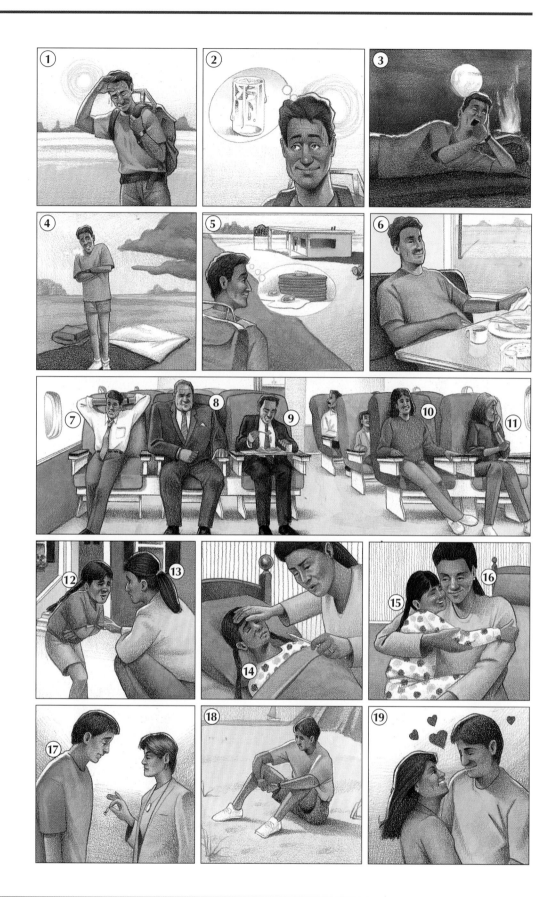

More vocabulary

furious: very angry

terrified: very scared

overjoyed: very happy

exhausted: very tired

starving: very hungry

humiliated: very embarrassed

Talk about your feelings.

I feel <u>happy</u> when I see <u>my friends</u>.

I feel <u>homesick</u> when I think about <u>my family</u>.

20. sad
悲しい

21. homesick
ホームシックにかかった

22. proud
誇りに思って

23. excited
興奮して

24. scared
怖い

25. embarrassed
恥ずかしい

26. bored
退屈な

27. confused
混乱して

28. frustrated
不満な

29. angry
怒って

30. upset
気が転倒して

31. surprised
驚いて

32. happy
うれしい/幸せな

33. tired
疲れた

Use the new language.

Look at **Clothing I**, page **64**, and answer the questions.

1. How does the runner feel?

2. How does the man at the bus stop feel?

3. How does the woman at the bus stop feel?

4. How do the teenagers feel?

5. How does the little boy feel?

A Graduation 卒業

The Ceremony

1. **graduating class**
   卒業学年

2. **gown**
   ガウン

3. **cap**
   帽子

4. **stage**
   ステージ

5. **podium**
   演壇

6. **graduate**
   卒業生

7. **diploma**
   卒業証書

8. **valedictorian**
   卒業生代表

9. **guest speaker**
   ゲストスピーカー

10. **audience**
    観客

11. **photographer**
    写真屋

A. **graduate**
   卒業する

B. **applaud / clap**
   拍手する

C. **cry**
   泣く

D. **take** a picture
   写真を撮る

E. **give** a speech
   スピーチをする

Talk about what the people in the pictures are doing.

She is
- tak**ing** a picture.
- giv**ing** a speech.
- smil**ing**.
- laugh**ing**.

He is
- mak**ing** a toast.
- clap**ping**.

They are
- graduat**ing**.
- hug**ging**.
- kiss**ing**.
- applaud**ing**.

The Party

12. caterer
仕出し屋/宴会サービス係

13. buffet
ビュッフェ

14. guests
ゲスト

15. banner
横断幕

16. dance floor
ダンスフロアー

17. DJ (disc jockey)
デスクジョッキー/DJ

18. gifts
贈り物

F. kiss
キスする

G. hug
抱き合う

H. laugh
笑う

I. make a toast
乾杯する

J. dance
踊る

Share your answers.

1. Did you ever go to a graduation? Whose?

2. Did you ever give a speech? Where?

3. Did you ever hear a great speaker? Where?

4. Did you ever go to a graduation party?

5. What do you like to eat at parties?

6. Do you like to dance at parties?

33

1. the city/an urban area
都市/都会

2. the suburbs
郊外

3. a small town
小さい町

4. the country/a rural area
田舎/地方

5. apartment building
アパート

6. house
家

7. townhouse
タウンハウス

8. mobile home
モービルホーム

9. college dormitory
大学寮

10. shelter
避難所

11. nursing home
老人ホーム

12. ranch
牧場

13. farm
農場

More vocabulary

duplex house: a house divided into two homes

condominium: an apartment building where each apartment is owned separately

co-op: an apartment building owned by the residents

Share your answers.

1. Do you like where you live?

2. Where did you live in your country?

3. What types of housing are there near your school?

Renting an apartment　アパートを借りる

A. look for a new apartment
新しいアパートを探す

B. talk to the manager
管理人と話す

C. sign a rental agreement
賃貸契約に署名する

D. move in
引っ越しする

E. unpack
荷物を解く

F. pay the rent
家賃を払う

Buying a house　家を買う

G. talk to the Realtor
不動産業者と話す

H. make an offer
買値を伝える

I. get a loan
ローンを受ける

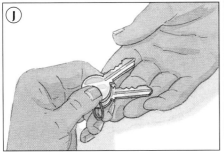

J. take ownership
持ち主となる

K. arrange the furniture
家具を配置する

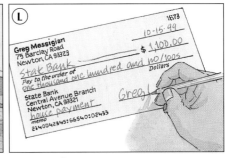

L. pay the mortgage
住宅ローンを払う

More vocabulary

lease: a rental agreement for a specific period of time

utilities: gas, water, and electricity for the home

Practice talking to an apartment manager.

How much is the rent?

Are utilities included?

When can I move in?

Entrance

Laundry Room

Recreation Room

Garage

1. first floor
1階

2. second floor
2階

3. third floor
3階

4. fourth floor
4階

5. roof garden
屋上

6. playground
遊び場

7. fire escape
非常口

8. intercom / speaker
インターコム／スピーカー

9. security system
警備保障システム

10. doorman
ドアマン

11. vacancy sign
空部屋の表示

12. manager / superintendent
管理人

13. security gate
警備ゲート

14. storage locker
物置

15. parking space
駐車場

More vocabulary

rec room: a short way of saying **recreation room**

basement: the area below the street level of an apartment or a house

Talk about where you live.

I live in Apartment 3 near the entrance.

I live in Apartment 11 on the second floor near the fire escape.

Hallway

Entryway

Office

Lobby

16. swimming pool
プール

17. balcony
バルコニー

18. courtyard
中庭

19. air conditioner
冷房

20. trash bin
ごみ入れ

21. alley
路地

22. neighbor
隣近所

23. fire exit
非常口

24. trash chute
トラッシュシュート

25. smoke detector
煙探知器

26. stairway
階段

27. peephole
のぞき穴

28. door chain
ドアのチェーン

29. dead-bolt lock
内鍵

30. doorknob
取っ手/ドアノブ

31. key
鍵

32. landlord
家主

33. tenant
借家人

34. elevator
エレベーター

35. stairs
階段

36. mailboxes
郵便受け

Grammar point: *there is, there are*

singular: *there is*   plural: *there are*

There is *a fire exit in the hallway.*

There are *mailboxes in the lobby.*

Talk about apartments.

My apartment has <u>an elevator</u>, <u>a lobby</u>, and <u>a rec room</u>.

My apartment doesn't have <u>a pool</u> or <u>a garage</u>.

My apartment needs <u>air conditioning</u>.

1. floor plan
   間取り

2. backyard
   裏庭

3. fence
   垣根

4. mailbox
   郵便受け

5. driveway
   ドライブウエイ

6. garage
   車庫

7. garage door
   車庫の戸

8. screen door
   網戸

9. porch light
   ポーチの電灯

10. doorbell
    呼び鈴

11. front door
    玄関のドア

12. storm door
    雨戸

13. steps
    階段

14. front walk
    前道

15. front yard
    前庭

16. deck
    デッキ

17. window
    窓

18. shutter
    シャッター

19. gutter
    雨樋

20. roof
    屋根

21. chimney
    煙突

22. TV antenna
    テレビのアンテナ

More vocabulary

two-story house: a house with two floors

downstairs: the bottom floor

upstairs: the part of a house above the bottom floor

Share your answers.

1. What do you like about this house?

2. What's something you don't like about the house?

3. Describe the perfect house.

1. hedge 生け垣	**8.** sprinkler スプリンクラー	**15.** pruning shears 刈込み用植木ばさみ	**22.** lawn mower 芝刈り機
2. hammock ハンモック	**9.** hose ホース	**16.** wheelbarrow 一輪車	**A.** **weed** the flower bed 花壇の草むしりをする
3. garbage can ごみ入れ	**10.** compost pile 堆肥の山	**17.** watering can じょうろ	**B.** **water** the plants 植木に水をやる
4. leaf blower ブローアー	**11.** rake 熊手	**18.** flowerpot 植木鉢	**C.** **mow** the lawn 芝生を刈る
5. patio furniture テラス用家具	**12.** hedge clippers 木ばさみ	**19.** flower 花	**D.** **plant** a tree 木を植える
6. patio テラス	**13.** shovel シャベル	**20.** bush 低木/茂み	**E.** **trim** the hedge 生け垣を刈込む
7. barbecue grill バーベキューグリル	**14.** trowel スコップ	**21.** lawn 芝生	**F.** **rake** the leaves 落ち葉を集める

Talk about your yard and gardening.

I like to *plant trees*.

I don't like to *weed*.

I like/don't like to work in the yard/garden.

Share your answers.

1. What flowers, trees, or plants do you see in the picture? (Look at **Trees, Plants, and Flowers**, pages **128–129** for help.)

2. Do you ever use a barbecue grill to cook?

1. cabinet 戸だな	**8.** shelf たな	**15.** toaster oven オーブントースター	**22.** counter 調理台
2. paper towels ペーパータオル	**9.** refrigerator 冷蔵庫	**16.** pot 鍋	**23.** drawer 引き出し
3. dish drainer 水切りかご	**10.** freezer 冷凍庫	**17.** teakettle やかん	**24.** pan 平鍋
4. dishwasher 皿洗い機	**11.** coffeemaker コーヒーメーカー	**18.** stove レンジ	**25.** electric mixer 電気ミキサー
5. garbage disposal 生ごみ処理機	**12.** blender ミキサー	**19.** burner バーナー	**26.** food processor フードプロセッサー
6. sink 流し台	**13.** microwave oven 電子レンジ	**20.** oven オーブン	**27.** cutting board まな板
7. toaster トースター	**14.** electric can opener 電気缶切り	**21.** broiler ブロイラー	

Talk about the location of kitchen items.

The toaster oven is _on the counter_ _near the stove_.

The microwave is _above the stove_.

Share your answers.

1. Do you have a garbage disposal? a dishwasher? a microwave?

2. Do you eat in the kitchen?

21	22	23	24	25	26	27	28

1. china cabinet
食器だな

2. set of dishes
食器一式

3. platter
大皿

4. ceiling fan
天井扇風機

5. light fixture
電燈

6. serving dish
大皿

7. candle
ろうそく

8. candlestick
ろうそく立て

9. vase
花瓶

10. tray
盆

11. teapot
ティーポット

12. sugar bowl
砂糖入れ

13. creamer
クリーム入れ

14. saltshaker
塩入れ

15. pepper shaker
コショウ入れ

16. dining room chair
食堂の椅子

17. dining room table
ダイニングテーブル / 食卓

18. tablecloth
テーブルクロス

19. napkin
ナプキン

20. place mat
ランチョンマット

21. fork
フォーク

22. knife
ナイフ

23. spoon
スプーン

24. plate
皿

25. bowl
ボール

26. glass
グラス

27. coffee cup
コーヒー茶碗

28. mug
マグカップ

Practice asking for things in the dining room.

Please pass the platter.

May I have the creamer?

Could I have a fork, please?

Share your answers.

1. What are the women in the picture saying?

2. In your home, where do you eat?

3. Do you like to make dinner for your friends?

A Living Room   居間

1. **bookcase**
   本棚

2. **basket**
   バスケット

3. **track lighting**
   移動式電燈

4. **lightbulb**
   電球

5. **ceiling**
   天井

6. **wall**
   壁

7. **painting**
   絵画

8. **mantel**
   暖炉棚

9. **fireplace**
   暖炉

10. **fire**
    火

11. **fire screen**
    暖炉のスクリーン

12. **logs**
    まき

13. **wall unit**
    壁取付棚/ウォールユニット

14. **stereo system**
    ステレオ

15. **floor lamp**
    フロアランプ

16. **drapes**
    カーテン

17. **window**
    窓

18. **plant**
    植木

19. **sofa/couch**
    ソファー

20. **throw pillow**
    クッション

21. **end table**
    サイドテーブル

22. **magazine holder**
    雑誌入れ

23. **coffee table**
    コーヒーテーブル

24. **armchair/easy chair**
    ひじかけ椅子

25. **love seat**
    ラブシート/二人用ソファー

26. **TV (television)**
    テレビ

27. **carpet**
    カーペット

Use the new language.

Look at **Colors**, page **12**, and describe this room.

There is a gray sofa and a gray armchair.

Talk about your living room.

In my living room I have a sofa, two chairs, and a coffee table.

I don't have a fireplace or a wall unit.

1. hamper
洗濯物かご

2. bathtub
浴槽

3. rubber mat
ゴムマット

4. drain
排水口

5. hot water
お湯

6. faucet
蛇口

7. cold water
水

8. towel rack
タオルかけ

9. tile
タイル

10. showerhead
シャワーヘッド

11. (mini)blinds
(ミニ)ブラインド

12. bath towel
バスタオル

13. hand towel
ハンドタオル / 手拭

14. washcloth
身体を洗うタオル

15. toilet paper
トイレットペーパー

16. toilet brush
トイレットブラシ

17. toilet
便器

18. mirror
鏡

19. medicine cabinet
戸棚

20. toothbrush
歯ブラシ

21. toothbrush holder
歯ブラシ立て

22. sink
洗面台

23. soap
石鹸

24. soap dish
石鹸箱

25. wastebasket
くずかご

26. scale
体重計

27. bath mat
バスマット

More vocabulary

half bath: a bathroom without a shower or bathtub

linen closet: a closet or cabinet for towels and sheets

stall shower: a shower without a bathtub

Share your answers.

1. Do you turn off the water when you brush your teeth? wash your hair? shave?

2. Does your bathroom have a bathtub or a stall shower?

1. mirror 鏡	**8.** bed ベッド	**15.** headboard ヘッドボード	**22.** dust ruffle ダストラッフル
2. dresser / bureau ドレッサー/化粧台	**9.** pillow 枕	**16.** clock radio ラジオ時計	**23.** rug じゅうたん
3. drawer 引き出し	**10.** pillowcase 枕カバー	**17.** lamp ランプ	**24.** floor 床
4. closet 押し入れ	**11.** bedspread ベッドカバー/上掛け	**18.** lampshade ランプの笠/シェード	**25.** mattress マットレス
5. curtains カーテン	**12.** blanket 毛布	**19.** light switch スイッチ	**26.** box spring ボックススプリング
6. window shade ブラインド	**13.** flat sheet フラットシーツ	**20.** outlet コンセント	**27.** bed frame ベッド枠
7. photograph 写真	**14.** fitted sheet フィッテッドシーツ	**21.** night table ナイトテーブル/ ベッドサイドテーブル	

Use the new language.

Describe this room. (See **Describing Things**, page **11,** for help.)

I see a soft pillow and a beautiful bedspread.

Share your answers.

1. What is your favorite thing in your bedroom?

2. Do you have a clock in your bedroom? Where is it?

3. Do you have a mirror in your bedroom? Where is it?

1. bunk bed 二段ベッド	**7.** bumper pad パッド	**13.** diaper pail 汚れたおむつ入れ	**19.** cradle ゆりかご
2. comforter 掛け布団	**8.** chest of drawers たんす（箪笥）	**14.** dollhouse おもちゃの家	**20.** coloring book ぬりえ
3. night-light ナイトライト	**9.** baby monitor ベビーモニター	**15.** blocks 積み木	**21.** crayons クレヨン
4. mobile モビール	**10.** teddy bear テディベア	**16.** ball ボール	**22.** puzzle パズル
5. wallpaper 壁紙	**11.** smoke detector 煙探知器	**17.** picture book 絵本	**23.** stuffed animals ぬいぐるみ
6. crib ベビーベッド	**12.** changing table おむつ交換台	**18.** doll 人形	**24.** toy chest おもちゃ箱

Talk about where items are in the room.

The dollhouse is near *the coloring book*.

The teddy bear is on *the chest of drawers*.

Share your answers.

1. Do you think this is a good room for children? Why?

2. What toys did you play with when you were a child?

3. What children's stories do you know?

A. **dust** the furniture
家具のほこりをはらう

B. **recycle** the newspapers
新聞紙をリサイクルする

C. **clean** the oven
オーブンを掃除する

D. **wash** the windows
窓を洗う

E. **sweep** the floor
床を掃く

F. **empty** the wastebasket
くずかごを空にする

G. **make** the bed
ベッドを整える

H. **put away** the toys
おもちゃをしまう

I. **vacuum** the carpet
カーペットに掃除器をかける

J. **mop** the floor
床をモップでふく

K. **polish** the furniture
家具をみがく

L. **scrub** the floor
床をみがく

M. **wash** the dishes
皿を洗う

N. **dry** the dishes
皿を拭く

O. **wipe** the counter
調理台を拭く

P. **change** the sheets
シーツを換える

Q. **take out** the garbage
ごみを出す

Talk about yourself.

I wash <u>the dishes</u> every day.

I change <u>the sheets</u> every week.

I never <u>dry the dishes</u>.

Share your answers.

1. Who does the housework in your family?

2. What is your favorite cleaning job?

3. What is your least favorite cleaning job?

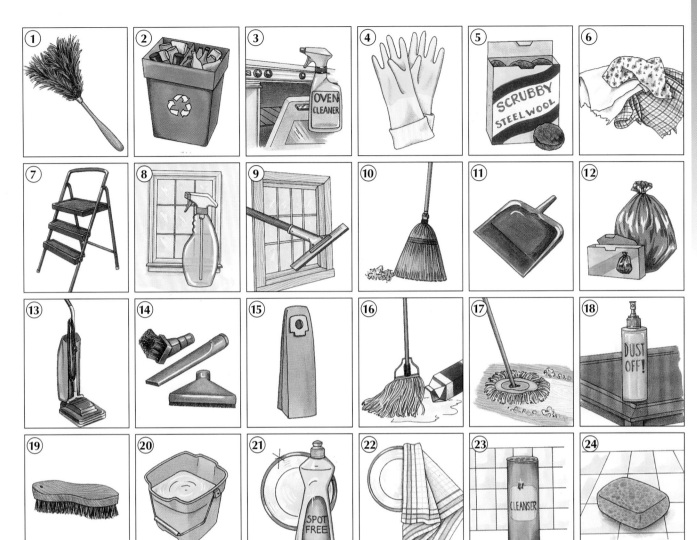

1. feather duster
はたき

2. recycling bin
リサイクル品入れ

3. oven cleaner
オーブンクリーナー

4. rubber gloves
ゴム手袋

5. steel-wool soap pads
石鹸付金属たわし

6. rags
ぞうきん

7. stepladder
脚立

8. glass cleaner
ガラスクリーナー

9. squeegee
ゴムぞうきん

10. broom
ほうき

11. dustpan
ちりとり

12. trash bags
ごみ袋

13. vacuum cleaner
掃除機

14. vacuum cleaner attachments
掃除機の付属品

15. vacuum cleaner bag
掃除機の中の袋

16. wet mop
ぬれモップ

17. dust mop
ほこり払いモップ

18. furniture polish
家具のつやだし

19. scrub brush
たわし

20. bucket / pail
バケツ

21. dishwashing liquid
食器用洗剤

22. dish towel
皿拭き用タオル／布巾

23. cleanser
クレンザー

24. sponge
スポンジ

Practice asking for the items.

I want to wash the windows.

Please hand me the squeegee.

I have to sweep the floor.

Can you get me the broom, please?

1. The water heater is **not working**.
   温水ボイラー（湯沸器）が**故障し
   ている**

2. The power is **out**.
   停電している

3. The roof is **leaking**.
   屋根から雨漏りがする

4. The wall is **cracked**.
   壁にひびが入っている

5. The window is **broken**.
   窓が**割れている**

6. The lock is **broken**.
   鍵が**壊れている**

7. The steps are **broken**.
   階段が**壊れている**

8. roofer
   屋根の修理屋

9. electrician
   電気屋

10. repair person
    修理人

11. locksmith
    鍵屋

12. carpenter
    大工

13. fuse box
    ヒューズの箱

14. gas meter
    ガスメーター

Use the new language.

Look at **Tools and Building Supplies**, pages **150–151**.

Name the tools you use for household repairs.

I use <u>a hammer and nails</u> to fix <u>a broken step</u>.

I use <u>a wrench</u> to repair <u>a dripping faucet</u>.

15. The furnace is **broken**.
暖房炉が**故障している**

16. The faucet is **dripping**.
蛇口から**水漏れがする**

17. The sink is **overflowing**.
洗面台が**あふれている**

18. The toilet is **stopped up**.
便器が**詰まっている**

19. The pipes are **frozen**.
水道管が**凍結している**

20. plumber
配管工

21. exterminator
害虫駆除業者

Household pests
家に住む害虫

22. termite(s)
白あり

23. flea(s)
蚤

24. ant(s)
あり

25. cockroach(es)
ごきぶり

26. mice*
はつかねずみ

27. rat(s)
ねずみ

*Note: *one mouse, two mice*

More vocabulary

fix: to repair something that is broken

exterminate: to kill household pests

pesticide: a chemical that is used to kill household pests

Share your answers.

1. Who does household repairs in your home?

2. What is the worst problem a home can have?

3. What is the most expensive problem a home can have?

1. grapes
   ぶどう

2. pineapples
   パイナップル

3. bananas
   バナナ

4. apples
   りんご

5. peaches
   もも

6. pears
   なし

7. apricots
   あんず

8. plums
   プラム

9. grapefruit
   グレープフルーツ

10. oranges
    オレンジ

11. lemons
    レモン

12. limes
    ライム

13. tangerines
    みかん

14. avocadoes
    アボカド

15. cantaloupes
    カンタロープ / メロン

16. cherries
    サクランボ

17. strawberries
    いちご

18. raspberries
    ラズベリー

19. blueberries
    ブルーベリー

20. papayas
    パパイヤ

21. mangoes
    マンゴ

22. coconuts
    ココナッツ

23. nuts
    ナッツ

24. watermelons
    スイカ

25. dates
    ナツメヤシの実

26. prunes
    プルーン

27. raisins
    レーズン

28. not ripe
    熟していない

29. ripe
    熟している

30. rotten
    腐った

Language note: *a bunch of*

We say *a bunch of grapes* and *a bunch of bananas*.

Share your answers.

1. Which fruits do you put in a fruit salad?

2. Which fruits are sold in your area in the summer?

3. What fruits did you have in your country?

1. lettuce レタス	**9.** celery セロリ	**17.** scallions ねぎ	**25.** string beans いんげん
2. cabbage キャベツ	**10.** parsley パセリ	**18.** eggplants なす	**26.** mushrooms マッシュルーム
3. carrots 人参	**11.** spinach ほうれんそう	**19.** peas エンドウまめ	**27.** corn とうもろこし
4. zucchini ズッキーニ	**12.** cucumbers きゅうり	**20.** artichokes アーティチョーク	**28.** onions たまねぎ
5. radishes ハツカダイコン	**13.** squash スクワッシュ	**21.** potatoes じゃがいも	**29.** garlic にんにく
6. beets ビート	**14.** turnips かぶ	**22.** yams ヤムイモ	
7. sweet peppers ピーマン	**15.** broccoli ブロッコリー	**23.** tomatoes トマト	
8. chili peppers 唐辛子	**16.** cauliflower カリフラワー	**24.** asparagus アスパラガス	

Language note: *a bunch of, a head of*

We say *a bunch of carrots*, *a bunch of celery*, and *a bunch of spinach*.

We say *a head of lettuce*, *a head of cabbage*, and *a head of cauliflower*.

Share your answers.

1. Which vegetables do you eat raw? cooked?

2. Which vegetables need to be in the refrigerator?

3. Which vegetables don't need to be in the refrigerator?

Beef 牛肉

1. roast beef
ローストビーフ

2. steak
ステーキ用肉

3. stewing beef
シチュー用牛肉

4. ground beef
挽肉

5. beef ribs
骨付のあばら肉

6. veal cutlets
子牛の肉

7. liver
レバー

8. tripe
第一胃と第二胃の食用部分

Pork 豚肉

9. ham
ハム

10. pork chops
豚肉の厚切り

11. bacon
ベーコン

12. sausage
ソーセージ

Lamb 子羊の肉

13. lamb shanks
子羊のすね肉

14. leg of lamb
子羊の足

15. lamb chops
子羊肉の厚切り

16. chicken
鶏肉

17. turkey
七面鳥の肉

18. duck
かも肉

19. breasts
胸肉

20. wings
手羽

21. thighs
もも肉

22. drumsticks
鶏の骨付脚肉

23. gizzards
（鶏の）砂嚢

24. **raw** chicken
生の鶏肉

25. **cooked** chicken
調理済みの鶏肉

More vocabulary

vegetarian: a person who doesn't eat meat

Meat and poultry without bones are called **boneless**.

Poultry without skin is called **skinless**.

Share your answers.

1. What kind of meat do you eat most often?

2. What kind of meat do you use in soup?

3. What part of the chicken do you like the most?

1. white bread
白パン

2. wheat bread
小麦パン

3. rye bread
ライ麦パン

4. smoked turkey
七面鳥の薫製

5. salami
サラミ

6. pastrami
牛の肩肉の薫製
または塩漬け肉

7. roast beef
ローストビーフ

8. corned beef
コーンビーフ

9. American cheese
アメリカンチーズ

10. cheddar cheese
チェダーチーズ

11. Swiss cheese
スイスチーズ

12. jack cheese
ジャックチーズ

13. potato salad
ポテトサラダ

14. coleslaw
コールスロー

15. pasta salad
パスタサラダ

Fish 魚

16. trout
鱒 (ます)

17. catfish
鯰 (なまず)

18. whole salmon
鮭まるごと一匹

19. salmon steak
鮭のステーキ

20. halibut
オヒョウ

21. filet of sole
シタビラメ

Shellfish 甲殻類

22. crab
蟹

23. lobster
ロブスター

24. shrimp
小エビ

25. scallops
ホタテ貝

26. mussels
ムール貝

27. oysters
カキ

28. clams
ハマグリ

29. **fresh** fish
新鮮な魚

30. **frozen** fish
冷凍の魚

Practice ordering a sandwich.

I'd like <u>roast beef</u> and <u>American cheese</u> on <u>rye bread</u>.

Tell what you want on it.

Please put <u>tomato</u>, <u>lettuce</u>, <u>onions</u>, and <u>mustard</u> on it.

Share your answers.

1. Do you like to eat fish?
2. Do you buy fresh or frozen fish?

1. bottle return 瓶の返却口	**3.** shopping cart ショッピングカート	**6.** baked goods パン/焼菓子製品	**9.** dairy section 乳製品売り場
2. meat and poultry section 肉と鳥肉売り場	**4.** canned goods 缶詰類	**7.** shopping basket ショッピングかご	**10.** pet food ペットフード
	5. aisle 通路	**8.** manager 店長	**11.** produce section 青果売り場

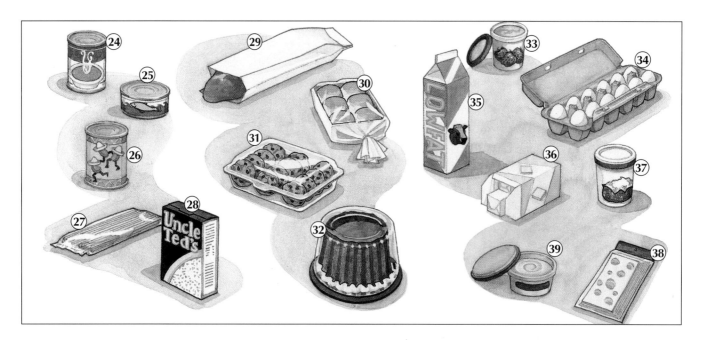

24. soup （缶の）スープ	**28.** rice 米	**32.** cake ケーキ	**36.** butter バター
25. tuna ツナ（缶）	**29.** bread パン	**33.** yogurt ヨーグルト	**37.** sour cream サワークリーム
26. beans 豆（の缶）	**30.** rolls ロールパン	**34.** eggs 卵	**38.** cheese チーズ
27. spaghetti スパゲッティ	**31.** cookies クッキー	**35.** milk ミルク	**39.** margarine マーガリン

12. frozen foods 冷凍食品	15. beverages 飲料	18. cash register レジ	21. bagger 袋詰め係
13. baking products パン/焼菓子の材料	16. snack foods スナック菓子	19. checker 勘定係/レジ係	22. paper bag 紙袋
14. paper products 紙製品	17. checkstand レジ台	20. line 列	23. plastic bag ポリ袋

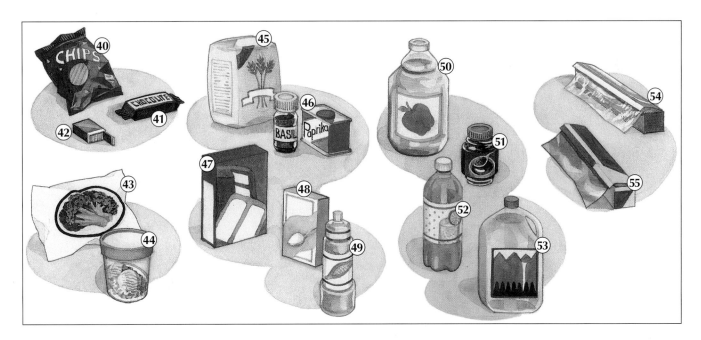

40. potato chips ポテトチップ	44. ice cream アイスクリーム	48. sugar 砂糖	52. soda 炭酸飲料
41. candy bar 板チョコ	45. flour 小麦粉	49. oil 油	53. bottled water ペットボトル水
42. gum ガム	46. spices 香辛料	50. apple juice りんごジュース	54. plastic wrap サランラップ
43. frozen vegetables 冷凍野菜	47. cake mix ケーキミックス	51. instant coffee インスタントコーヒー	55. aluminum foil アルミフォイル

1. bottle
ボトル

2. jar
瓶

3. can
缶

4. carton
カートン

5. container
容器

6. box
箱

7. bag
袋

8. package
パッケージ

9. six-pack
6本入り
のパック

10. loaf
塊

11. roll
巻

12. tube
チューブ

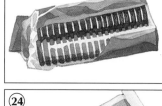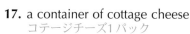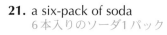

13. a bottle of soda
1本のソーダ

14. a jar of jam
1瓶のジャム

15. a can of soup
1缶のスープ

16. a carton of eggs
卵1パック

17. a container of cottage cheese
コテージチーズ1パック

18. a box of cereal
1箱のシリアル

19. a bag of flour
1袋の小麦粉

20. a package of cookies
クッキー1箱

21. a six-pack of soda
6本入りのソーダ1パック

22. a loaf of bread
パン1個

23. a roll of paper towels
ペーパータオル1巻

24. a tube of toothpaste
練歯みがき1つ

Grammar point: *How much? How many?*

Some foods can be counted: *one apple, two apples.*

How many apples do you need? I need ***two*** apples.

Some foods cannot be counted, like liquids, grains, spices, or dairy foods. For these, count containers: *one box of rice, two boxes of rice.*

How much rice do you need? I need ***two boxes.***

A. Measure the ingredients.
材料を測定する

B. Weigh the food.
食品を計量する

3.25 lb.

C. Convert the measurements.
計量値を換算する

1 cup = 237 milliliters

Liquid measures 液体の計量

① 1 fl. oz.

② 1 c.

③ Frozen YOGURT 1 pt.

④ MILK 1 qt.

⑤ 1 gal.

Dry measures 乾物類の計量

⑥ 1 tsp.

⑦ Sugar 1 TBS.

⑧ Brown Sugar 1/4 c.

⑨ 1/2 c.

⑩ FLOUR 1 c.

Weight 重さ

⑪ **.06 lb.**

⑫ **1.00 lb.**

1. a fluid ounce of water
   水1 オンス

2. a cup of oil
   油1 カップ

3. a pint of yogurt
   ヨーグルト1 パイント

4. a quart of milk
   牛乳1 クオート

5. a gallon of apple juice
   りんごジュース1 ガロン

6. a teaspoon of salt
   塩小さじ1 杯

7. a tablespoon of sugar
   砂糖大さじ1 杯

8. a 1/4 cup of brown sugar
   赤砂糖1/4 カップ

9. a 1/2 cup of raisins
   レーズン1/2 カップ

10. a cup of flour
    小麦粉1 カップ

11. an ounce of cheese
    チーズ1 オンス

12. a pound of roast beef
    ローストビーフ1 ポンド

VOLUME
1 fl. oz. = 30 milliliters (ml.)
1 c. = 237 ml.
1 pt. = .47 liters (l.)
1 qt. = .95 l.
1 gal. = 3.79 l.

EQUIVALENCIES	
3 tsp. = 1 TBS.	2 c. = 1 pt.
2 TBS. = 1 fl. oz.	2 pt. = 1 qt.
8 fl. oz. = 1 c.	4 qt. = 1 gal.

WEIGHT
1 oz. = 28.35 grams (g.)
1 lb. = 453.6 g.
2.205 lbs. = 1 kilogram
1 lb. = 16 oz.

Scrambled eggs いり卵

A. **Break** 3 eggs.
卵3個を割る

B. **Beat** well.
よく混ぜる

C. **Grease** the pan.
フライパンに油
をひく

D. **Pour** the eggs into
the pan.
フライパンに卵を
流し込む

E. **Stir.**
かき混ぜる

F. **Cook** until done.
でき上がるまで
調理する

Vegetable casserole 野菜のオーブン焼

G. **Chop** the onions.
玉葱を切る

H. **Sauté** the onions.
玉葱を炒める

I. **Steam** the broccoli.
ブロッコリーを蒸す

J. **Grate** the cheese.
チーズをおろす

K. **Mix** the ingredients.
材料を混ぜ合わせる

L. **Bake** at 350° for
45 minutes.
350度のオーブンで
45分焼く

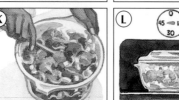

Chicken soup チキンスープ

M. **Cut up** the chicken.
鶏肉を切る

N. **Peel** the carrots.
人参の皮をむく

O. **Slice** the carrots.
人参をうす切り
にする

P. **Boil** the chicken.
鶏肉を茹でる

Q. **Add** the vegetables.
野菜を加える

R. **Simmer** for 1 hour.
1時間煮込む

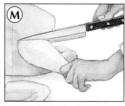
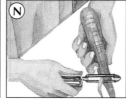
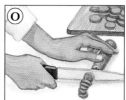

Five ways to cook chicken 5通りの鶏肉調理法

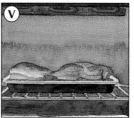
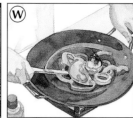

S. **fry**
揚げる

T. **barbecue / grill**
バーベキュー /
グリル

U. **roast**
オーブンで焼く

V. **broil**
あぶり焼きにする

W. **stir-fry**
炒める

Talk about the way you prepare these foods.

I _fry_ eggs.

I _bake_ potatoes.

Share your answers.

1. What are popular ways in your country to make rice?
vegetables? meat?

2. What is your favorite way to cook chicken?

1. can opener
   缶切り

2. grater
   おろしがね

3. plastic storage
   container
   プラスチック
   保存容器

4. steamer
   蒸し器

5. frying pan
   フライパン

6. pot
   鍋

7. ladle
   おたま、しゃく

8. double boiler
   二重鍋

9. wooden spoon
   木のスプーン

10. garlic press
    ニンニク圧搾器

11. casserole dish
    キャセロール皿

12. carving knife
    肉切り用ナイフ

13. roasting pan
    天板

14. roasting rack
    天板棚

15. vegetable peeler
    野菜の皮剥き器

16. paring knife
    果物ナイフ

17. colander
    水きり器

18. kitchen timer
    キッチンタイマー

19. spatula
    フライ返し

20. eggbeater
    卵の泡立器

21. whisk
    泡立器

22. strainer
    ざる

23. tongs
    トング

24. lid
    蓋

25. saucepan
    シチュー鍋

26. cake pan
    ケーキ用焼き型

27. cookie sheet
    クッキーシート

28. pie pan
    パイ用焼き型

29. pot holders
    なべつかみ

30. rolling pin
    麺棒

31. mixing bowl
    ボール

Talk about how to use the utensils.

You use a peeler to peel potatoes.

You use a pot to cook soup.

Use the new language.

Look at **Food Preparation**, page 58.

Name the different utensils you see.

1. hamburger
ハンバーガー

2. french fries
フライドポテト

3. cheeseburger
チーズバーガー

4. soda
ソーダ

5. iced tea
アイスティー

6. hot dog
ホットドック

7. pizza
ピザ

8. green salad
野菜サラダ

9. taco
タコス

10. nachos
ナチョス

11. frozen yogurt
フローズンヨーグルト

12. milk shake
ミルクシェイク

13. counter
勘定台

14. muffin
マフィン

15. doughnut
ドーナッツ

16. salad bar
サラダバー

17. lettuce
レタス

18. salad dressing
サラダドレッシング

19. booth
ブース

20. straw
ストロー

21. sugar
砂糖

22. sugar substitute
砂糖代替品

23. ketchup
ケチャップ

24. mustard
辛子

25. mayonnaise
マヨネーズ

26. relish
薬味

A. **eat**
食べる

B. **drink**
飲む

More vocabulary

donut: doughnut (spelling variation)

condiments: relish, mustard, ketchup, mayonnaise, etc.

Share your answers.

1. What would you order at this restaurant?

2. Which fast foods are popular in your country?

3. How often do you eat fast food? Why?

Breakfast

Lunch

Dinner

Desserts

Beverages

1. scrambled eggs
   いり卵

2. sausage
   ソーセージ

3. toast
   トースト

4. waffles
   ワッフル

5. syrup
   シロップ

6. pancakes
   ホットケーキ

7. bacon
   ベーコン

8. grilled cheese
   sandwich
   グリルチーズ
   サンドイッチ

9. chef's salad
   シェフのサラダ

10. soup of the day
    本日のスープ

11. mashed potatoes
    マッシュポテト

12. roast chicken
    ローストチキン

13. steak
    ステーキ

14. baked potato
    ベークドポテト

15. pasta
    パスタ

16. garlic bread
    ガーリックブレッド

17. fried fish
    魚のフライ

18. rice pilaf
    ピラフ

19. cake
    ケーキ

20. pudding
    プリン

21. pie
    パイ

22. coffee
    コーヒー

23. decaf coffee
    カフェイン抜きの
    コーヒー

24. tea
    紅茶

Practice ordering from the menu.

I'd like <u>a grilled cheese sandwich</u> and <u>some soup</u>.

I'll have <u>the chef's salad</u> and <u>a cup of decaf coffee</u>.

Use the new language.

Look at **Fruit,** page **50.**

Order a slice of pie using the different fruit flavors.

Please give me a slice of <u>apple</u> pie.

1. hostess
案内係

2. dining room
食堂

3. menu
メニュー

4. server / waiter
給士 / ウエイター

5. patron / diner
顧客 / 食事客

A. set the table
テーブルを整える

B. seat the customer
お客様を席に案内する

C. pour the water
水を注ぐ

D. order from the menu
メニューで注文をする

E. take the order
注文を受ける

F. serve the meal
料理を出す

G. clear the table
テーブルをかたずける

H. carry the tray
お盆を運ぶ

I. pay the check
勘定を支払う

J. leave a tip
チップを置く

More vocabulary

eat out: to go to a restaurant to eat

take out: to buy food at a restaurant and take it home
to eat

Practice giving commands.

Please <u>set the table</u>.

I'd like you to <u>clear the table</u>.

It's time to <u>serve the meal</u>.

6. server / waitress 給士／ウエイトレス	**8.** bread basket パン用のバスケット	**10.** kitchen 調理場	**12.** dishroom 食器用の部屋
7. dessert tray デザート用のトレー	**9.** busperson 食後のテーブルを片づける人	**11.** chef シェフ	**13.** dishwasher 食器を洗う人

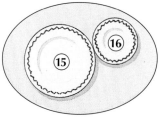
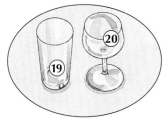

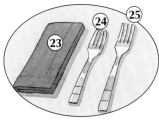
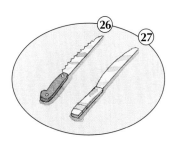
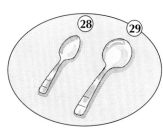

14. place setting 一人分の食器	**18.** soup bowl スープ皿	**22.** saucer 受け皿／ソーサー	**26.** steak knife ステーキナイフ
15. dinner plate ディナー皿	**19.** water glass 水を入れるコップ	**23.** napkin ナプキン	**27.** knife ナイフ
16. bread-and-butter plate パンとバター用の皿	**20.** wine glass ワイングラス	**24.** salad fork サラダフォーク	**28.** teaspoon ティースプーン
17. salad plate サラダ用の皿	**21.** cup コーヒー（紅茶）カップ	**25.** dinner fork ディナーフォーク	**29.** soupspoon スープスプーン

Talk about how you set the table in your home.

The glass is on the right.

The fork goes on the left.

The napkin is next to the plate.

Share your answers.

1. Do you know anyone who works in a restaurant? What does he or she do?

2. In your opinion, which restaurant jobs are hard? Why?

1. three-piece suit 三つ揃え	**6.** sports coat スポーツコート	**11.** pullover sweater セーター
2. suit スーツ	**7.** turtleneck タートルネック	**12.** T-shirt ティーシャツ
3. dress ワンピース	**8.** slacks/pants スラックス	**13.** shorts ショートパンツ
4. shirt シャツ	**9.** blouse ブラウス	**14.** sweatshirt スウェットシャツ/トレーナー
5. jeans ジーパン/ジーンズ	**10.** skirt スカート	**15.** sweatpants スウエットパンツ

More vocabulary:

outfit: clothes that look nice together

When clothes are popular, they are **in fashion.**

Talk about what you're wearing today and what you wore yesterday.

I'm wearing a gray sweater, a red T-shirt, and blue jeans.

Yesterday I wore a green pullover sweater, a white shirt, and black slacks.

16. jumpsuit
ジャンプスーツ

17. uniform
制服

18. jumper
ジャンパースカート

19. maternity dress
妊婦服

20. knit shirt
ニットシャツ

21. overalls
オーバーオール

22. tunic
チュニック

23. leggings
レギンズ / スパッツ

24. vest
チョッキ / ベスト

25. split skirt
キュロットスカート

26. sports shirt
スポーツシャツ

27. cardigan sweater
カーディガン

28. tuxedo
タキシード

29. evening gown
夜会服 / ロングドレス

Use the new language.

Look at **A Graduation**, pages **32–33**.

Name the clothes you see.

The man at the podium is wearing a suit.

Share your answers.

1. Which clothes in this picture are in fashion now?

2. Who is the best-dressed person in this line? Why?

3. What do you wear when you go to the movies?

1. hat
帽子

2. overcoat
コート

3. leather jacket
皮のジャケット

4. wool scarf/muffler
ウールのスカーフ/襟巻

5. gloves
手袋

6. cap
野球帽/キャップ

7. jacket
ジャケット/上着

8. parka
フード付き上着

9. mittens
ミトン

10. ski cap
スキー帽

11. tights
タイツ

12. earmuffs
防寒用耳あて

13. down vest
ダウンベスト

14. ski mask
スキーマスク

15. down jacket
ダウンジャケット

16. umbrella
傘

17. raincoat
レインコート

18. poncho
ポンチョ

19. rain boots
雨靴/長靴

20. trench coat
トレンチコート

21. sunglasses
サングラス

22. swimming trunks
海水パンツ

23. straw hat
麦わら帽子

24. windbreaker
ウインドブレーカー

25. cover-up
上着

26. swimsuit/bathing suit
水着

27. baseball cap
野球帽

Use the new language.

Look at **Weather**, page **10**.

Name the clothing for each weather condition.

Wear a jacket when it's windy.

Share your answers.

1. Which is better in the rain, an umbrella or a poncho?

2. Which is better in the cold, a parka or a down jacket?

3. Do you have more summer clothes or winter clothes?

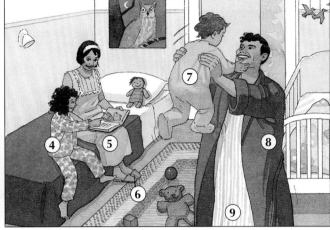

1. leotard
レオタード

2. tank top
タンクトップ

3. bike shorts
自転車競技用半ズボン

4. pajamas
パジャマ

5. nightgown
ガウン

6. slippers
スリッパ

7. blanket sleeper
毛布

8. bathrobe
バスローブ

9. nightshirt
寝間着

10. undershirt
下着

11. long underwear
ズボン下

12. boxer shorts
ボックス型ショーツ

13. briefs
ブリーフ型ショーツ

14. athletic supporter / jockstrap
男性用スポーツサポーター

15. socks
靴下

16. (bikini) panties
(ビキニ型) パンティー

17. briefs / underpants
パンツ

18. girdle
ガードル

19. garter belt
ガーターベルト

20. bra
ブラジャー

21. camisole
キャミソール

22. full slip
スリップ

23. half slip
ペチコート

24. knee-highs
膝丈ソックス

25. kneesocks
ハイソックス

26. stockings
ストッキング

27. pantyhose
パンティーストッキング

More vocabulary

lingerie: underwear or sleepwear for women

loungewear: clothing (sometimes sleepwear) people
wear around the home

Share your answers.

1. What do you wear when you exercise?

2. What kind of clothing do you wear for sleeping?

Shoes and Accessories 靴とアクセサリー

1. salesclerk
販売員

2. suspenders
ズボンつり

3. shoe department
靴売り場

4. silk scarves*
シルクのスカーフ

5. hats
帽子

12. sole
靴底

13. heel
かかと

14. shoelace
靴ひも

15. toe
つまさき

16. pumps
パンプス

17. high heels
ハイヒール

18. boots
ブーツ

19. loafers
ローファー

20. oxfords
オックスフォードシューズ

21. hiking boots
ハイキング（登山用）ブーツ

22. tennis shoes
テニス靴

23. athletic shoes
運動靴

24. sandals
サンダル

*Note: *one scarf, two scarves*

Talk about the shoes you're wearing today.

I'm wearing a pair of <u>white sandals</u>.

Practice asking a salesperson for help.

Could I try on these <u>sandals</u> in size <u>10</u>?

Do you have any <u>silk scarves</u>?

Where are <u>the hats</u>?

6. purses/handbags ハンドバック	**8.** jewelry 宝石類	**10.** ties ネクタイ
7. display case ショーケース	**9.** necklaces ネックレス	**11.** belts ベルト

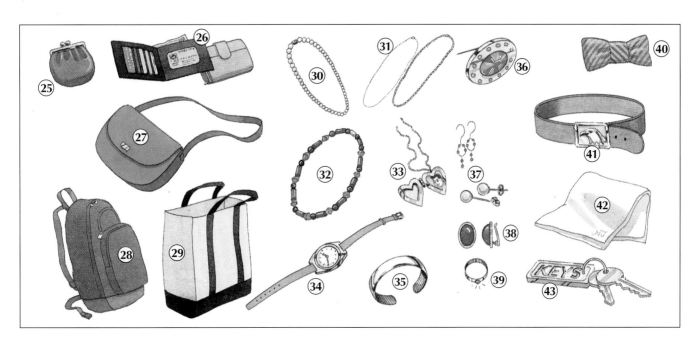

25. change purse 小銭入れ	**30.** string of pearls パール（の鎖）	**35.** bracelet ブレスレット	**40.** bow tie 蝶ネクタイ
26. wallet 財布	**31.** chain 鎖	**36.** pin ブローチ	**41.** belt buckle ベルトのバックル
27. shoulder bag ショルダーバッグ	**32.** beads ビーズ	**37.** pierced earrings ピアス	**42.** handkerchief ハンカチ
28. backpack/bookbag バックパック	**33.** locket ロケット	**38.** clip-on earrings イヤリング	**43.** key chain キーホルダー
29. tote bag 大型手さげ袋	**34.** (wrist)watch （腕）時計	**39.** ring 指輪	

Share your answers.

1. Which of these accessories are usually worn by women? by men?

2. Which of these do you wear every day?

3. Which of these would you wear to a job interview? Why?

4. Which accessory would you like to receive as a present? Why?

Describing Clothes 衣服の説明

Sizes サイズ

1. extra small
特小

2. small
小

3. medium
中

4. large
大

5. extra large
特大

Patterns 柄

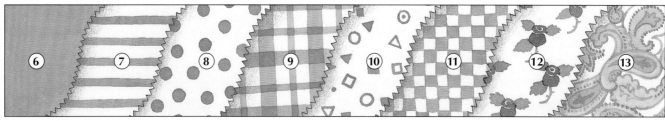

6. solid green
無地の緑

7. striped
縞模様

8. polka-dotted
水玉模様

9. plaid
格子柄

10. print
プリント柄

11. checked
チェック柄

12. floral
花柄

13. paisley
ペーズリー柄

Types of material 素材のタイプ

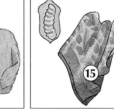 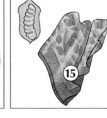  

14. wool sweater
ウールのセーター

15. silk scarf
シルクのスカーフ

16. cotton T-shirt
綿のティーシャツ

17. linen jacket
麻のジャケット

18. leather boots
皮のブーツ

19. nylon stockings*
ナイロンストッキング

Problems 問題

 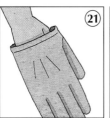  

20. too small
小さすぎる

21. too big
大きすぎる

22. stain
しみ

23. rip/tear
破れ/ほつれ

24. broken zipper
壊れたファスナー

25. missing button
行方不明のボタン

***Note:** Nylon, polyester, rayon, and plastic are synthetic materials.

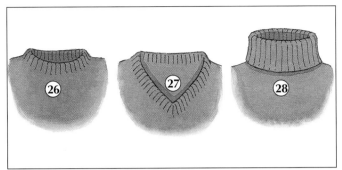

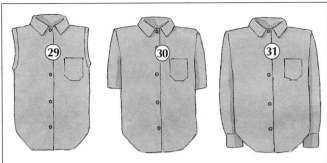

26. crewneck sweater
丸首のセーター

27. V-neck sweater
Vネックのセーター

28. turtleneck sweater
タートルネックのセーター

29. sleeveless shirt
袖なしシャツ

30. short-sleeved shirt
半袖シャツ

31. long-sleeved shirt
長袖シャツ

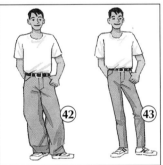
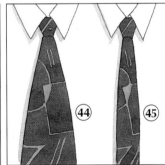
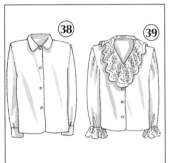
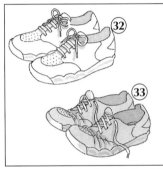
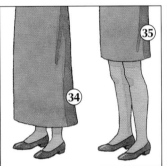

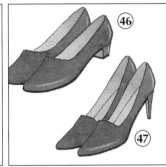

32. new shoes
新しい靴

33. old shoes
古い靴

34. long skirt
長いスカート

35. short skirt
短いスカート

36. formal dress
盛装用ドレス

37. casual dress
カジュアルな服／普段着

38. plain blouse
無地のブラウス

39. fancy blouse
装飾の多いブラウス

40. light jacket
薄手のジャケット

41. heavy jacket
厚手のジャケット

42. loose pants/**baggy** pants
ゆるい／だぶだぶのズボン

43. tight pants
きついズボン

44. wide tie
太いネクタイ

45. narrow tie
細いネクタイ

46. low heels
低いヒール

47. high heels
高いヒール

Talk about yourself.

I like <u>long-sleeved</u> shirts and <u>baggy</u> pants.

I like <u>short skirts</u> and <u>high heels</u>.

I usually wear <u>plain</u> clothes.

Share your answers.

1. What type of material do you usually wear in the summer? in the winter?

2. What patterns do you see around you?

3. Are you wearing casual or formal clothes?

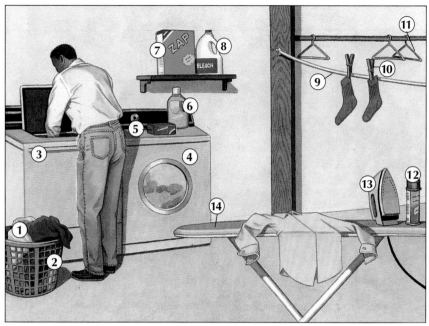
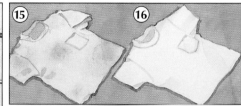
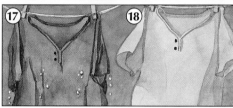
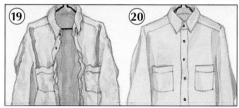

1. laundry
洗濯物

2. laundry basket
洗濯かご

3. washer
洗濯機

4. dryer
乾燥機

5. dryer sheets
乾燥機用のシート

6. fabric softener
柔軟仕上げ剤

7. laundry detergent
洗濯用洗剤

8. bleach
ブリーチ/漂白剤

9. clothesline
物干し綱

10. clothespin
洗濯ばさみ

11. hanger
ハンガー

12. spray starch
スプレー糊

13. iron
アイロン

14. ironing board
アイロン台

15. **dirty** T-shirt
汚れたTシャツ

16. **clean** T-shirt
きれいなTシャツ

17. **wet** T-shirt
濡れたTシャツ

18. **dry** T-shirt
乾いたTシャツ

19. **wrinkled** shirt
しわだらけのシャツ

20. **ironed** shirt
アイロンのかかった
シャツ

A. **Sort** the laundry.
洗濯物を仕分ける

B. **Add** the detergent.
洗剤を加える

C. **Load** the washer.
洗濯機に入れる

D. **Clean** the lint trap.
糸くずを**取り除く**

E. **Unload** the dryer.
乾燥機から洗濯物を**取り出す**

F. **Fold** the laundry.
洗濯物をたたむ

G. **Iron** the clothes.
服にアイロンをかける

H. **Hang up** the clothes.
服をハンガーにかける

More vocabulary

dry cleaners: a business that cleans clothes using chemicals, not water and detergent

 wash in cold water only

 no bleach

 line dry

 dry-clean only, do not wash

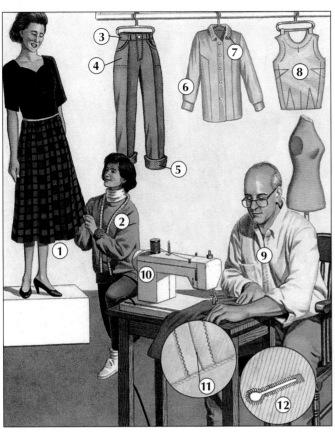

A. sew by hand
手で縫う

B. sew by machine
ミシンで縫う

C. lengthen
長くする

D. shorten
短くする

E. take in
幅を詰める

F. let out
幅を広げる

1. hemline ドレス/スカート などの裾	**4.** pocket ポケット	**7.** collar 襟	**10.** sewing machine ミシン
2. dressmaker （婦人用）仕立て屋	**5.** cuff そで口/カフス	**8.** pattern パターン	**11.** seam 縫い目
3. waistband ウエストバンド	**6.** sleeve 袖	**9.** tailor （紳士用）仕立て屋	**12.** buttonhole ボタンホール

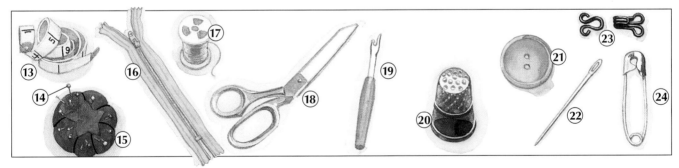

13. tape measure 巻尺	**16.** zipper ファスナー	**19.** seam ripper 糸ぬき	**22.** needle 針
14. pin ピン	**17.** spool of thread 1巻の糸	**20.** thimble 指ぬき	**23.** hook and eye ホック
15. pin cushion 針山	**18.** (pair of) scissors はさみ（1丁）	**21.** button ボタン	**24.** safety pin 安全ピン

More vocabulary

pattern maker: a person who makes patterns

garment worker: a person who works in a
clothing factory

fashion designer: a person who makes original clothes

Share your answers.

1. Do you know how to use a sewing machine?

2. Can you sew by hand?

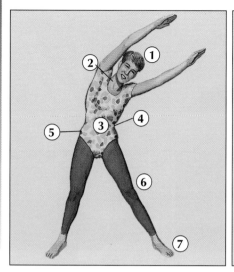

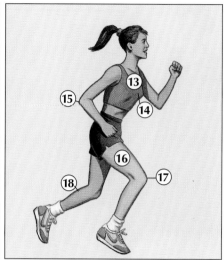

1. head
頭

2. neck
首

3. abdomen
腹

4. waist
胴

5. hip
腰

6. leg
脚

7. foot
足（くるぶしから下）

8. hand
手

9. arm
腕

10. shoulder
肩

11. back
背中

12. buttocks
尻

13. chest
胸

14. breast
乳房

15. elbow
肘

16. thigh
大腿部

17. knee
膝

18. calf
ふくらはぎ

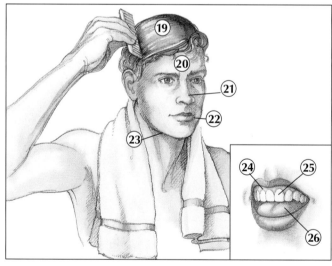

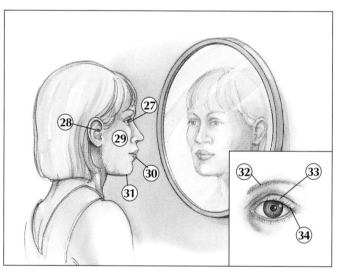

The face
顔

19. hair
髪

20. forehead
ひたい

21. nose
鼻

22. mouth
口

23. jaw
下あご

24. gums
歯茎

25. teeth
歯

26. tongue
舌

27. eye
目

28. ear
耳

29. cheek
頬

30. lip
唇

31. chin
あご先

32. eyebrow
眉毛

33. eyelid
まぶた

34. eyelashes
まつげ

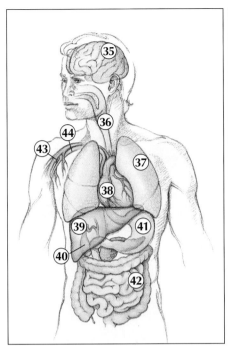

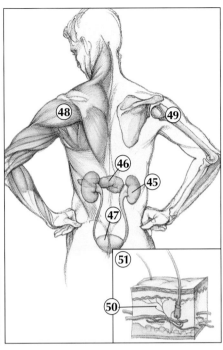

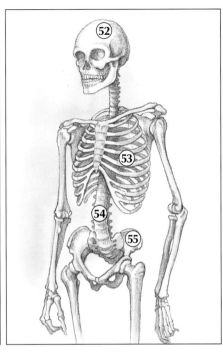

Inside the body
体内

35. brain
脳

36. throat
喉

37. lung
肺

38 heart
心臓

39. liver
肝臓

40. gallbladder
胆のう

41. stomach
胃

42. intestines
腸

43. artery
動脈

44. vein
静脈

45. kidney
腎臓

46. pancreas
膵臓

47. bladder
膀胱

48. muscle
筋肉

49. bone
骨

50. nerve
神経

51. skin
皮膚

The skeleton
骨格

52. skull
頭蓋骨

53. rib cage
胸郭

54. spinal column
脊柱

55. pelvis
骨盤

The Hand

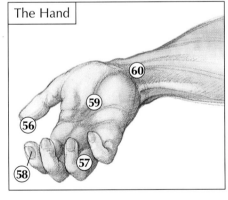

The Foot

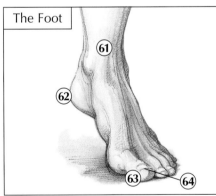

The Senses

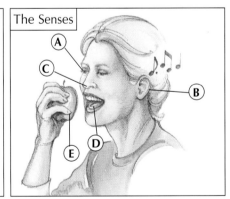

56. thumb
親指

57. fingers
指

58. fingernail
つめ

59. palm
手のひら

60. wrist
手首

61. ankle
足首

62. heel
かかと

63. toe
つま先

64. toenail
足のつめ

A. **see**
見る

B. **hear**
聴く

C. **smell**
臭いをかぐ

D. **taste**
味わう

E. **touch**
触れる

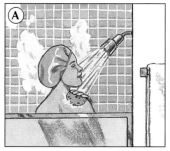

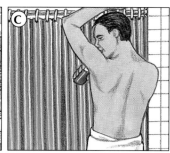

A. take a shower
シャワーを浴びる

B. bathe / take a bath
風呂にはいる

C. use deodorant
体臭防止剤を使う

D. put on sunscreen
日焼け止めをぬる

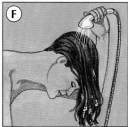
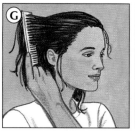
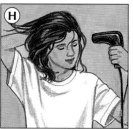

1. shower cap
   シャワーキャップ

2. soap
   石鹸

3. bath powder / talcum powder
   タルカムパウダー

4. deodorant
   体臭防止剤／デオドラント

5. perfume / cologne
   香水／コロン

6. sunscreen
   日焼け止め

7. body lotion
   ボディーローション

8. moisturizer
   モイスチャライザー

E. wash…hair
髪を洗う

F. rinse…hair
髪をすすぐ

G. comb…hair
髪をとかす

H. dry…hair
髪を乾かす

I. brush…hair
ブラシをかける

9. shampoo
   シャンプー

10. conditioner
    コンディショナー

11. hair gel
    ジェル

12. hair spray
    ヘアースプレー

13. comb
    櫛

14. brush
    ブラシ

15. curling iron
    こて

16. blow dryer
    ドライヤー

17. hair clip
    髪用クリップ

18. barrette
    髪止めピン

19. bobby pins
    ボビーピン

J. brush…teeth
歯を磨く

K. floss…teeth
歯にフロスを
かける

L. gargle
うがいをする

M. shave
髭を剃る

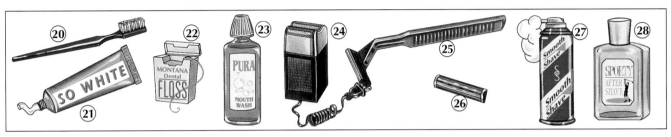

20. toothbrush
歯ブラシ

21. toothpaste
歯磨粉

22. dental floss
デンタルフロス

23. mouthwash
口腔内洗浄剤

24. electric shaver
電気かみそり

25. razor
かみそり

26. razor blade
かみそりの刃

27. shaving cream
シェービングクリーム

28. aftershave
アフターシェーブローション

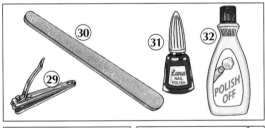

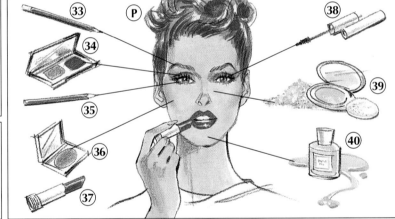

N. cut…nails
つめを切る

O. polish…nails
つめを磨く

P. put on…makeup
化粧をする

29. nail clipper
つめきり

30. emery board
つめやすり

31. nail polish
マニキュア液

32. nail polish remover
マニキュアおとし

33. eyebrow pencil
眉墨

34. eye shadow
アイシャドー

35. eyeliner
アイライナー

36. blush / rouge
ほお紅

37. lipstick
口紅

38. mascara
マスカラ

39. face powder
おしろい

40. foundation
ファンデーション

More vocabulary

A product without perfume or scent is **unscented.**

A product that is better for people with allergies is **hypoallergenic.**

Share your answers.

1. What is your morning routine if you stay home? if you go out?

2. Do women in your culture wear makeup? How old are they when they begin to use it?

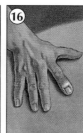
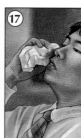

1. **headache**
頭痛

2. **toothache**
歯痛

3. **earache**
耳の痛み

4. **stomachache**
胃痛

5. **backache**
腰痛

6. **sore throat**
のどの炎症

7. **nasal congestion**
鼻づまり

8. **fever / temperature**
熱

9. **chills**
寒気

10. **rash**
湿疹

A. **cough**
せき

B. **sneeze**
くしゃみ

C. **feel** dizzy
めまいがする

D. **feel** nauseous
吐き気がする

E. **throw up / vomit**
おう吐

11. **insect bite**
虫さされ

12. **bruise**
打ち身

13. **cut**
切り傷

14. **sunburn**
日焼け

15. **blister**
水ぶくれ

16. **swollen** finger
腫れた指

17. **bloody** nose
鼻血

18. **sprained** ankle
足首のねんざ

Use the new language.

Look at **Health Care,** pages 80–81.

Tell what medication or treatment you would use for each health problem.

Share your answers.

1. For which problems would you go to a doctor? use medication? do nothing?

2. What do you do for a sunburn? for a headache?

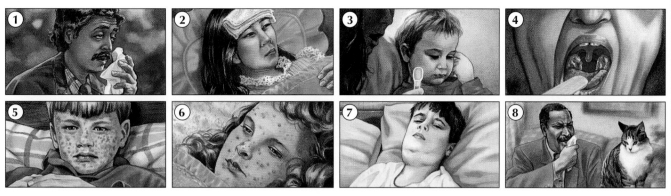

Common illnesses and childhood diseases　一般的な疾患と子供がよくかかる病気

1. cold
風邪

2. flu
流感

3. ear infection
耳の感染

4. strep throat
咽頭炎

5. measles
はしか

6. chicken pox
水ぼうそう

7. mumps
おたふくかぜ

8. allergies
アレルギー

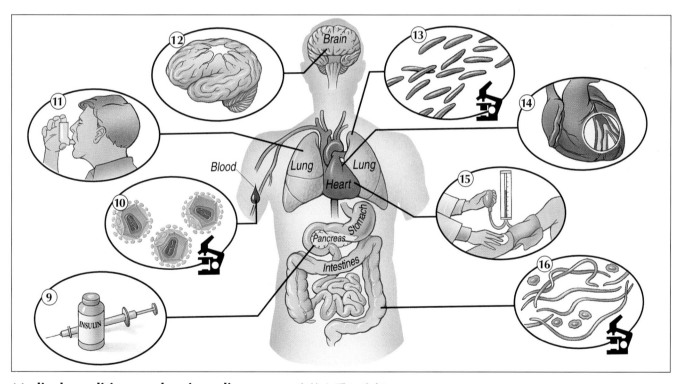

Medical conditions and serious diseases　症状と重い病気

9. diabetes
糖尿病

10. HIV (human immunodeficiency virus)
HIV

11. asthma
喘息

12. brain cancer
脳がん

13. TB (tuberculosis)
結核

14. heart disease
心臓病

15. high blood pressure
高血圧

16. intestinal parasites
腸の寄生虫

More vocabulary

AIDS (acquired immunodeficiency syndrome): a medical condition that results from contracting the HIV virus

influenza: flu

hypertension: high blood pressure

infectious disease: a disease that is spread through air or water

Share your answers.

Which diseases on this page are infectious?

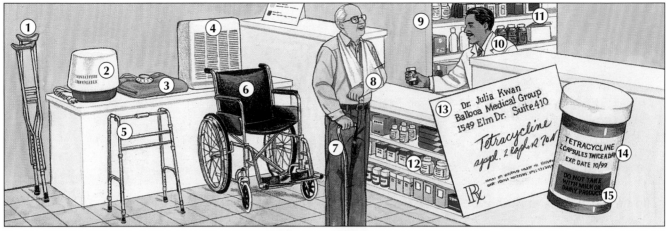

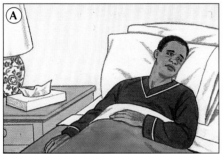

1. crutches
まつば杖

2. humidifier
加湿器

3. heating pad
ヒーティングパッド
（電気毛布など）

4. air purifier
空気清浄器

5. walker
歩行器

6. wheelchair
車椅子

7. cane
つえ

8. sling
つり包帯

9. pharmacy
薬局

10. pharmacist
薬剤師

11. prescription medication
処方薬

12. over-the-counter medication
売薬

13. prescription
処方箋

14. prescription label
薬のラベル

15. warning label
注意書き

A. **Get** bed rest.
ベッドで安静にする

B. **Drink** fluids.
水分を補給する

C. **Change** your diet.
食餌を変える

D. **Exercise.**
運動する

E. **Get** an injection.
注射をうつ

F. **Take** medicine.
薬を飲む

More vocabulary

dosage: how much medicine you take and how many times a day you take it

expiration date: the last day the medicine can be used

treatment: something you do to get better

Staying in bed, drinking fluids, and getting physical therapy are treatments.

An injection that stops a person from getting a serious disease is called **an immunization** or **a vaccination.**

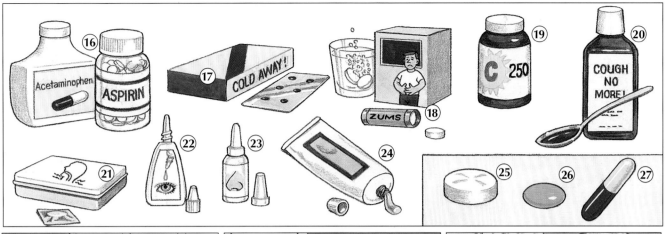

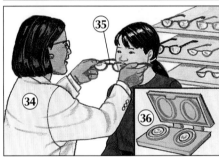

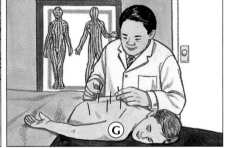

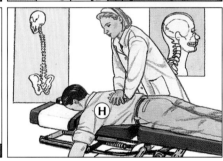

16. pain reliever 鎮痛剤	**24.** ointment 軟こう	**32.** audiologist 聴覚訓練士
17. cold tablets 風邪の錠剤	**25.** tablet 錠剤	**33.** hearing aid 補聴器
18. antacid 制酸薬	**26.** pill 丸薬	**34.** optometrist 検眼検査士
19. vitamins ビタミン剤	**27.** capsule カプセル	**35.** (eye)glasses 眼鏡
20. cough syrup せき止めのシロップ	**28.** orthopedist 整形外科医	**36.** contact lenses コンタクトレンズ
21. throat lozenges のど飴	**29.** cast ギプス包帯	**G. Get** acupuncture. 針治療を受ける
22. eyedrops 目薬	**30.** physical therapist 理学療法士	**H. Go** to a chiropractor. カイロプラクティックに行く
23. nasal spray 鼻のスプレー	**31.** brace 固定装具	

Share your answers.

1. What's the best treatment for a headache? a sore throat? a stomachache? a fever?

2. Do you think vitamins are important? Why or why not?

3. What treatments are popular in your culture?

A. **be injured / be hurt**
ケガをする

B. **be** unconscious
意識を失う

C. **be** in shock
衝撃を受ける

D. **have** a heart attack
心臓発作をおこす

E. **have** an allergic reaction
アレルギー反応をおこす

F. **get** an electric shock
電気ショックを受ける

G. **get** frostbite
しもやけになる

H. **burn** (your)self
火傷をする

I. **drown**
溺れる

J. **swallow** poison
毒物を飲む

K. **overdose** on drugs
薬を過量にとる

L. **choke**
のどがつまる

M. **bleed**
出血する

N. **can't breathe**
呼吸ができない

O. **fall**
倒れる

P. **break** a bone
骨折する

Grammar point: past tense

burn	—	burned	choke	—	choked	bleed	—	bled
drown	—	drowned	be	—	was, were	can't	—	couldn't
swallow	—	swallowed	have	—	had	fall	—	fell
overdose	—	overdosed	get	—	got	break	—	broke

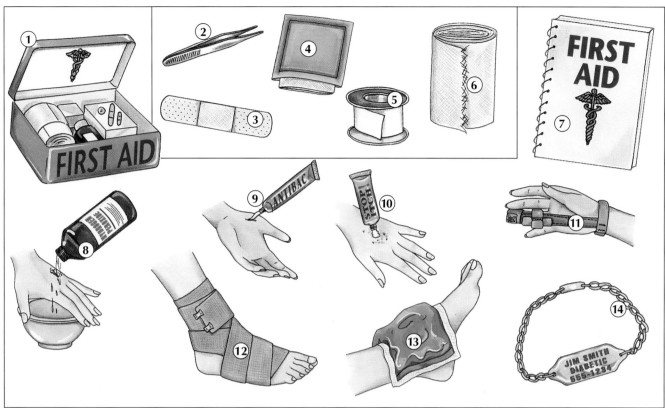

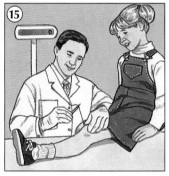
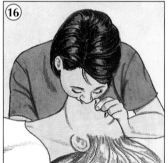
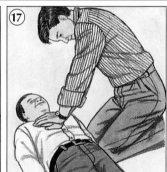

1. first aid kit
   救急箱

2. tweezers
   ピンセット/毛ぬき

3. adhesive bandage
   ばんそうこう

4. sterile pad
   無菌ガーゼ

5. tape
   テープ

6. gauze
   ガーゼ

7. first aid manual
   応急処置の手引き書

8. hydrogen peroxide
   過酸化水素

9. antibacterial ointment
   抗菌性軟膏

10. antihistamine cream
    抗ヒステミンのクリーム

11. splint
    添え木

12. elastic bandage
    伸縮性のある包帯

13. ice pack
    氷嚢

14. medical emergency bracelet
    救急用の医療腕輪

15. stitches
    傷口を縫う

16. rescue breathing
    人口呼吸

17. CPR (cardiopulmonary resuscitation)
    心肺蘇生法

18. Heimlich maneuver
    ハイムリッヒ法

Important Note: Only people who are properly trained should give stitches or do CPR.

Share your answers.

1. Do you have a First Aid kit in your home? Where can you buy one?

2. When do you use hydrogen peroxide? an elastic support bandage? antihistamine cream?

3. Do you know first aid? Where did you learn it?

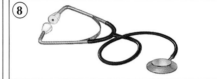

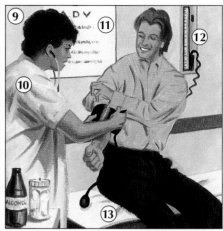

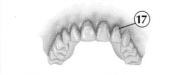

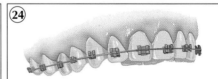

Medical clinic 診療所

1. waiting room
   待合室

2. receptionist
   受付

3. patient
   患者

4. insurance card
   保険証

5. insurance form
   保険請求用紙

6. doctor
   医者

7. scale
   体重計

8. stethoscope
   聴診器

9. examining room
   診察室

10. nurse
    看護婦

11. eye chart
    視力検査表

12. blood pressure gauge
    血圧計

13. examination table
    診察台

14. syringe
    注射器

15. thermometer
    体温計

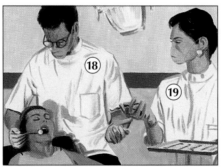
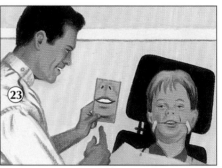

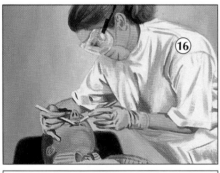

Dental clinic 歯科

16. dental hygienist
    歯科衛生士

17. tartar
    歯石

18. dentist
    歯科医

19. dental assistant
    歯科助手

20. cavity
    虫歯

21. drill
    穴を開ける

22. filling
    詰め物

23. orthodontist
    歯列矯正医

24. braces
    矯正器

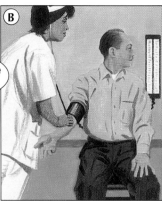

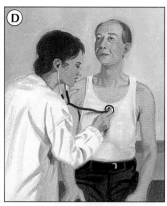

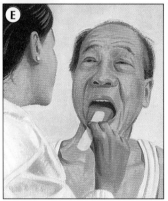

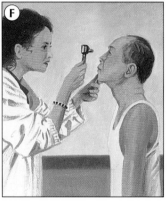

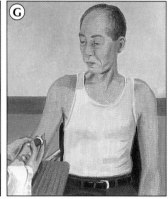

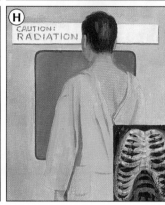

A. **make** an appointment
予約をとる

B. **check**…blood pressure
血圧をはかる

C. **take**…temperature
熱をはかる

D. **listen** to…heart
心音を聴く

E. **look** in…throat
喉を見る

F. **examine**…eyes
目の検査を行う

G. **draw**…blood
血液をとる

H. **get** an X ray
X線写真を撮る

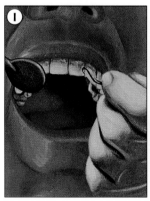

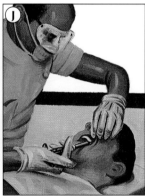

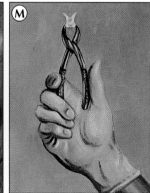

I. **clean**…teeth
歯のクリーニングを行う

J. **give**…a shot of anesthetic
麻酔をうつ

K. **drill** a tooth
歯に穴を開ける

L. **fill** a cavity
虫歯を埋める

M. **pull** a tooth
歯を抜く

More vocabulary

get a checkup: to go for a medical exam

extract a tooth: to pull out a tooth

Share your answers.

1. What is the average cost of a medical exam in your area?

2. Some people are nervous at the dentist's office. What can they do to relax?

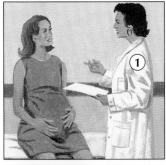
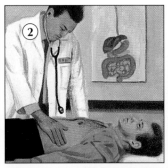

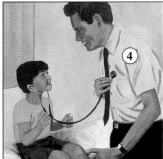

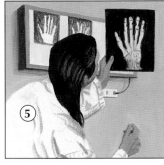
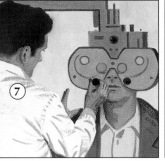
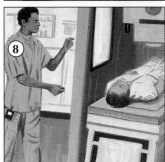

Hospital staff　病院の職員

1. obstetrician
産科医

2. internist
内科専門医

3. cardiologist
心臓専門医

4. pediatrician
小児科医

5. radiologist
放射線医

6. psychiatrist
精神科医

7. ophthalmologist
眼科医

8. X-ray technician
X線技士

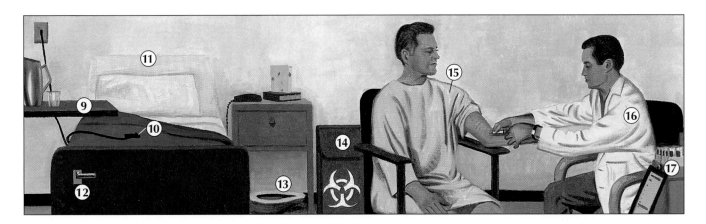

Patient's room　病室

9. bed table
ベッドテーブル

10. call button
呼び出しボタン

11. hospital bed
病院のベッド

12. bed control
ベッド調整

13. bedpan
便器／おまる

14. medical waste disposal
医療廃棄物用ゴミ箱

15. hospital gown
診察用ガウン

16. lab technician
検査技師

17. blood work／blood test
血液検査

More vocabulary

nurse practitioner: a nurse licensed to give medical exams

specialist: a doctor who only treats specific medical problems

gynecologist: a specialist who examines and treats women

nurse midwife: a nurse practitioner who examines pregnant women and delivers babies

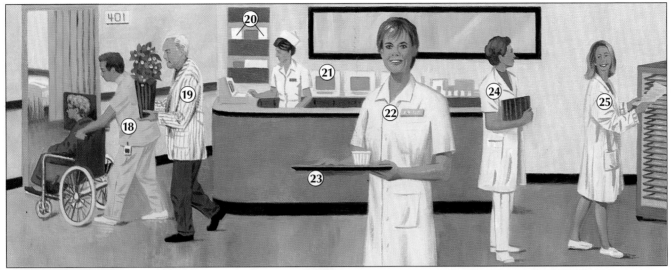

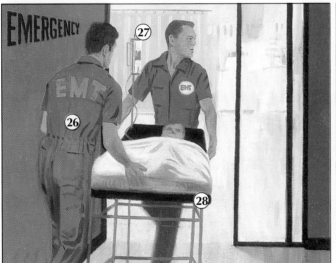

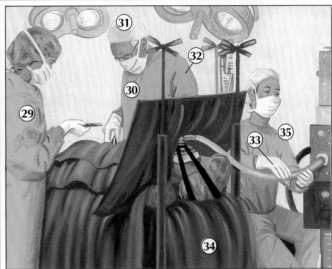

Nurse's station
ナースステーション

18. orderly
規則正しい

19. volunteer
ボランティア

20. medical charts
カルテ

21. vital signs monitor
呼吸数・脈拍を示すモニター

22. RN (registered nurse)
登録看護婦

23. medication tray
薬品用トレイ

24. LPN (licensed practical nurse) /
LVN (licensed vocational nurse)
公認准看護婦

25. dietician
栄養士

Emergency room
救急病院

26. emergency medical technician
(EMT)
救急医療士

27. IV (intravenous drip)
点滴

28. stretcher / gurney
車輪つき担架

Operating room
手術室

29. surgical nurse
手術看護婦

30. surgeon
外科医

31. surgical cap
手術帽

32. surgical gown
手術用ガウン

33. latex gloves
ゴム製手袋

34. operating table
手術台

35. anesthesiologist
麻酔専門医

Practice asking for the hospital staff.

Please get the nurse. I have a question for her.

Where's the anesthesiologist? I need to talk to her.

I'm looking for the lab technician. Have you seen him?

Share your answers.

1. Have you ever been to an emergency room? Who helped you?

2. Have you ever been in the hospital? How long did you stay?

1. fire station
   消防署

2. coffee shop
   コーヒーショップ

3. bank
   銀行

4. car dealership
   自動車販売店

5. hotel
   ホテル

6. church
   教会

7. hospital
   病院

8. park
   公園

9. synagogue
   ユダヤ教会

10. theater
    劇場

11. movie theater
    映画館

12. gas station
    ガソリンスタンド

13. furniture store
    家具屋

14. hardware store
    金物屋

15. barber shop
    床屋

More vocabulary

skyscraper: a very tall office building

downtown / city center: the area in a city with the city hall, courts, and businesses

Practice giving your destination.

I'm going to go <u>downtown</u>.

I have to go to <u>the post office</u>.

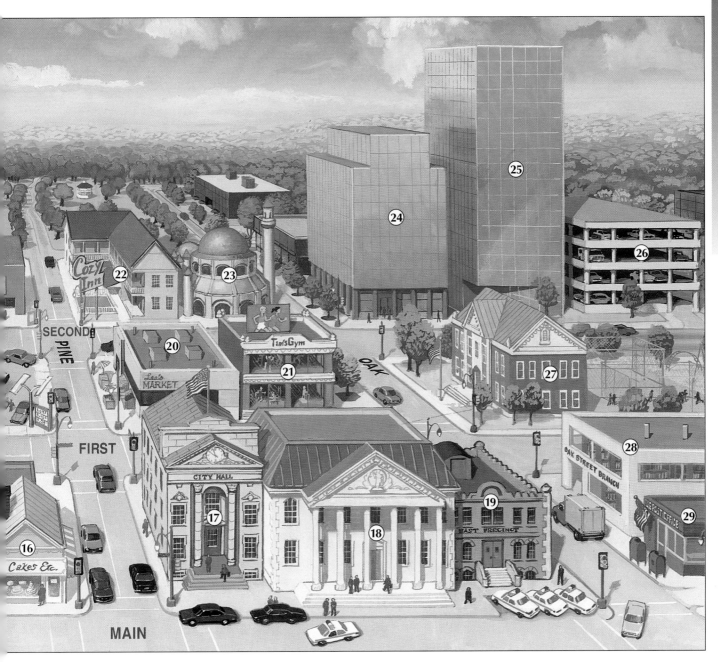

16. bakery
パン屋

17. city hall
市役所

18. courthouse
裁判所

19. police station
警察署

20. market
スーパー

21. health club
ヘルスクラブ

22. motel
モーテル

23. mosque
モスク

24. office building
オフィスビル

25. high-rise building
高層ビル

26. parking garage
駐車場

27. school
学校

28. library
図書館

29. post office
郵便局

Practice asking for and giving the locations of buildings.

Where's the post office?

  It's on Oak Street.

Share your answers.

1. Which of the places in this picture do you go to every week?

2. Is it good to live in a city? Why or why not?

3. What famous cities do you know?

89

1. Laundromat
   コインランドリー

2. drugstore / pharmacy
   薬局

3. convenience store
   コンビニエンスストアー

4. photo shop
   写真店

5. parking space
   駐車場

6. traffic light
   交通信号

7. pedestrian
   歩行者

8. crosswalk
   横断歩道

9. street
   道

10. curb
    縁石

11. newsstand
    新聞雑誌店

12. mailbox
    郵便ポスト

13. drive-thru window
    ドライブスルー用の窓

14. fast food restaurant
    ファーストフードレストラン

15. bus
    バス

A. **cross** the street
   道を**渡る**

B. **wait** for the light
   信号を**待つ**

C. **drive** a car
   車を**運転する**

More vocabulary

neighborhood: the area close to your home

do errands: to make a short trip from your home to buy or pick up something

Talk about where to buy things.

You can buy <u>newspapers</u> at <u>a newsstand</u>.

You can buy <u>donuts</u> at <u>a donut shop</u>.

You can buy <u>food</u> at <u>a convenience store</u>.

16. bus stop バス停留所	**22.** copy center / print shop コピー屋／印刷屋	**28.** fire hydrant 消火栓
17. corner 曲がり角	**23.** streetlight 街灯	**29.** sign 看板
18. parking meter 駐車メーター	**24.** dry cleaners ドライクリーニング店	**30.** street vendor 屋台
19. motorcycle オートバイ	**25.** nail salon ネールサロン	**31.** cart カート
20. donut shop ドーナツ屋	**26.** sidewalk 歩道	**D.** **park** the car 駐車する
21. public telephone 公衆電話	**27.** garbage truck ごみ収集車	**E.** **ride** a bicycle 自転車に乗る

Share your answers.

1. Do you like to do errands?

2. Do you always like to go to the same stores?

3. Which businesses in the picture are also in your neighborhood?

4. Do you know someone who has a small business? What kind?

5. What things can you buy from a street vendor?

1. music store
   楽器店

2. jewelry store
   宝石店

3. candy store
   菓子屋

4. bookstore
   本屋

5. toy store
   おもちゃ屋

6. pet store
   ペットショップ

7. card store
   カードショップ

8. optician
   眼鏡店

9. travel agency
   旅行代理店

10. shoe store
    靴屋

11. fountain
    噴水

12. florist
    花屋

More vocabulary

beauty shop: hair salon

men's store: a store that sells men's clothing

dress shop: a store that sells women's clothing

Talk about where you want to shop in this mall.

Let's go to the card store.

I need to buy a card for Maggie's birthday.

13. department store デパート	**17.** maternity shop マタニティ用品店	**21.** escalator エスカレーター
14. food court レストラン街	**18.** electronics store 電気屋	**22.** information booth 案内所
15. video store ビデオ屋	**19.** directory 案内板	
16. hair salon 美容院	**20.** ice cream stand アイスクリーム屋	

Practice asking for and giving the location of different shops.

Where's <u>the maternity shop</u>?

  It's on <u>the first floor</u>, next to <u>the hair salon</u>.

Share your answers.

1. Do you like shopping malls? Why or why not?
2. Some people don't go to the mall to shop.
   Name some other things you can do in a mall.

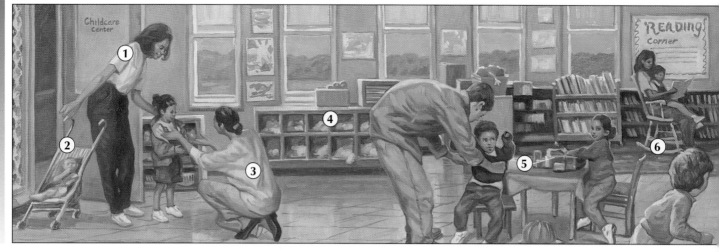

1. parent
親

2. stroller
ベビーカー

3. childcare worker
託児所職員

4. cubby
幼児用整理棚

5. toys
おもちゃ

6. rocking chair
ロッキングチェア

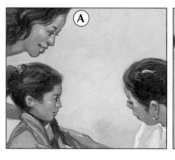

A. drop off
預ける

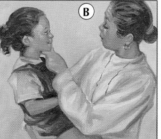

B. hold
抱く

C. nurse
世話をする

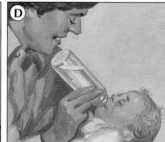

D. feed
授乳する

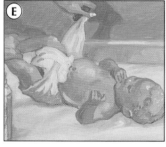

E. change diapers
おむつを替える

F. read a story
物語を読む

G. pick up
迎えに行く

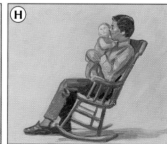

H. rock
揺らす

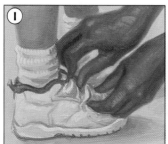

I. tie shoes
靴紐をむすぶ

J. dress
服を着せる

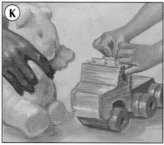

K. play
遊ぶ

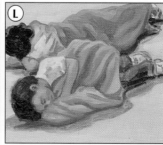

L. take a nap
昼寝する

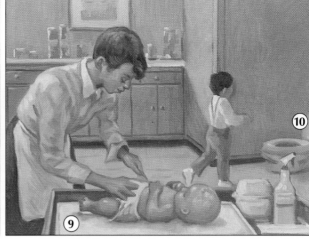

7. high chair
小児用の食事椅子

8. bib
よだれ掛け

9. changing table
おむつ交換台

10. potty seat
おまる

11. playpen
ベビーサークル

12. walker
歩行器

13. car safety seat
車用安全椅子

14. baby carrier
ベビーキャリヤー

15. baby backpack
ベビーバックパック

16. carriage
乳母車

17. wipes
ふき取りペーパー

18. baby powder
ベビーパウダー

19. disinfectant
消毒剤

20. disposable diapers
使い捨ておむつ

21. cloth diapers
布おむつ

22. diaper pins
おむつピン

23. diaper pail
おむつ用バケツ

24. training pants
トイレットトレーニングパンツ

25. formula
調合乳

26. bottle
ほ乳びん

27. nipple
（ほ乳びんの）乳首

28. baby food
ベビーフード

29. pacifier
おしゃぶり

30. teething ring
環状のおしゃぶり

31. rattle
ガラガラ

1. envelope
封筒

2. letter
手紙

3. postcard
ハガキ

4. greeting card
グリーティングカード

5. package
小包

6. letter carrier
郵便集配人

7. return address
差出人住所

8. mailing address
宛先

9. postmark
消印

10. stamp / postage
切手 / 郵便料金

11. certified mail
配達証明郵便

12. priority mail
プライオリティメール

13. air letter / aerogramme
航空便

14. ground post /
parcel post
小包郵便

15. Express Mail /
overnight mail
翌日配達郵便

A. **address** a postcard
ハガキに宛名を書く

B. **send** it / **mail** it
送る / 郵送する

C. **deliver** it
配達する

D. **receive** it
受取る

Emily Rose
1543 Oak Lane
Springvale, CA 91254
⑦

SPRINGVALE
5-7-99
CA
⑨

USA
⑩

Alyson Shepard
249 Courtney Drive
Newton, NY 10043
⑧

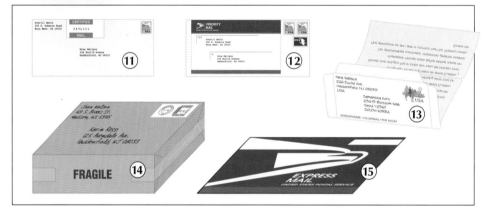

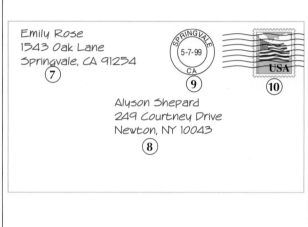

FRAGILE

EXPRESS
MAIL
UNITED STATES POSTAL SERVICE

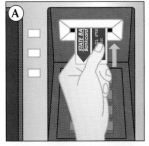

1. teller
   銀行の窓口係

2. vault
   金庫室

3. ATM (automated teller machine)
   ATM/キャッシュディスペンサー

4. security guard
   警備員

5. passbook
   銀行通帳

6. savings account number
   普通預金口座番号

7. checkbook
   小切手帳

8. checking account number
   当座預金口座番号

9. ATM card
   キャッシュカード

10. monthly statement
    月々の貸借表

11. balance
    残高

12. deposit slip
    預金伝票

13. safe-deposit box
    貸金庫

Using the ATM machine　ATMを使う

A. **Insert** your ATM card.
   キャッシュカードを挿入する

B. **Enter** your PIN number.*
   暗唱番号を押す

C. **Make** a deposit.
   預金する

D. **Withdraw** cash.
   現金を引き出す

E. **Transfer** funds.
   資金を振替える

F. **Remove** your ATM card.
   キャッシュカードを抜き取る

*PIN: personal identification number

More vocabulary

overdrawn account: When there is not enough money in an account to pay a check, we say the account is overdrawn.

Share your answers.

1. Do you use a bank?

2. Do you use an ATM card?

3. Name some things you can put in a safe-deposit box.

1. **reference librarian**
   司書

2. **reference desk**
   司書デスク

3. **atlas**
   地図帳

4. **microfilm reader**
   マイクロフィルム
   読み取り機

5. **microfilm**
   マイクロフィルム

6. **periodical section**
   定期刊行物セクション

7. **magazine**
   雑誌

8. **newspaper**
   新聞

9. **online catalog**
   オンラインカタログ

10. **card catalog**
    カード式索引

11. **media section**
    メディアセクション

12. **audiocassette**
    カセットテープ

13. **videocassette**
    ビデオテープ

14. **CD (compact disc)**
    CD（コンパクトディスク）

15. **record**
    レコード

16. **checkout desk**
    貸し出しカウンター

17. **library clerk**
    図書館員

18. **encyclopedia**
    百科事典

19. **library card**
    図書館カード

20. **library book**
    図書館の本

21. **title**
    書名

22. **author**
    著者

More vocabulary

check a book out: to borrow a book from the library

nonfiction: real information, history or true stories

fiction: stories from the author's imagination

Share your answers.

1. Do you have a library card?

2. Do you prefer to buy books or borrow them from the library?

You have the right to remain silent…

Bail is set at $20,000.

A. arrest a suspect
容疑者を**逮捕**する

1. police officer
警察官

2. handcuffs
手錠

B. hire a lawyer / **hire** an attorney
弁護士を**雇**う

3. guard
監視

4. defense attorney
被告側の弁護士

C. appear in court
出廷する

5. defendant
被告人

6. judge
裁判官

D. stand trial
裁判を受ける

7. courtroom
法廷

8. jury
陪審員

9. evidence
証拠

10. prosecuting attorney
検察官

11. witness
目撃者

12. court reporter
法廷記者

13. bailiff
廷吏

Guilty.

7 years.

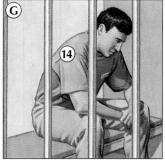

E. give the verdict*
判決をくだす

F. sentence the defendant
刑を**宣告**する

G. go to jail / **go** to prison
刑務所に入る

14. convict
有罪を宣告する

H. be released
釈放される

***Note:** There are two possible verdicts, "guilty" and "not guilty."

Share your answers.

1. What are some differences between the legal system in the United States and the one in your country?

2. Do you want to be on a jury? Why or why not?

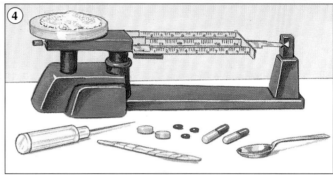

1. vandalism
故意の破壊行為

2. gang violence
暴力団乱暴行為

3. drunk driving
飲酒運転

4. illegal drugs
不法の薬物

5. mugging
強盗

6. burglary
住居侵入 / 押込み

7. assault
暴行

8. murder
殺人

9. gun
拳銃

More vocabulary

commit a crime: to do something illegal

criminal: someone who commits a crime

victim: someone who is hurt or killed by someone else

Share your answers.

1. Is there too much crime on TV? in the movies?

2. Do you think people become criminals from watching crime on TV?

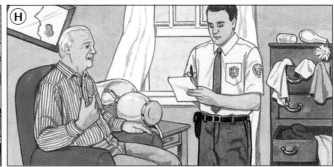

A. **Walk** with a friend.
友達と**歩く**

B. **Stay** on well-lit streets.
明るい道を**選ぶ**

C. **Hold** your purse close to your body.
鞄はなるべく体の近くでもつ

D. **Protect** your wallet.
財布を**守る**

E. **Lock** your doors.
ドアに鍵をかける

F. **Don't open** your door to strangers.
知らない人にドアを**開けない**

G. **Don't drink** and **drive**.
飲酒運転をしない

H. **Report** crimes to the police.
警察に犯罪を**通報する**

More vocabulary

Neighborhood Watch: a group of neighbors who watch for criminals in their neighborhood

designated drivers: people who don't drink alcoholic beverages so that they can drive drinkers home

Share your answers.

1. Do you feel safe in your neighborhood?

2. Look at the pictures. Which of these things do you do?

3. What other things do you do to stay safe?

1. lost child
迷子

2. car accident
交通事故

3. airplane crash
飛行機事故

4. explosion
爆発

5. earthquake
地震

6. mudslide
土砂崩れ

7. fire
火災

8. firefighter
消防士

9. fire truck
消防車

Practice reporting a fire.

This is <u>Lisa Broad</u>. There is a fire.

The address is <u>323 Oak Street</u>.

Please send someone quickly.

Share your answers.

1. Can you give directions to your home if there is a fire?

2. What information do you give to the other driver if you are in a car accident?

10. drought
干ばつ

11. blizzard
大吹雪

12. hurricane
ハリケーン

13. tornado
トルネード／大たつまき

14. volcanic eruption
火山の噴火

15. tidal wave
大津波

16. flood
洪水

17. search and rescue team
捜索救助隊

Share your answers.

1. Which disasters are common in your area? Which never happen?

2. What can you do to prepare for emergencies?

3. Do you have emergency numbers near your telephone?

4. What organizations will help you in an emergency?

1. bus stop バス停	**7.** passenger 乗客	**13.** train station 駅	**19.** taxi stand タクシー乗り場
2. route ルート	**8.** bus driver バスの運転手	**14.** ticket 切符	**20.** taxi driver タクシーの運転手
3. schedule 時刻表	**9.** subway 地下鉄	**15.** platform プラットホーム	**21.** meter メーター
4. bus バス	**10.** track 線路	**16.** conductor 車掌	**22.** taxi license タクシー許可証
5. fare 料金	**11.** token トークン（代用硬貨）	**17.** train 電車	**23.** ferry フェリー
6. transfer 乗り換え	**12.** fare card 料金カード	**18.** taxi/cab タクシー	

More vocabulary

hail a taxi: to get a taxi driver's attention by raising your hand

miss the bus: to arrive at the bus stop late

Talk about how you and your friends come to school.

I take the bus to school.   *He drives to school.*

You take the train.   *She walks to school.*

We take the subway.   *They ride bikes.*

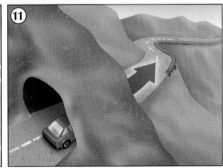

1. **under** the bridge
   橋の下

2. **over** the bridge
   橋の上

3. **across** the water
   水上を横切って

4. **into** the taxi
   タクシーの中へ

5. **out of** the taxi
   タクシーの外へ

6. **onto** the highway
   ハイウエイへ

7. **off** the highway
   ハイウエイを出る

8. **down** the stairs
   階段を下に

9. **up** the stairs
   階段を上に

10. **around** the corner
    角を曲がって

11. **through** the tunnel
    トンネルをぬけて

Grammar point: *into, out of, on, off*

We say, *get **into** a taxi or a car.*

But we say, *get **on** a bus, a train, or a plane.*

We say, *get **out of** a taxi or a car.*

But we say, *get **off** a bus, a train, or a plane.*

1. subcompact
   準小型車

2. compact
   小型車

3. midsize car
   中型車

4. full-size car
   大型車

5. convertible
   オープンカー

6. sports car
   スポーツカー

7. pickup truck
   小型トラック

8. station wagon
   ステーションワゴン

9. SUV (sports utility
   vehicle)
   スポーツ
   ユーティリティー車

10. minivan
    ミニバン

11. camper
    キャンパー

12. dump truck
    ダンプカー

13. tow truck
    レッカー車

14. moving van
    移動バン

15. tractor trailer/semi
    トレーラートラック/
    セミトレーラー

16. cab
    タクシー

17. trailer
    トレーラー

More vocabulary

make: the name of the company that makes the car

model: the style of car

Share your answers.

1. What is your favorite kind of car?

2. What kind of car is good for a big family? for a single person?

Directions　方向

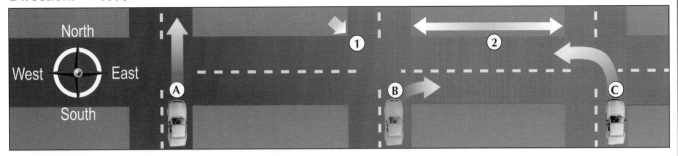

A. go straight
まっすぐ行く

B. turn right
右にまがる

C. turn left
左にまがる

1. corner
かど

2. block
ブロック

Signs　標識

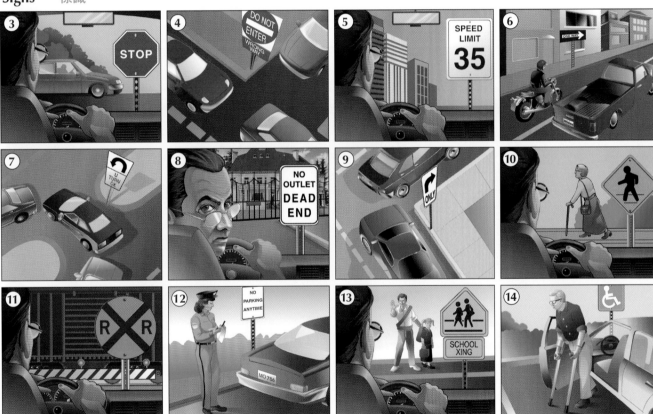

3. stop
止まれ

4. do not enter / wrong way
進入禁止

5. speed limit
制限速度

6. one way
一方通行

7. U-turn OK
UターンOK

8. no outlet / dead end
行き止まり

9. right turn only
右折のみ

10. pedestrian crossing
横断歩道

11. railroad crossing
踏切

12. no parking
駐車禁止

13. school crossing
通学路

14. handicapped parking
身体障害者用の駐車スペース

More vocabulary

right-of-way: the right to go first

yield: to give another person or car the right-of-way

Share your answers.

1. Which traffic signs are the same in your country?

2. Do pedestrians have the right-of-way in your city?

3. What is the speed limit in front of your school?
your home?

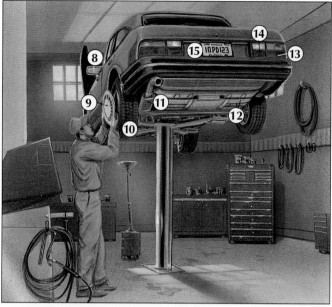

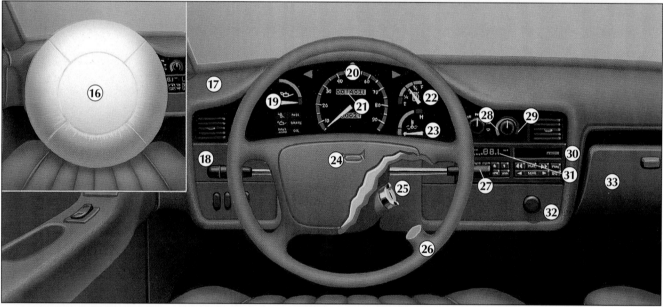

1. **rearview mirror**
バックミラー

2. **windshield**
フロントグラス

3. **windshield wipers**
ワイパー

4. **turn signal**
方向指示灯

5. **headlight**
ヘッドライト

6. **hood**
ボンネット

7. **bumper**
バンパー

8. **sideview mirror**
サイドミラー

9. **hubcap**
ハブキャップ

10. **tire**
タイヤ

11. **muffler**
マフラー

12. **gas tank**
燃料タンク

13. **brake light**
ブレーキライト

14. **taillight**
尾灯

15. **license plate**
ナンバープレート

16. **air bag**
エアバッグ

17. **dashboard**
ダッシュボード

18. **turn signal**
方向指示灯

19. **oil gauge**
オイルゲージ

20. **speedometer**
速度計

21. **odometer**
走行距離計

22. **gas gauge**
燃料計

23. **temperature gauge**
温度計

24. **horn**
クラクション

25. **ignition**
イグニション
（エンジンの点火装置）

26. **steering wheel**
ハンドル

27. **gearshift**
変速装置

28. **air conditioning**
エアコン

29. **heater**
ヒーター

30. **tape deck**
テープデッキ

31. **radio**
ラジオ

32. **cigarette lighter**
ライター

33. **glove compartment**
グローブボックス

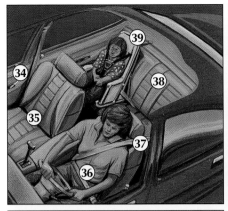

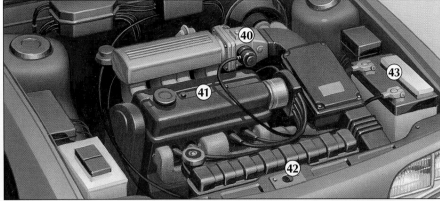

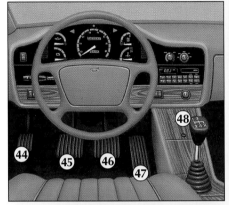

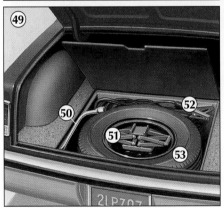

34. lock
    鍵

35. front seat
    前部席

36. seat belt
    シートベルト

37. shoulder harness
    シートベルト（腰）

38. backseat
    後部席

39. child safety seat
    子供用安全シート

40. fuel injection system
    燃料噴射装置

41. engine
    エンジン

42. radiator
    ラジエーター

43. battery
    バッテリー

44. emergency brake
    サイドブレーキ

45. clutch*
    クラッチ

46. brake pedal
    ブレーキペダル

47. accelerator/gas pedal
    アクセル/ガスペダル

48. stick shift
    シフトレバー

49. trunk
    トランク

50. lug wrench
    ラグレンチ

51. jack
    ジャッキ

52. jumper cables
    ジャンパーケーブル

53. spare tire
    予備タイヤ

54. The car needs **gas**.
    この車は**ガソリン**が必要です

55. The car needs **oil**.
    この車は**オイル**が必要です

56. The radiator needs **coolant**.
    このラジエーターは**クーラント**が
    必要です

57. The car needs **a smog check**.
    この車は**スモッグ検査**が必要です

58. The battery needs **recharging**.
    このバッテリは**再充電**が必要です

59. The tires need **air**.
    このタイヤは**空気**が必要です

*Note: Standard transmission cars have a clutch; automatic transmission cars do not.

1. airline terminal
航空会社のターミナル

2. airline representative
航空会社の係員

3. check-in counter
搭乗手続カウンター

4. arrival and departure monitors
発着便表示モニター

5. gate
ゲート

6. boarding area
搭乗口

7. control tower
管制塔

8. helicopter
ヘリコプター

9. airplane
飛行機

10. overhead compartment
頭上の収納用スペース

11. cockpit
操縦室

12. pilot
操縦士／パイロット

13. flight attendant
客室乗務員

14. oxygen mask
酸素マスク

15. airsickness bag
エチケット袋

16. tray table
テーブル

17. baggage claim area
手荷物受取所

18. carousel
カルーセル／ターンテーブル

19. luggage carrier
手荷物運搬人

20. customs
税関

21. customs officer
税関検査官

22. declaration form
申告書

23. passenger
乗客

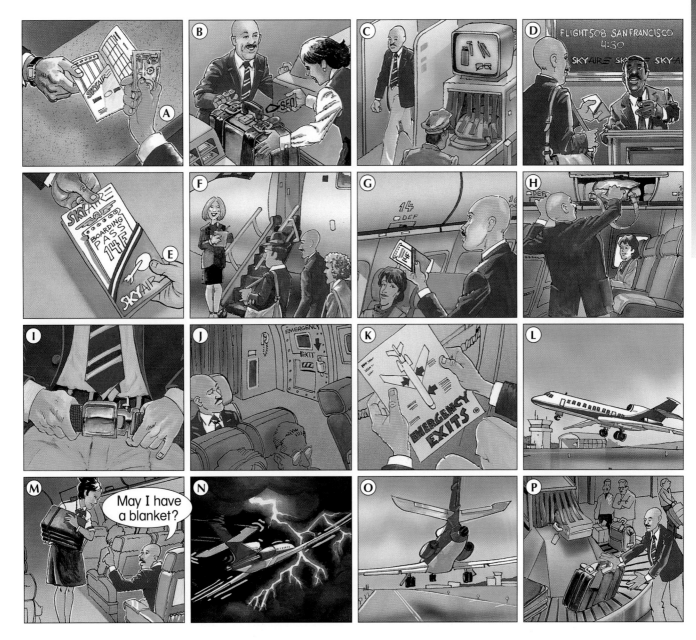

A. **buy** your ticket
航空券を買う

B. **check** your bags
荷物を預ける

C. **go through** security
セキュリティーチェックを
受ける

D. **check in** at the gate
ゲートで搭乗手続きをする

E. **get** your boarding pass
搭乗券を受け取る

F. **board** the plane
搭乗する

G. **find** your seat
席を見つける

H. **stow** your carry-on bag
持ち込み荷物をしまう

I. **fasten** your seat belt
シートベルトを締める

J. **look for** the emergency exit
非常口を確認する

K. **look at** the emergency card
非常時のガイドを見る

L. **take off / leave**
離陸 / 出発

M. **request** a blanket
毛布を頼む

N. **experience** turbulence
揺れを感じる

O. **land / arrive**
着陸 / 到着

P. **claim** your baggage
荷物を受け取る

More vocabulary

destination: the place the passenger is going

departure time: the time the plane takes off

arrival time: the time the plane lands

direct flight: a plane trip between two cities with no stops

stopover: a stop before reaching the destination, sometimes to change planes

111

1. public school
公立学校

2. private school
私立学校

3. parochial school
教区学校／カトリック系の学校

4. preschool
保育園、幼稚園

5. elementary school
小学校

**6. middle school /
junior high school**
中学校

7. high school
高校

8. adult school
成人学校

9. vocational school / trade school
職業訓練校／専門学校

10. college / university
単科大学／総合大学

Note: In the U.S. most children begin school at age 5 (in kindergarten) and graduate from high school at 17 or 18.

More vocabulary

When students graduate from a college or university they receive a **degree**:

Bachelor's degree—usually 4 years of study

Master's degree—an additional 1–3 years of study

Doctorate—an additional 3–5 years of study

community college: a two-year college where students can get an Associate of Arts degree

graduate school: a school in a university where students study for their master's degrees and doctorates

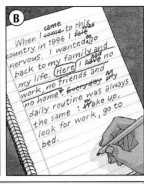

1. writing assignment
レポートの課題

A. Write a first draft.
初稿を書く

B. Edit your paper.
レポートを編集する

C. Get feedback.
フィードバックを受ける

D. Rewrite your paper.
レポートを書き直す

E. Turn in your paper.
レポートを提出する

2. paper / composition
論文／作文

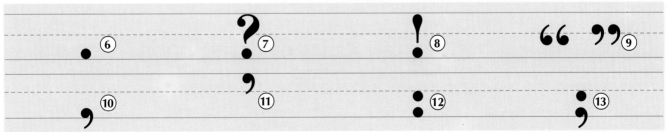

③
④ **My life in the U.S.**

⑤ I arrived in this country in 1996. My family did not come with me. I was homesick, nervous, and a little excited. I had no job and no friends here. I lived with my aunt and my daily routine was always the same: get up, look for a job, go to bed. At night I remembered my mother's words to me, "Son, you can always come home!" I was homesick and scared, but I did not go home.

I started to study English at night. English is a difficult language and many times I was too tired to study. One teacher, Mrs. Armstrong, was very kind to me. She showed me many

3. title
題

4. sentence
文

5. paragraph
段落

Punctuation　句読法

6. period
ピリオド

7. question mark
クエスチョンマーク

8. exclamation mark
エクスクラメーションマーク／
感嘆符

9. quotation marks
クォーテーションマーク

10. comma
コンマ

11. apostrophe
アポストロフィ

12. colon
コロン

13. semicolon
セミコロン

Exploration

War

Immigration

Historical and Political Events 歴史的及び政治的出来事	**1492 →** French, Spanish, English explorers フランス、スペイン、イギリスの探検家	**1607–1750** Colonies along Atlantic coast founded by Northern Europeans 北欧人が開拓した大西洋沿岸の植民地	**1619** 1st African slave sold in Virginia バージニアで最初のアフリカ人奴隷売買 **1653** 1st Indian reservation in Virginia バージニアでの最初のインディアン居留地

Before 1700 · 1700

Immigration* 移民	**1607** 1st English in Virginia バージニアに最初のイギリス人	**1610** Spanish at Santa Fe サンタフェにスペイン人	
Population** 人口	Before 1700: Native American: 1,000,000+ アメリカンインディアン：1,000,000+		1700: colonists: 250,000 入植者：250,000

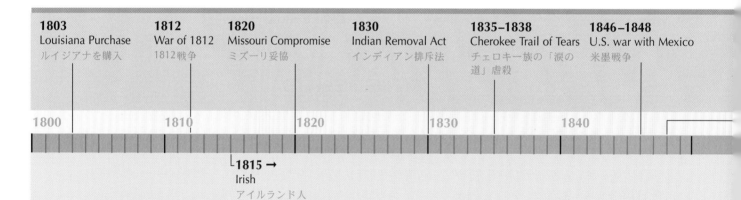

1803 Louisiana Purchase ルイジアナを購入	**1812** War of 1812 1812戦争	**1820** Missouri Compromise ミズーリ妥協	**1830** Indian Removal Act インディアン排斥法	**1835–1838** Cherokee Trail of Tears チェロキー一族の「涙の道」虐殺	**1846–1848** U.S. war with Mexico 米墨戦争

1800 · 1810 · 1820 · 1830 · 1840

1815 →
Irish
アイルランド人

1800: citizens and free blacks: 5,300,000　slaves: 450,000
市民および自由黒人：5,300,000　奴隷：450,000

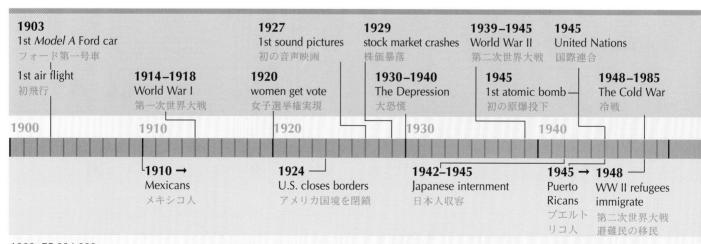

1903 1st *Model A* Ford car フォード第一号車 1st air flight 初飛行	**1914–1918** World War I 第一次世界大戦	**1927** 1st sound pictures 初の音声映画 **1920** women get vote 女子選挙権実現	**1929** stock market crashes 株価暴落 **1930–1940** The Depression 大恐慌	**1939–1945** World War II 第二次世界大戦 **1945** 1st atomic bomb 初の原爆投下	**1945** United Nations 国際連合 **1948–1985** The Cold War 冷戦

1900 · 1910 · 1920 · 1930 · 1940

1910 →
Mexicans
メキシコ人

1924
U.S. closes borders
アメリカ国境を閉鎖

1942–1945
Japanese internment
日本人収容

1945 →
Puerto Ricans
プエルトリコ人

1948
WW II refugees immigrate
第二次世界大戦避難民の移民

1900: 75,994,000

*Immigration dates indicate a time when large numbers of that group first began to immigrate to the U.S.
**All population figures before 1790 are estimates. Figures after 1790 are based on the official U.S. census.

Movement

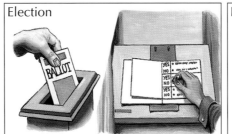

Election

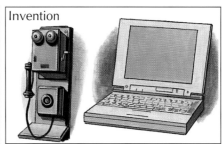

Invention

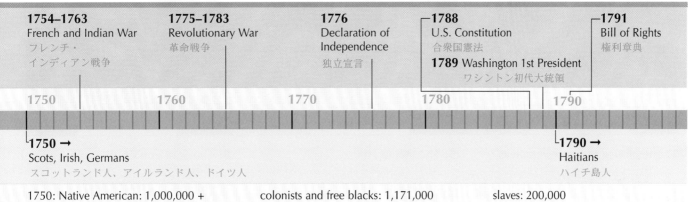

1754–1763
French and Indian War
フレンチ・
インディアン戦争

1775–1783
Revolutionary War
革命戦争

1776
Declaration of
Independence
独立宣言

1788
U.S. Constitution
合衆国憲法
1789 Washington 1st President
ワシントン初代大統領

1791
Bill of Rights
権利章典

1750　　1760　　1770　　1780　　1790

1750 →
Scots, Irish, Germans
スコットランド人、アイルランド人、ドイツ人

1790 →
Haitians
ハイチ島人

1750: Native American: 1,000,000 +
アメリカンインディアン：1,000,000 +
colonists and free blacks: 1,171,000
入植者及び自由黒人：1,171,000
slaves: 200,000
奴隷：200,000

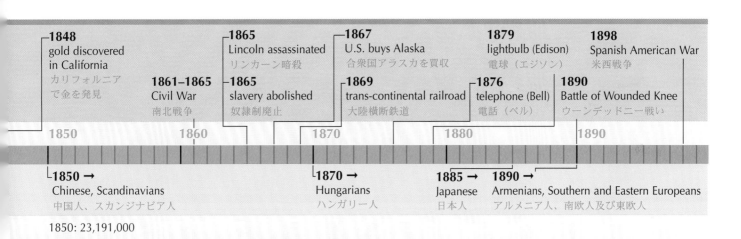

1848
gold discovered
in California
カリフォルニア
で金を発見

1865
Lincoln assassinated
リンカーン暗殺
1861–1865
Civil War
南北戦争
1865
slavery abolished
奴隷制廃止

1867
U.S. buys Alaska
合衆国アラスカを買収
1869
trans-continental railroad
大陸横断鉄道

1879
lightbulb (Edison)
電球（エジソン）
1876
telephone (Bell)
電話（ベル）

1898
Spanish American War
米西戦争
1890
Battle of Wounded Knee
ウーンデッドニー戦い

1850　　1860　　1870　　1880　　1890

1850 →
Chinese, Scandinavians
中国人、スカンジナビア人

1870 →
Hungarians
ハンガリー人

1885 →
Japanese
日本人

1890 →
Armenians, Southern and Eastern Europeans
アルメニア人、南欧人及び東欧人

1850: 23,191,000

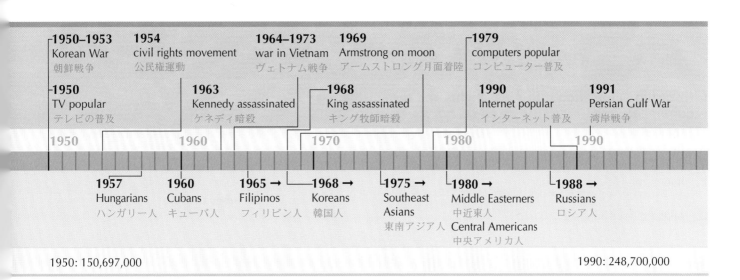

1950–1953
Korean War
朝鮮戦争
1950
TV popular
テレビの普及

1954
civil rights movement
公民権運動
1963
Kennedy assassinated
ケネディ暗殺

1964–1973
war in Vietnam
ヴェトナム戦争
1968
King assassinated
キング牧師暗殺

1969
Armstrong on moon
アームストロング月面着陸

1979
computers popular
コンピューター普及
1990
Internet popular
インターネット普及

1991
Persian Gulf War
湾岸戦争

1950　　1960　　1970　　1980　　1990

1957
Hungarians
ハンガリー人

1960
Cubans
キューバ人

1965 →
Filipinos
フィリピン人

1968 →
Koreans
韓国人

1975 →
Southeast
Asians
東南アジア人

1980 →
Middle Easterners
中近東人
Central Americans
中央アメリカ人

1988 →
Russians
ロシア人

1950: 150,697,000

1990: 248,700,000

BRANCHES OF GOVERNMENT

Legislative | Executive | Judicial

1. The House of Representatives
下院

2. congresswoman / congressman
下院女性議員／下院議員

3. The Senate
上院

4. senator
上院議員

5. The White House
ホワイトハウス

6. president
大統領

7. vice president
副大統領

8. The Supreme Court
最高裁判所

9. chief justice
連邦最高裁判所長官

10. justices
最高裁判所判事

Citizenship application requirements
市民権申請の必要条件

A. **be** 18 years old
18歳に達している

B. **live** in the U.S. for five years
アメリカに5年以上住んでいる

C. **take** a citizenship test
市民権の試験を受ける

Rights and responsibilities
権利と責務

D. **vote**
投票する

E. **pay** taxes
納税する

F. **register** with Selective Service*
選抜徴兵に登録する

G. **serve** on a jury
陪審員をつとめる

H. **obey** the law
法律に従う

*Note: All males 18 to 26 who live in the U.S. are required to register with Selective Service.

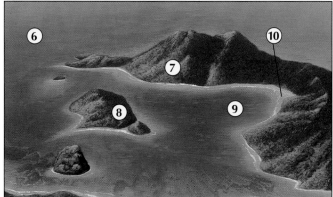

1. rain forest
熱帯雨林

2. waterfall
滝

3. river
河川

4. desert
砂漠

5. sand dune
砂丘

6. ocean
海洋

7. peninsula
半島

8. island
島

9. bay
湾

10. beach
浜辺

11. forest
森林

12. shore
岸

13. lake
湖

14. mountain peak
山頂

15. mountain range
山脈

16. hills
丘

17. canyon
大峡谷

18. valley
谷

19. plains
平野

20. meadow
採草地、牧草地

21. pond
池

More vocabulary

a body of water: a river, lake, or ocean

stream/creek: a very small river

Talk about where you live and where you like to go.

I live in a valley. There is a lake nearby.

I like to go to the beach.

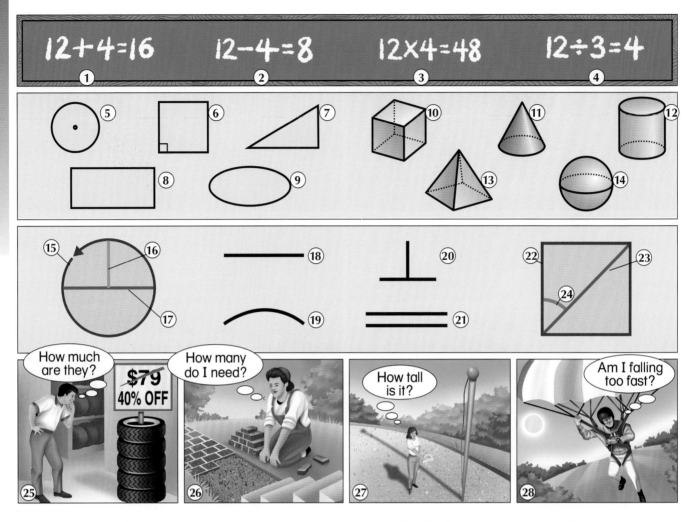

Operations
演算

1. addition
足し算

2. subtraction
引き算

3. multiplication
掛け算

4. division
割り算

Shapes
図形

5. circle
円

6. square
正方形

7. triangle
三角形

8. rectangle
長方形

9. oval / ellipse
楕円形

Solids
立体

10. cube
立方体

11. cone
円錐

12. cylinder
円柱

13. pyramid
角錐

14. sphere
球体

Parts of a circle
円の部位

15. circumference
円周

16. radius
半径

17. diameter
直径

Lines
線

18. straight
直線

19. curved
曲線

20. perpendicular
垂線

21. parallel
平行線

Parts of a square
正方形の部位

22. side
側面

23. diagonal
対角線

24. angle
角

Types of math
数学の種類

25. algebra
代数学

26. geometry
幾何学

27. trigonometry
三角法

28. calculus
微積分学

More vocabulary

total: the answer to an addition problem

difference: the answer to a subtraction problem

product: the answer to a multiplication problem

quotient: the answer to a division problem

pi (π): the number when you divide the circumference of a circle by its diameter (approximately = 3.14)

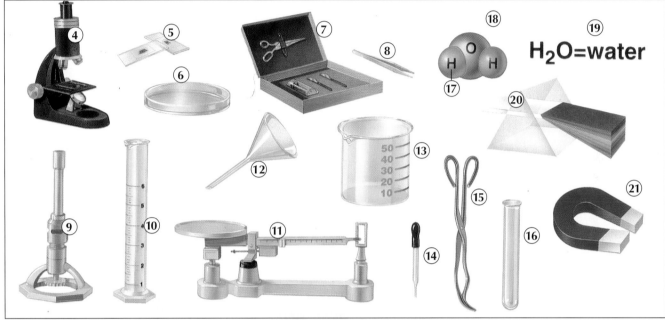

H₂O=water

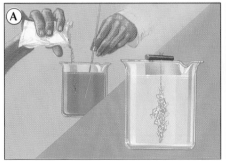

1. biology 生物学	**9.** Bunsen burner ブンゼンバーナー	**17.** atom 原子
2. chemistry 化学	**10.** graduated cylinder 目盛付シリンダー	**18.** molecule 分子
3. physics 物理学	**11.** balance 天秤	**19.** formula 公式
4. microscope 顕微鏡	**12.** funnel ろうと	**20.** prism プリズム
5. slide スライド	**13.** beaker ビーカー	**21.** magnet 磁石
6. petri dish ペトリ皿	**14.** dropper スポイト	**A.** **do** an experiment 実験をする
7. dissection kit 解剖器具	**15.** crucible tongs るつぼばさみ	**B.** **observe** 観察する
8. forceps 鉗子、ピンセット	**16.** test tube 試験管	**C.** **record** results 結果を記録する

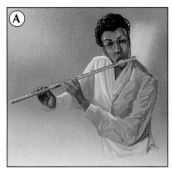

A. play an instrument
楽器を**演奏する**

B. sing a song
歌をうたう

1. orchestra
オーケストラ

2. rock band
ロックバンド

Woodwinds

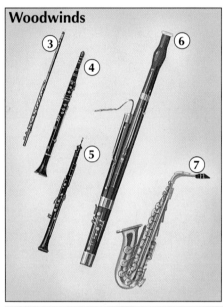

Strings

Brass

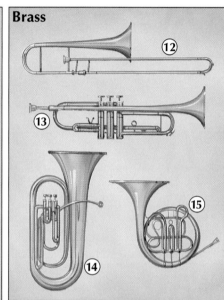

Percussion

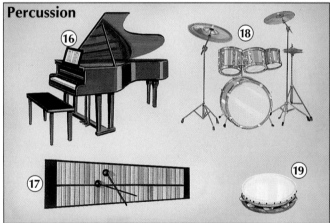

Other Instruments

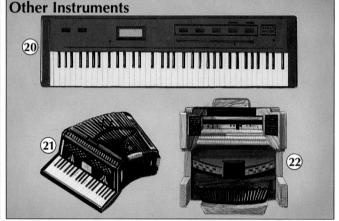

3. flute フルート	**8.** violin ヴァイオリン	**13.** trumpet / horn トランペット	**18.** drums ドラム
4. clarinet クラリネット	**9.** cello チェロ	**14.** tuba チューバ	**19.** tambourine タンバリン
5. oboe オーボエ	**10.** bass バス	**15.** French horn フレンチホルン	**20.** electric keyboard 電子キーボード
6. bassoon バスーン	**11.** guitar ギター	**16.** piano ピアノ	**21.** accordion アコーディオン
7. saxophone サクソフォーン	**12.** trombone トロンボーン	**17.** xylophone 木琴	**22.** organ オルガン

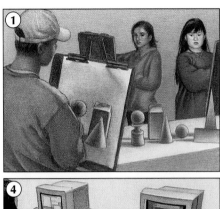

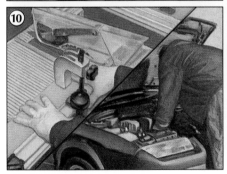

1. art
美術

2. business education
職業教育

3. chorus
コーラス

4. computer science
コンピューターサイエンス

5. driver's education
自動車運転教習

6. economics
経済学

7. English as a second language
第二言語としての英語

8. foreign language
外国語

9. home economics
家政学

10. industrial arts / shop
工芸技術 / 技術工作

11. PE (physical education)
体育

12. theater arts
演劇

More vocabulary

core course: a subject students have to take

elective: a subject students choose to take

Share your answers.

1. What are your favorite subjects?

2. In your opinion, what subjects are most important? Why?

3. What foreign languages are taught in your school?

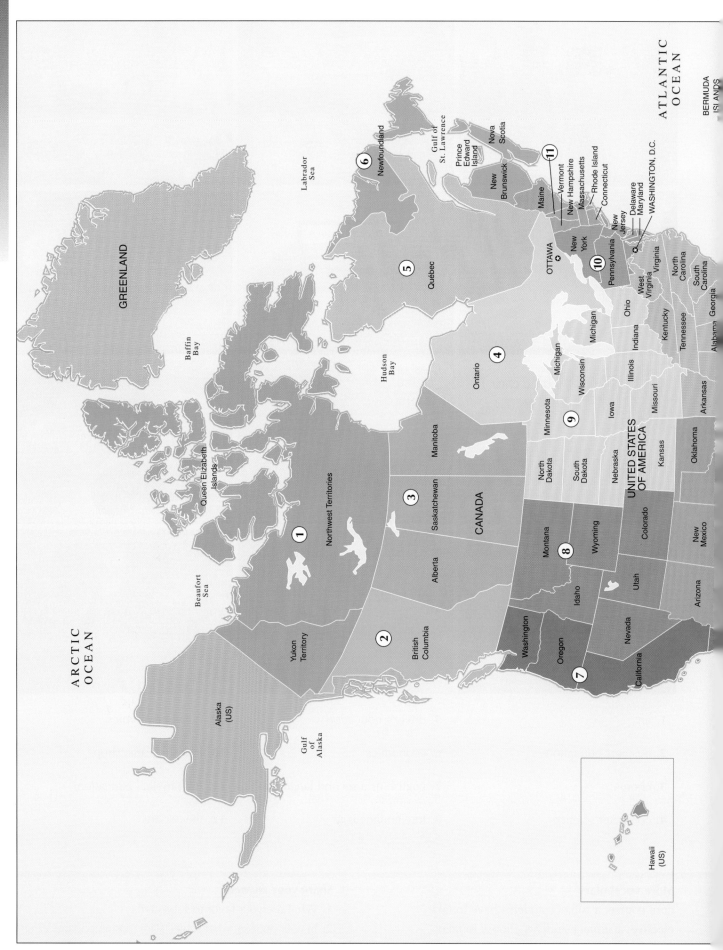

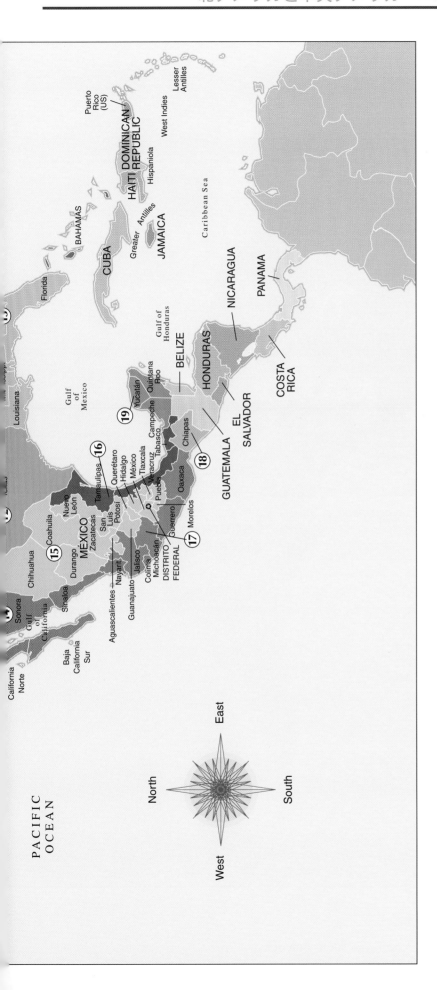

Regions of Canada
カナダの各地方

1. Northern Canada
   カナダ北部
2. British Columbia
   ブリティッシュコロンビア
3. The Prairie Provinces
   プレーリー諸州
4. Ontario
   オンタリオ
5. Québec
   ケベック
6. The Atlantic Provinces
   大西洋諸州

Regions of the United States
アメリカ合衆国の各地方

7. The Pacific States / the West Coast
   太平洋諸州 / 西海岸
8. The Rocky Mountain States
   ロッキー山脈諸州
9. The Midwest
   中西部
10. The Mid-Atlantic States
    中大西洋諸州
11. New England
    ニューイングランド地方
12. The Southwest
    南西部
13. The Southeast / the South
    南東部 / 南部

Regions of Mexico
メキシコの各地方

14. The Pacific Northwest
    太平洋北西部
15. The Plateau of Mexico
    メキシコ高原
16. The Gulf Coastal Plain
    湾岸平野
17. The Southern Uplands
    南部台地
18. The Chiapas Highlands
    チャパス高地
19. The Yucatan Peninsula
    ユカタン半島

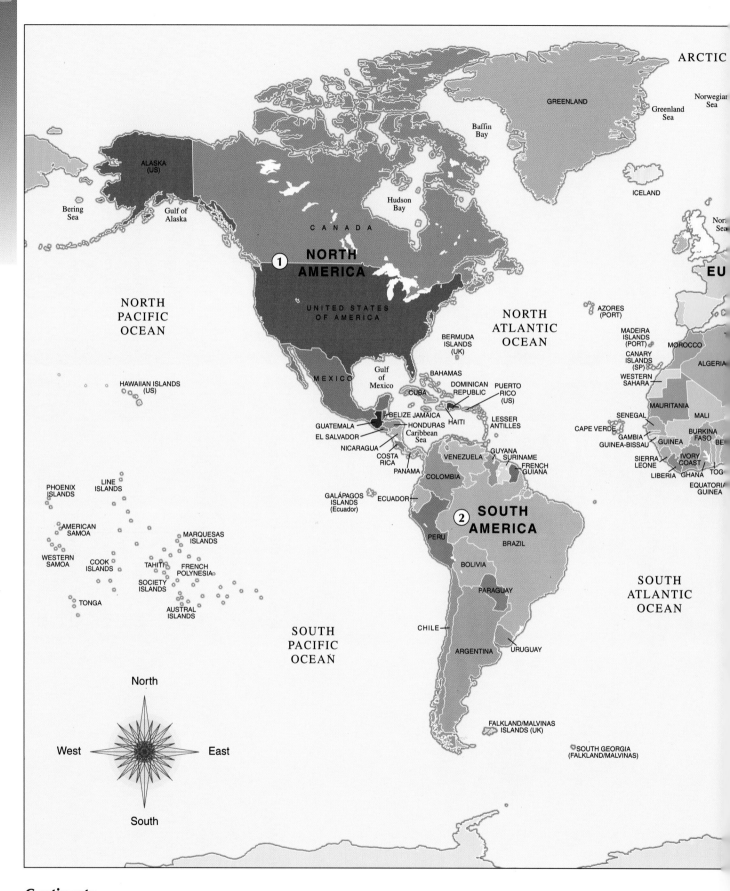

ARCTIC

Norwegian
Sea

GREENLAND

Greenland
Sea

Baffin
Bay

ICELAND

ALASKA
(US)

Bering
Sea

Gulf of
Alaska

Hudson
Bay

C A N A D A

**① NORTH
AMERICA**

NORTH
PACIFIC
OCEAN

UNITED STATES
OF AMERICA

NORTH
ATLANTIC
OCEAN

EU

AZORES
(PORT)

MADEIRA
ISLANDS
(PORT)

MOROCCO

BERMUDA
ISLANDS
(UK)

CANARY
ISLANDS
(SP)

ALGERIA

M E X I C O

Gulf
of
Mexico

BAHAMAS

WESTERN
SAHARA

HAWAIIAN ISLANDS
(US)

CUBA

DOMINICAN
REPUBLIC

PUERTO
RICO
(US)

MAURITANIA

MALI

SENEGAL

CAPE VERDE

BELIZE JAMAICA

GUATEMALA

HONDURAS

HAITI

LESSER
ANTILLES

GAMBIA

GUINEA-BISSAU

BURKINA
FASO

BE

EL SALVADOR

Caribbean
Sea

GUINEA

NICARAGUA

SIERRA
LEONE

IVORY
COAST

TOG

COSTA
RICA

VENEZUELA

GUYANA
SURINAME

LIBERIA

GHANA

PHOENIX
ISLANDS

LINE
ISLANDS

PANAMA

COLOMBIA

FRENCH
GUIANA

EQUATORIA
GUINEA

GALÁPAGOS
ISLANDS
(Ecuador)

ECUADOR

**② SOUTH
AMERICA**

AMERICAN
SAMOA

MARQUESAS
ISLANDS

PERU

BRAZIL

WESTERN
SAMOA

COOK
ISLANDS

TAHITI

FRENCH
POLYNESIA

BOLIVIA

SOUTH
ATLANTIC
OCEAN

SOCIETY
ISLANDS

PARAGUAY

TONGA

AUSTRAL
ISLANDS

SOUTH
PACIFIC
OCEAN

CHILE

North

ARGENTINA

URUGUAY

West

East

FALKLAND/MALVINAS
ISLANDS (UK)

South

SOUTH GEORGIA
(FALKLAND/MALVINAS)

Continents
大陸

1. North America
北アメリカ

2. South America
南アメリカ

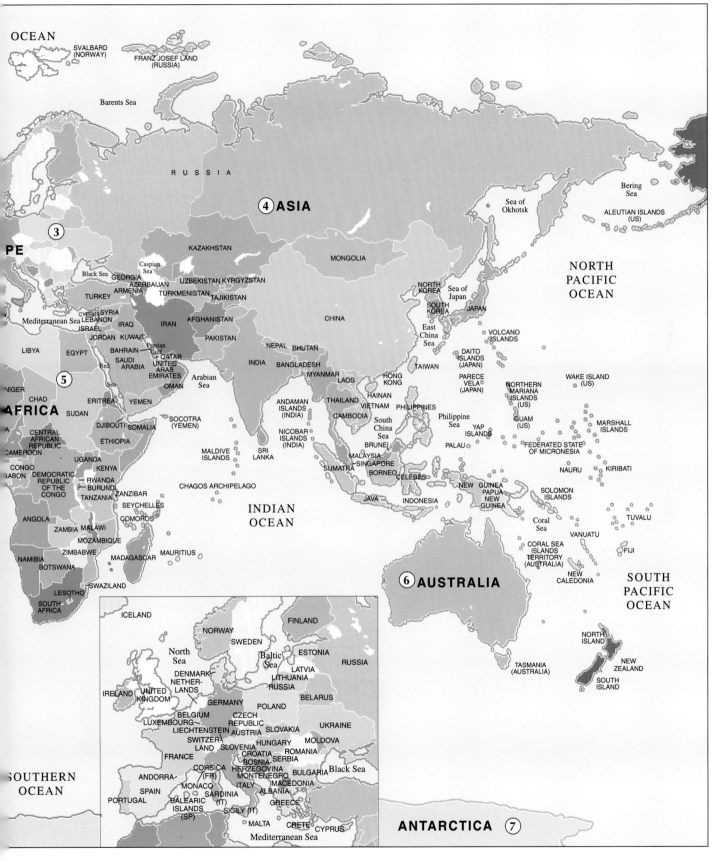

3. Europe
ヨーロッパ

4. Asia
アジア

5. Africa
アフリカ

6. Australia
オーストラリア

7. Antarctica
南極大陸

Energy and the Environment　エネルギーと環境

Energy resources　エネルギー源

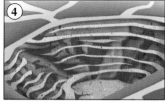

1. solar energy
太陽エネルギー

2. wind
風力

3. natural gas
天然ガス

4. coal
石炭

5. hydroelectric power
水力発電

6. oil/petroleum
石油

7. geothermal energy
地熱エネルギー

8. nuclear energy
原子力エネルギー

Pollution　汚染

9. hazardous waste
危険廃棄物

10. air pollution/smog
大気汚染/スモッグ

11. acid rain
酸性雨

12. water pollution
水質汚染

13. radiation
放射能

14. pesticide poisoning
農薬汚染

15. oil spill
重油流出

Conservation　節約

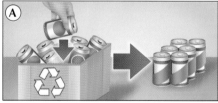

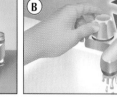

A. **recycle**
再生利用する

B. **save** water/**conserve** water
水を節約する

C. **save** energy/**conserve** energy
エネルギーを節約する

Share your answers.

1. How do you heat your home?

2. Do you have a gas stove or an electric stove?

3. What are some ways you can save energy when it's cold?

4. Do you recycle? What products do you recycle?

5. Does your market have recycling bins?

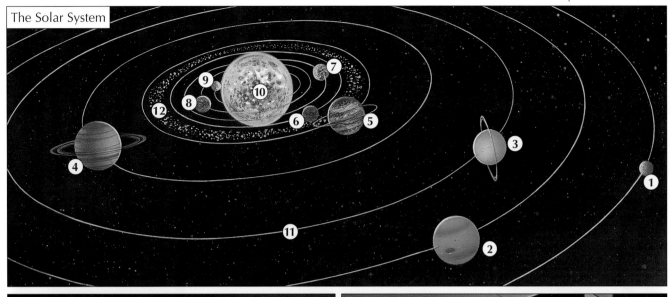

The Solar System

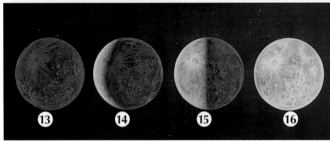

The planets
惑星

1. Pluto
冥王星

2. Neptune
海王星

3. Uranus
天王星

4. Saturn
土星

5. Jupiter
木星

6. Mars
火星

7. Earth
地球

8. Venus
金星

9. Mercury
水星

10. sun
太陽

11. orbit
軌道

12. asteroid belt
小惑星帯

13. new moon
新月

14. crescent moon
三日月

15. quarter moon
弦月

16. full moon
満月

17. astronaut
宇宙飛行士

18. space station
宇宙ステーション

19. observatory
天文台 / 観測所

20. astronomer
天文学者

21. telescope
望遠鏡

22. space
宇宙

23. star
星

24. constellation
星座

25. comet
彗星

26. galaxy
銀河系 / 星雲

More vocabulary

lunar eclipse: when the earth is between the sun and the moon

solar eclipse: when the moon is between the earth and the sun

Share your answers.

1. Do you know the names of any constellations?

2. How do you feel when you look up at the night sky?

3. Is the night sky in the U.S. the same as in your country?

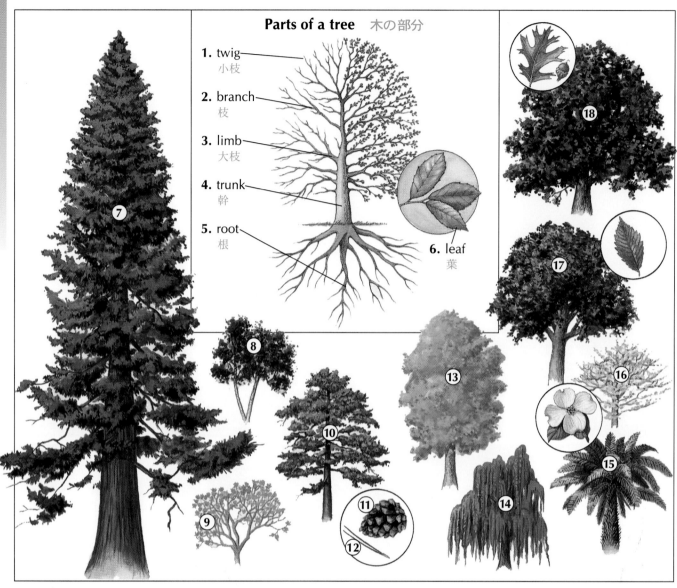

Parts of a tree 木の部分

1. twig
小枝

2. branch
枝

3. limb
大枝

4. trunk
幹

5. root
根

6. leaf
葉

7. redwood
セコイア

8. birch
シラカバ

9. magnolia
モクレン属の花木

10. pine
マツ

11. pinecone
松傘/まつぼっくり

12. needle
針状葉

13. maple
カエデ

14. willow
ヤナギ

15. palm
ヤシ

16. dogwood
ハナミズキ

17. elm
ニレ

18. oak
オーク

Plants 植物

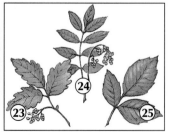

19. holly
セイヨウヒイラギ

20. berries
ベリー/液果

21. cactus
サボテン

22. vine
ブドウの木

23. poison oak
ポイズンオーク
（触れるとかぶれる）

24. poison sumac
ポイズンスマク
（触れるとかぶれる）

25. poison ivy
ウルシ/ツタウルシ

Parts of a flower　花の部分

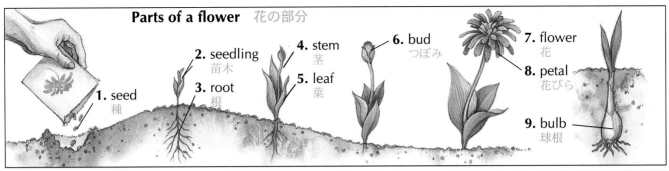

1. seed
種
2. seedling
苗木
3. root
根
4. stem
茎
5. leaf
葉
6. bud
つぼみ
7. flower
花
8. petal
花びら
9. bulb
球根

10. sunflower
ヒマワリ

11. tulip
チューリップ

12. hibiscus
ハイビスカス

13. marigold
マリーゴールド

14. daisy
デイジー

15. rose
バラ

16. gardenia
クチナシ

17. orchid
ラン

18. carnation
カーネーション

19. chrysanthemum
キク

20. iris
アイリス

21. jasmine
ジャスミン

22. violet
スミレ

23. poinsettia
ポインセチア

24. lily
ユリ

25. crocus
クロッカス

26. daffodil
スイセン

27. bouquet
ブーケ、花束

28. thorn
とげ

29. houseplant
室内の鉢植え植物

Marine Life, Amphibians, and Reptiles 海の生物、両生類、は虫類

Parts of a fish 魚の部位　　　Sea animals 海洋動物

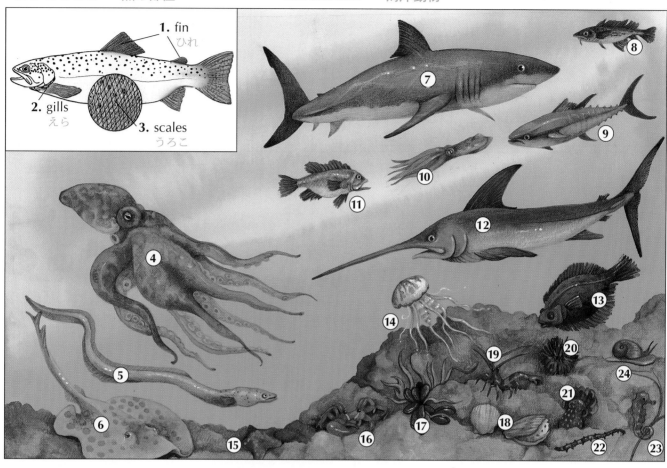

1. fin
ひれ

2. gills
えら

3. scales
うろこ

4. octopus
タコ

5. eel
ウナギ

6. ray
エイ

7. shark
サメ

8. cod
タラ

9. tuna
マグロ

10. squid
イカ

11. bass
バス、スズキ

12. swordfish
メカジキ

13. flounder
カレイ/ヒラメ

14. jellyfish
クラゲ

15. starfish
ヒトデ

16. crab
カニ

17. mussel
ムラサキイガイ

18. scallop
ホタテガイ

19. shrimp
エビ

20. sea urchin
ウニ

21. sea anemone
イソギンチャク

22. worm
フナクイムシ

23. sea horse
タツノオトシゴ

24. snail
巻貝

Amphibians 両生類

25. frog
カエル

26. newt
イモリ

27. salamander
サンショウウオ

28. toad
ヒキガエル

Sea mammals　海に住む哺乳類

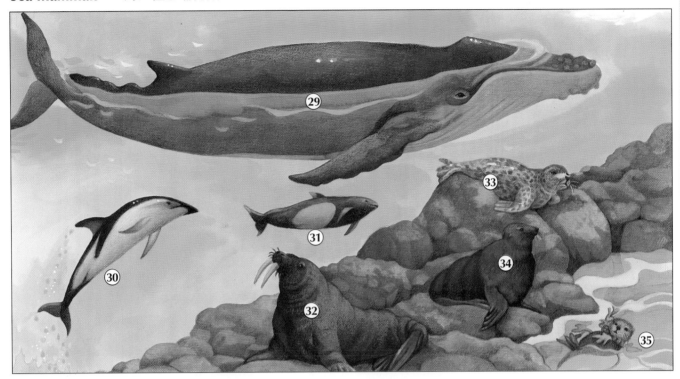

29. whale クジラ	**31.** porpoise ネズミイルカ	**33.** seal アザラシ	**35.** otter ラッコ
30. dolphin イルカ	**32.** walrus セイウチ	**34.** sea lion トド	

Reptiles　は虫類

36. alligator アリゲーター / ワニ	**38.** rattlesnake ガラガラヘビ	**40.** cobra コブラ	**42.** turtle カメ
37. crocodile クロコダイル / ワニ	**39.** garter snake ガーターヘビ	**41.** lizard トカゲ	

Birds, Insects, and Arachnids 鳥、昆虫、蛛形類

Parts of a bird 鳥の部位

1. beak / bill
   くちばし
2. wing
   つばさ
3. nest
   巣
4. claw
   （かぎ）つめ
5. feather
   羽

6. owl フクロウ	**9.** woodpecker キツツキ	**12.** penguin ペンギン	**15.** peacock クジャク
7. blue jay アオカケス	**10.** eagle ワシ	**13.** duck カモ／アヒル	**16.** pigeon ハト
8. sparrow スズメ	**11.** hummingbird ハチドリ	**14.** goose ガン／ガチョウ	**17.** robin ヨーロッパコマドリ

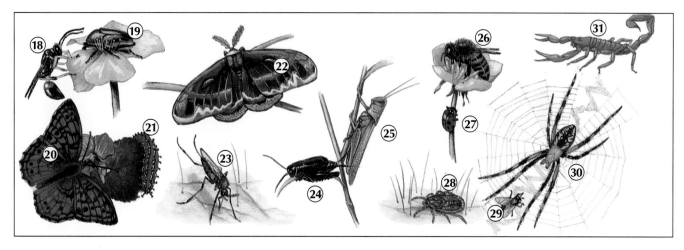

18. wasp スズメバチ	**22.** moth ガ（蛾）	**26.** honeybee ミツバチ	**30.** spider クモ
19. beetle カブトムシ	**23.** mosquito カ（蚊）	**27.** ladybug テントウムシ	**31.** scorpion サソリ
20. butterfly チョウ	**24.** cricket コオロギ	**28.** tick ダニ	
21. caterpillar イモムシ／毛虫	**25.** grasshopper バッタ	**29.** fly ハエ	

Farm animals　農場の動物

1. goat
ヤギ

2. donkey
ロバ

3. cow
乳牛

4. horse
馬

5. hen
雌鶏

6. rooster
雄鶏

7. sheep
羊

8. pig
ブタ

Pets　ペット

9. cat
猫

10. kitten
子猫

11. dog
犬

12. puppy
子犬

13. rabbit
うさぎ

14. guinea pig
モルモット

15. parakeet
インコ

16. goldfish
金魚

Rodents　げっ歯動物

17. mouse
ハツカネズミ

18. rat
ネズミ

19. gopher
ジリス

20. chipmunk
シマリス

21. squirrel
リス

22. prairie dog
プレーリードッグ

More vocabulary

Wild animals live, eat, and raise their young away from people, in the forests, mountains, plains, etc.

Domesticated animals work for people or live with them.

Share your answers.

1. Do you have any pets? any farm animals?

2. Which of these animals are in your neighborhood? Which are not?

1. **moose**
   ムース

2. **mountain lion**
   アメリカンライオン

3. **coyote**
   コヨーテ

4. **opossum**
   フクロネズミ

5. **wolf**
   オオカミ

6. **buffalo/bison**
   スイギュウ/ヤギュウ

7. **bat**
   コウモリ

8. **armadillo**
   アルマジロ

9. **beaver**
   ビーバー

10. **porcupine**
    ヤマアラシ

11. **bear**
    クマ

12. **skunk**
    スカンク

13. **raccoon**
    タヌキ

14. **deer**
    シカ

15. **fox**
    キツネ

16. **antler**
    枝角

17. **hoof**
    ひづめ

18. **whiskers**
    ひげ

19. **coat/fur**
    外被/毛皮

20. **paw**
    かぎつめのある足

21. **horn**
    角

22. **tail**
    尾

23. **quill**
    はり

24. anteater アリクイ	**30.** gorilla ゴリラ	**36.** lion ライオン	**42.** elephant ゾウ
25. leopard ヒョウ	**31.** hyena ハイエナ	**37.** tiger トラ	**43.** hippopotamus カバ
26. llama ラマ	**32.** baboon ヒヒ	**38.** camel ラクダ	**44.** kangaroo カンガルー
27. monkey サル	**33.** giraffe キリン	**39.** panther ヒョウ/ピューマ	**45.** koala コアラ
28. chimpanzee チンパンジー	**34.** zebra シマウマ	**40.** orangutan オランウータン	**46.** platypus カモノハシ
29. rhinoceros サイ	**35.** antelope アンテロープ	**41.** panda パンダ	

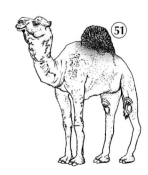

47. trunk
胴体

48. tusk
牙

49. mane
たてがみ

50. pouch
袋

51. hump
こぶ

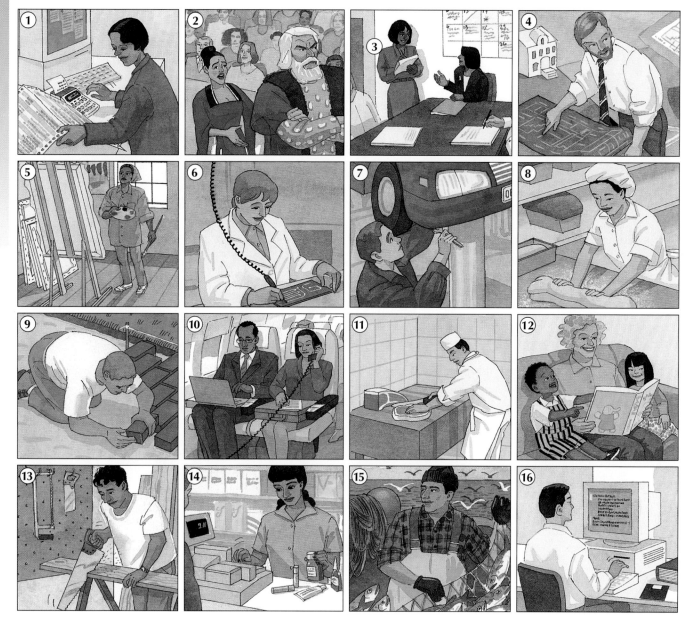

1. accountant
   会計士

2. actor
   俳優

3. administrative assistant
   経営管理アシスタント／秘書

4. architect
   建築家

5. artist
   芸術家

6. assembler
   組立工

7. auto mechanic
   自動車修理工

8. baker
   パン屋

9. bricklayer
   れんが積み職人

10. businessman/businesswoman
    ビジネスマン／ビジネスウーマン

11. butcher
    肉屋

12. caregiver/baby-sitter
    子守／ベビーシッター

13. carpenter
    大工

14. cashier
    レジ係／キャッシャー

15. commercial fisher
    漁師

16. computer programmer
    コンピュータープログラマー

Use the new language.

1. Who works outside?

2. Who works inside?

3. Who makes things?

4. Who uses a computer?

5. Who wears a uniform?

6. Who sells things?

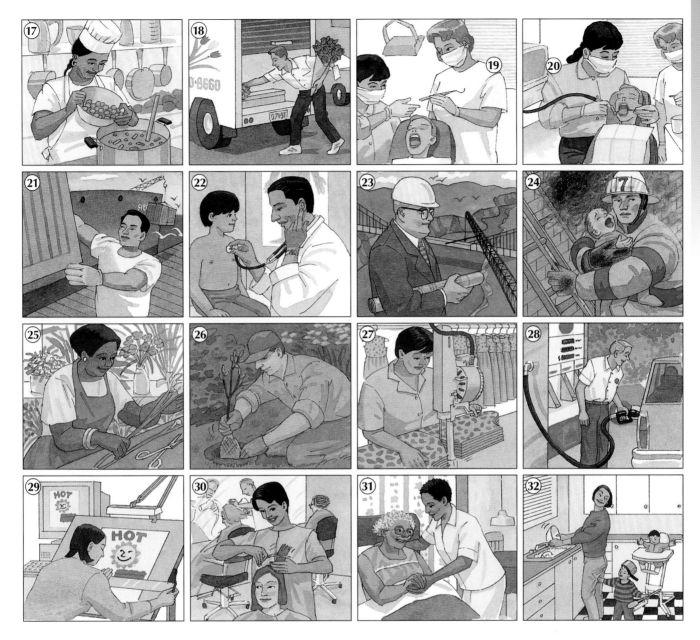

17. cook コック	**23.** engineer エンジニア	**29.** graphic artist グラフィックアーティスト
18. delivery person 配達人	**24.** firefighter 消防士	**30.** hairdresser 美容師
19. dental assistant 歯科助手	**25.** florist 花屋	**31.** home attendant ホームヘルパー
20. dentist 歯医者	**26.** gardener 庭師	**32.** homemaker 主婦
21. dockworker 港湾労働者	**27.** garment worker 裁縫師	
22. doctor 医者/医師	**28.** gas station attendant ガソリンスタンド従業員	

Share your answers.

1. Do you know people who have some of these jobs?
What do they say about their work?

2. Which of these jobs are available in your city?

3. For which of these jobs do you need special training?

Jobs and Occupations, H–W 仕事と職業

33. housekeeper
家政婦

34. interpreter / translator
通訳 / 翻訳家

35. janitor / custodian
用務員 / 管理人

36. lawyer
法律家 / 弁護士

37. machine operator
機械オペレータ

38. messenger / courier
メッセージ / 宅配の配達人

39. model
モデル

40. mover
引越し業者

41. musician
ミュージシャン / 音楽家

42. nurse
看護婦

43. painter
ペンキ屋

44. police officer
警察官

45. postal worker
郵便局員

46. printer
印刷工

47. receptionist
受付係

48. repair person
修理工

Talk about each of the jobs or occupations.

She's a housekeeper. She works in a hotel.

He's an interpreter. He works for the government.

She's a nurse. She works with patients.

49. reporter
リポーター

50. salesclerk / salesperson
販売員

51. sanitation worker
公衆衛生員

52. secretary
秘書

53. server
給仕人

54. serviceman / servicewoman
軍人

55. stock clerk
在庫管理事務員

56. store owner
店主

57. student
学生

58. teacher / instructor
教師 / 講師

59. telemarketer
テレマーケッター

60. travel agent
旅行案内業者 / 旅行社社員

61. truck driver
トラック運転手

62. veterinarian
獣医

63. welder
溶接工

64. writer / author
ライター / 作家

Talk about your job or the job you want.

What do you do?

I'm a salesclerk. I work in a store.

What do you want to do?

I want to be a veterinarian. I want to work with animals.

A. assemble components
部品を組み立てる

B. assist medical patients
患者を補助する

C. cook
料理する

D. do manual labor
手仕事をする

E. drive a truck
トラックを運転する

F. operate heavy machinery
重機械を操作する

G. repair appliances
機器を修理する

H. sell cars
車を販売する

I. sew clothes
服を縫う

J. speak another language
別の言語を話す

K. supervise people
人を管理する

L. take care of children
子供の世話をする

M. type
タイプを打つ

N. use a cash register
レジを使う

O. wait on customers
お客に給仕する

P. work on a computer
コンピューターで仕事をする

More vocabulary

act: to perform in a play, movie, or TV show

fly: to pilot an airplane

teach: to instruct, to show how to do something

Share your answers.

1. What job skills do you have? Where did you learn them?

2. What job skills do you want to learn?

A. **talk** to friends
友人に相談する

B. **look** at a job board
求人掲示板を見る

C. **look** for a help wanted sign
求人掲示を探す

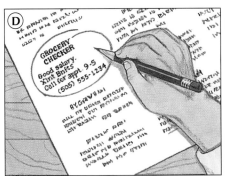

D. **look** in the classifieds
求人広告欄で探す

E. **call** for information
電話をかけて情報を集める

F. **ask** about the hours
勤務時間についてたずねる

G. **fill out** an application
申込書に記入する

H. **go** on an interview
面接に行く

I. **talk** about your experience
経歴を話す

J. **ask** about benefits
福利厚生についてたずねる

K. **inquire** about the salary
給料についてたずねる

L. **get hired**
採用される

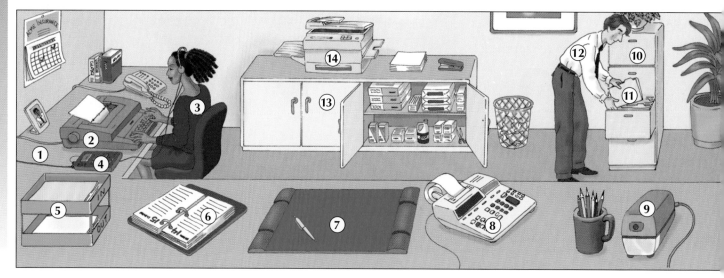

1. **desk**
   デスク

2. **typewriter**
   タイプライター

3. **secretary**
   秘書

4. **microcassette transcriber**
   マイクロカセット
   トランスクライバー

5. **stacking tray**
   書類トレー

6. **desk calendar**
   卓上カレンダー

7. **desk pad**
   デスクパッド

8. **calculator**
   計算機

9. **electric pencil sharpener**
   電気鉛筆削り

10. **file cabinet**
    ファイルキャビネット

11. **file folder**
    ファイルホルダー

12. **file clerk**
    資料整理係

13. **supply cabinet**
    備品キャビネット

14. **photocopier**
    コピー機

A. **take** a message
   伝言を受ける

B. **fax** a letter
   手紙をファックスする

C. **transcribe** notes
   要件を書き写す

D. **type** a letter
   手紙をタイプする

E. **make** copies
   コピーをとる

F. **collate** papers
   書類を照合する

G. **staple**
   ホチキスでとめる

H. **file** papers
   書類をファイルする

Practice taking messages.

Hello. My name is <u>Sara Scott</u>. Is <u>Mr. Lee</u> in?

  Not yet. Would you like to leave a message?

Yes. Please ask <u>him</u> to call me at <u>555-4859</u>.

Share your answers.

1. Which office equipment do you know how to use?
2. Which jobs does a file clerk do?
3. Which jobs does a secretary do?

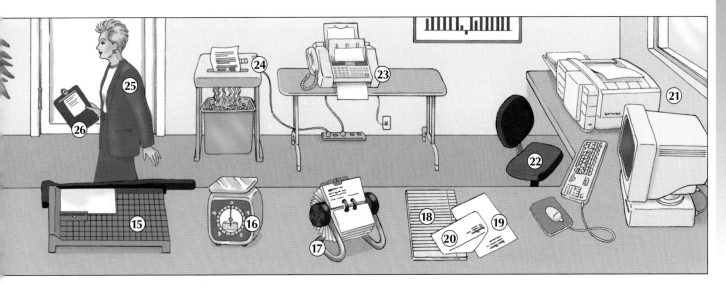

15. paper cutter
裁断機

16. postal scale
郵便料金メーター

17. rotary card file
回転式カードファイル

18. legal pad
リーガルパッド

19. letterhead paper
レターヘッド紙

20. envelope
封筒

21. computer workstation
コンピューターワークステーション

22. swivel chair
回転椅子

23. fax machine
ファクシミリ

24. paper shredder
シュレッダー

25. office manager
オフィスマネージャー

26. clipboard
クリップボード

27. appointment book
スケジュール管理帳

28. stapler
ホチキス

29. staple
ホチキスの針

30. organizer
オーガナイザー

31. typewriter cartridge
タイプライター
カートリッジ

32. mailer
郵送用パッケージ/封筒

33. correction fluid
修正液

34. Post-it notes
付箋紙

35. label
ラベル

36. notepad
ノートパッド

37. glue
糊

38. rubber cement
ゴム糊

39. clear tape
クリアテープ

40. rubber stamp
ゴム印

41. ink pad
スタンプ台

42. packing tape
梱包用テープ

43. pushpin
押しピン

44. paper clip
クリップ

45. rubber band
輪ゴム

Use the new language.

1. Which items keep things together?

2. Which items are used to mail packages?

3. Which items are made of paper?

Share your answers.

1. Which office supplies do students use?

2. Where can you buy them?

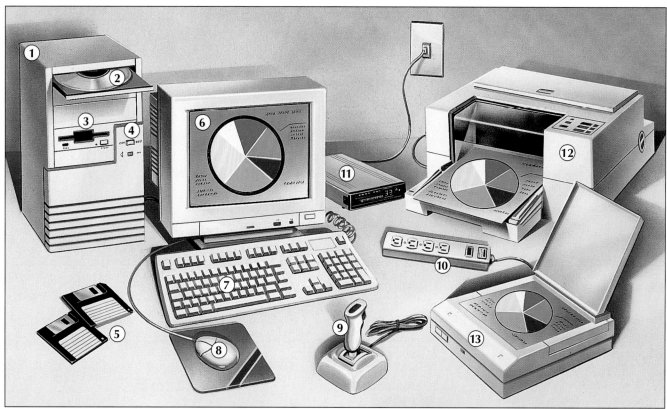

Hardware
ハードウェア

1. CPU (central processing unit)
   CPU (中央処理装置)

2. CD-ROM disc
   CD ROM ディスク

3. disk drive
   ディスクドライブ

4. power switch
   電源

5. disk / floppy
   ディスク/フロッピー

6. monitor / screen
   モニター/スクリーン

7. keyboard
   キーボード

8. mouse
   マウス

9. joystick
   ジョイスティック

10. surge protector
    サージ保安器

11. modem
    モデム

12. printer
    プリンタ

13. scanner
    スキャナー

14. laptop
    ラップトップ

15. trackball
    トラックボール

16. cable
    ケーブル

17. port
    ポート

18. motherboard
    マザーボード

19. slot
    スロット

20. hard disk drive
    ハードディスクドライブ

Software
ソフトウェア

21. program / application
    プログラム/アプリケーション

22. user's manual
    ユーザーマニュアル

More vocabulary

data: information that a computer can read

memory: how much data a computer can hold

speed: how fast a computer can work with data

Share your answers.

1. Can you use a computer?

2. How did you learn? in school? from a book? by yourself?

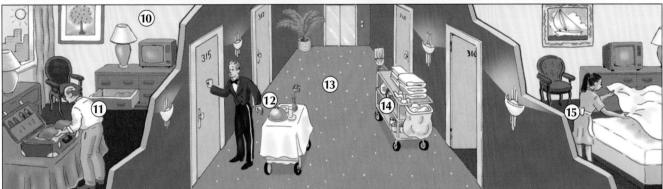

1. valet parking
バレーパーキング

2. doorman
ドアマン

3. lobby
ロビー

4. bell captain
ベルキャプテン

5. bellhop
メッセンジャー

6. luggage cart
手荷物運搬カート

7. gift shop
ギフトショップ

8. front desk
フロント

9. desk clerk
フロント係

10. guest room
客室

11. guest
客

12. room service
ルームサービス

13. hall
廊下

14. housekeeping cart
清掃カート

15. housekeeper
清掃係

16. pool
プール

17. pool service
プールサービス

18. ice machine
製氷器

19. meeting room
会議室

20. ballroom
舞踏場

More vocabulary

concierge: the hotel worker who helps guests find restaurants and interesting places to go

service elevator: an elevator for hotel workers

Share your answers.

1. Does this look like a hotel in your city? Which one?

2. Which hotel job is the most difficult?

3. How much does it cost to stay in a hotel in your city?

1. front office
   本部

2. factory owner
   工場所有者

3. designer
   設計士

4. time clock
   タイムレコーダー

5. line supervisor
   ライン管理者

6. factory worker
   工場労働者

7. parts
   部品

8. assembly line
   組立ライン

9. warehouse
   倉庫

10. order puller
    注文品取揃え係

11. hand truck
    台車

12. conveyor belt
    ベルトコンベヤー

13. packer
    梱包係

14. forklift
    フォークリフト

15. shipping clerk
    出荷係

16. loading dock
    荷積みドック

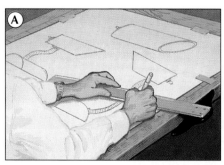

A. design
    設計する

B. manufacture
    製造する

C. ship
    出荷する

1. electrical hazard
高圧危険

2. flammable
引火性

3. poison
有毒

4. corrosive
腐食性

5. biohazard
生物学的危険

6. radioactive
放射性

7. hazardous materials
危険物質

8. dangerous situation
危険な状況

9. safety goggles
防護ゴーグル

10. safety glasses
防護めがね

11. safety visor
防護バイザー

12. respirator
防毒マスク

13. earplugs
耳栓

14. safety earmuffs
防護耳おおい

15. safety vest
防護ベスト

16. back support
バックサポーター

17. latex gloves
ゴム手袋

18. hair net
ヘアネット

19. hard hat
ヘルメット / 保安帽

20. safety boot
安全靴

21. toe guard
爪先保護

22. fire extinguisher
消火器

23. careless
不注意な

24. careful
注意深い

Crops 作物

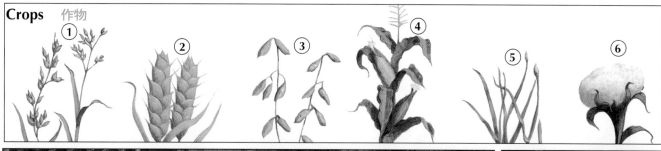

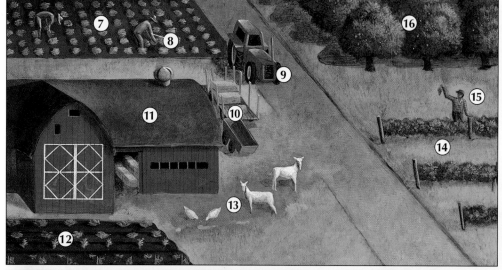

1. rice
米

2. wheat
小麦

3. soybeans
大豆

4. corn
トウモロコシ

5. alfalfa
アルファルファ

6. cotton
綿

7. field
畑

8. farmworker
農園労働者

9. tractor
トラクター

10. farm equipment
農耕機具

11. barn
納屋

12. vegetable garden
菜園

13. livestock
家畜

14. vineyard
ブドウ園

15. farmer / grower
農場主 / 飼育者

16. orchard
果樹園

17. corral
畜舎 / 囲い柵

18. hay
干し草

19. fence
囲い

20. hired hand
農場労働者

21. steers / cattle
雄の子牛 / 畜牛

22. rancher
牧場主 / 牧場労働者

A. plant
植える

B. harvest
収穫する

C. milk
乳をしぼる

D. feed
餌をやる

1. construction worker
   現場労働者

2. ladder
   はしご

3. I beam/girder
   I 形鋼/けた

4. scaffolding
   足場

5. cherry picker
   チェリークレーン
   （移動式クレーン）

6. bulldozer
   ブルドーザー

7. crane
   クレーン

8. backhoe
   バックホー

9. jackhammer/pneumatic drill
   手持ち削岩機/空気ドリル

10. concrete
    コンクリート

11. bricks
    煉瓦

12. trowel
    こて

13. insulation
    断熱材

14. stucco
    化粧しっくい

15. window pane
    窓ガラス

16. plywood
    合板/ベニヤ板

17. wood/lumber
    材木

18. drywall
    石壁/ドライ壁

19. shingles
    屋根板

20. pickax
    つるはし

21. shovel
    シャベル

22. sledgehammer
    大ハンマー

A. **paint**
   ペンキを塗る

B. **lay** bricks
   れんがを積む

C. **measure**
   寸法をはかる

D. **hammer**
   釘をうつ

1. hammer
金槌

2. mallet
つち

3. ax
おの

4. handsaw
のこぎり

5. hacksaw
弓のこ

6. C-clamp
C型クランプ

7. pliers
やっとこ／ペンチ

8. electric drill
電気ドリル

9. power sander
動力式サンダー

10. circular saw
丸のこ

11. blade
刃

12. router
くり抜き機

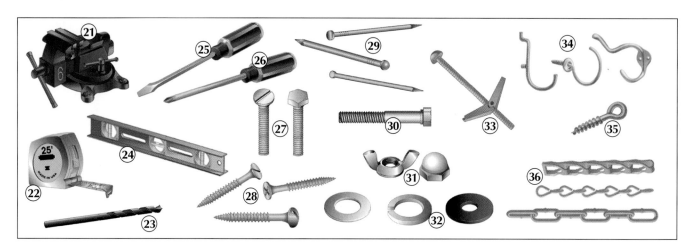

21. vise
万力

22. tape measure
巻き尺

23. drill bit
きり先

24. level
水準儀

25. screwdriver
ねじまわし

26. Phillips screwdriver
プラスのねじまわし

27. machine screw
小ねじ

28. wood screw
木ねじ

29. nail
釘

30. bolt
ボルト

31. nut
ナット（留めねじ）

32. washer
ワッシャー

33. toggle bolt
トグルボルト

34. hook
かぎ／フック

35. eye hook
アイフック

36. chain
チェーン

Use the new language.

1. Which tools are used for plumbing?

2. Which tools are used for painting?

3. Which tools are used for electrical work?

4. Which tools are used for working with wood?

13. wire
針金

14. extension cord
延長コード

15. yardstick
もの差し

16. pipe
パイプ

17. fittings
管継手

18. wood
材木

19. spray gun
スプレーガン

20. paint
ペンキ

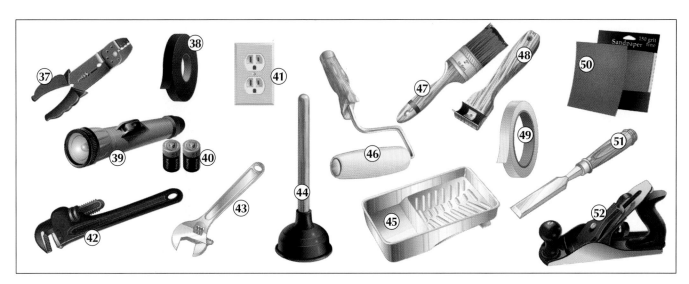

37. wire stripper
ワイヤーストリッパー

38. electrical tape
絶縁テープ

39. flashlight
懐中電灯

40. battery
電池

41. outlet
コンセント

42. pipe wrench
パイプレンチ

43. wrench
レンチ／スパナ

44. plunger
プランジャー

45. paint pan
ペンキ入れ

46. paint roller
ペンキローラー

47. paintbrush
ペンキはけ

48. scraper
削り器

49. masking tape
マスキングテープ

50. sandpaper
紙ヤスリ

51. chisel
のみ

52. plane
かんな

Use the new language.

Look at **Household Problems and Repairs,** pages **48–49.**

Name the tools you use to fix the problems you see.

Share your answers.

1. Which tools do you have in your home?

2. Which tools can be dangerous to use?

1. zoo
動物園

2. animals
動物

3. zookeeper
動物園職員

4. botanical gardens
植物園

5. greenhouse
温室

6. gardener
庭師

7. art museum
美術館

8. painting
絵画

9. sculpture
彫刻

10. the movies
映画

11. seat
席

12. screen
画面

13. amusement park
遊園地

14. puppet show
人形劇

15. roller coaster
ジェットコースター

16. carnival
カーニバル／巡回見世物

17. rides
乗り物

18. game
ゲーム

19. county fair
郡の農産物・家畜品評会

20. first place/first prize
一等賞

21. exhibition
展覧会／展示会

22. swap meet/flea market
のみの市

23. booth
ブース

24. merchandise
商品

25. baseball game
野球の試合

26. stadium
競技場／球場

27. announcer
アナウンサー

Talk about the places you like to go.

I like <u>animals</u>, so I go to <u>the zoo</u>.

I like <u>rides</u>, so I go to <u>carnivals</u>.

Share your answers.

1. Which of these places is interesting to you?

2. Which rides do you like at an amusement park?

3. What are some famous places to go to in your country?

1. ball field
球技場

2. bike path
自転車道

3. cyclist
サイクリスト

4. bicycle/bike
自転車

5. jump rope
なわとびの縄

6. duck pond
池

7. tennis court
テニスコート

8. picnic table
ピクニックテーブル

9. tricycle
三輪車

10. bench
ベンチ

11. water fountain
噴水式水飲み場

12. swings
ブランコ

13. slide
すべり台

14. climbing apparatus
ジャングルジム

15. sandbox
砂場

16. seesaw
シーソー

A. **pull** the wagon
ワゴンを引っ張る

B. **push** the swing
ブランコを押す

C. **climb** on the bars
棒によじ登る

D. **picnic/have** a picnic
ピクニック/ピクニックをする

1. camping
キャンプする

2. boating
ボートを漕ぐ

3. canoeing
カヌーを漕ぐ

4. rafting
いかだを漕ぐ

5. fishing
魚釣りをする

6. hiking
ハイキングをする

7. backpacking
バックパックを背負って歩く

8. mountain biking
マウンテンバイクに乗る

9. horseback riding
馬に乗る

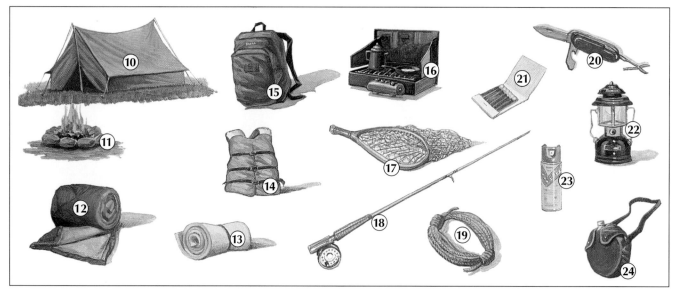

10. tent
テント

11. campfire
キャンプファイア

12. sleeping bag
寝袋

13. foam pad
気泡マット

14. life vest
救命胴衣

15. backpack
バックパック

16. camping stove
キャンプ用コンロ

17. fishing net
魚捕り網

18. fishing pole
釣竿

19. rope
ロープ

20. multi-use knife
多目的ナイフ

21. matches
マッチ

22. lantern
手提げランプ

23. insect repellent
虫避けスプレー

24. canteen
水筒

1. ocean/water 海/水	**9.** beach umbrella ビーチパラソル	**17.** sunbather 日光浴をしている人
2. fins ひれ/フリッパー	**10.** sand castle 砂の城	**18.** lifeguard 救助員/監視員
3. diving mask ダイビングマスク	**11.** cooler クーラー	**19.** lifesaving device 救命道具
4. sailboat 帆船/ヨット	**12.** shade 日陰	**20.** lifeguard station 監視塔
5. surfboard サーフボード	**13.** sunscreen/sunblock 日焼け止め	**21.** seashell 貝殻
6. wave 波	**14.** beach chair ビーチチェアー	**22.** pail/bucket バケツ
7. wet suit ウェットスーツ	**15.** beach towel ビーチタオル	**23.** sand 砂
8. scuba tank 潜水用タンク	**16.** pier 埠頭	**24.** rock 岩/石

More vocabulary

seaweed: a plant that grows in the ocean

tide: the level of the ocean. The tide goes in and out every twelve hours.

Share your answers.

1. Are there any beaches near your home?

2. Do you prefer to spend more time on the sand or in the water?

3. Where are some of the world's best beaches?

155

Sports Verbs　スポーツ関連の動詞

A. walk 歩く	**E. catch** キャッチする	**I. shoot** シュートする	**M. tackle** タックルする
B. jog ジョギングする	**F. pitch** （ボールを）投げる	**J. jump** ジャンプする	
C. run 走る	**G. hit** 打つ	**K. dribble/bounce** ドリブルする	
D. throw 投げる	**H. pass** パスする	**L. kick** キックする	

Practice talking about what you can do.

I can <u>swim</u>, but I can't <u>dive</u>.

I can <u>pass the ball</u> well, but I can't <u>shoot</u> too well.

Use the new language.

Look at **Individual Sports**, page **159**.

Name the actions you see people doing.

The man in number 18 is riding a horse.

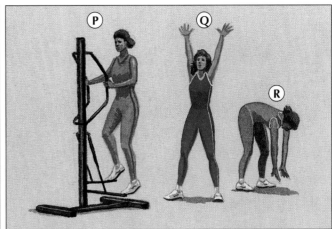

N. serve
サーブする

O. swing
スウィングする

P. exercise / work out
運動する

Q. stretch
伸ばす

R. bend
曲げる

S. dive
飛び込む

T. swim
泳ぐ

U. ski
スキーをする

V. skate
スケートをする

W. ride
乗る

X. start
スタートする

Y. race
競争する

Z. finish
ゴールインする

Share your answers.

1. What do you like to do?

2. What do you have difficulty doing?

3. How often do you exercise? Once a week? Two or three times a week? More? Never?

4. Which is more difficult, throwing a ball or catching it?

1. score
スコア

2. coach
コーチ

3. team
チーム

4. fan
ファン

5. player
選手

6. official/referee
審判員/レフリー

7. basketball court
バスケットボールコート

8. basketball
バスケットボール

9. baseball
野球

10. softball
ソフトボール

11. football
フットボール

12. soccer
サッカー

13. ice hockey
アイスホッケー

14. volleyball
バレーボール

15. water polo
ウォーターポロ/水球

More vocabulary

captain: the team leader

umpire: in baseball, the name for referee

Little League: a baseball league for children

win: to have the best score

lose: the opposite of win

tie: to have the same score as the other team

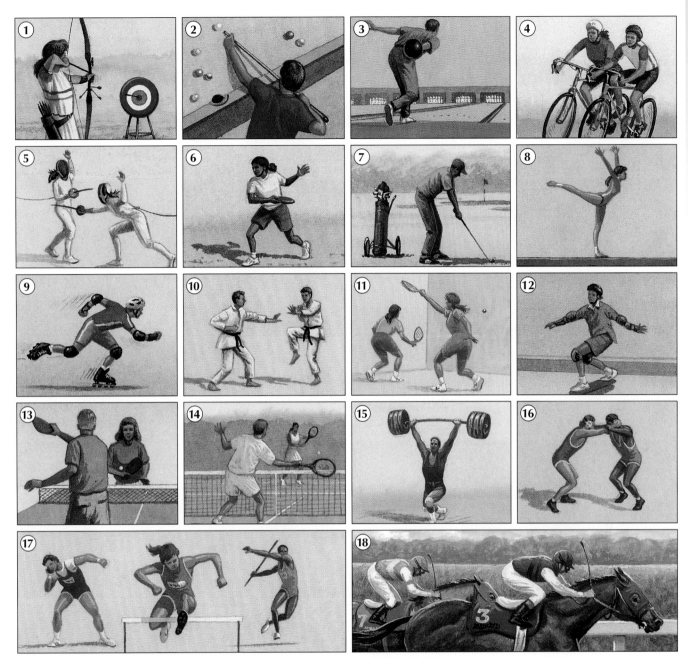

1. archery
アーチェリー

2. billiards/pool
ビリヤード

3. bowling
ボーリング

4. cycling/biking
サイクリング

5. fencing
フェンシング

6. flying disc*
フリスビー

7. golf
ゴルフ

8. gymnastics
体操

9. inline skating
インラインスケート

10. martial arts
武道

11. racquetball
ラケットボール

12. skateboarding
スケートボード

13. table tennis/
Ping-Pong™
卓球/ピンポン

14. tennis
テニス

15. weightlifting
ウエイトリフティング

16. wrestling
レスリング

17. track and field
陸上競技

18. horse racing
競馬

*Note: one brand is Frisbee®
(Mattel, Inc.)

Talk about sports.

Which sports do you like?

　I like <u>tennis</u> but I don't like <u>golf</u>.

Share your answers.

1. Which sports are good for children to learn? Why?
2. Which sport is the most difficult to learn? Why?
3. Which sport is the most dangerous? Why?

1. **downhill skiing**
   ダウンヒルスキー

2. **snowboarding**
   スノーボード

3. **cross-country skiing**
   クロスカントリースキー

4. **ice skating**
   アイススケート

5. **figure skating**
   フィギュアスケート

6. **sledding**
   そり遊び

7. **waterskiing**
   水上スキー

8. **sailing**
   セーリング

9. **surfing**
   サーフィン

10. **sailboarding**
    ウィンドサーフィン

11. **snorkeling**
    シュノーケル

12. **scuba diving**
    スキューバダイビング

Use the new language.

Look at **The Beach,** page **155.**

Name the sports you see.

Share your answers.

1. Which sports are in the Winter Olympics?

2. Which sports do you think are the most exciting to watch?

1. golf club
ゴルフクラブ

2. tennis racket
テニスラケット

3. volleyball
バレーボール

4. basketball
バスケットボール

5. bowling ball
ボーリングのボール

6. bow
弓

7. arrow
矢

8. target
標的

9. ice skates
アイススケート靴

10. inline skates
インラインスケート靴

11. hockey stick
ホッケースティック

12. soccer ball
サッカーボール

13. shin guards
すね当て

14. baseball bat
野球のバット

15. catcher's mask
キャッチャーマスク

16. uniform
ユニフォーム

17. glove
グローブ

18. baseball
野球のボール

19. weights
ウェート／おもり

20. football helmet
フォトボールヘルメット

21. shoulder pads
ショルダーパッド

22. football
フットボール

23. snowboard
スノーボード

24. skis
スキー

25. ski poles
スキーストック

26. ski boots
スキー靴

27. flying disc*
フリスビー

*Note: one brand is Frisbee®
(Mattel, Inc.)

Share your answers.

1. Which sports equipment is used for safety reasons?

2. Which sports equipment is heavy?

3. What sports equipment do you have at home?

Use the new language.

Look at **Individual Sports,** page **159.**

Name the sports equipment you see.

161

A. collect things
ものを**集める**

B. play games
ゲームをする

C. build models
模型を組み立てる

D. do crafts
工作をする

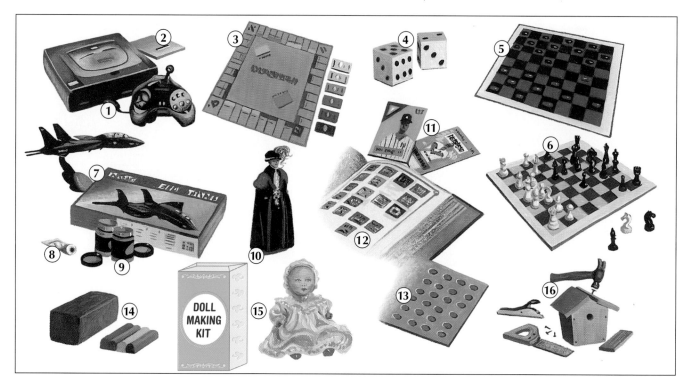

1. video game system
ビデオゲーム機

2. cartridge
カートリッジ

3. board game
盤上ゲーム

4. dice
さいころ

5. checkers
チェッカー

6. chess
チェス

7. model kit
モデルキット

8. glue
のり

9. acrylic paint
アクリル絵具

10. figurine
置物（像）

11. baseball card
ベースボールカード

12. stamp collection
切手収集

13. coin collection
コイン収集

14. clay
粘土

15. doll making kit
人形作りキット

16. woodworking kit
木工キット

Talk about how much time you spend on your hobbies.

I *do crafts* all the time.

I *play chess* sometimes.

I never *build models*.

Share your answers.

1. How often do you play video games? Often?
Sometimes? Never?

2. What board games do you know?

3. Do you collect anything? What?

E. paint
絵を描く

F. knit
編み物をする

G. pretend
まねをする

H. play cards
トランプをする

17. yarn
毛糸

18. knitting needles
編み針

19. embroidery
刺繍

20. crochet
かぎ針編み

21. easel
画架/イーゼル

22. canvas
キャンバス

23. paintbrush
絵筆

24. oil paint
油絵具

25. watercolor
水彩絵具

26. clubs
クラブ

27. diamonds
ダイアモンド

28. spades
スペード

29. hearts
ハート

30. paper doll
着せ替え人形

31. action figure
キャラクター人形

32. model trains
電車の模型

Share your answers.

1. Do you like to play cards? Which games?

2. Did you pretend a lot when you were a child? What did you pretend to be?

3. Is it important to have hobbies? Why or why not?

4. What's your favorite game?

5. What's your hobby?

1. clock radio
時計付きラジオ

2. portable radio-cassette player
ラジカセ

3. cassette recorder
カセットレコーダー

4. microphone
マイクロホン

5. shortwave radio
短波ラジオ

6. TV (television)
テレビ

7. portable TV
携帯テレビ

8. VCR (videocassette recorder)
VCR／ビデオテープレコーダー

9. remote control
リモコン（リモートコントロール）

10. videocassette
ビデオテープ

11. speakers
スピーカー

12. turntable
ターンテーブル

13. tuner
チューナー

14. CD player
CD プレーヤー

15. personal radio-cassette player
ヘッドホンステレオ

16. headphones
ヘッドホン

17. adapter
アダプタ

18. plug
プラグ

  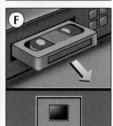

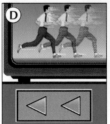

19. video camera ビデオカメラ	**27.** camera case カメラケース	**35.** underexposed 露光不足の
20. tripod 三脚	**28.** screen スクリーン	**A.** **record** 録音する
21. camcorder カムコーダー	**29.** carousel slide projector ドーナツ型スライド映写機	**B.** **play** 再生する
22. battery pack バッテリーパック	**30.** slide tray スライドトレー	**C.** **fast forward** 早送りする
23. battery charger バッテリーチャージャー	**31.** slides スライド	**D.** **rewind** 巻き戻しする
24. 35 mm camera 35ミリカメラ	**32.** photo album アルバム	**E.** **pause** 一時停止する
25. zoom lens ズームレンズ	**33.** out of focus ピンぼけ	**F.** **stop** and **eject** 停止して取り出す
26. film フィルム	**34.** overexposed 露光過度の	

Types of entertainment 娯楽の種類

1. film/movie
映画

2. play
芝居

3. television program
テレビ番組

4. radio program
ラジオ番組

5. stand-up comedy
お笑い芸

6. concert
コンサート

7. ballet
バレー

8. opera
オペラ

Types of stories ストーリーの種類

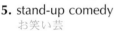

9. western
西部劇

10. comedy
喜劇

11. tragedy
悲劇

12. science fiction story
SF (サイエンス
フィクション)

13. action story/
adventure story
アクション/冒険もの

14. horror story
ホラー

15. mystery
ミステリー

16. romance
恋愛もの

Types of TV programs　テレビ番組の種類

17. news
ニュース

18. sitcom (situation comedy)
連続ホームコメディ

19. cartoon
漫画

20. talk show
トークショー

21. soap opera
メロドラマ

22. nature program
自然ドキュメンタリー

23. game show/quiz show
ゲームショー/クイズショー

24. children's program
子供番組

25. shopping program
ショッピング番組

26. serious book
まじめな本

27. funny book
面白い本

28. sad book
悲しい本

29. boring book
退屈な本

30. interesting book
興味深い本

1. **New Year's Day**
   元日

2. **parade**
   パレード

3. **confetti**
   紙吹雪

4. **Valentine's Day**
   バレンタインデー

5. **card**
   カード

6. **heart**
   ハート

7. **Independence Day / 4th of July**
   アメリカ独立記念日

8. **fireworks**
   花火

9. **flag**
   旗

10. **Halloween**
    ハロウィーン

11. **jack-o'-lantern**
    かぼちゃの提灯

12. **mask**
    仮面

13. **costume**
    衣装

14. **candy**
    キャンディ

15. **Thanksgiving**
    感謝祭

16. **feast**
    ごちそう

17. **turkey**
    七面鳥

18. **Christmas**
    クリスマス

19. **ornament**
    飾り

20. **Christmas tree**
    クリスマスツリー

A. **plan** a party
パーティを計画する

B. **invite** the guests
客（ゲスト）を招待する

C. **decorate** the house
家を飾り付けする

D. **wrap** a gift
贈り物を包む

E. **hide**
隠れる

F. **answer** the door
玄関で応対する

G. **shout** "surprise!"
「びっくりー」と叫ぶ

H. **light** the candles
ロウソクに灯をともす

I. **sing** "Happy Birthday"
「ハッピーバースディ」を歌う

J. **make** a wish
願い事をする

K. **blow out** the candles
ロウソクを吹き消す

L. **open** the presents
プレゼントを開ける

Practice inviting friends to a party.

I'd love for you to come to my party <u>next week</u>.

Could <u>you and your friend</u> come to my party?

Would <u>your friend</u> like to come to a party I'm giving?

Share your answers.

1. Do you celebrate birthdays? What do you do?

2. Are there birthdays you celebrate in a special way?

3. Is there a special birthday song in your country?

Verb Guide

Verbs in English are either regular or irregular in the past tense and past participle forms.

Regular Verbs

The regular verbs below are marked 1, 2, 3, or 4 according to four different spelling patterns.
(See page 172 for the **irregular verbs** which do not follow any of these patterns.)

Spelling Patterns for the Past and the Past Participle	Example		
1. Add **-ed** to the end of the verb.	**ASK**	→	**ASKED**
2. Add **-d** to the end of the verb.	**LIVE**	→	**LIVED**
3. Double the final consonant and add **-ed** to the end of the verb.	**DROP**	→	**DROPPED**
4. Drop the final y and add **-ied** to the end of the verb.	**CRY**	→	**CRIED**

The Oxford Picture Dictionary List of Regular Verbs

act (1)
add (1)
address (1)
answer (1)
apologize (2)
appear (1)
applaud (1)
arrange (2)
arrest (1)
arrive (2)
ask (1)
assemble (2)
assist (1)
bake (2)
barbecue (2)
bathe (2)
board (1)
boil (1)
borrow (1)
bounce (2)
brainstorm (1)
breathe (2)
broil (1)
brush (1)
burn (1)
call (1)
carry (4)
change (2)
check (1)
choke (2)
chop (3)
circle (2)
claim (1)
clap (3)
clean (1)
clear (1)
climb (1)
close (2)
collate (2)

collect (1)
color (1)
comb (1)
commit (3)
compliment (1)
conserve (2)
convert (1)
cook (1)
copy (4)
correct (1)
cough (1)
count (1)
cross (1)
cry (4)
dance (2)
design (1)
deposit (1)
deliver (1)
dial (1)
dictate (2)
die (2)
discuss (1)
dive (2)
dress (1)
dribble (2)
drill (1)
drop (3)
drown (1)
dry (4)
dust (1)
dye (2)
edit (1)
eject (1)
empty (4)
end (1)
enter (1)
erase (2)
examine (2)
exchange (2)

exercise (2)
experience (2)
exterminate (2)
fasten (1)
fax (1)
file (2)
fill (1)
finish (1)
fix (1)
floss (1)
fold (1)
fry (4)
gargle (2)
graduate (2)
grate (2)
grease (2)
greet (1)
grill (1)
hail (1)
hammer (1)
harvest (1)
help (1)
hire (2)
hug (3)
immigrate (2)
inquire (2)
insert (1)
introduce (2)
invite (2)
iron (1)
jog (3)
join (1)
jump (1)
kick (1)
kiss (1)
knit (3)
land (1)
laugh (1)
learn (1)

lengthen (1)
listen (1)
live (2)
load (1)
lock (1)
look (1)
mail (1)
manufacture (2)
mark (1)
match (1)
measure (2)
milk (1)
miss (1)
mix (1)
mop (3)
move (2)
mow (1)
need (1)
nurse (2)
obey (1)
observe (2)
open (1)
operate (2)
order (1)
overdose (2)
paint (1)
park (1)
pass (1)
pause (2)
peel (1)
perm (1)
pick (1)
pitch (1)
plan (3)
plant (1)
play (1)
point (1)
polish (1)
pour (1)
pretend (1)
print (1)
protect (1)

pull (1)
push (1)
race (2)
raise (2)
rake (2)
receive (2)
record (1)
recycle (2)
register (1)
relax (1)
remove (2)
rent (1)
repair (1)
repeat (1)
report (1)
request (1)
return (1)
rinse (2)
roast (1)
rock (1)
sauté (2)
save (2)
scrub (3)
seat (1)
sentence (2)
serve (2)
share (2)
shave (2)
ship (3)
shop (3)
shorten (1)
shout (1)
sign (1)
simmer (1)
skate (2)
ski (1)
slice (2)
smell (1)
sneeze (2)
sort (1)
spell (1)
staple (2)

start (1)
stay (1)
steam (1)
stir (3)
stir-fry (4)
stop (3)
stow (1)
stretch (1)
supervise (2)
swallow (1)
tackle (2)
talk (1)
taste (2)
thank (1)
tie (2)
touch (1)
transcribe (2)
transfer (3)
travel (1)
trim (3)
turn (1)
type (2)
underline (2)
unload (1)
unpack (1)
use (2)
vacuum (1)
vomit (1)
vote (2)
wait (1)
walk (1)
wash (1)
watch (1)
water (1)
weed (1)
weigh (1)
wipe (2)
work (1)
wrap (3)
yield (1)

Verb Guide

Irregular Verbs

These verbs have irregular endings in the past and/or the past participle.

The Oxford Picture Dictionary List of Irregular Verbs

simple	past	past participle	simple	past	past participle
be	was	been	leave	left	left
beat	beat	beaten	lend	lent	lent
become	became	become	let	let	let
begin	began	begun	light	lit	lit
bend	bent	bent	make	made	made
bleed	bled	bled	pay	paid	paid
blow	blew	blown	picnic	picnicked	picnicked
break	broke	broken	put	put	put
build	built	built	read	read	read
buy	bought	bought	rewind	rewound	rewound
catch	caught	caught	rewrite	rewrote	rewritten
come	came	come	ride	rode	ridden
cut	cut	cut	run	ran	run
do	did	done	say	said	said
draw	drew	drawn	see	saw	seen
drink	drank	drunk	sell	sold	sold
drive	drove	driven	send	sent	sent
eat	ate	eaten	set	set	set
fall	fell	fallen	sew	sewed	sewn
feed	fed	fed	shoot	shot	shot
feel	felt	felt	sing	sang	sung
find	found	found	sit	sat	sat
fly	flew	flown	speak	spoke	spoken
get	got	gotten	stand	stood	stood
give	gave	given	sweep	swept	swept
go	went	gone	swim	swam	swum
hang	hung	hung	swing	swung	swung
have	had	had	take	took	taken
hear	heard	heard	teach	taught	taught
hide	hid	hidden	throw	threw	thrown
hit	hit	hit	wake	woke	woken
hold	held	held	wear	wore	worn
keep	kept	kept	withdraw	withdrew	withdrawn
lay	laid	laid	write	wrote	written

Index

Two numbers are shown after words in the index: the first refers to the page where the word is illustrated and the second refers to the item number of the word on that page. For example, cool [kōol] **10**-3 means that the word *cool* is item number 3 on page 10. If only the bold page number appears, then that word is part of the unit title or subtitle, or is found somewhere else on the page. A bold number followed by ✦ means the word can be found in the exercise space at the bottom of that page.

Words or combinations of words that appear in **bold** type are used as verbs or verb phrases. Words used as other parts of speech are shown in ordinary type. So, for example, **file** (in bold type) is the verb *file*, while file (in ordinary type) is the noun *file*. Words or phrases in small capital letters (for example, HOLIDAYS) form unit titles.

Phrases and other words that form combinations with an individual word entry are often listed underneath it. Rather than repeating the word each time it occurs in combination with what is listed under it, the word is replaced by three dots (...), called an ellipsis. For example, under the word *bus*, you will find ...driver and ...stop meaning *bus driver* and *bus stop*. Under the word *store* you will find shoe... and toy..., meaning *shoe store* and *toy store*.

Pronunciation Guide

The index includes a pronunciation guide for all the words and phrases illustrated in the book. This guide uses symbols commonly found in dictionaries for native speakers. These symbols, unlike those used in pronunciation systems such as the International Phonetic Alphabet, tend to use English spelling patterns and so should help you to become more aware of the connections between written English and spoken English.

Consonants

[b] as in back [băk]　　　　　[k] as in key [kē]　　　　　[sh] as in shoe [shōo]

[ch] as in cheek [chēk]　　　[l] as in leaf [lēf]　　　　　[t] as in tape [tāp]

[d] as in date [dāt]　　　　　[m] as in match [măch]　　　[th] as in three [thrē]

[dh] as in this [dhĭs]　　　　[n] as in neck [něk]　　　　　[v] as in vine [vīn]

[f] as in face [fās]　　　　　[ng] as in ring [rĭng]　　　　[w] as in wait [wāt]

[g] as in gas [găs]　　　　　[p] as in park [pärk]　　　　[y] as in yams [yămz]

[h] as in half [hăf]　　　　　[r] as in rice [rīs]　　　　　[z] as in zoo [zōo]

[j] as in jam [jăm]　　　　　[s] as in sand [sănd]　　　　[zh] as in measure [mězh*/*ər]

Vowels

[ā] as in bake [bāk]　　　　[ī] as in lip [lĭp]　　　　　[ow] as in cow [kow]

[ă] as in back [băk]　　　　[ï] as in near [nïr]　　　　[oy] as in boy [boy]

[ä] as in car [kär] or box [bäks]　　[ō] as in cold [kōld]　　　[ŭ] as in cut [kŭt]

[ē] as in beat [bēt]　　　　[ö] as in short [shört]　　　[ü] as in curb [kürb]

[ĕ] as in bed [bĕd]　　　　　　　　　　or claw [klö]　　　[ə] as in above [ə bŭv*/*]

[ë] as in bear [bër]　　　　[ōo] as in cool [kōol]

[ī] as in line [līn]　　　　　[ōo] as in cook [kŏok]

All the pronunciation symbols used are alphabetical except for the schwa [ə]. The schwa is the most frequent vowel sound in English. If you use the schwa appropriately in unstressed syllables, your pronunciation will sound more natural.

Vowels before [r] are shown with the symbol [¨] to call attention to the special quality that vowels have before [r]. (Note that the symbols [ä] and [ö] are also used for vowels not followed by [r], as in *box* or *claw*.) You should listen carefully to native speakers to discover how these vowels actually sound.

Stress

This index follows the system for marking stress used in many dictionaries for native speakers.

1. Stress is not marked if a word consisting of a single syllable occurs by itself.

2. Where stress is marked, two levels are distinguished:

a bold accent [*/*] is placed after each syllable with primary (or strong) stress, a light accent [/] is placed after each syllable with secondary (or weaker) stress.

In phrases and other combinations of words, stress is indicated for each word as it would be pronounced within the whole phrase or other unit. If a word consisting of a single syllable is stressed in the combinations listed below it, the accent mark indicating the degree of stress it has in the phrases (primary or secondary) is shown in parentheses. A hyphen replaces any part of a word or phrase that is omitted. For example, bus [bŭs(*/*–)] shows that the word *bus* is said with primary stress in the combinations shown below it. The word ...driver [–drī/vər], listed under *bus*, shows that *driver* has secondary stress in the combination *bus driver*: [bŭs*/* drī/vər].

Syllable Boundaries

Syllable boundaries are indicated by a single space or by a stress mark.

Note: The pronunciations shown in this index are based on patterns of American English. There has been no attempt to represent all of the varieties of American English. Students should listen to native speakers to hear how the language actually sounds in a particular region.

abdomen [ăb/də mən] **74**–3
above [ə bŭv/] **13**–6
accelerator [ĭk sĕl/ə rā/tər] **109**–47
ACCESSORIES [ĭk sĕs/ə rēz] **68–69**
accident [ăk/sə dənt] **102**–2
accordion [ə kör/dē ən] **120**–21
accountant [ə kown/tnt] **136**–1
acid rain [ăs/əd rān/] **126**–11
across [ə krös/] **105**–3
acrylic paint [ə krĭl/ĭk pānt/] **162**–9
act [ăkt] **140** ✦
action [ăk/shən]
    ...figure [–fĭg/yər] **163**–31
    ...story [–stör/ē] **166**–13
actor [ăk/tər] **136**–2
acupuncture [ăk/yə pŭngk/chər] **81**–G
adapter [ə dăp/tər] **164**–17
add [ăd] **58**–Q, **72**–B
addition [ə dĭsh/ən] **118**–1
address [ə drĕs/] **96**–A
address [ə drĕs/, ă/drĕs] **4**–5, **96**–7,8
adhesive bandage [əd hē/sĭv băn/dĭj] **83**–3
administrative assistant [əd mĭn/ə strā/tĭv ə sĭs/tənt] **136**–3
administrator [əd mĭn/ə strā/tər] **5** ✦
adults [ə dŭlts/, ăd/ŭlts] **22**–9
adult school [ə dŭlt/ skool/, ăd/ŭlt–] **112**–8
adventure story [əd vĕn/chər stör/ē] **166**–13
aerogramme [ĕr/ə grăm/] **96**–13
afternoon [ăf/tər noon/] **17**–18
aftershave [ăf/tər shāv/] **77**–28
AGE AND PHYSICAL DESCRIPTION [āj/ ən fĭz/ĭ kəl dĭ skrĭp/shən] **22**
AIDS (acquired immunodeficiency syndrome) [ādz] **79** ✦
air [ĕr(/–)] **109**–59
    ...bag [–băg/] **108**–16
    ...conditioner [–kən dĭsh/ə nər] **37**–19
    ...conditioning [–kən dĭsh/ə nĭng] **108**–28
    ...letter [–lĕt/ər] **96**–13
    ...pollution [–pə loo/shən] **126**–10
    ...purifier [–pyoor/ə fī ər] **80**–4
airline [ĕr/līn/]
    ...representative [–rĕp rĭ zĕn/tə tĭv] **110**–2
    ...terminal [–tür/mə nəl] **110**–1
airplane [ĕr/plān/] **110**–9
    ...crash [–krăsh/] **102**–3
AIRPORT [ĕr/pört/] **110**
airsickness bag [ĕr/sĭk/nəs băg/] **110**–15
aisle [īl] **54**–5
Alaska time [ə lăs/kə tīm/] **17**–25
alfalfa [ăl făl/fə] **148**–5
algebra [ăl/jə brə] **118**–25
allergies [ăl/ər jēz] **79**–8
alley [ăl/ē] **37**–21
alligator [ăl/ə gā/tər] **131**–36
alphabet [ăl/fə bĕt/] **3**–30
ALTERATIONS [öl/tə rā/shənz] **73**
aluminum foil [ə loo/mə nəm foyl/] **55**–55
a.m. [ā/ĕm/] **16** ✦
American cheese [ə mĕr/ə kən chēz/] **53**–9
AMPHIBIANS [ăm fĭb/ē ənz] **130–131**
amusement park [ə myooz/mənt pärk/] **152**–13
anesthesiologist [ăn/əs thē/zē ăl/ə jĭst] **87**–35
angle [ăng/gəl] **118**–24
angry [ăng/grē] **31**–29
animals [ăn/ə məlz] **152**–2
ANIMALS, DOMESTIC [də mĕs/tĭk ăn/ə məlz] **133**

ankle [ăng/kəl] **75**–61, **78**–18
anniversary [ăn/ə vür/sə rē] **19**–42
announcer [ə nown/sər] **152**–27
answer [ăn/sər]
    ...a question [–ə kwĕs/chən] **6**–H
    ...the door [–dhə dör/] **169**–F
answering machine [ăn/sə rĭng mə shēn/] **9**–14
answer sheet [ăn/sər shēt/] **7**–T
antacid [ănt ăs/əd] **81**–18
anteater [ănt/ē/tər] **135**–24
antelope [ăn/tə lōp/] **135**–35
antibacterial ointment [ăn/tē băk tïr/ē əl oynt/mənt] **83**–9
antihistamine cream [ăn/tĭ hĭs/tə mēn krēm/] **83**–10
antler [ănt/lər] **134**–16
ants [ănts] **49**–24
apartment [ə pärt/mənt]
    ...building [–bĭl/dĭng] **34**–5
    ...number [–nŭm/bər] **4**–6
APARTMENTS [ə pärt/mənts] **36–37**
apologize [ə päl/ə jīz/] **8**–I
apostrophe [ə päs/trə fē] **113**–11
appear in court [ə pïr/ ĭn kört/] **99**–C
applaud [ə plöd/] **32**–B
apple juice [ăp/əl joos/] **55**–50, **57**–5
apples [ăp/əlz] **50**–4
application [ăp/lə kā/shən] **144**–21
appointment [ə poynt/mənt] **19**–45, **85**
    ...book [–book/] **143**–27
apricots [ăp/rə käts/] **50**–7
April [ā/prəl] **19**–28
archery [är/chə rē] **159**–1
architect [är/kə tĕkt/] **136**–4
area [ĕr/ē ə] **34**–(1, 4)
area code [ĕr/ē ə kōd/] **4**–10
arm [ärm] **74**–9
armadillo [är/mə dĭl/ō] **134**–8
armchair [ärm/chĕr/] **42**–24
around [ə rownd/] **105**–10
arrange [ə rānj/] **35**–K
arrest [ə rĕst/] **99**–A
arrival and departure monitors [ə rī/vəl ən dĭ pär/chər män/ə tərz] **110**–4
arrival time [ə rī/vəl tīm/] **111** ✦
arrive [ə rīv/] **111**–O
arrow [ăr/ō] **161**–7
art [ärt] **121**–1
artery [är/tə rē] **75**–43
artichokes [är/tə chōks/] **51**–20
artist [är/tĭst] **136**–5
art museum [ärt/ myoo zē/əm] **152**–7
ask [ăsk(/–)]
    ...about benefits [–ə bowt/ bĕn/ə fĭts] **141**–J
    ...about the hours [–ə bowt/ dhē ow/ərz] **141**–F
    ...a question [–ə kwĕs/chən] **6**–G
asparagus [ə spăr/ə gəs] **51**–24
assault [ə sölt/] **100**–7
assemble [ə sĕm/bəl] **140**–A
assembler [ə sĕm/blər] **136**–6
assembly line [ə sĕm/blē līn/] **146**–8
assist [ə sĭst/] **140**–B
Associate of Arts (AA) [ə sō/shē ĭt əv ärts/, –sē ĭt–] / [ā/ā/] **112** ✦
asteroid belt [ăs/tə royd bĕlt/] **127**–12
asthma [ăz/mə] **79**–11
astronaut [ăs/trə nöt/] **127**–17
astronomer [ə strän/ə mər] **127**–20

athletic [ăth lĕt/ĭk]
…shoes [–shōōz/] **68**–23
…supporter [–sə pör/tər] **67**–14
Atlantic time [ət lăn/tĭk tīm/] **17**–30
atlas [ăt/ləs] **98**–3
ATM (automated teller machine) [ā/tē/ĕm/] **97**–3
ATM card [ā/tē/ĕm/ kärd/] **97**–9
atom [ăt/əm] **119**–17
attorney [ə tür/nē] **99**–4
attractive [ə trăk/tĭv] **22**–23
audience [ö/dē əns] **32**–10
audiocassette [ö/dē ō kə sĕt/] **98**–12
audiologist [ö/dē äl/ə jĭst] **81**–32
auditorium [ö/də tör/ē əm] **5**–3
August [ö/gəst] **19**–32
aunt [ănt] **24**–10
author [ö/thər] **98**–22, **139**–64
automatic transmission
   [ö/tə măt/ĭk trănz mĭsh/ən, –trăns–] **109**
auto mechanic [ö/tō mə kăn/ĭk] **136**–7
average [ăv/rĭj]
…height [–hīt/] **22**–17
…weight [–wāt/] **22**–21
avocadoes [ä/və kä/dōz, ăv/ə–] **50**–14
ax [ăks] **150**–3
baboon [bă bōōn/] **135**–32
baby [bā/bē] **22**–2
…backpack [–băk/păk/] **95**–15
…carrier [–kăr/ē ər] **95**–14
…food [–fōōd/] **95**–28
…monitor [–män/ə tər] **45**–9
…powder [–pow/dər] **95**–18
baby-sitter [bā/bē sĭt/ər] **136**–12
Bachelor's degree [băch/lərz də grē/] **112** ✦
back [băk(/–)] **74**–11
…support [–sə pört/] **147**–16
backache [băk/āk/] **78**–5
backhoe [băk/hō/] **149**–8
backpack [băk/păk/] **69**–28, **95**–15, **154**–15
backpacking [băk/păk/ĭng] **154**–7
backseat [băk/sēt/] **109**–38
backyard [băk/yärd/] **38**–2
bacon [bā/kən] **52**–11, **61**–7
bad [băd] **11**–18
bag [băg] (market) **55**–22, 23, **56**–7, 19 (purse) **69**–27, 28, 29
baggage claim area [băg/ĭj klăm/ ër/ē ə] **110**–17
bagger [băg/ər] **55**–21
baggy [băg/ē] **71**–42
bag of flour [băg/ əv flow/ər] **56**–19
bags (luggage) [băgz] **111**–B
bailiff [bā/ləf] **99**–13
bake [bāk] **58**–L
baked [bākt(/–)]
…goods [–gōōdz/] **54**–6
…potato [–pə tā/tō] **61**–14
baker [bā/kər] **136**–8
bakery [bā/kə rē] **89**–16
baking products [bā/kĭng präd/ŭkts] **55**–13
balance [băl/əns] (bank) **97**–11, (science) **119**–11
balcony [băl/kə nē] **37**–17
bald [böld] **23**–12
ball [böl] **45**–16, **161**–3, 4, 5, 12, 18, 22
ballet [bă lā/] **166**–7
ball field [böl/ fēld/] **153**–1
ballroom [böl/rōōm/] **145**–20

bananas [bə năn/əz] **50**–3
bandage [băn/dĭj] **83**–3, 12
bangs [băngz] **23**–8
BANK [băngk] **97**
bank [băngk] **88**–3
banner [băn/ər] **33**–15
barbecue [bär/bĭ kyōō/] **58**–T
barbecue grill [bär/bĭ kyōō grĭl/] **39**–7
barber shop [bär/bər shäp/] **88**–15
bar code [bär/ kōd/] **21**–4
barn [bärn] **148**–11
barrette [bə rĕt/] **76**–18
baseball [bās/böl/] **158**–9, **161**–18
…bat [–băt/] **161**–14
…cap [–kăp/] **66**–27
…card [–kärd/] **162**–11
…game [–gām/] **152**–25
basement [bās/mənt] **36** ✦
basket [băs/kət] **42**–2
basketball [băs/kət böl/] **158**–8, **161**–4
…court [–kört/] **158**–7
bass (fish) [băs] **130**–11
bass (instrument) [bās] **120**–10
bassoon [bə sōōn/] **120**–6
bat [băt] (animal) **134**–7, (baseball) **161**–14
bath [băth(/–)]
…mat [–măt/] **43**–27
…powder [–pow/dər] **76**–3
…towel [–tow/əl] **43**–12
bathe [bādh] **76**–B
bathing suit [bā/dhĭng sōōt/] **66**–26
bathrobe [băth/rōb/] **67**–8
BATHROOM [băth/rōōm/] **43**
bathtub [băth/tŭb/] **43**–2
battery [băt/ə rē] (car) **109**–43, (flashlight) **151**–40
…charger [–chär/jər] **165**–23
…pack [–păk/] **165**–22
bay [bā] **117**–9
be [bē]
…18 years old [–ā/tēn/ yïrz/ ōld/] **116**–A
…born [–börn/] **28**–A
…hurt [–hürt/] **82**–A
…injured [–ĭn/jərd] **82**–A
…in school [–ĭn skōōl/] **26**–J
…in shock [–ĭn shäk/] **82**–C
…released [–rĭ lēst/] **99**–H
…unconscious [–ŭn kän/shəs] **82**–B
BEACH [bēch] **155**
beach [bēch(/–)] **117**–10
…chair [–chër/] **155**–14
…towel [–tow/əl] **155**–15
…umbrella [–ŭm brĕl/ə] **155**–9
beads [bēdz] **69**–32
beak [bēk] **132**–1
beaker [bē/kər] **119**–13
beam [bēm] **149**–3
beans [bēnz] **51**–25, **54**–26
bear [bër] **134**–11
beard [bïrd] **23**–6
beat [bēt] **58**–B
beautiful [byōō/tə fəl] **11**–21
beauty shop [byōō/tē shäp/] **92** ✦
beaver [bē/vər] **134**–9
become a citizen [bĭ kŭm/ ə sĭt/ə zən] **28**–H
bed [bĕd(/–)] **44**–8

Index

...control [–kən trōl/] **86**–12
...frame [–frām/] **44**–27
...table [–tā/bəl] **86**–9
bedpan [bĕd/păn/] **86**–13
BEDROOM [bĕd/rōōm/] **44**
bedspread [bĕd/sprĕd/] **44**–11
Beef [bēf] **52**
beef ribs [bēf/ rĭbz/] **52**–5
beetle [bēt/l] **132**–19
beets [bēts] **51**–6
begin [bĭ gĭn/] **8**–B
behind [bĭ hīnd/] **13**–3
beige [bāzh] **12**–9
bell captain [bĕl/ kăp/tən] **145**–4
bellhop [bĕl/häp/] **145**–5
below [bĭ lō/] **13**–7
belt buckle [bĕlt/ bŭk/əl] **69**–41
belts [bĕlts] **69**–11
bench [bĕnch] **153**–10
bend [bĕnd] **157**–R
berries [bĕr/ēz] **128**–20
between [bĭ twēn/] **13**–10
beverages [bĕv/rə jəz] **55**–15, **61**
bib [bĭb] **95**–8
bicycle [bī/sĭ kəl] **153**–4
big [bĭg] **11**–2
bike [bīk(/–)] **153**–4
...path [–păth/] **153**–2
...shorts [–shörts/] **67**–3
biking [bī/kĭng] **159**–4
bikini panties [bə kē/nē păn/tēz] **67**–16
bill (bird) [bĭl] **132**–1
bill (invoice) [bĭl] **21** ✦
billiards [bĭl/yərdz] **159**–2
billion [bĭl/yən] **14**
bills (paper money) [bĭlz] **20, 20** ✦
bin [bĭn] **37**–20
binder [bīn/dər] **3**–24
biohazard [bī/ō hăz/ərd] **147**–5
biology [bī äl/ə jē] **119**–1
birch [bürch] **128**–8
BIRDS, INSECTS, AND ARACHNIDS
  [bürdz/ ĭn/sĕkts ən ə răk/nĭdz] **132**
birth certificate [bürth/ sər tĭf/ə kət] **29**–1
birthday [bürth/dā/] **19**–41, **169**–I
bison [bī/sən] **134**–6
black [blăk(/–)] **12**–15
...hair [–hër/] **23**–15
bladder [blăd/ər] **75**–47
blade [blād] **150**–11
blanket [blăng/kət] **44**–12
...sleeper [–slē/pər] **67**–7
bleach [blēch] **72**–8
bleachers [blē/chərz] **5**–10
bleed [blēd] **82**–M
blender [blĕn/dər] **40**–12
blind [blīnd] **22**–26
blinds [blīndz] **43**–11
blister [blĭs/tər] **78**–15
blizzard [blĭz/ərd] **103**–11
block [blăk] **107**–2
blocks [blăks] **45**–15
blond [bländ] **23**–16
blood [blŭd(/–)] **79**–15
...pressure gauge [–prĕsh/ər gāj/] **84**–12

...test [–tĕst/] **86**–17
...work [–würk/] **86**–17
bloody nose [blŭd/ē nōz/] **78**–17
blouse [blows] **64**–9
blow dryer [blō/ drī/ər] **23**–20, **76**–16
blow out [blō/ owt/] **169**–K
blue [blōō] **12**–1
blueberries [blōō/bĕr/ēz] **50**–19
blue jay [blōō/ jā/] **132**–7
blush [blŭsh] **77**–36
board game [börd/ gām/] **162**–3
boarding area [bör/dĭng ër/ē ə] **110**–6
board the plane [börd/ dhə plān/] **111**–F
boating [bō/tĭng] **154**–2
bobby pins [bäb/ē pĭnz/] **76**–19
BODY [bäd/ē] **74**–**75**
body lotion [bäd/ē lō/shən] **76**–7
body of water [bäd/ē əv wö/tər] **117** ✦
boil [boyl] **58**–P
bolt [bōlt] **37**–29, **150**–30, 33
bone [bōn] (body) **75**–49, (broken) **82**–P
boneless [bōn/ləs] **52** ✦
bookbag [bŏŏk/băg/] **69**–28
bookcase [bŏŏk/kās/] **3**–8, **42**–1
bookstore [bŏŏk/stör/] **92**–4
booth [bōōth] **60**–19, **152**–23
boots [bōōts] **68**–18
bored [börd] **31**–26
boring [bör/ĭng] **167**–29 ✦
borrow [bär/ō, bör/ō] **20** ✦
botanical gardens [bə tăn/ĭ kəl gär/dnz] **152**–4
bottle [bät/l] **56**–1, **95**–26
...of soda [–əv sō/də] **56**–13
bottled water [bät/ld wö/tər] **55**–53
bottle return [bät/l rĭ türn/] **54**–1
bounce [bowns] **156**–K
bouquet [bō kā/, bōō–] **129**–27
bow [bō] **161**–6
bowl [bōl] **41**–25
bowling [bō/lĭng] **159**–3
...ball [–böl/] **161**–5
bow tie [bō/ tī/] **69**–40
box [bäks(/–)] **56**–6
...of cereal [–əv sïr/ē əl] **56**–18
...spring [–sprĭng/] **44**–26
boxer shorts [bäk/sər shörts/] **67**–12
boy [boy] **22**–4, 7
bra [brä] **67**–20
brace [brās] **81**–31
bracelet [brās/lət] **69**–35, **83**–14
braces [brā/səz] **84**–24
brain [brān(/–)] **75**–35
...cancer [–kăn/sər] **79**–12
brainstorm [brān/störm/] **6**–K
brake [brāk(/–)]
...light [–līt/] **108**–13
...pedal [–pĕd/l] **109**–46
branch [brănch] **128**–2
Branches of government [brăn/chəz əv gŭv/ər mənt] **116**
Brass [brăs] **120**
bread [brĕd(/–)] **53**–1, 2, 3, **54**–29
...basket [–băs/kət] **63**–8
bread-and-butter plate [brĕd/ n bŭt/ər plāt/] **63**–16
break [brāk(/–)]
...a bone [–ə bōn/] **82**–P

...three eggs [–thrē/ ĕgz/] **58**–A

Breakfast [brĕk/fəst] **61**

breast (body) [brĕst] **74**–14

breasts (chicken) [brĕsts] **52**–19

bricklayer [brĭk/lā/ər] **136**–9

bricks [brĭks] **149**–11

bridge [brĭj] **105**–2

briefs [brēfs] **67**–13, 17

broccoli [bräk/ə lē] **51**–15, **58**–I

broil [broyl] **58**–V

broiler [broy/lər] **40**–21

broken [brō/kən] **48**–5, 6, 7, **49**–15, **70**–24

broom [bro͞om] **47**–10

brother [brŭdh/ər] / [–brŭdh/ər] **24**–9

  half... [hăf/–] **25**–29

brother-in-law [brŭdh/ər ĭn lö/] **24**–16

brown [brown(/–)] **12**–11

  ...hair [–hër/] **23**–17

bruise [bro͞oz] **78**–12

brush [brŭsh(/–)]

  ...hair [–hër/] **76**–I

  ...teeth [–tēth/] **77**–J

brush [(–)brŭsh(/)] **23**–18, **76**–14

  paint... [pānt/–] **151**–47, **163**–23

  scrub... [skrŭb/–] **47**–19

  toilet... [toy/lət–] **43**–16

bucket [bŭk/ət] **47**–20, **155**–22

buckle [bŭk/əl] **69**–41

bud [bŭd] **129**–6

buffalo [bŭf/ə lō] **134**–6

buffet [bə fā/] **33**–13

building [bĭl/dĭng] **34**–5

BUILDING SUPPLIES [bĭl/dĭng sə plīz/] **150–151**

build models [bĭld/ mäd/lz] **162**–C

bulb [bŭlb] **129**–9

bulldozer [bo͞ol/dō/zər] **149**–6

bulletin board [bo͞ol/ə tn börd/] **3**–14

bumper [bŭm/pər] **108**–7

bumper pad [bŭm/pər păd/] **45**–7

bunk [bŭngk] **45**–1

Bunsen burner [bŭn/sən bür/nər] **119**–9

bureau [byo͞or/ō] **44**–2

burglary [bür/glə rē] **100**–6

burner [bür/nər] **40**–19

burn (your)self [bürn/ (yər)sĕlf/] **82**–H

bus [bŭs(/–)] **90**–15, **104**–4

  ...driver [–drī/vər] **104**–8

  ...stop [–stäp/] **91**–16, **104**–1

bush [bo͞osh] **39**–20

business education [bĭz/nəs ĕj ə kā/shən] **121**–2

businessman [bĭz/nəs măn/] **136**–10

businesswoman [bĭz/nəs wo͞om/ən] **136**–10

busperson [bŭs/pür/sən] **63**–9

butcher [bo͞och/ər] **136**–11

butter [bŭt/ər] **54**–36

butterfly [bŭt/ər flī/] **132**–20

buttocks [bŭt/əks] **74**–12

button [bŭt/n] **73**–21

buttonhole [bŭt/n hōl/] **73**–12

buy [bī(/–)] **21**–C

  ...a house [–ə hows/] **29**–O

  ...your ticket [–yər tĭk/ət] **111**–A

Buying a house [bī/ĭng ə hows/] **35**

cab [kăb] **104**–18, **106**–16

cabbage [kăb/ĭj] **51**–2

cabinet [kăb/ə nət] **40**–1

cable [kā/bəl] **144**–16

cactus [kăk/təs] **128**–21

cafeteria [kăf/ə tïr/ē ə] **5**–4

cake [kāk(/–)] **54**–32, **61**–19

  ...mix [–mĭks/] **55**–47

  ...pan [–păn/] **59**–26

calculator [kăl/kyə lā/tər] **142**–8

calculus [kăl/kyə ləs] **118**–28

CALENDAR [kăl/ən dər] **18–19**

calf [kăf] **74**–18

call [köl] **141**–E

call button [köl/ bŭt/n] **86**–10

calm [käm] **30**–10

camcorder [kăm/kör/dər] **165**–21

camel [kăm/əl] **135**–38

camera [kăm/rə] **165**–19, 24, 27

  ...case [–kās/] **165**–27

camisole [kăm/ə sōl/] **67**–21

camper [kăm/pər] **106**–11

campfire [kămp/fīr/] **154**–11

camping [kăm/pĭng] **154**–1

  ...stove [–stōv/] **154**–16

can [kăn(/–)] **56**–3

  ...of soup [–əv so͞op/] **56**–15

  ...opener [–ō/pə nər] **40**–14, **59**–1

cancer [kăn/sər] **79**–12

candle [kăn/dl] **41**–7

candles [kăn/dlz] **169**–H, K

candlestick [kăn/dl stĭk/] **41**–8

candy [kăn/dē] **55**–41, **168**–14

  ...bar [–bär/] **55**–41

  ...store [–stör/] **92**–3

cane [kān] **80**–7

canned goods [kănd/ go͞odz/] **54**–4

canoeing [kə no͞o/ĭng] **154**–3

cantaloupes [kăn/tə lōps/] **50**–15

can't breathe [kănt/ brēdh/] **82**–N

canteen [kăn tēn/] **154**–24

canvas [kăn/vəs] **163**–22

canyon [kăn/yən] **117**–17

cap [kăp] (graduation) **32**–3, (clothing) **66**–6

capsule [kăp/səl] **81**–27

captain [kăp/tən] **158** ✦

car [kär(/–)]

  ...accident [–ăk/sə dənt] **102**–2

  ...dealership [–dē/lər shĭp] **88**–4

  ...safety seat [–sāf/tē sēt/] **95**–13

card [kärd(/–)] **96**–4, **168**–5

  ...catalog [–kăt/l ög, –äg] **98**–10

  ...store [–stör/] **92**–7

cardigan sweater [kär/də gən swĕt/ər] **65**–27

Cardinals [kärd/nəlz] **14**

cardiologist [kär/dē äl/ə jĭst] **86**–3

cards [kärdz] **163**–H

careful [kër/fəl] **147**–24

caregiver [kër/gĭv/ər] **136**–12

careless [kër/ləs] **147**–23

CAR MAINTENANCE [kär/ mān/tn əns] **108–109**

carnation [kär nā/shən] **129**–18

carnival [kär/nə vəl] **152**–16

carousel [kär/ə sĕl/] **110**–18

carousel slide projector [kär/ə sĕl/ slīd/ prə jĕk/tər] **165**–29

carpenter [kär/pən tər] **48**–12, **136**–13

carpet [kär/pət] **42**–27

Index

carriage [kăr/ĭj] **95**–16
carrots [kăr/əts] **51**–3
carry [kăr/ē] **62**–H
carry-on bag [kăr/ē än băg/, –ön–] **111**–H
CARS AND TRUCKS [kärz/ ən trŭks/] **106**
cart [kärt] **54**–3, **91**–31
carton [kär/tn] **56**–4
   ...of eggs [əv ĕgz/] **56**–16
cartoon [kär tōōn/] **167**–19
cartridge [kär/trĭj] / [–kär/trĭj] **162**–2
   typewriter... [tīp/rī/tər–] **143**–31
carving knife [kär/vĭng nīf/] **59**–12
cash [kăsh(/–)] **20**–13, **97**–D
   ...register [–rĕj/ə stər] **55**–18, **140**–N
cashier [kă shïr/] **136**–14
casserole dish [kăs/ə rōl dĭsh/] **59**–11
cassette [kə sĕt/]
   ...player [–plā/ər] **3**–11, **164**–2, 15
   ...recorder [–rĭ kör/dər] **164**–3
cast [kăst] **81**–29
casual [kăzh/ōō əl] **71**–37
cat [kăt] **133**–9
catch [kăch] **156**–E
catcher's mask [kăch/ərz măsk/] **161**–15
caterer [kā/tər ər] **33**–12
caterpillar [kăt/ə pĭl/ər, kăt/ər–] **132**–21
catfish [kăt/fĭsh/] **53**–17
cattle [kăt/l] **148**–21
cauliflower [kö/lĭ flow/ər, kä/–] **51**–16
cavity [kăv/ə tē] **84**–20
C-clamp [sē/klămp/] **150**–6
CD (compact disc) [sē/dē/] **98**–14
   ...player [–plā/ər] **164**–14
   ...ROM disc [–räm/ dĭsk/] **144**–2
ceiling [sē/lĭng] **42**–5
   ...fan [–făn/] **41**–4
celery [sĕl/ə rē] **51**–9
cello [chĕl/ō] **120**–9
cellular phone [sĕl/yə lər fōn/] **9**–13
Celsius [sĕl/sē əs] **10**
cent [sĕnt] **20**–1
centimeter (cm) [sĕn/tə mē/tər] **15**–12
CENTRAL AMERICA [sĕn/trəl ə mĕr/ə kə] **122**–**123**
central time [sĕn/trəl tīm/] **17**–28
cents [sĕnts] **20**–2, 3, 4
cereal [sïr/ē əl] **56**–18
Ceremony [sĕr/ə mō/nē] **32**
Certificate of Naturalization
   [sər tĭf/ə kət əv năch/rə lə zā/shən] **29**–6
certified mail [sür/tə fīd/ māl/] **96**–11
chain [chān] (hardware) **37**–28, **150**–36, (jewelry) **69**–31
chair [(–)chër(/)] **2**–7
   dining room... [dī/nĭng rōōm/–] **41**–16
   easy... [ē/zē–] **42**–24
   high... [hī/–] **95**–7
   rocking... [räk/ĭng–] **94**–6
   swivel... [swĭv/əl–] **143**–22
chalk [chök] **3**–16
chalkboard [chök/börd/] **2**–1
   ...eraser [–ĭ rā/sər] **3**–17
change [chānj(/–)] **21**–9
   ...purse [–pürs/] **69**–25
change [chānj(/–)]
   ...diapers [–dī/pərz] **94**–E
   ...the sheets [–dhə shēts/] **46**–P

...your diet [–yər dī/ət] **80**–C
changing table [chān/jĭng tā/bəl] **45**–12, **95**–9
cheap [chēp] **11**–20
check [chĕk(/–)]
   ...blood pressure [–blŭd/ prĕsh/ər] **85**–B
   ...your bags [–yər băgz/] **111**–B
   ...your work [–yər würk/] **7**–Y
checkbook [chĕk/bŏŏk/] **97**–7
checked [chĕkt] **70**–11
checker [chĕk/ər] **55**–19
checkers [chĕk/ərz] **162**–5
check in [chĕk/ ĭn/] **111**–D
check-in counter [chĕk/ĭn kown/tər] **110**–3
checking account number [chĕk/ĭng ə kownt/ nŭm/bər] **97**–8
check out [chĕk/ owt/] **98** ✦
checkout desk [chĕk/owt dĕsk/] **98**–16
checkstand [chĕk/stănd/] **55**–17
cheddar cheese [chĕd/ər chēz/] **53**–10
cheek [chēk] **74**–29
cheese [chēz] **53**–9, 10, 11, 12, **54**–38
cheeseburger [chēz/bür/gər] **60**–3
chef [shĕf] **63**–11
chef's salad [shĕfs/ săl/əd] **61**–9
chemistry [kĕm/ə strē] **119**–2
cherries [chĕr/ēz] **50**–16
cherry picker [chĕr/ē pĭk/ər] **149**–5
chess [chĕs] **162**–6
chest (body) [chĕst] **74**–13
chest of drawers [chĕst/ əv drörz/] **45**–8
chicken [chĭk/ən] **52**–16, **61**–12
   ...soup [–sōōp/] **58**
chicken pox [chĭk/ən päks/] **79**–6
Chief Justice [chēf/ jŭs/təs] **116**–9
CHILDCARE CENTER [chīld/kër sĕn/tər] **94**–**95**
childcare worker [chīld/kër wür/kər] **94**–3
Childhood diseases [chīld/hŏŏd dĭ zē/zəz] **79**
children [chĭl/drən] **11**–11, 12, **22**–1
CHILDREN'S BEDROOM [chĭl/drənz bĕd/rōōm] **45**
children's program [chĭl/drənz prō/grăm] **167**–24
child safety seat [chīld/ sāf/tē sēt/] **109**–39
chili peppers [chĭl/ē pĕp/ərz] **51**–8
chills [chĭlz] **78**–9
chimney [chĭm/nē] **38**–21
chimpanzee [chĭm/păn zē/] **135**–28
chin [chĭn] **74**–31
china cabinet [chī/nə kăb/ə nət] **41**–1
chipmunk [chĭp/mŭngk/] **133**–20
chiropractor [kī/rə präk/tər] **81**–H
chisel [chĭz/əl] **151**–51
choke [chōk] **82**–L
chop [chäp] **58**–G
chorus [kör/əs] **121**–3
Christmas [krĭs/məs] **168**–18
   ...tree [–trē/] **168**–20
chrysanthemum [krĭ săn/thə məm] **129**–19
church [chürch] **88**–6
cigarette lighter [sĭg/ə rĕt/ lī/tər, sĭg/ə rĕt–] **108**–32
circle [sür/kəl] **7**–5
circle [sür/kəl] **118**–5
circular saw [sür/kyə lər sö/] **150**–10
circumference [sər kŭm/frəns] **118**–15
Citizen application requirements
   [sĭt/ə zən ăp/lə kā/shən rĭ kwïr/mənts] **116**
CITIZENSHIP [sĭt/ə zən shĭp/] **116**
city [sĭt/ē] **4**–7, **34**–1

...center [–sĕn/tər] **88** ✦
...hall [–höl/] **89**–17
CITY STREETS [sĭt/ē strēts/] **88–89**
claim your baggage [klām/ yər băg/ĭj] **111**–P
clams [klămz] **53**–28
clap [klăp] **32**–B
clarinet [klăr/ə nĕt/] **120**–4
CLASSROOM [klăs/rōōm/] **2–3**
classroom [klăs/rōōm/] **5**–1
Class work [klăs/ würk/] **7**
claw [klö] **132**–4
clay [klā] **162**–14
clean [klēn] (household) **27**–N, **46**–C, **72**–D, (teeth) **85**–I
clean [klēn] **72**–16
CLEANING SUPPLIES [klē/nĭng sə plīz/] **47**
cleanser [klĕn/zər] **47**–23
clear [klïr(/–)] **10**–6
...tape [–tāp/] **143**–39
clear [klïr] **62**–G
clear [klïr] **10**–6
clerk [(–)klürk(/)] **5**–18
desk... [dĕsk/–] **145**–8
file... [fīl/–] **142**–12
library... [lī/brër ē–] **98**–17
shipping... [shĭp/ĭng–] **146**–15
stock... [stäk/–] **139**–55
climb [klīm] **153**–C
climbing apparatus [klī/mĭng ăp ə răt/əs] **153**–14
CLINICS [klĭn/ĭks] **84**
clipboard [klĭp/börd/] **143**–26
clip-on earrings [klĭp/än ïr/ĭngz, –ön–] **69**–38
clock [kläk(/–)] **3**–10
...radio [–rā/dē ō] **44**–16, **164**–1
close [klōz] **2**–J
closet [kläz/ət] **11**–15, 16, **43** ✦, **44**–4
cloth diapers [klöth/ dī/pərz] **95**–21
clothesline [klōz/līn/] **72**–9
clothespin [klōz/pĭn/] **72**–10
CLOTHING I, II, III [klō/dhĭng] **64–67**
cloudy [klow/dē] **10**–7
clubs [klŭbz] **163**–26
clutch [klŭch] **109**–45
coach [kōch] **5** ✦, **158**–2
coal [kōl] **126**–4
coat [kōt] (clothing) **66**, (animal) **134**–19
cobra [kō/brə] **131**–40
cockpit [käk/pĭt/] **110**–11
cockroaches [käk/rō/chəz] **49**–25
coconuts [kō/kə nŭts/] **50**–22
cod [käd] **130**–8
coffee [kö/fē] **55**–51, **61**–22
...cup [–kŭp/] **41**–27
...shop [–shäp/] **88**–2
...table [–tā/bəl] **42**–23
instant... [ĭn/stənt–] **55**–51
coffeemaker [kö/fē mā/kər] **40**–11
COFFEE SHOP MENU [kö/fē shäp/ mĕn/yōō] **61**
coin collection [koyn/ kə lĕk/shən] **162**–13
Coins [koynz] **20**
colander [käl/ən dər] **59**–17
cold [kōld] (weather) **10**–4, (feeling) **30**–4
cold (illness) [kōld(/–)] **79**–1
...tablets [–tăb/ləts] **81**–17
cold water [kōld/ wö/tər] **43**–7
coleslaw [kōl/slö/] **53**–14

collar [käl/ər] **73**–7
collate [kō/lāt/, kə lāt/] **142**–F
collect [kə lĕkt/]
...the papers [–dhə pā/pərz] **7**–Q
...things [–thĭngz/] **162**–A
collection [kə lĕk/shən] **162**–12, 13
college [käl/ĭj] **112**–10
...degree [–də grē/] **29**–7
...dormitory [–dör/mə tör/ē] **34**–9
community... [kə myōō/nə tē–] **112** ✦
cologne [kə lōn/] **76**–5
colon [kō/lən] **113**–12
color hair [kŭl/ər hër/] **23**–D
coloring book [kŭl/ə rĭng bŏŏk/] **45**–20
COLORS [kŭl/ərz] **12**
comb...hair [kōm/ hër/] **76**–G
comb [kōm] **23**–22, **76**–13
comedy [käm/ə dē] **166**–10
come home [kŭm/ hōm/] **27**–Q
comet [käm/ət] **127**–25
comfortable [kŭmf/tə bəl, –tər–] **30**–7
comforter [kŭm/fər tər] **45**–2
comma [käm/ə] **113**–10
commercial fisher [kə mür/shəl fĭsh/ər] **136**–15
commit a crime [kə mĭt/ ə krīm/] **100** ✦
Common illnesses and childhood diseases
[käm/ən ĭl/nə səz ən chīld/hŏŏd dĭ zē/zəz] **79**
community college [kə myōō/nə tē käl/ĭj] **112** ✦
compact [käm/păkt] **106**–2
compact disc (CD) [käm/păkt dĭsk/] **98**–14
compliment [käm/plə mĕnt/] **8**–G
components [kəm pō/nənts] **140**–A
composition [käm/pə zĭsh/ən] **113**–2
compost pile [käm/pōst pīl/] **39**–10
computer [kəm pyōō/tər] **3**–15
...programmer [–prō/grăm ər] **136**–16
...science [–sī/əns] **121**–4
...workstation [–würk/stā/shən] **143**–21
COMPUTERS [kəm pyōō/tərz] **144**
concert [kän/sərt] **166**–6
concierge [kän/sē ërzh/, kōn/–] **145** ✦
concrete [käng/krēt, kän krēt/] **149**–10
condiments [kän/də mənts] **60** ✦
conditioner [kən dĭsh/ə nər] **76**–10
condominium [kän/də mĭn/ē əm] **34** ✦
conductor [kən dŭk/tər] **104**–16
cone [kōn] **118**–11
confetti [kən fĕt/ē] **168**–3
confused [kən fyōōzd/] **31**–27
congestion [kən jĕs/chən] **78**–7
Congressman [käng/grəs mən] **116**–2
Congresswoman [käng/grəs wŏŏm/ən] **116**–2
Conservation [kän/sər vā/shən] **126**
conserve [kən sürv/] **126**–B, C
constellation [kän/stə lā/shən] **127**–24
CONSTRUCTION [kən strŭk/shən] **149**
construction worker [kən strŭk/shən wür/kər] **149**–1
contact lenses [kän/täkt lĕn/zəz] **81**–36
container [kən tā/nər] **56**–5, **59**–3
...of cottage cheese [–əv kät/ĭj chēz/] **56**–17
CONTAINERS AND PACKAGED FOODS
[kən tā/nərz ən păk/ĭjd fōōdz/] **56**
Continents [kän/tə nənts] **124**
control tower [kən trōl/ tow/ər] **110**–7
convenience store [kən vēn/yəns stör/] **90**–3

Index

CONVERSATION, EVERYDAY [ĕv/rē dā/ kän/vər sā/shən] **8**
convertible [kən vür/tə bəl] **106**–5
convert the measurements
  [kən vürt/ dhə mĕzh/ər mənts] **57**–C
conveyor belt [kən vā/ər bĕlt/] **146**–12
convict [kən vĭkt/] **99**–14
cook [kŏŏk] **27**–P, **58**–F, **140**–C
cook [kŏŏk] **137**–17
cooked chicken [kŏŏkt/ chĭk/ən] **52**–25
cookies [kŏŏk/ēz] **54**–31, **56**–20
cookie sheet [kŏŏk/ē shēt/] **59**–27
cool [kōōl] **10**–3
coolant [kōō/lənt] **109**–56
cooler [kōō/lər] **155**–11
co-op [kō/äp/] **34** ✦
copy [käp/ē] **6**–F
copy center [käp/ē sĕn/tər] **91**–22
cord [körd] **9**–3, **151**–14
cordless phone [körd/ləs fōn/] **9**–12
core course [kör/ körs/] **121** ✦
corn [körn] **51**–27, **148**–4
corned beef [körnd/ bēf/] **53**–8
corner [kör/nər] **91**–17, **105**–10, **107**–1
corral [kə răl/] **148**–17
correct [kə rĕkt/] **7**–Z
correction fluid [kə rĕk/shən flōō/əd] **143**–33
corrosive [kə rō/sĭv] **147**–4
cost [köst] **21**–6
costume [käs/tōōm] **168**–13
cottage cheese [kät/ĭj chēz/] **56**–17
cotton [kät/n] **70**–16, **148**–6
couch [kowch] **42**–19
cough [köf] **78**–A
cough syrup [köf/ sĭr/əp, –sür/–] **81**–20
counselor [kown/slər] **5**–16
counselor's office [kown/slərz ö/fəs] **5**–15
count [kownt] **15** ✦
counter [kown/tər] **40**–22, **46**–O, **60**–13, **80**–12, **110**–3
country [kŭn/trē] **34**–4
county fair [kown/tē fër/] **152**–19
courier [kür/ē ər, kŏŏr/–] **138**–38
court [kört(/–)] **99**–C
  …reporter [–rĭ pör/tər] **99**–12
courthouse [kört/hows/] **89**–18
courtroom [kört/rōōm/] **99**–7
courtyard [kört/yärd/] **37**–18
cousin [kŭz/ən] **24**–12
cover-up [kŭv/ər ŭp/] **66**–25
cow [kow] **133**–3
coyote [kī ō/tē, kī/ōt/] **134**–3
CPR (cardiopulmonary resuscitation) [sē/pē/är/] **83**–17
CPU (central processing unit) [sē/pē/yōō/] **144**–1
crab [krăb] **53**–22, **130**–16
cracked [krăkt] **48**–4
cradle [krād/l] **45**–19
crane [krān] **149**–7
crash [krăsh] **102**–3
crayons [krā/änz] **45**–21
creamer [krē/mər] **41**–13
credit card [krĕd/ət kärd/] **20**–15
creek [krēk, krĭk] **117** ✦
crescent moon [krĕs/ənt mōōn/] **127**–14
crewneck sweater [krōō/nĕk/ swĕt/ər] **71**–26
crib [krĭb] **45**–6
cricket [krĭk/ət] **132**–24

CRIME [krīm] **100**
criminal [krĭm/ə nəl] **100** ✦
crochet [krō shā/] **163**–20
crocodile [kräk/ə dīl/] **131**–37
crocus [krō/kəs] **129**–25
Crops [kräps] **148**
cross-country skiing [krös/kŭn/trē skē/ĭng] **160**–3
cross out [krös/ owt/] **7**–U
cross the street [krös/ dhə strēt/] **90**–A
crosswalk [krös/wök/] **90**–8
crucible tongs [krōō/sə bəl tängz/, –töngz/] **119**–15
crutches [krŭch/əz] **80**–1
cry [krī] **32**–C
cubby [kŭb/ē] **94**–4
cube [kyōōb] **118**–10
cucumbers [kyōō/kŭm bərz] **51**–12
cuff [kŭf] **73**–5
cup [kŭp(/–)] **63**–21
  …of flour [–əv flow/ər] **57**–10
  …of oil [–əv oyl/] **57**–2
curb [kürb] **90**–10
curling iron [kür/lĭng ī/ərn] **76**–15
curly [kür/lē] **23**–11
curtains [kür/tnz] **44**–5
curved [kürvd] **118**–19
custodian [kŭ stō/dē ən] **138**–35
customs [kŭs/təmz] **110**–20
  …officer [–ö/fə sər] **110**–21
cut [kŭt] **23**–A, **77**–N
cut [kŭt] **78**–13
cute [kyōōt] **22**–24
cutting board [kŭt/ĭng börd/] **40**–27
cut up [kŭt/ ŭp/] **58**–M
cycling [sī/klĭng] **159**–4
cyclist [sī/klĭst] **153**–3
cylinder [sĭl/ən dər] **118**–12
daffodil [dăf/ə dĭl/] **129**–26
DAILY ROUTINES [dā/lē rōō tēnz/] **26**–27
dairy section [dër/ē sĕk/shən] **54**–9
daisy [dā/zē] **129**–14
dance [dăns] **33**–J
dance floor [dăns/ flör/] **33**–16
dangerous situation [dān/jər əs sĭ ch/ōō ā/shən] **147**–8
dark blue [därk/ blōō/] **12**–2
dashboard [dăsh/börd/] **108**–17
data [dā/tə, dăt/ə] **144** ✦
date [dāt(/–)] **18**–14
  …of birth [–əv bürth/] **4**–16
dates (fruit) [dāts] **50**–25
daughter [dö/tər] **24**–21
daughter-in-law [dö/tər ĭn lö/] **24** ✦
day [dā] **18**–10
daylight saving time [dā/līt/ sā/vĭng tīm/] **17**–33
Days of the week [dāz/ əv dhə wēk/] **18**
dead-bolt lock [dĕd/bōlt/ läk/] **37**–29
dead end [dĕd/ĕnd/] **107**–8
deaf [dĕf] **22**–27
decaf coffee [dē/kăf/ kö/fē] **61**–23
December [dĭ sĕm/bər] **19**–36
deck [dĕk] **38**–16
declaration form [dĕk/lə rā/shən förm/] **110**–22
decorate [dĕk/ə rāt/] **169**–C
deer [dïr] **134**–14
defendant [dĭ fĕn/dənt] **99**–5
defense attorney [dĭ fĕns/ ə tür/nē] **99**–4

degree [də grē/] **29**–7, **112** ✦
degrees [də grēz/]
  ...Celsius [–sĕl/sē əs] **10**
  ...Fahrenheit [–făr/ən hīt/] **10**
DELI AND SEAFOOD [dĕl/ē ən sē/food/] **53**
deliver [də lĭv/ər] **96**–C
delivery person [də lĭv/ə rē pür/sən] **137**–18
dental [dĕn/təl]
  ...assistant [–ə sĭs/tənt] **84**–19, **137**–19
  ...floss [–flös/, –fläs/] **77**–22
  ...hygienist [–hī jē/nĭst, –jĕn/ĭst] **84**–16
Dental clinic [dĕn/təl klĭn/ĭk] **84**
DENTAL EXAMS [dĕn/təl ĭg zămz/] **85**
dentist [dĕn/tĭst] **84**–18, **137**–20
deodorant [dē ō/dər ənt] **76**–4
department store [dĭ pärt/mənt stör/] **93**–13
departure time [dĭ pär/chər tīm/] **111** ✦
deposit [dĭ päz/ət] **9**–C
deposit [dĭ päz/ət] **97**–C
  ...slip [–slĭp/] **97**–12
depth [dĕpth] **15**–15
DESCRIBING CLOTHES [dĭ skrī/bĭng klōz/] **70**–**71**
DESCRIBING HAIR [dĭ skrī/bĭng hër/] **23**
DESCRIBING THINGS [dĭ skrī/bĭng thĭngz/] **11**
desert [dĕz/ərt] **117**–4
design [dĭ zīn/] **146**–A
designated drivers [dĕz/ĭg nā/təd drī/vərz] **101** ✦
designer [dĭ zī/nər] **146**–3
desk [dĕsk/–] **2**–6, **142**–1
  ...calendar [–kăl/ən dər] **142**–6
  ...clerk [–klürk/] **145**–9
  ...pad [–păd/] **142**–7
dessert tray [dĭ zürt/ trā/] **63**–7
destination [dĕs/tə nā/shən] **111** ✦
diabetes [dī/ə bē/tēz, –təs] **79**–9
diagonal [dī ăg/ə nəl, –ăg/nəl] **118**–23
dial [dī/əl] **9**–D
dial tone [dī/əl tōn/] **9**–B
diameter [dī ăm/ə tər] **118**–17
diamonds [dī/məndz] **163**–27
diaper [dī/pər]
  ...pail [–pāl/] **45**–13, **95**–23
  ...pins [–pĭnz/] **95**–22
dice [dīs] **162**–4
dictate [dĭk/tāt] **6**–N
dictionary [dĭk/shə nër/ē] **3**–28
Dictionary work [dĭk/shə nër ē würk/] **6**
die [dī] **29**–R
dietician [dī/ə tĭsh/ən] **87**–25
difference [dĭf/rəns] **118** ✦
difficult [dĭf/ĭ kŭlt/] **11**–24
dime [dīm] **20**–3
Dimensions [də mĕn/shənz] **15**
diner [dī/nər] **62**–5
DINING AREA [dī/nĭng ër/ē ə] **41**
dining room [dī/nĭng room/] **62**–2
  ...chair [–chër/] **41**–16
  ...table [–tā/bəl] **41**–17
dinner [dĭn/ər]
  ...fork [–förk/] **63**–25
  ...plate [–plāt/] **63**–15
diploma [də plō/mə] **29**–2, **32**–7
direct flight [də rĕkt/ flīt/, dī–] **111** ✦
Directions [də rĕk/shənz, dī–] **107**

DIRECTIONS AND TRAFFIC SIGNS
  [də rĕk/shənz ən trăf/ĭk sīnz/, dī–] **107**
directory [də rĕk/tə rē, dī–] **9**–8, **93**–19
directory assistance (411) [də rĕk/tə rē ə sĭs/təns, dī–] **9**–8
dirty [dür/tē] **72**–15
discuss [dĭ skŭs/] **6**–L
disgusted [dĭ skŭs/təd] **30**–9
dish [dĭsh/–]
  ...drainer [–drā/nər] **40**–3
  ...towel [–tow/əl] **47**–22
dishroom [dĭsh/room/] **63**–12
dishwasher [dĭsh/wä/shər, –wö/–] (machine) **40**–4,
  (person) **63**–13
dishwashing liquid [dĭsh/wä/shĭng lĭk/wəd, –wö/–] **47**–21
disinfectant [dĭs/ən fĕk/tənt] **95**–19
disk [dĭsk/–] **144**–5
  ...drive [–drīv/] **144**–3
display case [dĭ splā/ kās/] **69**–7
disposable diapers [dĭ spō/zə bəl dī/pərz] **95**–20
dissection kit [dĭ sĕk/shən kĭt/, dī–] **119**–7
dive [dīv] **157**–5
diving mask [dī/vĭng măsk/] **155**–3
division [də vĭzh/ən] **118**–4
divorced [də vörst/] **25**–24
DJ (disc jockey) [dē/jā/] / [dĭsk/ jäk/ē] **33**–17
do [doo/–]
  ...an experiment [–ən ĭk spĕr/ə mənt] **119**–A
  ...crafts [–krăfts/] **162**–A
  ...errands [–ĕr/əndz] **90** ✦
  ...homework [–hōm/würk/] **27**–T
  ...manual labor [–măn/yoo əl lā/bər] **140**–D
dockworker [däk/wür/kər] **137**–21
doctor [däk/tər] **84**–6, **137**–22
Doctorate [däk/tər ət] **112** ✦
dog [dög] **11**–17, 18, **133**–11
dogwood [dög/wood/] **128**–16
DOING THE LAUNDRY [doo/ĭng dhə lön/drē] **72**–2
doll [däl] **45**–18
dollar [däl/ər] **20**–7
dollhouse [däl/hows/] **45**–14
doll making kit [däl/ mā/kĭng kĭt/] **162**–15
dolphin [däl/fən, döl–] **131**–30
DOMESTIC ANIMALS AND RODENTS
  [də mĕs/tĭk ăn/ə məlz ən rōd/nts] **133**
domesticated animals [də mĕs/tə kā/təd ăn/ə məlz] **133** ✦
donkey [däng/kē, dŭng/–, döng/–] **133**–2
do not enter [doo/ nät/ ĕn/tər] **107**–4
do not wash [doo/ nät/ wäsh/, –wösh/] **72** ✦
don't [dōnt/–]
  ...**drink** and **drive** [–drĭngk/ ən drīv/] **101**–G
  ...**open** [–ō/pən] **101**–F
donut shop [dō/nŭt shäp/] **91**–20
doorbell [dör/bĕl/] **38**–10
door chain [dör/ chān/] **37**–28
doorknob [dör/näb/] **37**–30
doorman [dör/măn/] **36**–10, **145**–2
dosage [dō/sĭj] **80** ✦
double boiler [dŭb/əl boy/lər] **59**–8
doughnut [dō/nŭt] **60**–15, **60** ✦
down (feathers) [down/–]
  ...jacket [–jăk/ət] **66**–15
  ...vest [–vĕst/] **66**–13
down (preposition) [down] **105**–8
downhill skiing [down/hĭl/ skē/ĭng] **160**–1
downstairs [down/stërz/] **38** ✦

Index

downtown [down/town/] **88** ✦
drain [drān] **43**–4
drapes [drāps] **42**–16
draw a picture [drö/ ə pĭk/chər] **6**–M
draw blood [drö/ blŭd/] **85**–G
drawer [drör] **40**–23, **44**–3
dress [(–)drĕs(/)] **64**–3
  maternity... [mə tür/nə tē–] **65**–19
dress [drĕs] **94**–J
dresser [drĕs/ər] **44**–2
dressmaker [drĕs/mā/kər] **73**–2
dress shop [drĕs/ shäp/] **92** ✦
dribble [drĭb/əl] **156**–K
drill [drĭl(/–)] **84**–21, **150**–8, 23
  ...bit [–bĭt/] **150**–23
drill a tooth [drĭl/ ə tōōth/] **85**–K
drink [drĭngk(/–)] / [–drĭngk/] **60**–B
  ...fluids [–flōō/ədz] **80**–B
  don't... [dōnt/–] **101**–G
dripping [drĭp/ĭng] **49**–16
drive [drīv] **26**–I, **90**–C, **140**–E
drive (computer) [drīv] **144**–3, 20
driver's [drī/vərz]
  ...education [–ĕj/ə kā/shən] **121**–5
  ...license [–lī/səns] **29**–4
drive-thru window [drīv/thrōō/ wĭn/dō] **90**–13
driveway [drīv/wā/] **38**–5
drop off [dräp/ öf/] **94**–A
dropper [dräp/ər] **119**–14
drought [drowt] **103**–10
drown [drown] **82**–I
drugs [drŭgz] **100**–4
drugstore [drŭg/stör/] **90**–2
drums [drŭmz] **120**–18
drumsticks [drŭm/stĭks/] **52**–22
drunk driving [drŭngk/ drī/vĭng] **100**–3
dry [drī(/–)]
  ...hair [–hër/] **76**–H
  ...the dishes [–dhə dĭsh/əz] **46**–N
dry [drī] **72**–18
dry-clean [drī/klēn/] **72** ✦
dry cleaners [drī/ klē/nərz] **72** ✦, **91**–24
dryer [drī/ər] **72**–4
  ...sheets [–shēts/] **72**–5
Dry measures [drī/ mĕzh/ərz] **57**
drywall [drī/wöl/] **149**–18
duck [dŭk(/–)] **52**–18, **132**–13
  ...pond [–pänd/] **153**–6
dump truck [dŭmp/ trŭk/] **106**–12
duplex house [dōō/plĕks hows/] **34** ✦
dust [dŭst] **46**–A
dust [dŭst(/–)]
  ...mop [–mäp/] **47**–17
  ...ruffle [–rŭf/əl] **44**–22
  ...storm [–störm/] **10**–21
dustpan [dŭst/păn/] **47**–11
dye hair [dī/ hër/] **23**–D
eagle [ē/gəl] **132**–10
ear [ïr(/–)] **74**–28
  ...infection [–ĭn fĕk/shən] **79**–3
earache [ïr/āk/] **78**–3
early [ür/lē] **17**–22
earmuffs [ïr/mŭfs/] (outdoor) **66**–12, (safety) **147**–14
earplugs [ïr/plŭgz/] **147**–13
earrings [ïr/ĭngz] **69**–37

Earth [ürth] **127**–7
earthquake [ürth/kwāk/] **102**–5
easel [ē/zəl] **163**–21
east [ēst] **107, 123, 124**
eastern time [ē/stərn tīm/] **17**–29
easy [ē/zē] **11**–23
  ...chair [–chër/] **42**–24
cat [ĕt(/–)] **60**–B
  ...breakfast [–brĕk/fəst] **26**–E
eat out [ēt/ owt/] **62** ✦
eclipse [ĭ klĭps/]
  lunar... [lōō/nər–] **127** ✦
  solar... [sō/lər–] **127** ✦
economics [ĕk/ə näm/ĭks, ē/kə–] **121**–6
edit [ĕd/ət] **113**–B
eel [ēl] **130**–5
eggbeater [ĕg/bē/tər] **59**–20
eggplants [ĕg/plănts/] **51**–18
eggs [(–)ĕgz(/)] **54**–34
  scrambled... [skrăm/bəld–] **61**–1
eight [āt] **14**
eighteen [ā/tēn/] **14**
eighteenth [ā/tēnth/] **14**
eighth [ātth, āth] **14, 15**–1
eighty [ā/tē] **14, 15**–10
eject [ĭ jĕkt/] **165**–F
elastic bandage [ĭ lăs/tĭk băn/dĭj] **83**–12
elbow [ĕl/bō] **74**–15
elderly [ĕl/dər lē] **22**–15
Election [ĭ lĕk/shən] **115**
elective [ĭ lĕk/tĭv] **121** ✦
electric [ĭ lĕk/trĭk]
  ...can opener [–kăn/ ō/pə nər] **40**–14
  ...drill [–drĭl/] **150**–8
  ...keyboard [–kē/börd/] **120**–20
  ...mixer [–mĭk/sər] **40**–25
  ...pencil sharpener [–pĕn/səl shär/pə nər] **142**–9
  ...shaver [–shā/vər] **77**–24
electrical [ĭ lĕk/trĭ kəl] **151**–38
  ...hazard [–hăz/ərd] **147**–1
  ...tape [–tāp/] **151**–38
electrician [ĭ lĕk trĭsh/ən] **48**–9
ELECTRONICS AND PHOTOGRAPHY
  [ĭ lĕk trän/ĭks ən fə tä/grə fē] **164–165**
electronics store [ĭ lĕk trän/ĭks stör/] **93**–18
elementary school [ĕl/ə mĕn/trē skōōl/] **112**–5
elephant [ĕl/ə fənt] **135**–42
elevator [ĕl/ə vā/tər] **37**–34, **145** ✦
eleven [ĭ lĕv/ən] **14**
eleventh [ĭ lĕv/ənth] **14**
ellipse [ĭ lĭps/] **118**–9
elm [ĕlm] **128**–17
embarrassed [ĭm băr/əst] **31**–25
embroidery [ĭm broy/də rē] **163**–19
EMERGENCIES AND NATURAL DISASTERS [ĭ mür/jən sēz ən
  năch/rəl dĭ zăs/tərz, –năch/ər əl–] **102–103**
emergency [ĭ mür/jən sē]
  ...brake [–brāk/] **109**–44
  ...card [–kärd/] **111**–K
  ...exit [–ĕg/zət, –ĕk/sət] **111**–J
  ...medical technician (EMT)
    [–mĕd/ĭ kəl tĕk nĭsh/ən] / [ē/ĕm/tē/] **87**–26
  ...service (911) [–sür/vəs] **9**–9
Emergency room [ĭ mür/jən sē rōōm/] **87**
emery board [ĕm/ə rē börd/, ĕm/rē–] **77**–30

empty [ĕmp/tē] **46**–F
empty [ĕmp/tē] **11**–10
encyclopedia [ĭn sī/klə pē/dē ə] **98**–18
end table [ĕnd/ tā/bəl] **42**–21
end the conversation[ĕnd/ dhə kän/vər sā/shən] **8**–C
ENERGY AND THE ENVIRONMENT
　[ĕn/ər jē ən dhē ĭn vī/rən mənt, –vī/ərn–] **126**
Energy resources [ĕn/ər jē rē/sör səz, –rĭ sör/səz] **126**
engine [ĕn/jən] **109**–41
engineer [ĕn/jə nïr/] **137**–23
English as a second language
　[ĭng/glĭsh əz ə sĕk/ənd lăng/gwĭj] **121**–7
ENGLISH COMPOSITION [ĭng/glĭsh käm/pə zĭsh/ən] **113**
ENTERTAINMENT [ĕn/tər tān/mənt] **166**–**167**
enter your PIN number [ĕn/tər yər pĭn/ nŭm/bər] **97**–B
entrance [ĕn/trəns] **36** ✦
Entryway [ĕn/trē wā/] **37**
envelope [ĕn/və lōp/] **96**–1, **143**–20
ENVIRONMENT [ĭn vī/rən mənt, –vī/ərn–] **126**
Equivalents [ĭ kwĭv/ə lənts] **15**
erase [ĭ rās/] **2**–H
eraser [ĭ rā/sər] **3**–21
escalator [ĕs/kə lā/tər] **93**–21
evening [ēv/nĭng] **17**–19
　...gown [–gown/] **65**–29
every day [ĕv/rē dā/] **18**–21
EVERYDAY CONVERSATION [ĕv/rē dā/ kän/vər sā/shən] **8**
evidence [ĕv/ə dəns] **99**–9
examination table [ĭg zăm/ə nā/shən tā/bəl] **84**–13
examine [ĭg zăm/ən] **85**–F
examining room [ĭg zăm/ə nĭng rōōm/] **84**–9
exchange [ĭks chānj/] **21**–G
excited [ĭk sī/təd] **31**–23
exclamation mark [ĕk/sklə mā/shən märk/] **113**–8
Excuse me. [ĭk skyōōz/ mē] **8**
Executive [ĭg zĕk/yə tĭv] **116**
exercise [ĕk/sər sīz/] **27**–W, **80**–D, **157**–P
exhausted [ĭg zö/stəd] **30** ✦
exhibition [ĕk/sə bĭsh/ən] **152**–21
expensive [ĭk spĕn/sĭv] **11**–19
experience turbulence [ĭk spïr/ē əns tür/byə ləns] **111**–N
expiration date [ĕk/spə rā/shən dāt/] **80** ✦
Exploration [ĕk/splə rā/shən] **114**
explosion [ĭk splō/zhən] **102**–4
Express Mail [ĭk sprĕs/ māl/] **96**–15
extension cord [ĭk stĕn/shən körd/] **151**–14
exterminate [ĭk stür/mə nāt/] **49** ✦
exterminator [ĭk stür/mə nā/tər] **49**–21
extra [ĕk/strə]
　...large [–lärj/] **70**–5
　...small [–smöl/] **70**–1
extract a tooth [ĭk străkt/ ə tōōth/] **85** ✦
eye [ī(/–)] / [–ī/] **73**–23, **74**–27
　...chart [–chärt/] **84**–11
　...glasses [–glăs/əz] **81**–35
　...hook [–hōōk/] **150**–35
　...shadow [–shăd/ō] **77**–34
　hook and... [hōōk/ ən–] **73**–23
eyebrow [ī/brow/] **74**–32
　...pencil [–pĕn/səl] **77**–33
eyedrops [ī/drăps/] **81**–22
eyelashes [ī/lăsh/əz] **74**–34
eyelid [ī/lĭd/] **74**–33
eyeliner [ī/lī/nər] **77**–35
fabric softener [făb/rĭk sö/fə nər] **72**–6

Face [fās] **74, 77**
face powder [fās/ pow/dər] **77**–39
FACTORY [făk/tə rē, –trē] **146**
factory [făk/tə rē, –trē]
　...owner [–ō/nər] **146**–2
　...worker [–wür/kər] **146**–6
fall [föl] **82**–O
fall [föl] **19**–39
fall in love [föl/ ĭn lŭv/] **28**–K
FAMILY [făm/lē, făm/ə lē] **24**–**25**
fan [făn] (appliance) **41**–4, (person) **158**–4
fancy [făn/sē] **71**–39
fare [fër(/–)] **104**–5
　...card [–kärd/] **104**–12
far from [fär/ frŭm/, –frəm] **13** ✦
farm [färm(/–)] **34**–13
　...equipment [–ĭ kwĭp/mənt] **148**–10
Farm animals [färm/ ăn/ə məlz] **133**
farmer [fär/mər] **148**–15
FARMING AND RANCHING [fär/mĭng ən răn/chĭng] **148**
farmworker [färm/wür/kər] **148**–8
fashion designer [făsh/ən dĭ zī/nər] **73** ✦
fast [făst] **11**–3
fasten your seat belt [făs/ən yər sēt/ bĕlt/] **111**–I
FAST FOOD [făst/ fōōd/] **60**
fast food restaurant [făst/ fōōd/ rĕs/tə rənt, –ränt] **90**–14
fast forward [făst/ för/wərd] **165**–C
fat [făt] **11**–7
father [fä/dhər] **24**–6, **25**–26
father-in-law [fä/dhər ĭn lö/] **24**–14
faucet [fö/sət] **43**–6, **49**–16
fax [făks] **142**–B
fax machine [făks/ mə shēn/] **143**–23
feast [fēst] **168**–16
feather [fĕdh/ər] **132**–5
　...duster [–dŭs/tər] **47**–1
February [fĕb/yōō ër/ē, fĕb/rōō–] **19**–26
feed [fēd] **94**–D, **148**–D
feel [fēl(/–)]
　...dizzy [–dĭz/ē] **78**–C
　...nauseous [–nö/shəs, –zē əs] **78**–D
FEELINGS [fē/lĭngz] **30**–**31**
feet [fēt] **15** ✦
female [fē/māl/] **4**–14
fence [fĕns] **38**–3, **148**–19
fencing [fĕn/sĭng] **159**–5
ferry [fĕr/ē] **104**–23
fever [fē/vər] **78**–8
fiction [fĭk/shən] **98, 166**
field [fēld] (school) **5**–12, (farm) **148**–7, (sports) **159**–17
fifteen [fĭf/tēn/] **14**
fifteenth [fĭf/tēnth/] **14**
fifth [fĭfth] **14**
fifty [fĭf/tē] **14**
　...dollars [–däl/ərz] **20**–11
　...percent [–pər sĕnt/] **15**–9
figure skating [fĭg/yər skā/tĭng] **160**–5
figurine [fĭg/yə rēn/] **162**–10
file [fīl] **142**–H
file [fīl(/–)]
　...cabinet [–kăb/ə nət] **142**–10
　...clerk [–klürk/] **142**–12
　...folder [–fōl/dər] **142**–11
filet of sole [fĭ lā/ əv sōl/] **53**–21
fill a cavity [fĭl/ ə kăv/ə tē] **85**–L

fill in the blank [fĭl′ ĭn dhə blăngk′] **7**–R
fill out [fĭl′ owt′] / [fĭl′ owt/–]
  ...a form [–ə förm′] **4**–B
  ...an application [–ən ăp/lə kā′shən] **141**–G
filling [fĭl/ĭng] **84**–22
film [fĭlm] (camera) **165**–26, (movie) **166**–1
fin [fĭn] **130**–1
find your seat [fīnd′ yər sēt′] **111**–G
FINDING A HOME [fīn/dĭng ə hōm′] **35**
fingernail [fĭng/gər nāl′] **75**–58
fingers [fĭng/gərz] **75**–57
finish [fĭn/ĭsh] **157**–Z
fins [fĭnz] **155**–2
fire [fīr(′–)] **42**–10, **102**–7
  ...escape [–ĭ skāp′] **36**–7
  ...exit [–ĕg/zət, –ĕk/sət] **37**–23
  ...extinguisher [–ĭk stĭng/gwĭ shər] **147**–22
  ...hydrant [–hī/drənt] **91**–28
  ...screen [–skrēn′] **42**–11
  ...station [–stā/shən] **88**–1
  ...truck [–trŭk′] **102**–9
firefighter [fīr/fī/tər] **102**–8, **137**–24
fireplace [fīr/plās′] **42**–9
fireworks [fīr/würks′] **168**–8
first [fürst(′–)] **14**
  ...draft [–drăft′] **113**–A
  ...floor [–flör′] **36**–1
  ...name [–nām′] **4**–2
  ...place [–plās′] **152**–20
  ...prize [–prīz′] **152**–20
FIRST AID [fürst′ ād′] **83**
first aid [fürst′ ād′]
  ...kit [–kĭt′] **83**–1
  ...manual [–măn/yōō əl] **83**–7
Fish [fĭsh] **53**
fish [fĭsh] **61**–17, **130**–12, 14, 15
fishing [fĭsh/ĭng] **154**–5
  ...net [–nĕt′] **154**–17
  ...pole [–pōl′] **154**–18
fitted sheet [fĭt/əd shēt′] **44**–14
fittings [fĭt/ĭngz] **151**–17
five [fīv(′–)] **14**–5, 20
  ...after one [–ăf/tər wŭn′] **16**–5
  ...to two [tə tōō′] **16**–15
Five ways to cook chicken [fīv′ wāz′ tə kōōk′ chĭk/ən] **58**
fix [fĭks] **49** ✦
flag [flăg] **168**–9
flammable [flăm/ə bəl] **147**–2
flashlight [flăsh/līt′] **151**–39
flat sheet [flăt′ shēt′] **44**–13
flea market [flē′ mär/kət] **152**–22
fleas [flēz] **49**–23
flight attendant [flīt′ ə tĕn/dənt] **110**–13
flood [flŭd] **103**–16
floor [flör(′–)] / [–flör′] **44**–24
  ...lamp [–lămp′] **42**–15
  ...plan [–plăn′] **38**–1
  dance... [dăns′–] **33**–16
floppy [fläp/ē] **144**–5
floral [flör/əl] **70**–12
florist [flör/ĭst] **92**–12, **137**–25
floss [flös, fläs] **77**–K
flounder [flown/dər] **130**–13
flour [flow/ər] **55**–45, **57**–10
flower [flow/ər] **39**–19, **129**–7

  ...bed [–bĕd′] **39**–A
  ...pot [–pät′] **39**–18
  Parts of a... [pärts′ əv ə–] **129**
FLOWERS [flow/ərz] **129**
flu [flōō] **79**–2
fluid ounce [flōō/əd owns′] **57**–1
flute [flōōt] **120**–3
fly [flī] **140** ✦
fly [flī] **132**–29
flying disc [flī/ĭng dĭsk′] **159**–6, **161**–27
foam pad [fōm′ păd′] **154**–13
foggy [fö/gē, fäg/ē–] **10**–11
fold [fōld] **72**–F
Follow directions [fäl/ō də rek/shənz, –dī–] **7**
food [fōōd(′–)]
  ...court [–kört′] **93**–14
  ...processor [–prä/sĕ sər] **40**–26
FOOD PREPARATION [fōōd′ prĕp ə rā/shən] **58**
Foot [fōōt] **75**
foot [fōōt] (measurement) **15** ✦, (body) **74**–7
football [fōōt/böl′] **158**–11, **161**–22
  ...helmet [–hĕl/mət] **161**–20
forceps [för/səps, –sĕps] **119**–8
forehead [för/əd, –hĕd′, fär′–] **74**–20
foreign language [för/ən lăng/gwĭj, fär′–] **121**–8
forest [för/əst, fär′–] **117**–11
fork [förk] **41**–21, **63**–24, 25, ✦
forklift [förk/lĭft′] **146**–14
form [(–)förm(′)]
  declaration... [dĕk/lə rā/shən–] **110**–22
  registration... [rĕj/ə strā/shən–] **4**
formal [för/məl] **71**–36
former husband [för/mər hŭz/bənd] **25** ✦
former wife [för/mər wīf′] **25** ✦
formula [för/myə lə] **95**–25, **119**–19
forty [för/tē] **14**, **16**–12
foundation [fown dā/shən] **77**–40
fountain [fown/tn] / [–fown/tn] **92**–11
  water... [wö/tər–] **153**–11
four [för] **14**
fourteen [för/tēn′] **14**
fourteenth [för/tēnth′] **14**
fourth [förth(′–)] **14**, **15**–2
  ...floor [–flör′] **36**–4
fox [fäks] **134**–15
Fractions [frăk/shənz] **15**
freezer [frē/zər] **40**–10
freezing [frē/zĭng] **10**–5
french fries [frĕnch′ frīz′] **60**–2
French horn [frĕnch′ hörn′] **120**–15
fresh [frĕsh] **53**–29
Friday [frī/dā, –dē] **18**–6
fried [frīd] **61**–17
frog [frög, fräg] **130**–25
front... [frŭnt(′–)]
  ...desk [–dĕsk′] **145**–8
  ...door [–dör′] **38**–11
  ...office [–ö/fəs] **146**–1
  ...seat [–sēt′] **109**–35
  ...walk [–wök′] **38**–14
  ...yard [–yärd′] **38**–15
frozen [frō/zən]
  ...fish [–fĭsh′] **53**–30
  ...foods [–fōōdz′] **55**–12
  ...vegetables [–vĕj/tə bəlz] **55**–43

...yogurt [–yō/gərt] **60**–11
FRUIT [fro͞ot] **50**
frustrated [frŭs/trā/təd] **31**–28
fry [frī] **58**–5
frying pan [frī/ĭng păn/] **59**–5
fuel injection system [fyo͞o/əl ĭn jĕk/shən sĭs/təm] **109**–40
full [fo͞ol] (not empty) **11**–9, (satisfied) **30**–6
full [fo͞ol(/–)]
...moon [–mo͞on/] **127**–16
...slip [–slĭp/] **67**–22
full-size car [fo͞ol/sīz/ kär/] **106**–4
funnel [fŭn/əl] **119**–12
funny [fŭn/ē] **167**–27
fur [für] **134**–19
furious [fyo͝or/ē əs] **30** ◆
furniture [für/nĭ chər] / [–für/nĭ chər] **35**–K
...polish [–päl/ĭsh] **47**–18
...store [–stör/] **88**–13
patio... [păt/ē ō–] **39**–5
fuse box [fyo͞oz/ băks/] **48**–13
galaxy [găl/ək sē] **127**–26
gallbladder [göl/blăd/ər] **75**–40
gallon [găl/ən] **57**–5
game [gām(/–)] **152**–18
...show [–shō/] **167**–23
GAMES [gām(/–)] **162**–**163**
gang violence [găng/ vī/ə ləns] **100**–2
garage [gə räzh/, –räj/] / [–gə räzh/, –räj/] **36, 38**–6
...door [–dör/] **38**–7
garbage [gär/bĭj] **46**–Q
...can [–kăn/] **39**–3
...disposal [–dĭ spō/zəl] **40**–5
...truck [–trŭk/] **91**–27
garden [gär/dn] (vegetable) **148**–12, (botanical) **152**–4
gardener [gärd/nər, gär/dn ər] **137**–26, **152**–6
gardenia [gär dēn/yə] **129**–16
gargle [gär/gəl] **77**–L
garlic [gär/lĭk] **51**–29
...bread [–brĕd/] **61**–16
...press [–prĕs/] **59**–10
garment worker [gär/mənt wür/kər] **73** ◆, **137**–27
garter belt [gär/tər bĕlt/] **67**–19
garter snake [gär/tər snāk/] **131**–39
gas [găs(/–)] / [–găs/] **109**–54
...gauge [–gāj/] **108**–22
...meter [–mē/tər] **48**–14
...pedal [–pĕd/l] **109**–47
...station [–stā/shən] **88**–12, **137**–28
...station attendant [–stā/shən ə tĕn/dənt] **137**–28
...tank [–tăngk/] **108**–12
natural... [năch/rəl–, năch/ər əl–] **126**–3
gate [gāt] (garage) **36**, (airport) **110**–5, **111**–D
gauge [gāj] **84**–12, **108**–19, 22, 23
gauze [göz] **83**–6
gearshift [gĭr/shĭft/] **108**–27
GEOGRAPHY [jē ăg/rə fē] **117**
geometry [jē äm/ə trē] **118**–26
geothermal energy [jē/ō thür/məl ĕn/ər jē] **126**–7
get [gĕt(/–)]
...a checkup [–ə chĕk/ŭp/] **85** ◆
...acupuncture [–ăk/yə pŭngk/chər] **81**–G
...a job [–ə jäb/] **28**–G
...a loan [–ə lōn/] **35**–I
...an electric shock [–ən ĭ lĕk/trĭk shäk/] **82**–F
...an injection [–ən ĭn jĕk/shən] **80**–E

...an X ray [–ən ĕks/ rā/] **85**–H
...bed rest [–bĕd/ rĕst/] **80**–A
...feedback [–fēd/băk/] **113**–C
...frostbite [–fröst/bīt/] **82**–G
...home [–hōm/] **27**–Q
...your boarding pass [–yər bör/dĭng păs/] **111**–E
get dressed [gĕt/ drĕst/] **26**–D
get hired [gĕt/ hīrd/] **141**–L
get married [gĕt/ măr/ēd] **28**–L
get up [gĕt/ ŭp/] **26**–B
gift [gĭft(/–)] **169**–D
...shop [–shäp/] **145**–7
gifts [gĭfts] **33**–18
gills [gĭlz] **130**–2
giraffe [jə răf/] **135**–33
girder [gür/dər] **149**–3
girdle [gür/dl] **67**–18
girl [gürl] **22**–5, 8
give [gĭv(/–)] **21**–D
...a shot of anesthetic [–ə shät/ əv ăn/əs thet/ĭk] **85**–J
...a speech [–ə spēch/] **32**–E
...the verdict [–dhə vür/dĭkt] **99**–E
gizzards [gĭz/ərdz] **52**–23
glass [glăs(/–)] **11**–9, 10, **41**–26, **63**–19, 20, ◆
...cleaner [–klē/nər] **47**–8
glasses [glăs/əz] **81**–35
globe [glōb] **3**–9
glove [glŭv(/–)] **161**–17
...compartment [–kəm pärt/mənt] **108**–33
gloves [glŭvz] **66**–5
glue [glo͞o] **143**–37, **162**–8
go [gō(/–)]
...on an interview [–än ən ĭn/tər vyo͞o/, –ön–] **141**–H
...straight [–strāt/] **107**–A
...through security [–thro͞o sĭ kyo͝or/ə tē] **111**–C
...to a chiropractor [–to͞o ə kī/rə prăk/tər] **81**–H
...to bed [–tə bĕd/] **27**–X
...to college [–tə käl/ĭj] **28**–J
...to jail [–tə jāl/] **99**–G
...to prison [–tə prĭz/ən] **99**–G
...to sleep [–tə slēp/] **27**–Y
...to the market [–tə dhə mär/kət] **26**–L
...to work [–tə würk/] **26**–I
goat [gōt] **133**–1
goggles [gäg/əlz] **147**–9
goldfish [gōld/fĭsh/] **133**–16
golf [gälf(/–), gölf(/–)] **159**–7
...club [–klŭb/] **161**–1
good [go͝od] **11**–17
good-bye [go͝od bī/, gə–] **8**
goose [go͞os] **132**–14
gopher [gō/fər] **133**–19
gorilla [gə rĭl/ə] **135**–30
gown [gown] **32**–2, **65**–29
graduate [grăj/o͞o āt/] **28**–D, **32**–A
graduate [grăj/o͞o ət] **32**–6
...school [–sko͞ol/] **112** ◆
graduated cylinder [grăj/o͞o ā/təd sĭl/ən dər] **119**–10
graduating class [grăj/o͞o ā/tĭng klăs/] **32**–1
GRADUATION [grăj/o͞o ā/shən] **32**–**33**
grams [grămz] **57** ◆
grandchild [grăn/chīld/, grănd/–] **29**–Q
granddaughters [grăn/dö/tərz] **24** ◆
grandfather [grăn/fä/dhər, grănd/–] **24**–3
grandmother [grăn/mŭdh/ər, grănd/–] **24**–2

Index

grandparents [grăn/për/ənts, gränd/–] **24**–1
grandson [grăn/sŭn/, gränd/–] **24**–7
grapefruit [grāp/frōōt/] **50**–9
grapes [grāps] **50**–1
graphic artist [grăf/ĭk är/tĭst] **137**–29
grasshopper [grăs/häp/ər] **132**–25
grate [grāt] **58**–J
grater [grā/tər] **59**–2
gray [grā(/–)] **12**–5
  ...hair [–hër/] **23**–13
grease [grēs] **58**–C
green [grēn] **12**–8
greenhouse [grēn/hows/] **152**–5
green salad [grēn/ săl/əd] **60**–8
greeting card [grē/tĭng kärd/] **96**–4
greet someone [grēt/ sŭm/wŭn] **8**–A
grill [grĭl] **58**–T
grilled cheese sandwich [grĭld/ chēz/ săn/wĭch, –sănd/–] **61**–8
ground beef [grownd/ bēf/] **52**–4
ground post [grownd/ pōst/] **96**–14
grower [grō/ər] **148**–15
guard [gärd] **97**–4, **99**–3
guest [gĕst(/–)] **32**–9, **145**–11
  ...room [–rōōm/] **145**–10
  ...speaker [–spē/kər] **32**–9
guests [gĕsts] **33**–14, **169**–B
guilty [gĭl/tē] **99**
guinea pig [gĭn/ē pĭg/] **133**–14
guitar [gĭ tär/] **120**–11
gum [gŭm] **55**–42
gums [gŭmz] **74**–24
gun [gŭn] **100**–9
gurney [gür/nē] **87**–28
gutter [gŭt/ər] **38**–19
gym [jĭm] **5**–9
gymnastics [jĭm năs/tĭks] **159**–8
gynecologist [gī/nə käl/ə jĭst] **86** ✦
hacksaw [hăk/sö/] **150**–5
hail [hāl] **10**–19
hail a taxi [hāl/ ə tăk/sē] **104** ✦
hailstorm [hāl/störm/] **10**–18
hair [hër(/–)] **23**, **74**–19
  ...clip [–klĭp/] **76**–17
  ...gel [–jĕl/] **76**–11
  ...net [–nĕt/] **147**–18
  ...salon [–sə län/] **23** ✦, **93**–16
  ...spray [–sprā/] **76**–12
  ...stylist [–stī/lĭst] **23** ✦
hairdresser [hër/drĕs/ər] **137**–30
half [hăf(/–)] **15**–4, **16**–10, **20**–5
  ...bath [–băth/] **43** ✦
  ...brother [–brŭdh/ər] **25**–29
  ...cup of raisins [–kŭp/ əv rā/zənz] **57**–9
  ...past one [–păst/ wŭn/] **16**
  ...sister [–sĭs/tər] **25**–30
  ...slip [–slĭp/] **67**–23
halibut [hăl/ə bət] **53**–20
hall [höl] **89**–17, **145**–13
Halloween [hăl/ə wēn/, häl/–] **168**–10
Hallway [höl/wā/] **37**
ham [hăm] **52**–9
hamburger [hăm/bür/gər] **60**–1
hammer [hăm/ər] **149**–D
hammer [hăm/ər] **150**–1
hammock [hăm/ək] **39**–2

hamper [hăm/pər] **43**–1
Hand [hănd] **75**
hand [hănd(/–)] **2**, **11**, **74**–8
  ...towel [–tow/əl] **43**–13
  ...truck [–trŭk/] **146**–11
handbags [hănd/băgz/] **69**–6
handcuffs [hănd/kŭfs/] **99**–2
handicapped parking [hăn/dē kăpt pär/kĭng] **107**–14
handkerchief [hăng/kər chĭf, –chēf/] **69**–42
handsaw [hănd/sö/] **150**–4
hanger [hăng/ər] **72**–11
hang up [hăng/ ŭp/] / [hăng/ ŭp/–]
  ...the clothes [–dhə klōz/] **72**–H
  ...the receiver [–dhə rĭ sē/vər] **9**–F
happy [hăp/ē] **31**–32
Happy Birthday [hăp/ē bürth/dā] **169**
hard [härd] (surface) **11**–5, (difficult) **11**–24
hard [härd(/–)]
  ...disk drive [–dĭsk/ drīv/] **144**–20
  ...hat [–hăt/] **147**–19
Hardware [härd/wër/] **144**
hardware [härd/wër/] **150**
  ...store [–stör/] **88**–14
harvest [här/vəst] **148**–B
hat [hăt] **66**–1
hats [hăts] **68**–5
have [hăv(/–)]
  ...a baby [–ə bā/bē] **29**–M
  ...a grandchild [–ə grăn/chīld/, gränd/–] **29**–Q
  ...a heart attack [–ə härt/ ə tăk/] **82**–D
  ...an allergic reaction [–ən ə lür/jĭk rē ăk/shən] **82**–E
  ...a picnic [–ə pĭk/nĭk] **153**–D
  ...dinner [–dĭn/ər] **27**–R
Hawaii-Aleutian time [hə wī/ē ə lōō/shən tīm/] **17**–24
hay [hā] **148**–18
hazardous [hăz/ər dəs]
  ...materials [–mə tïr/ē əlz] **147**–7
  ...waste [–wāst/] **126**–9
head [hĕd] **74**–1
headache [hĕd/āk/] **78**–1
headboard [hĕd/börd/] **44**–15
headlight [hĕd/līt/] **108**–5
headphones [hĕd/fōnz/] **164**–16
HEALTH CARE [hĕlth/ kër/] **80**–81
health [hĕlth(/–)]
  ...club [–klŭb/] **89**–21
  ...insurance card [–ĭn shōōr/əns kärd/] **84**
hear [hïr] **75**–B
hearing aid [hïr/ĭng ād/] **81**–33
hearing impaired [hïr/ĭng ĭm përd/] **22**–27
heart (symbol) [härt] **168**–6
heart (body) [härt(/–)] **75**–38, **79**–14
  ...disease [–dĭ zēz/] **79**–14
  listen to... [lĭs/ən tə–] **85**–D
hearts [härts] **163**–29
heater [hē/tər] **48**–1, **108**–29
heating pad [hē/tĭng păd/] **80**–3
heat wave [hēt/ wāv/] **10**–15
heavy [hĕv/ē] **11**–13, **71**–41
  ...machinery [–mə shē/nə rē] **140**–F
heavyset [hĕv/ē sĕt/] **22**–20
hedge [hĕj(/–)] **39**–1
  ...clippers [–klĭp/ərz] **39**–12
heel [hēl] (shoe) **68**–13, (foot) **75**–62
height [hīt] **15**–14, **22**

Heimlich maneuver [hīm/lĭk mə noo/vər] **83**–18

helicopter [hĕl/ə käp/tər] **110**–8

hello [hə lō/, hĕ–] **8**

help [hĕlp] **6**–J

help wanted sign [hĕlp/ wän/təd sīn/, –wön/–] **141**–C

hemline [hĕm/līn/] **73**–1

hen [hĕn] **133**–5

Hi! [hī] **8**

hibiscus [hī bĭs/kəs, hĭ–] **129**–12

hide [hīd] **169**–E

high [hī(/–)]

...chair [–chër/] **95**–7

...heels [–hēlz/] **68**–17, **71**–47

high blood pressure [hī/ blŭd/ prĕsh/ər] **79**–15

high-rise building [hī/rīz/ bĭl/dĭng] **89**–25

high school [hī/ skool/] **112**–7

hiking [hī/kĭng] **154**–6

...boots [–boots/] **68**–21

hills [hĭlz] **117**–16

hip [hĭp] **74**–5

hippopotamus [hĭp/ə pät/ə məs] **135**–43

hire [hīr] **99**–B

hired hand [hīrd/ hănd/] **148**–20

hit [hĭt] **156**–G

HIV (human immunodeficiency virus) [ăch/ī/vē/]
[hyoo/mən ĭm/yə nō dĭ fĭsh/ən sē vī/rəs] **79**–10

HOBBIES AND GAMES [häb/ēz ən gāmz/] **162**–163

hockey stick [häk/ē stĭk/] **161**–11

hold [hōld] **94**–B, **101**–C

holiday [häl/ə dā/] **19**–43, 44

HOLIDAYS [häl/ə dāz/] **168**

holly [häl/ē] **128**–19

home [hōm(/–)]

...attendant [–ə tĕn/dənt] **137**–31

...economics [–ĕk/ə näm/ĭks, –ē/kə–] **121**–9

homemaker [hōm/mā/kər] **137**–32

homesick [hōm/sĭk/] **31**–21

honeybee [hŭn/ē bē/] **132**–26

hood [hood] **108**–6

hoof [hoof] **134**–17

hook [hook(/–)] **150**–34, 35

...and eye [–ən ī/] **73**–23

horn [hörn] (car) **108**–24, (music) **120**–13, (animal) **134**–21

horror story [hör/ər stör/ē, här/–] **166**–14

horse [hörs(/–)] **133**–4

...racing [–rā/sĭng] **159**–18

horseback riding [hörs/băk rī/dĭng] **154**–9

hose [hōz] **39**–9

HOSPITAL [häs/pĭ tl] **86**–87

hospital [häs/pĭ tl] **88**–7

...bed [–bĕd/] **86**–11

...gown [–gown/] **86**–15

Hospital staff [häs/pĭ tl stăf/] **86**

hostess [hō/stəs] **62**–1

hot [hät] (weather) **10**–1, (feeling) **30**–1

hot dog [hät/ dög/] **60**–6

HOTEL [hō tĕl/] **145**

hotel [hō tĕl/] **88**–5

hot water [hät/ wö/tər] **43**–5

hour [ow/ər] **16**–3

HOUSE [hows] **38**

house [(–)hows(/)] **34**–6

buy a... [bī/ ə–] **29**–O

clean the... [klēn/ dhə–] **27**–N

Household Pests [hows/hōld/ pĕsts/] **49**

HOUSEHOLD PROBLEMS AND REPAIRS
[hows/hōld/ präb/ləmz ən rĭ përz/] **48**–49

housekeeper [hows/kē/pər] **138**–33, **145**–15

housekeeping cart [hows/kē/pĭng kärt/] **145**–14

House of Representatives [hows/ əv rĕp/rĭ zĕn/tə tĭvz] **116**–1

houseplant [hows/plănt/] **129**–29

HOUSEWORK [hows/würk/] **46**

hubcap [hŭb/kăp/] **108**–9

hug [hŭg] **33**–G

humid [hyoo/məd] **10**–12

humidifier [hyoo mĭd/ə fī/ər] **80**–2

humiliated [hyoo mĭl/ē ā/təd] **30** ✦

hummingbird [hŭm/ĭng bürd/] **132**–11

hump [hŭmp] **135**–51

hundred [hŭn/drəd] **14**

hungry [hŭng/grē] **30**–5

hurricane [hür/ə kān/] **103**–12

hurt [hürt] (feeling) **30**–17, (medical) **82**–A

husband [hŭz/bənd] **24**–19

hydrant [hī/drənt] **91**–28

hydroelectric power [hī/drō ĭ lĕk/trĭk pow/ər] **126**–5

hydrogen peroxide [hī/drə jən pə räk/sīd] **83**–8

hyena [hī ē/nə] **135**–31

hygienist [hī jē/nĭst, –jĕn/ĭst] **84**–16

hypertension [hī/pər tĕn/shən] **79** ✦

hypoallergenic [hī/pō ăl/ər jĕn/ĭk] **77** ✦

I beam [ī/ bēm/] **149**–3

ice [īs(/–)]

...hockey [–häk/ē] **158**–13

...machine [–mə shēn/] **145**–18

...pack [–păk/] **83**–13

...skates [–skāts/] **161**–9

...skating [–skā/tĭng] **160**–4

ice cream [īs/ krēm/] **55**–44

ice cream stand [īs/ krēm stănd/] **93**–20

iced tea [īst/ tē/] **60**–5

icy [ī/sē] **10**–13

ignition [ĭg nĭsh/ən] **108**–25

illegal drugs [ĭ lē/gəl drŭgz/] **100**–4

ILLNESSES AND MEDICAL CONDITIONS
[ĭl/nə səz ən mĕd/ĭ kəl kən dĭsh/ənz] **79**

immigrate [ĭm/ə grāt/] **28**–C

Immigration [ĭm/ə grā/shən] **114**

immunization [ĭm/yə nə zā/shən] **80** ✦

in [ĭn] **13**–5

...fashion [–făsh/ən] **64** ✦

...front of [–frŭnt/ əv] **13**–4

...love [–lŭv/] **28**–K, **30**–19

...pain [–pān/] **30**–12

...shock [–shäk/] **82**

inch (in.) [ĭnch] **15**–13

Independence Day [ĭn/də pĕn/dəns dā/] **168**–7

INDIVIDUAL SPORTS [ĭn/də vĭj/oo əl spörts/] **159**

industrial arts [ĭn dŭs/trē əl ärts/] **121**–10

infectious disease [ĭn fĕk/shəs dĭ zēz/] **79** ✦

influenza [ĭn/floo ĕn/zə] **79** ✦

information booth [ĭn/fər mā/shən booth/] **93**–22

ingredients [ĭn grē/dē ənts] **58**–K

INJURIES [ĭn/jə rēz] **78**

ink pad [ĭngk/ păd/] **143**–41

inline [ĭn/līn/]

...skates [–skāts/] **161**–10

...skating [–skā/tĭng] **159**–9

inquire about the salary [ĭn kwīr/ ə bowt/ dhə săl/ə rē] **141**–K

insect [ĭn/sĕkt]

Index

...bite [–bīt/] **78**–11
...repellent [–rĭ pĕl/ənt] **154**–23
INSECTS [ĭn/sĕkts] **132**
insert [ĭn sürt/] **97**–A
Inside the body [ĭn/sīd/ dhə bäd/ē] **75**
instant coffee [ĭn/stənt kö/fē] **55**–51
instructor [ĭn strŭk/tər] **5 ✦, 139**–58
instrument [ĭn/strə mənt] **120**–A
insulation [ĭn/sə lā/shən] **149**–13
insurance [ĭn shoor/əns]
...card [–kärd/] **84**–4
...form [–förm/] **84**–5
intercom [ĭn/tər käm/] **36**–8
interesting [ĭn/trə stĭng, ĭn/tə rĕs/tĭng] **167**–30
international call [ĭn/tər năsh/ə nəl köl/] **9**–6
internist [ĭn/tür/nĭst] **86**–2
interpreter [ĭn tür/prə tər] **138**–34
INTERSECTION [ĭn/tər sĕk/shən] **90**–**91**
interview [ĭn/tər vyōō/] **141**–H
intestinal parasites [ĭn tĕs/tə nəl păr/ə sīts/] **79**–16
intestines [ĭn tĕs/tənz] **75**–42
into [ĭn/tōō, –tə] **105**–4
introduce [ĭn/trə dōōs/] **8**–D, F
Invention [ĭn vĕn/shən] **115**
invite [ĭn vīt/] **169**–B
iris [ī/rəs] **129**–20
iron [ī/ərn] **72**–G
iron [ī/ərn] **72**–13
ironed shirt [ī/ərnd shürt/] **72**–20
ironing board [ī/ər nĭng börd/] **72**–14
island [ī/lənd] **117**–8
IV (intravenous drip) [ī/vē/] / [ĭn/trə vē/nəs drĭp/] **87**–27
jack [jăk] **109**–51
jack cheese [jăk/ chēz/] **53**–12
jacket [jăk/ət] **66**–7
jack hammer [jăk/ hăm/ər] **149**–9
jack-o'-lantern [jăk/ə lăn/tərn] **168**–11
jam [jăm] **56**–14
janitor [jăn/ə tər] **138**–35
January [jăn/yōō ër/ē] **19**–25
jar [jär(/–)] **56**–2
...of jam [–əv jăm/] **56**–14
jasmine [jăz/mən] **129**–21
jaw [jö] **74**–23
jeans [jēnz] **64**–5
jellyfish [jĕl/ē fĭsh/] **130**–14
jewelry [jōō/əl rē] **69**–8
...store [–stör/] **92**–2
job [jäb(/–)] / [–jäb/]
...board [–börd/] **141**–B
get a... [gĕt/ ə–] **28**–G
JOB SAFETY [jäb/ sāf/tē] **147**
JOB SEARCH [jäb/ sürch/] **141**
JOB SKILLS [jäb/ skĭlz/] **140**
JOBS AND OCCUPATIONS A-H [jäbz/ ən äk/yə pā/shənz] **136**–**137**
JOBS AND OCCUPATIONS H-W [jäbz/ ən äk/yə pā/shənz] **138**–**139**
jockstrap [jäk/străp/] **67**–14
jog [jäg] **156**–B
join the army [joyn/ dhē är/mē] **28**–F
joystick [joy/stĭk/] **144**–9
judge [jŭj] **99**–6
Judicial [jōō dĭsh/əl] **116**
July [jōō lī/] **19**–31, **168**–7
jump [jŭmp] **156**–J

jumper [jŭm/pər] **65**–18
jumper cables [jŭm/pər kā/bəlz] **109**–52
jump rope [jŭmp/ rōp/] **153**–5
jumpsuit [jŭmp/sōōt/] **65**–16
June [jōōn] **19**–30
junior high school [jōōn/yər hī/ skōōl] **112**–6
Jupiter [jōō/pə tər] **127**–5
jury [joor/ē] **99**–8, **116**
Justices [jŭs/tə səz] **116**–10
kangaroo [kăng/gə rōō/] **135**–44
keep [kēp] **21**–E
ketchup [kĕch/əp, kăch/–] **60**–23
key [kē(/–)] **37**–31
...chain [–chān/] **69**–43
keyboard [kē/börd/] **120**–20, **144**–7
kick [kĭk] **156**–L
kidney [kĭd/nē] **75**–45
kilometers [kĭ läm/ə tərz, kĭl/ə mē/tərz] **15 ✦**
kiss [kĭs] **33**–F
KITCHEN [kĭch/ən] **40**
kitchen [kĭch/ən] **63**–10
...timer [–tī/mər] **59**–18
KITCHEN UTENSILS [kĭch/ən yōō tĕn/səlz] **59**
kitten [kĭt/n] **133**–10
knee [nē(/–)] **74**–17
...socks [–säks/] **67**–25
knee-highs [nē/hīz/] **67**–24
knife [(–)nīf(/)] **41**–22, **63**–27
carving... [kär/vĭng–] **59**–12
multi-use... [mŭl/tē yōōs/–, mŭl/tī–] **154**–20
paring... [për/ĭng–] **59**–16
knit [nĭt] **163**–F
knit shirt [nĭt/ shürt/] **65**–20
knitting needles [nĭt/ĭng nēd/lz] **163**–18
koala [kō ä/lə] **135**–45
label [lā/bəl] / [–lā/bəl] **143**–35
prescription... [prĭ skrĭp/shən–] **80**–14
lab technician [lăb/ tĕk nĭsh/ən] **86**–16
ladder [lăd/ər] **149**–2
ladle [lād/l] **59**–7
ladybug [lā/dē bŭg/] **132**–27
lake [lāk] **117**–13
lamb [lăm(/–)] **52**–13, 14, 15
...chops [–chäps/] **52**–15
...shanks [–shăngks/] **52**–13
lamp [lămp] **42**–15, **44**–17
lampshade [lămp/shād/] **44**–18
land [lănd] **111**–O
landlord [lănd/lörd/] **37**–32
language [lăng/gwĭj]
English as a second... [ĭng/glĭsh əz ə sĕk/ənd–] **141**–7
foreign... [för/ən–, fär/–] **141**–8
speak another... [spēk/ ə nä/thər] **140**–J
use the new... [yōōz/ thə nū/–] **143 ✦**
lantern [lăn/tərn] **154**–22
laptop [lăp/täp/] **144**–14
large [lärj] **70**–4
last [lăst(/–)]
...name [–nām/] **4**–4
...week [–wēk/] **18**–18
late [lāt] **17**–23
latex gloves [lā/tĕks glŭvz/] **87**–33, **147**–17
laugh [lăf] **33**–H
Laundromat [lön/drə măt/] **90**–1
laundry [lön/drē] **72**–1

...basket [–băs/kət] **72**–2
...detergent [–dĭ tür/jənt] **72**–7
...room [–rōōm/] **36**
lawn [lön(/–)] **39**–21
...mower [–mō/ər] **39**–22
lawyer [lö/yər] **99**–B, **138**–36
lay bricks [lā/ brĭks/] **149**–B
leaf [lēf(/–)] **128**–6, **129**–5
...blower [–blō/ər] **39**–4
leaking [lē/kĭng] **48**–3
learn to drive [lürn/ tə drīv/] **28**–E
lease [lēs] **35** ✦
leather [lĕdh/ər]
...boots [–bōōts/] **70**–18
...jacket [–jăk/ət] **66**–3
leave [lēv(/–)] **111**–L
...a message [–ə mĕs/ĭj] **9**–E
...a tip [–ə tĭp/] **62**–J
...work [–würk/] **26**–M
left [lĕft] **13**–1
leg [lĕg(/–)] **74**–6
...of lamb [–əv lăm/] **52**–14
legal [lē/gəl]
...holiday [–häl/ə dā/] **19**–43
...pad [–păd/] **143**–18
LEGAL SYSTEM [lē/gəl sĭs/təm] **99**
leggings [lĕg/ĭngz] **65**–23
Legislative [lĕj/əs lā/tĭv] **116**
lemons [lĕm/ənz] **50**–11
lend [lĕnd] **20** ✦
length [lĕngkth] **15**–16
lengthen [lĕngk/thən] **73**–C
leopard [lĕp/ərd] **135**–25
leotard [lē/ə tärd/] **67**–1
let out [lĕt/ owt/] **73**–F
letter [lĕt/ər] / [–lĕt/ər] **96**–2, **142**–B, D
...carrier [–kăr/ē ər] **96**–6
air... [ër/–] **96**–13
letterhead paper [lĕt/ər hĕd pā/pər] **143**–19
lettuce [lĕt/əs] **51**–1, **60**–17
level [lĕv/əl] **150**–24
librarian [lī brër/ē ən] **98**–1
LIBRARY [lī/brër ē] **98**
library [lī/brër ē] **5**–6, **89**–28, **98**–17, 19, 20
...book [–bōōk/] **98**–20
...card [–kärd/] **98**–19
...clerk [–klürk/] **98**–17
license plate [lī/səns plāt/] **108**–15
lid [lĭd] **59**–24
LIFE EVENTS [līf/ ĭ vĕnts/] **28**–29
lifeguard [līf/gärd/] **155**–18
...station [–stā/shən] **155**–20
lifesaving device [līf/sā/vĭng dĭ vīs/] **155**–19
life vest [līf/ vĕst/] **154**–14
light [līt] **169**–H
light [līt] (weight) **11**–14, **71**–40, (color) **12**–3
light (appliance) [līt(/–)] / [–līt/]
...fixture [–fĭks/chər] **41**–5
...switch [–swĭch/] **44**–19
porch... [pörch/–] **38**–9
lightbulb [līt/bŭlb/] **42**–4
lightning [līt/nĭng] **10**–17
lily [lĭl/ē] **129**–24
limb [lĭm] **128**–3
limes [līmz] **50**–12

line [līn(/–)] / [–līn/] **55**–20
...supervisor [–sōō/pər vī zər] **146**–5
assembly... [ə sĕm/blē–] **146**–8
line dry [līn/ drī/] **72** ✦
linen [lĭn/ən] **70**–17
linen closet [lĭn/ən kläz/ət] **43** ✦
Lines [līnz] **118**
lingerie [län/zhə rā/, –jə–] **67** ✦
lion [lī/ən] **135**–36
lip [lĭp] **74**–30
lipstick [lĭp/stĭk/] **77**–37
Liquid measures [lĭk/wəd mĕzh/ərz] **57**
list [lĭst] **6**–L
listen [lĭs/ən] **2**–C, **85**–D
listen for the dial tone [lĭs/ən fər dhə dī/əl tōn/] **9**–B
liters [lē/tərz] **57** ✦
little [lĭt/l] **11**–1
Little League [lĭt/l lēg/] **158** ✦
live [lĭv] **116**–B
liver [lĭv/ər] (food) **52**–7, (body) **75**–39
livestock [līv/stäk/] **148**–13
LIVING ROOM [lĭv/ĭng rōōm/] **42**
lizard [lĭz/ərd] **131**–41
llama [lä/mə] **135**–26
loading dock [lō/dĭng däk/] **146**–16
load the washer [lōd/ dhə wä/shər, –wö/–] **72**–C
loaf [lōf(/–)] **56**–10
...of bread [–əv brĕd/] **56**–22
loafers [lō/fərz] **68**–19
loan [lōn] **35**–I
Lobby [läb/ē] **37**
lobby [läb/ē] **145**–3
lobster [läb/stər] **53**–23
local call [lō/kəl köl/] **9**–4
lock [läk] **101**–E
lock [läk] (house) **37**–29, **48**–6, (car) **109**–34
lockers [läk/ərz] **5**–7
locket [läk/ət] **69**–33
locksmith [läk/smĭth/] **48**–11
logs [lögz, lägz] **42**–12
lonely [lōn/lē] **30**–18
long [löng(/–)] **23**–3, **71**–34
...underwear [–ŭn/dər wër/] **67**–11
long-distance call [löng/dĭs/təns köl/] **9**–5
long-sleeved shirt [löng/slēvd/ shürt/] **71**–31
look at [lōōk/ ăt/, –ət] **111**–K, **141**–B
look for [lōōk/ för/] / [lōōk/ fər]
...a help wanted sign [–ə hĕlp/ wän/təd sīn/, –wön/–] **141**–C
...a new apartment [–ə nōō/ ə pärt/mənt] **35**–A
...the emergency exit
[–dhē ĭ mür/jən sē ĕg/zət, –ĕk/sət] **111**–J
look in [lōōk/ ĭn]
...the classifieds [–dhə klăs/ə fīdz/] **141**–D
...throat [–thrōt/] **85**–E
look up a word [lōōk/ ŭp ə würd/] **6**–A
loose [lōōs] **71**–42
lose [lōōz] **158** ✦
lost child [löst/ chīld/] **102**–1
loud [lowd] **11**–11
loungewear [lownj/wër/] **67** ✦
love [lŭv(/–)] **30**–19
...seat [–sēt/] **42**–25
low [lō] **71**–46
LPN (licensed practical nurse)
[ĕl/pē/ĕn/] / [lī/sənst präk/tĭ kəl nürs/] **87**–24

luggage [lŭg/ĭj]
...carrier [–kăr/ē ər] **110**–19
...cart [–kärt/] **145**–6
lug wrench [lŭg/ rĕnch/] **109**–50
lumber [lŭm/bər] **149**–17, **151**
lunar eclipse [lōō/nər ĭ klĭps/] **127** ✦
lunch [lŭnch(/–)] **61**
...benches [–bĕn/chəz] **5**–5
lung [lŭng] **75**–37
LVN (licensed vocational nurse)
[ĕl/vē/ĕn] / [lī/sənst vō kā/shə nəl nürs/]**87**–24
machine [mə shēn/]
...operator [–äp/ə rā tər] **138**–37
...screw [–skrōō/] **150**–27
magazine [măg/ə zēn/, măg/ə zēn/] **98**–7
...holder [–hōl/dər] **42**–22
magnet [măg/nət] **119**–21
magnolia [măg nōl/yə] **128**–9
mailbox [māl/bäks/] **38**–4, **90**–12
mailboxes [māl/bäk/səz] **37**–36
mailer [mā/lər] **143**–32
mailing address [mā/lĭng ə drĕs/, –ă/drĕs] **96**–8
mail [māl/ ĭt] **96**–B
main office [mān/ ö/fəs] **5**–17
make [māk] **106** ✦
make [māk(/–)]
...a deposit [–ə dĭ päz/ət] **97**–C
...an appointment [–ən ə poynt/mənt] **85**–A
...an offer [–ən ö/fər] **35**–H
...a toast [–ə tōst/] **33**–I
...a wish [–ə wĭsh/] **169**–J
...copies [–käp/ēz] **142**–E
...lunch [–lŭnch/] **26**–F
...the bed [–dhə bĕd/] **46**–G
make sure you understand
[māk/ shōōr/ yōō ŭn/dər stănd/] **8**–E
male [māl] **4**–13
MALL [möl] **92**–93
mallet [măl/ət] **150**–2
MAMMALS [măm/əlz] **134**–135
Mammals, Sea [sē/ măm/əlz] **131**
man [măn] **22**–11
manager [măn/ĭ jər] **35**–B, **36**–12, **54**–8, **143**–25
mane [mān] **135**–49
mangoes [măng/gōz] **50**–21
mantel [măn/təl] **42**–8
manual [măn/yōō əl] **144**–22
manual labor [măn/yōō əl lā/bər] **140**–D
manufacture [măn/yə făk/chər] **146**–B
map [măp] **3**–12
maple [mā/pəl] **128**–13
March [märch] **19**–27
margarine [mär/jər ən] **54**–39
marigold [mär/ə gōld/] **129**–13
MARINE LIFE, AMPHIBIANS, AND REPTILES
[mə rēn/ līf/ ăm fĭb/ē ənz ən rĕp/tīlz] **130**–131
mark [märk] **7**–T
marker [mär/kər] **3**–19
MARKET [mär/kət] **54**–55
market [mär/kət] **89**–20
marriage license [mär/ĭj lī/səns] **29**–8
married [mär/ēd] **25**–23, **28**–L
Mars [märz] **127**–6
martial arts [mär/shəl ärts/] **159**–10
mascara [mă skăr/ə] **77**–38

mashed potatoes [măsht/ pə tā/tōz] **61**–11
mask [măsk] **168**–12
masking tape [măs/kĭng tāp/] **151**–49
Master's degree [măs/tərz də grē/] **112** ✦
match [măch] **7**–X
matches [măch/əz] **154**–21
maternity dress [mə tür/nə tē drĕs/] **65**–19
maternity shop [mə tür/nə tē shäp/] **93**–17
MATHEMATICS [măth/ə măt/ĭks] **118**
mattress [mă/trəs] **44**–25
May [mā] **19**–29
mayonnaise [mā/ə nāz/, mā/ə nāz/] **60**–25
meadow [mĕd/ō] **117**–20
measles [mē/zəlz] **79**–5
measure [mĕzh/ər] **15** ✦, **149**–C
Measurement [mĕzh/ər mənt] **15**
MEASUREMENTS [mĕzh/ər mənts] **14**–15
MEASURES [mĕzh/ərz] **57**
measure the ingredients [mĕzh/ər dhē ĭn grē/dē ənts] **57**–A
MEAT AND POULTRY [mēt/ n pōl/trē] **52**
meat and poultry section [mēt/ n pōl/trē sĕk/shən] **54**–2
media section [mē/dē ə sĕk/shən]**98**–11
medical [mĕd/ĭ kəl]
...charts [–chärts/] **87**–20
...emergency bracelet [–ĭ mür/jən sē brās/lət] **83**–14
...waste disposal [–wāst/ dĭ spō/zəl] **86**–14
MEDICAL AND DENTAL EXAMS
[mĕd/ĭ kəl ən dĕn/təl ĭg zămz/]**85**
Medical clinic [mĕd/ĭ kəl klĭn/ĭk] **84**
MEDICAL CONDITIONS [mĕd/ĭ kəl kən dĭsh/ənz]**79**
Medical conditions and serious diseases
[mĕd/ĭ kəl kən dĭsh/ənz ən sïr/ē əs dĭ zē/zəz] **79**
MEDICAL EMERGENCIES [mĕd/ĭ kəl ĭ mür/jən sēz] **82**
medication [mĕd/ə kā/shən] **80**–11, 12
...tray [–trā/] **87**–23
medicine cabinet [mĕd/ə sən kăb/ə nət] **43**–19
medium [mē/dē əm] **70**–3
meeting room [mē/tĭng rōōm/] **145**–19
memory [mĕm/ə rē] **144** ✦
men's store [mĕnz/ stör/] **90** ✦
menu [mĕn/yōō] **62**–3
MENU, COFFEE SHOP [kö/fē shäp/ mĕn/yōō] **61**
merchandise [mür/chən dīz/, –dīs/]**152**–24
Mercury [mür/kyə rē] **127**–9
messenger [mĕs/ən jər] **138**–38
messy [mĕs/ē]**11**–16
meter [mē/tər](measurement) **15**, (taxi) **104**–21
meter [mē/tər] / [–mē/tər]
gas... [găs/–]**48**–14
parking... [pär/kĭng–]**91**–18
mice [mīs] **49**–26
microcassette transcriber [mī/krō kə sĕt/ trăn skrī/bər] **142**–4
microfilm [mī/krə fĭlm/] **98**–5
microfilm reader [mī/krə fĭlm rē/dər] **98**–4
microphone [mī/krə fōn/] **164**–4
microscope [mī/krə skōp/] **119**–4
microwave oven [mī/krə wāv/ ŭv/ən] **40**–13
middle-aged [mĭd/l ājd/] **22**–14
middle initial [mĭd/l ĭ nĭsh/əl]**4**–3
middle school [mĭd/l skōōl/] **112**–6
midnight [mĭd/nīt/] **17**–21
midsize car [mĭd/sīz/ kär/] **106**–3
mile [mīl]**15** ✦
milk [mĭlk]**148**–C
milk [mĭlk(/–)] **54**–35

Index

...shake   [–shāk/] **60**–12
milliliters   [mĭl/ə lē/tərz] **57** ✦
million   [mĭl/yən] **14**
miniblinds   [mĭn/ē blīndz/] **43**–11
minivan   [mĭn/ē văn/] **106**–10
minute   [mĭn/ət] **16**–2
mirror   [mĭr/ər] **43**–18, **44**–1
   rearview...   [rĭr/vyōō/–] **108**–1
   sideview...   [sīd/vyōō/–] **108**–8
missing   [mĭs/ĭng] **70**–25
miss the bus   [mĭs/ dhə bŭs/] **104** ✦
mistake   [mĭ stāk/] **7**–2
mittens   [mĭt/nz] **66**–9
mix   [mĭks] **58**–K
mixing bowl   [mĭk/sĭng bōl/] **59**–31
mobile   [mō/bēl] **45**–4
mobile home   [mō/bəl hōm/] **34**–8
model (occupation)   [mäd/l] **138**–39
model (hobby)   [mäd/l] **106** ✦
   ...kit   [–kĭt/] **162**–7
   ...trains   [–trānz/] **163**–32
models   [mäd/lz] **162**–C
modem   [mō/dəm, –dĕm] **144**–11
moisturizer   [moys/chə rī/zər] **76**–8
molecule   [mäl/ĭ kyōōl/] **119**–18
Monday   [mŭn/dā, –dē] **18**–2
MONEY   [mŭn/ē] **20**
money order   [mŭn/ē ör/dər] **20**–16
monitor   [män/ə tər] **144**–6
monitors   [män/ə tərs] **110**–4
monkey   [mŭng/kē] **135**–27
month   [mŭnth] **4**–16, **18**–9
monthly statement   [mŭnth/lē stāt/mənt] **97**–10
Months of the year   [mŭnths/ əv dhə yïr/] **19**
moon   [mōōn] **127**–13, 14, 15, 16
moose   [mōōs] **134**–1
mop   [mäp] **46**–J
mop   [(–)mäp(/)]
   dust...   [dŭst/–] **47**–17
   wet...   [wĕt/–] **47**–16
MORE SCHOOL SUBJECTS   [mör/ skōōl/ sŭb/jĭkts] **121**
morning   [mör/nĭng] **17**–16
mosque   [mäsk] **89**–23
mosquito   [mə skē/tō] **132**–23
motel   [mō tĕl/] **89**–22
moth   [möth] **132**–22
mother   [mŭdh/ər] **24**–5, **25**–25
motherboard   [mŭdh/ər börd/] **144**–18
mother-in-law   [mŭdh/ər ĭn lö/] **24**–13
motorcycle   [mō/tər sī/kəl] **91**–19
mountain   [mown/tn]
   ...biking   [–bī/kĭng] **154**–8
   ...lion   [lī/ən] **134**–2
   ...peak   [–pēk/] **117**–14
   ...range   [–rānj/] **117**–15
   ...time   [–tīm/] **17**–27
mouse   [mows] (animal) **133**–17, (computer) **144**–8
mouth   [mowth] **74**–22
mouthwash   [mowth/wäsh/, –wösh/] **77**–23
move   [mōōv] **29**–P
move in   [mōōv/ ĭn/] **35**–D
Movement   [mōōv/mənt] **115**
mover   [mōō/vər] **138**–40
movie   [mōō/vē] **166**–1
movies   [mōō/vēz] **152**–10

movie theater   [mōō/vē thē/ə tər] **88**–11
moving van   [mōō/vĭng văn/] **106**–14
mow   [mō] **39**–C
mudslide   [mŭd/slīd/] **102**–6
muffin   [mŭf/ən] **60**–14
muffler   [mŭf/lər] (clothing) **66**–4, (car part) **108**–11
mug   [mŭg] **41**–28
mugging   [mŭg/ĭng] **100**–5
multiplication   [mŭl/tə plə kā/shən] **118**–3
multi-use knife   [mŭl/tē yōōs/ nīf/, mŭl/tī–] **154**–20
mumps   [mŭmps] **79**–7
murder   [mür/dər] **100**–8
muscle   [mŭs/əl] **75**–48
mushrooms   [mŭsh/rōōmz/] **51**–26
MUSIC   [myōō/zĭk] **120**
musician   [myōō zĭsh/ən] **138**–41
music store   [myōō/zĭk stör/] **92**–1
mussel   [mŭs/əl] **130**–17
mussels   [mŭs/əlz] **53**–26
mustache   [mŭs/tăsh] **23**–5
mustard   [mŭs/tərd] **60**–24
mystery   [mĭs/tə rē] **166**–15
nachos   [nä/chōz] **60**–10
nail (hardware)   [nāl] **150**–29
nail (body)   [nāl(/–)]
   ...clipper   [–klĭp/ər] **77**–29
   ...polish   [–päl/ĭsh] **77**–31
   ...polish remover   [–päl/ĭsh rĭ mōō/vər] **77**–32
   ...salon   [–sə län/] **91**–25
name   [nām] **4**–1, 2, 3, 4, A, C, D
napkin   [năp/kĭn] **41**–19, **63**–23
narrow   [năr/ō] **71**–45
nasal congestion   [nā/zəl kən jĕs/chən] **78**–7
nasal spray   [nā/zəl sprā/] **81**–23
NATURAL DISASTERS
   [năch/rəl dĭ zăs/tərz, năch/ər əl–] **102–103**
natural gas   [năch/rəl găs/, năch/ər əl–] **126**–3
nature program   [nā/chər prō/grăm] **167**–22
near   [nïr] **13** ✦
neat   [nēt] **11**–15
neck   [nĕk] **74**–2
necklaces   [nĕk/lə səz] **69**–9
need   [nēd] **109**–(54–59)
needle   [nēd/l] (sewing) **73**–22, (pine) **128**–12
neighbor   [nā/bər] **37**–22
neighborhood   [nā/bər hōōd/] **90** ✦
Neighborhood Watch
   [nā/bər hōōd/ wäch/, –wöch/] **101** ✦
nephew   [nĕf/yōō] **24**–18
Neptune   [nĕp/tōōn] **127**–2
nerve   [nürv] **75**–50
nervous   [nür/vəs] **30**–11
nest   [nĕst] **132**–5
new   [nōō(/–)] **71**–32
   ...moon   [–mōōn/] **127**–13
Newfoundland time   [nōō/fən lənd tīm/, –fənd–] **17**–31
news   [nōōz] **167**–17
newspaper   [nōōz/pā/pər] **98**–8
newsstand   [nōōz/stănd/] **90**–11
newt   [nōōt] **130**–26
New Year's Day   [nōō/ yïrz/ dā/] **168**–1
next to   [nĕkst/ tōō, –tə] **13**–1, 2
next week   [nĕkst/ wēk/] **18**–20
nickel   [nĭk/əl] **20**–2
niece   [nēs] **24**–17

Index

night [nīt] **17**–20
nightgown [nīt**/**gown**/**] **67**–5
night-light [nīt**/**līt**/**] **45**–3
nightshirt [nīt**/**shürt**/**] **67**–9
night table [nīt**/** tā/bəl] **44**–21
nine [nīn] **14**
nineteen [nīn/tēn**/**] **14**
nineteenth [nīn/tēnth**/**] **14**
nineteen-year-old [nīn/tēn/yïr ōld**/**] **22**–8
ninety [nīn/tē] **14**
ninth [nīnth] **14**
nipple [nĭp/əl] **95**–27
noisy children [noy/zē chĭl/drən] **11**–11
nonfiction [nän/fĭk/shən] **98** ✦
noon [nōōn] **17**–17
no outlet [nō**/** owt/lĕt, –lət] **107**–8
no parking [nō**/** pär/kĭng] **107**–12
north [nörth] **107, 123, 124**
NORTH AMERICA AND CENTRAL AMERICA
    [nörth**/** ə mĕr/ə kə ən sĕn/trəl ə mĕr/ə kə] **122**–123
nose [nōz] **74**–21
not [nät(**/**–)]
    ...guilty [–gĭl/tē] **99**
    ...ripe [–rīp] **50**–28
notebook [nōt/bŏŏk**/**] **3**–24
    ...paper [–pā/pər] **3**–25
note pad [nōt**/** pắd**/**] **143**–36
November [nō vĕm/bər] **19**–35
nuclear energy [nōō/klē ər ĕn/ər jē] **126**–8
numbers [nŭm/bərz] **3**–31
NUMBERS AND MEASUREMENTS
    [nŭm/bərz ən mĕzh/ər mənts] **14–15**
nurse [nürs] **94**–C
nurse [nürs(**/**–)] **84**–10, **87**–22, 24, 29, ✦, **138**–42, ✦
    ...midwife [–mĭd/wīf**/**] **86** ✦
    ...practitioner [–prăk tĭsh/ə nər] **86** ✦
Nurse's station [nür/səz stā/shən] **87**
nursing home [nür/sĭng hōm**/**] **34**–11
nut (hardware) [nŭt] **150**–31
nuts (food) [nŭts] **50**–23
nylon [nī/län] **70**–19
oak [ōk] **128**–18
obey the law [ō bā**/** dhə lö**/**] **116**–H
oboe [ō/bō] **120**–5
observatory [əb zür/və tör/ē] **127**–19
observe [əb zürv**/**] **119**–B
obstetrician [äb/stə trĭsh/ən] **86**–1
OCCUPATIONS (A-H) [äk/yə pā/shənz] **136–137**
OCCUPATIONS (H-W) [äk/yə pā/shənz] **138–139**
ocean [ō/shən] **117**–6, **155**–1
o'clock [ə kläk**/**] **16**–4
October [äk tō/bər] **19**–34
octopus [äk/tə pəs] **130**–4
odometer [ō däm/ə tər] **108**–21
off [öf] **105**–7
OFFICE [ö/fəs] **142–143**
Office [ö/fəs] **37**
office [ö/fəs] **5**–13, 15, 17, **146**–1
    ...building [–bĭl/dĭng] **89**–24
    ...manager [–măn/ĭ jər] **143**–25
official [ə fĭsh/əl] **158**–6
oil (cooking) [oyl] **55**–49, **57**–2
oil (petroleum) [oyl(**/**–)] **109**–55, **126**–6
    ...gauge [–gāj**/**] **108**–19
    ...paint [–pānt/] **163**–24

...spill [–spĭl**/**] **126**–15
ointment [oynt/mənt] **81**–24, **83**–9
old [ōld] **71**–33
on [än, ön] **13**–8
    ...the left [–dhə lĕft**/**] **13**–1
    ...the right [–dhə rīt**/**] **13**–2
once a week [wŭns/ə wēk**/**] **18**–22
one [wŭn(**/**–)] **14, 15**–1, 2, 3, 4, 5, 11, **16**–4, 15, **20**–1, 12
    ...o'clock [–ə kläk**/**] **16**–4
    ...way [–wā**/**] **107**–6
one billion [wŭn**/** bĭl/yən] **14**
one-eighth [wŭn**/** ātth**/**, –āth**/**] **15**–1
one-fifteen [wŭn**/** fĭf/tēn**/**] **16**–7
one-fifty [wŭn**/** fĭf/tē] **16**–14
one-forty [wŭn**/** för/tē] **16**–12
one-fourth [wŭn**/** förth**/**] **15**–2
one-half [wŭn**/** hăf**/**] **15**–4
one-hundred percent [wŭn**/** hŭn/drəd pər sĕnt**/**] **15**–11
one-oh-five [wŭn**/** ō fīv**/**] **16**–5
one-ten [wŭn**/** tĕn**/**] **16**–6
one-third [wŭn**/** thürd**/**] **15**–3
one-thirty [wŭn**/** thür/tē] **16**–10
one-twenty [wŭn**/** twĕn/tē] **16**–8
onions [ŭn/yənz] **51**–28, **58**–G, H
online catalog [än/līn**/** kăt/l ög**/**, –äg**/**, ön**/**–] **98**–9
on time [än**/** tīm**/**, ön**/**–] **17** ✦
onto [än/tōō, –tə, ön**/**–] **105**–6
open [ō/pən] **2**–I
    ...the presents [–dhə prĕz/ənts] **169**–L
    don't... [dōnt**/**–] **101**–F
opera [äp/rə] **166**–8
operate heavy machinery
    [äp/ə rāt**/** hĕv/ē mə shē/nə rē] **140**–F
Operating room [äp/ə rā/tĭng rōōm**/**] **87**
operating table [äp/ə rā/tĭng tā/bəl] **87**–34
Operations (math) [äp/ə rā/shənz] **118**
operator [äp/ə rā/tər] **9**–7
ophthalmologist [äf/thəl mäl/ə jĭst, –thə mäl**/**–, äp/–] **86**–7
opossum [ə päs/əm, päs/əm] **134**–4
optician [äp tĭsh/ən] **92**–8
optometrist [äp täm/ə trĭst] **81**–34
orange [ör/ənj, är**/**–] **12**–6
oranges [ör/ən jəz, är**/**–] **50**–10
orangutan [ə răng/ə tăng**/**, –tăn**/**] **135**–40
orbit [ör/bət] **127**–11
orchard [ör/chərd] **148**–16
orchestra [ör/kə strə] **120**–1
orchid [ör/kĭd] **129**–17
order [ör/dər] **62**–D
orderly [ör/dər lē] **87**–18
order puller [ör/dər pŏŏl/ər] **146**–10
Ordinals [ör/dn əlz, örd/nəlz] **14**
organ [ör/gən] **120**–22
organizer [ör/gə nī/zər] **143**–30
ornament [ör/nə mənt] **168**–19
orthodontist [ör/thə dän/tĭst] **84**–23
orthopedist [ör/thə pē/dĭst] **81**–28
Other instruments [ŭdh/ər ĭn/strə mənts] **120**
otter [ät/ər] **131**–35
ounce [owns] **57**–11
out [owt(**/**–)] **48**–2
    ...of focus [–əv fō/kəs] **165**–33
    ...of the taxi [–əv dhə tăk/sē] **105**–5
OUTDOOR RECREATION [owt/dör rĕk/rē ā/shən] **154**
outfit [owt/fĭt] **64** ✦

outlet [owt/lĕt, –lət] **44**–20, **107**–8, **151**–41
oval [ō/vəl] **118**–9
oven [ŭv/ən] **40**–20, **46**–C, **47**–3
  …cleaner [–klē/nər] **47**–3
  microwave…[mī/krə wāv/–] **40**–13
over [ō/vər] **105**–2
overalls [ō/vər ölz/] **65**–21
overcoat [ō/vər kōt/] **66**–2
overdose [ō/vər dōs/, ō/vər dōs/] **82**–K
overdrawn account [ō/vər drön/ ə kownt/] **97** ✦
overexposed [ō/vər ĭk spōzd/] **165**–34
overflowing [ō/vər flō/ĭng] **49**–17
overhead [ō/vər hĕd/]
  …compartment [–kəm pärt/mənt] **110**–10
  …projector [–prə jĕk/tər] **2**–4
overjoyed [ō/vər joyd/] **30** ✦
overnight mail [ō/vər nīt/ māl/] **96**–15
over-the-counter medication
  [ō/vər dhə kown/tər mĕd/ə kā/shən] **80**–12
owl [owl] **132**–6
owner [ō/nər] **139**–56
oxfords [äks/fərdz] **68**–20
oxygen mask [äk/sĭ jən mäsk/] **110**–14
oysters [oy/stərz] **53**–27
Pacific time [pə sĭf/ĭk tīm/] **17**–26
pacifier [päs/ə fī/ər] **95**–29
package [pȁk/ĭj] **56**–8, **96**–5
  …of cookies [–əv kook/ēz] **56**–20
PACKAGED FOODS [pȁk/ĭjd foodz/] **56**
packer [pȁk/ər] **146**–13
packing tape [pȁk/ĭng tāp/] **143**–42
pager [pā/jər] **9**–16
pail [pāl] **45**–13, **47**–20, **155**–22
pain [pān(/–)]
  …reliever [–rĭ lē/vər] **81**–16
paint [pānt] **149**–A, **163**–E
paint [pānt(/–)] / [–pānt/] **151**–20
  …pan [–pȁn/] **151**–45
  …roller [–rō/lər] **151**–46
  acrylic… [ə krĭl/ĭk–] **162**–47
paintbrush [pānt/brŭsh/] **151**–9, **163**–23
painter [pān/tər] **138**–43
painting [pān/tĭng] **42**–7, **152**–8
pair of scissors [për/ əv sĭz/ərz] **73**–18
paisley [pāz/lē] **70**–13
pajamas [pə jä/məz, –jä/–] **67**–4
palm [päm] (hand) **75**–59, (tree) **128**–15
pan [pȁn] **40**–24, **59**–5, 13, 26, 28
pancakes [pȁn/kāks/] **61**–6
pancreas [pȁng/krē əs] **75**–46
panda [pȁn/də] **135**–41
panther [pȁn/thər] **135**–39
panties [pȁn/tēz] **67**–16
pants [pȁnts] **64**–8
pantyhose [pȁn/tē hōz/] **67**–27
papayas [pə pī/əz] **50**–20
paper [pā/pər] (composition) **113**–2
paper [pā/pər] / [–pā/pər]
  …bag [–bȁg/] **55**–22
  …clip [–klĭp/] **143**–44
  …cutter [–kŭt/ər] **143**–15
  …doll [–däl/] **163**–30
  …products [–präd/ŭkts] **55**–14
  …shredder [–shrĕd/ər] **143**–24
  …towels [–tow/əlz] **40**–2, **56**–23

notebook… [nōt/book/–] **3**–24, 25, 26
parade [pə rād/] **168**–2
paragraph [pȁr/ə grȁf/] **113**–5
parakeet [pȁr/ə kēt/] **133**–15
parallel [pȁr/ə lĕl/] **118**–21
parcel post [pär/səl pōst/] **96**–14
parent [për/ənt] **94**–1
parents [për/ənts] **24**–4
paring knife [për/ĭng nīf/] **59**–16
park [pärk] **91**–D
park [pärk] **88**–8
parka [pär/kə] **66**–8
PARK AND PLAYGROUND [pärk/ ən plā/grownd/] **153**
parking [pär/kĭng]
  …garage [–gə räzh/, –räj/] **89**–26
  …meter [–mē/tər] **91**–18
  …space [–spās/] **36**–15, **90**–5
parochial school [pə rō/kē əl skool/] **112**–3
parsley [pär/slē] **51**–10
part [pärt] **23**–4
partner [pärt/nər] **6**–J
parts [pärts] **146**–7
Parts of a bird [pärts/ əv ə bürd/] **132**
PARTS OF A CAR AND CAR MAINTENANCE
  [pärts/ əv ə kär/ ən kär/ mān/tn əns] **108**–**109**
Parts of a circle [pärts/ əv ə sür/kəl] **118**
Parts of a fish [pärts/ əv ə fĭsh/] **130**
Parts of a flower [pärts/ əv ə flow/ər] **129**
Parts of a square [pärts/ əv ə skwër/] **118**
Parts of a tree [pärts/ əv ə trē/] **128**
PARTY [pär/tē] **169**
Party [pär/tē] **33**
pass [pȁs] **156**–H
passbook [pȁs/book/] **97**–5
passenger [pȁs/ən jər] **104**–7, **110**–23
pass out [pȁs/ owt/] **7**–O
passport [pȁs/pört/] **29**–9
pasta [päs/tə] **61**–15
  …salad [–sȁl/əd] **53**–15
pastrami [pə strä/mē] **53**–6
patient [pā/shənt] **84**–3
Patient's room [pā/shənts room/] **86**
patio [pȁt/ē ō] **39**–6
  …furniture [–für/nĭ chər] **39**–5
patron [pā/trən] **62**–5
pattern (clothes) [pȁt/ərn] **73**–8
pattern maker [pȁt/ərn mā/kər] **73** ✦
Patterns (fabric) [pȁt/ərnz] **70**
pause [pöz] **165**–E
paw [pö] **134**–42
pay [pā(/–)]
  …taxes [–tȁk/səz] **116**–E
  …the check [–dhə chĕk/] **62**–I
  …the mortgage [–dhə mör/gĭj] **35**–L
  …the rent [–dhə rĕnt/] **35**–F
pay phone [pā/ fōn] **9**–11
pay back [pā/ bȁk/] **20** ✦
pay for [pā/ för/, –fər] **21**–C
PE (physical education) [pē/ē] / [fĭz/ĭ kəl ĕj/ə kā/shən]
  121–11
peaches [pē/chəz] **50**–5
peacock [pē/käk/] **132**–15
peak [pēk] **117**–14
pearls [pürlz] **69**–30
pears [përz] **50**–6

peas [pēz] **51**–19
pedestrian [pə dĕs/trē ən] **90**–7
  ...crossing [–krö/sĭng] **107**–10
pediatrician [pē/dē ə trĭsh/ən] **86**–4
peel [pēl] **58**–N
peephole [pēp/hōl/] **37**–27
pelvis [pĕl/vəs] **75**–55
pen [pĕn] **3**–18
pencil [pĕn/səl] **3**–20
  ...eraser [–ĭ rā/sər] **3**–21
  ...sharpener [–shär/pə nər] **3**–13, **142**–9
penguin [pĕng/wĭn] **132**–12
peninsula [pə nĭn/sə lə] **117**–7
penny [pĕn/ē] **20**–1
peppers [pĕp/ərz] **51**–7
pepper shaker [pĕp/ər shā/kər] **41**–15
Percents [pər sĕnts/] **15**
Percussion [pər kŭsh/ən] **120**
perfume [pür/fyoom/, pər fyoom/] **76**–5
period [pïr/ē əd] **113**–6
periodical section [pïr/ē äd/ĭ kəl sĕk/shən] **98**–6
perm hair [pürm/ hër/] **23**–B
perpendicular [pür/pən dĭk/yə lər] **118**–20
personal check [pür/sə nəl chĕk/] **20**–14
PERSONAL HYGIENE [pür/sə nəl hī/jēn] **76**–**77**
personal identification number (PIN)
  [pür/sə nəl ī dĕn/tə fə kā/shən nŭm/bər] **97**–B
PERSONAL INFORMATION [pür/sə nəl ĭn/fər mā/shən] **4**
personal radio-cassette player
  [pür/sə nəl rā/dē ō kə sĕt/ plā/ər] **164**–15
pesticide [pĕs/tə sīd/] **49** ✦
  ...poisoning [–poy/zə nĭng] **126**–14
pet [pĕt(/–)]
  ...food [–food/] **54**–10
  ...store [–stör/] **92**–6
petal [pĕt/l] **129**–8
petri dish [pē/trē dĭsh/] **119**–6
petroleum [pə trō/lē əm] **126**–6
Pets [pĕts] **133**
pharmacist [fär/mə sĭst] **80**–10
pharmacy [fär/mə sē] **80**–9, **90**–2
Phillips screwdriver [fĭl/ĭps skroo/drī/vər] **150**–26
phone [fōn(/–)] **9**–1
  ...card [–kärd/] **9**–10
photo [fō/tō]
  ...album [–ăl/bəm] **165**–32
  ...shop [–shäp/] **90**–4
photocopier [fō/tə käp/ē ər] **142**–14
photograph [fō/tə grăf/] **44**–7
photographer [fə täg/rə fər] **32**–11
PHOTOGRAPHY [fə täg/rə fē] **164**–**165**
PHYSICAL DESCRIPTION [fĭz/ĭ kəl dĭ skrĭp/shən] **22**
physically challenged [fĭz/ĭ klē chăl/ənjd] **22**–25
physical therapist [fĭz/ĭ kəl thër/ə pĭst] **81**–30
physics [fĭz/ĭks] **119**–3
pi (π) [pī] **118** ✦
piano [pē ăn/ō] **120**–16
pickax [pĭk/ăks/] **149**–20
pick up [pĭk/ ŭp/] / [pĭk/ ŭp/–] **94**–G
  ...the children [–dhə chĭl/drən] **27**–O
  ...the receiver [–dhə rĭ sē/vər] **9**–A
pickup truck [pĭk/ŭp trŭk/] **106**–7
picnic [pĭk/nĭk] **153**–D
picnic table [pĭk/nĭk tā/bəl] **153**–8
picture [pĭk/chər]

...book [–book/] **45**–17
...dictionary [–dĭk/shə nër ē] **3**–29
pie [pī(/–)] **61**–21
  ...pan [–păn/] **59**–28
pier [pïr] **155**–16
pierced earrings [pïrst/ ïr/ĭngz] **69**–37
pig [pĭg] **133**–8
pigeon [pĭj/ən] **132**–16
pill [pĭl] **81**–26
pillow [pĭl/ō] **42**–20, **44**–9
pillowcase [pĭl/ō kās/] **44**–10
pilot [pī/lət] **110**–12
PIN (personal identification number) [pĭn] **97**–B
pin [pĭn] (jewelry) **69**–36, (sewing) **73**–14
pin [pĭn(/–)] / [–pĭn/]
  ...cushion [–koosh/ən] **73**–15
  push... [poosh/–] **143**–43
pine [pīn] **128**–10
pinecone [pīn/kōn/] **128**–11
pineapples [pī/năp/əlz] **50**–2
Ping-Pong [pĭng/päng/, –pöng/] **159**–13
pink [pĭngk] **12**–10
pint [pīnt] **57**–3
pipe [pīp(/–)] **151**–16
  ...wrench [–rĕnch/] **151**–43
pipes [pīps] **49**–19
pitch [pĭch] **156**–F
pizza [pēt/sə] **60**–7
place [plās(/–)]
  ...mat [–măt/] **41**–20
  ...setting [–sĕt/ĭng] **63**–14
place of birth [plās/ əv bürth/] **4**–17
PLACES TO GO [plā/səz tə gō/] **152**
PLACES TO LIVE [plā/səz tə lĭv/] **34**
plaid [plăd] **70**–9
plain [plān] **71**–38
plains [plānz] **117**–19
plan [plăn] **169**–A
plane (tool) [plān] **151**–52
PLANE TRIP [plān/ trĭp/] **111**
Planets [plăn/əts] **127**
plant [plănt] **39**–D, **148**–A
plant [plănt] **39**–B, **42**–18
PLANTS [plănts] **128**
plastic [plăs/tĭk] **70**
  ...bag [–băg/] **55**–23
  ...storage container [–stör/ĭj kən tā/nər] **59**–3
  ...wrap [–răp/] **55**–54
plate [plāt] **41**–24, **63**–15, 16, 17
platform [plăt/förm/] **104**–15
platter [plăt/ər] **41**–3
platypus [plăt/ĭ pəs, –poos/] **135**–46
play [plā(/–)] **94**–K, **165**–B
  ...an instrument [–ən ĭn/strə mənt] **120**–A
  ...cards [–kärdz/] **163**–H
  ...games [–gāmz/] **162**–C
play [plā] **166**–2
player [plā/ər] **158**–5, **164**–2, 14, 15
PLAYGROUND [plā/grownd/] **153**
playground [plā/grownd/] **36**–6
playpen [plā/pĕn/] **95**–11
pliers [plī/ərz] **150**–7
plug [plŭg] **164**–18
plumber [plŭm/ər] **49**–20
plums [plŭmz] **50**–8

plunger [plŭn/jər] **151**–44
Pluto [plōō/tō] **127**–1
plywood [plī/wŏŏd/] **149**–16
p.m. [pē/ĕm/] **16**
pneumatic drill [nŏŏ măt/ĭk drĭl/] **149**–9
pocket [päk/ət] **73**–4
podium [pō/dē əm] **32**–5
poinsettia [poyn sĕt/ē ə, –sĕt/ə] **129**–23
point [poynt] **2**–F
poison [poy/zən] **82**–J, **147**–3
...ivy [–ī/vē] **128**–25
...oak [–ōk/] **128**–23
...sumac [–sōō/măk, –shōō/–] **128**–24
police [pə lēs/]
...officer [–ö/fə sər] **99**–1, **138**–44
...station [–stā/shən] **89**–19
polish [päl/ĭsh]
...nails [–nālz/] **77**–O
...the furniture [–dhə für/nĭ chər] **46**–K
polka-dotted [pō/kə dät/əd] **70**–8
Pollution [pə lōō/shən] **126**
polyester [päl/ē ĕs/tər, päl/ē ĕs/tər] **70**
poncho [pän/chō] **66**–18
pond [pänd] **117**–21, **153**–6
pool (game) [pōōl] **159**–2
pool (swimming) [pōōl(/–)] **37**–16, **145**–16
...service [–sür/vəs] **145**–17
porch light [pörch/ līt/] **38**–9
porcupine [pör/kyə pīn/] **134**–10
Pork [pörk] **52**
pork chops [pörk/ chäps/] **52**–10
porpoise [pör/pəs] **131**–31
port [pört] **144**–17
portable [pör/tə bəl]
...radio-cassette player [–rā/dē ō kə sĕt/ plā/ər] **164**–2
...TV [–tē/vē/] **164**–7
postage [pō/stĭj] **96**–10
postal [pō/stəl]
...scale [–skāl/] **143**–16
...worker [–wür/kər] **138**–45
postcard [pōst/kärd/] **96**–3
Post-it notes [pōst/ĭt nōts/] **143**–34
postmark [pōst/märk/] **96**–9
post office [pōst/ ö/fəs] **89**–29
pot [pät(/–)] **40**–16, **59**–6
...holders [–hōl/dərz] **59**–29
potato [pə tā/tō]
...chips [–chĭps/] **55**–40
...salad [–săl/əd] **53**–13
potatoes [pə tā/tōz] **51**–21, **61**–11
potty seat [pät/ē sēt/] **95**–10
pouch [powch] **135**–50
POULTRY [pōl/trē] **52**
poultry section [pōl/trē sĕk/shən] **54**–2
pound [pownd] **57**–12
pour [pör(/–)]
...the eggs into the pan [–dhē ĕgz/ ĭn/tə dhə pän/] **58**–D
...the water [–dhə wö/tər] **62**–C
power [pow/ər] **48**–2
...sander [–săn/dər] **150**–9
...switch [–swĭch/] **144**–4
prairie dog [prër/ē dög/] **133**–22
pregnant [prĕg/nənt] **22**–19
PREPOSITIONS [prĕp/ə zĭsh/ənz] **13**
PREPOSITIONS OF MOTION [prĕp/ə zĭsh/ənz əv mō/shən] **105**

preschool [prē/skōōl/] **112**–4
prescription [prĭ skrĭp/shən] **80**–13
...label [–lā/bəl] **80**–14
...medication [–mĕd/ə kā/shən] **80**–11
President [prĕz/ə dənt] **116**–6
pretend [prĭ tĕnd/] **163**–G
price [prīs(/–)] **21**–6
...tag [–tăg/] **21**–1
principal [prĭn/sə pəl] **5**–14
principal's office [prĭn/sə pəlz ö/fəs] **5**–13
print [prĭnt] **4**–C
print [prĭnt] **70**–10
printer [prĭn/tər] (occupation) **138**–46, (computer) **144**–12
print shop [prĭnt/ shäp/] **91**–22
priority mail [prī ör/ə tē māl/, –är/–] **96**–12
prism [prĭz/əm] **119**–20
prison [prĭz/ən] **99**–G
private school [prī/vət skōōl/] **112**–2
Problems (clothing) [präb/ləmz] **70**
PROBLEMS, HOUSEHOLD [hows/hōld/ präb/ləmz] **48**–49
produce section [prō/dōōs sĕk/shən] **54**–11
product [präd/ŭkt] **118** ✦
program (computer) [prō/grăm] **144**–21
Programs (TV) [prō/grămz] **167**
projector [prə jĕk/tər] / [–prə jĕk/tər]
carousel slide... [kăr/ə sĕl/ slīd/–] **165**–29
overhead... [ō/vər hĕd/–] **2**–4
prosecuting attorney [präs/ĭ kyōō/tĭng ə tür/nē] **99**–10
protect your wallet [prə tĕkt/ yər wä/lət, –wö/–] **101**–D
proud [prowd] **31**–22
prunes [prōōnz] **50**–26
pruning shears [prōō/nĭng shïrz/] **39**–15
psychiatrist [sī kī/ə trĭst, sə–] **86**–6
PUBLIC SAFETY [pŭb/lĭk sāf/tē] **101**
public school [pŭb/lĭk skōōl/] **112**–1
public telephone [pŭb/lĭk tĕl/ə fōn/] **91**–21
PUBLIC TRANSPORTATION
[pŭb/lĭk trăns/pər tā/shən] **104**
pudding [pŏŏd/ĭng] **61**–20
pull [pŏŏl(/–)]
...a tooth [–ə tōōth/] **85**–M
...the wagon [–dhə wăg/ən] **153**–A
pullover sweater [pŏŏl/ō/vər swĕt/ər] **64**–11
pumps [pŭmps] **68**–16
Punctuation [pŭngk/chōō ā/shən] **113**
puppet show [pŭp/ət shō/] **152**–14
puppy [pŭp/ē] **133**–12
purple [pür/pəl] **12**–7
purses [pür/səz] **69**–6
push [pŏŏsh] **153**–B
pushpin [pŏŏsh/pĭn/] **143**–43
put away [pŏŏt/ə wā/] / [pŏŏt/ə wā/–]
...the toys [–dhə toyz/] **46**–H
...your pencil [–yər pĕn/səl] **2**–L
put in order [pŏŏt/ ĭn ör/dər] **7**–W
put on [pŏŏt/ än/, –ön/] / [pŏŏt/ än–, –ön–]
...makeup [–māk/ŭp/] **77**–P
...sunscreen [–sŭn/skrēn/] **76**–D
puzzle [pŭz/əl] **45**–22
pyramid [pïr/ə mĭd] **118**–13
quart [kwört] **57**–4
quarter [kwör/tər] (time) **16**, (money) **20**–4
quarter cup [kwör/tər kŭp/] **57**–8
quarter moon [kwör/tər mōōn/] **127**–15
question mark [kwĕs/chən märk/] **113**–7

Index

quiet [kwī/ət] **11**–12
quill [kwĭl] **134**–23
quiz show [kwĭz/ shō/] **167**–23
quotation marks [kwō tā/shən märks/] **113**–9
quotient [kwō/shənt] **118** ✦
rabbit [răb/ət] **133**–13
raccoon [ră kōōn/] **134**–13
race [rās] **157**–Y
racquetball [răk/ət böl/] **159**–11
radiation [rā/dē ā/shən] **126**–13
radiator [rā/dē ā/tər] **109**–42, 56
radio [rā/dē ō] **44**–16, **108**–31
   ...program [-prō/grăm] **166**–4
radioactive [rā/dē ō ăk/tĭv] **147**–6
radiologist [rā/dē äl/ə jĭst] **86**–5
radishes [răd/ĭ shəz] **51**–5
radius [rā/dē əs] **118**–16
rafting [răf/tĭng] **154**–4
rags [răgz] **47**–6
railroad crossing [rāl/rōd krö/sĭng] **107**–11
rain boots [rān/ bōōts/] **66**–19
raincoat [rān/kōt/] **66**–17
rain forest [rān/ för/əst, fär/–] **117**–1
raining [rā/nĭng] **10**–8
raise [rāz] **2**–A
raisins [rā/zənz] **50**–27
rake [rāk] **39**–F
rake [rāk] **39**–11
ranch [rănch] **34**–12
rancher [răn/chər] **148**–22
RANCHING [răn/chĭng] **148**
rash [răsh] **78**–10
raspberries [răz/bĕr/ēz] **50**–18
rat [răt] **133**–18
rats [răts] **49**–27
rattle [răt/l] **95**–31
rattlesnake [răt/l snāk/] **131**–38
raw [rö] **52**–24
ray [rā] **130**–6
rayon [rā/än] **70**
razor [rā/zər] **77**–25
   ...blade [–blād/] **77**–26
read [rēd] **6**–B, **27**–V, **94**–F
Realtor [rē/əl tər] **35**
rearview mirror [rĭr/vyōō/ mĭr/ər] **108**–1
receipt [rĭ sēt/] **21**–5
receive [rĭ sēv/] **96**–D
receiver [rĭ sē/vər] **9**–2
receptionist [rĭ sĕp/shə nĭst] **84**–2, **138**–47
recharging [rē chär/jĭng] **109**–58
record [rĕk/ərd] **98**–15
record [rĭ körd/] (science) **119**–C, (cassette player) **165**–A
Recreation room [rĕk/rē ā/shən rōōm/] **36**
rec room [rĕk/ rōōm/] **36** ✦
rectangle [rĕk/tăng/gəl] **118**–8
recycle [rē sī/kəl] **46**–B, **126**–A
recycling bin [rē sī/klĭng bĭn/] **47**–2
red [rĕd(/–)] **12**–13
   ...hair [–hër/] **23**–14
redwood [rĕd/wŏŏd/] **128**–1
referee [rĕf/ə rē/] **158**–6
reference [rĕf/rəns]
   ...desk [–dĕsk/] **98**–2
   ...librarian [lī brër/ē ən] **98**–1
refrigerator [rĭ frĭj/ə rā/tər] **40**–9

register [rĕj/ə stər] **116**–F
registered [rĕj/ə stərd]
   ...nurse (RN) [–nürs/] **87**–22
regular price [rĕg/yə lər prīs/] **21**–2
relax [rĭ lăks/] **27**–U
relieved [rĭ lēvd/] **30**–16
religious holiday [rĭ lĭj/əs häl/ə dā/] **19**–44
relish [rĕl/ĭsh] **60**–26
remarried [rē măr/ēd] **25**–27
remote control [rĭ mōt/ kən trōl/] **164**–9
remove [rĭ mōōv/] **97**–F
rent [rĕnt] **28**–I
Renting an apartment [rĕn/tĭng ən ə pärt/mənt] **35**
repair [rĭ për/] **140**–G
repair person [rĭ për/ pür/sən] **48**–10, **138**–48
REPAIRS [rĭ përz/] **48**–49
repeat [rĭ pēt/] **6**–D
report crimes [rĭ pört/ krīmz/] **101**–H
reporter [rĭ pör/tər] **99**–12, **139**–49
Reptiles [rĕp/tīlz] **131**
request [rĭ kwĕst/] **111**–M
rescue breathing [rĕs/kyōō brē/dhĭng] **83**–16
Resident Alien card [rĕz/ə dənt ā/lē ən kärd/] **29**–3
respirator [rĕs/pə rā/tər] **147**–12
Responsibilities (of citizenship)
   [rĭ spän/sə bĭl/ə tēz əv sĭt/ə zən shĭp/] **116**
RESTAURANT [rĕs/tə rənt, –ränt/] **62**–63
restaurant [rĕs/tə rənt, –ränt/] **90**–14
rest rooms [rĕst/ rōōmz/] **5**–8
retire [rĭ tīr/] **29** ✦
return [rĭ türn/] **21**–F
return address [rĭ türn/ ə drĕs/, –ā/drĕs] **96**–7
rewind [rē wīnd/] **165**–D
rewrite [rē rīt/] **113**–D
rhinoceros [rī näs/ər əs] **135**–29
rib cage [rĭb/ kāj/] **75**–53
rice [rīs(/–)] **54**–28, **148**–1
   ...pilaf [–pē/läf, –pĭ läf/] **61**–18
ride [rīd] **91**–E, **157**–W
rides [rīdz] **152**–17
right [rīt(/–)] / [–rīt/]
   ...turn only [–türn/ ōn/lē] **107**–9
   on the... [än dhə–, ön–] **13**–2
right-of-way [rīt/əv wā/] **107** ✦
Rights and responsibilities [rīts/ ən rĭ spän/sə bĭl/ə tēz] **116**
ring [rĭng] **69**–39
rinse [rĭns] **76**–F
rip [rĭp] **70**–23
ripe [rīp] **50**–29
river [rĭv/ər] **117**–3
RN (registered nurse) [är/ĕn/] **87**–22
roast [rōst] **58**–U
roast [rōst(/–)]
   ...beef [–bēf/] **52**–1, **53**–7, **57**–12
   ...chicken [–chĭk/ən] **61**–12
roasting [rō/stĭng]
   ...pan [–păn/] **59**–13
   ...rack [–răk/] **59**–14
robin [räb/ən] **132**–17
rock [räk] **94**–H
rock [räk(/–)] **155**–24
rock band [räk/ bănd/] **120**–2
rocking chair [räk/ĭng chër/] **94**–6
RODENTS [rōd/nts] **133**
roll [rōl(/–)] **56**–11

...of paper towels [–əv pā/pər tow/əlz] **56**–23
roller coaster [rō/lər kō/stər] **152**–15
rollers [rō/lərz] **23**–21
rolling pin [rō/lĭng pĭn/] **59**–30
rolls [rōlz] **54**–30
romance [rō măns/, rō/măns] **166**–16
Roman numerals [rō/mən nōō/mər əlz] **14**
roof [rōōf] **38**–20, **48**–3
roofer [rōō/fər] **48**–8
roof garden [rōōf/ gär/dn] **36**–5
room service [rōōm/ sür/vəs] **145**–12
rooster [rōō/stər] **133**–6
root [rōōt] **128**–5, **129**–3
rope [rōp] **154**–19
rose [rōz] **129**–15
rotary card file [rō/tə rē kärd/ fĭl/] **143**–17
rotten [rät/n] **50**–30
rouge [rōōzh] **77**–36
route [rōōt, rowt] **104**–2
router [row/tər] **150**–12
rubber [rŭb/ər]
...band [–bănd/] **143**–45
...cement [–sə mĕnt/] **143**–38
...gloves [–glŭvz/] **47**–4
...mat [–măt/] **43**–3
...stamp [–stămp/] **143**–40
rug [rŭg] **44**–23
ruler [rōō/lər] **3**–27
run [rŭn] **156**–C
rural area [rōōr/əl ër/ē ə] **34**–4
rye bread [rī/ brĕd/] **53**–3
sad [săd] **31**–20, **167**–28
safe-deposit box [sāf/dĭ päz/ət bäks/] **97**–13
safety [sāf/tē]
...boot [–bōōt/] **147**–20
...earmuffs [–ïr/mŭfs] **147**–14
...glasses [–glăs/əz] **147**–10
...goggles [–gäg/əlz] **147**–9
...pin [–pĭn/] **73**–24
...seat [–sēt/] **109**–39
...vest [–vĕst/] **147**–15
...visor [–vī/zər] **147**–11
SAFETY, PUBLIC [pŭb/lĭk sāf/tē] **101**
sailboarding [sāl/bör/dĭng] **160**–10
sailboat [sāl/bōt/] **155**–4
sailing [sā/lĭng] **160**–8
salad [săl/əd]
...bar [–bär/] **60**–16
...dressing [–drĕs/ĭng] **60**–18
...fork [–förk/] **63**–24
...plate [–plāt/] **63**–17
salamander [săl/ə măn/dər] **130**–27
salami [sə lä/mē] **53**–5
sale price [sāl/ prīs/] **21**–3
salesclerk [sālz/klürk/] **68**–1, **139**–50
salesperson [sālz/pür/sən] **139**–50
sales tax [sālz/ tăks/] **21**–7
salmon steak [săm/ən stāk/] **53**–19
saltshaker [sölt/shā/kər] **41**–14
sand [sănd(/–)] **155**–23
...castle [–kăs/əl] **155**–10
...dune [–dōōn/] **117**–5
sandals [săn/dlz] **68**–24
sandbox [sănd/bäks/] **153**–15
sandpaper [sănd/pā/pər] **151**–50

sanitation worker [săn/ə tā/shən wür/kər] **139**–51
Saturday [săt/ər dā/, –dē] **18**–7
Saturn [săt/ərn] **127**–4
saucepan [sös/păn/] **59**–25
saucer [sö/sər] **63**–22
sausage [sö/sĭj] **52**–12, **61**–2
sauté [sö tā/, sō–] **58**–H
save [sāv] **126**–B, C
savings account number [sā/vĭngz ə kownt/ nŭm/bər] **97**–6
saxophone [săk/sə fōn/] **120**–7
say [sā] **6**–C
scaffolding [skăf/əl dĭng] **149**–4
scale (weight) [skāl] **43**–26, **84**–7
scales (fish) [skālz] **130**–3
scallions [skăl/yənz] **51**–17
scallop [skăl/əp, skäl/–] **130**–18
scallops [skăl/əps, skäl/–] **53**–25
scanner [skăn/ər] **144**–13
scared [skërd] **31**–24
scarf [skärf] **66**–4, **70**–15
schedule [skĕj/ōōl, –ōō əl] **104**–3
SCHOOL [skōōl] **5**
school **89**–27
...crossing [–krö/sĭng] **107**–13
adult... [ə dŭlt/–, ăd/ŭlt–] **112**–8
elementary... [ĕl/ə mĕn/trē–] **112**–5
high... [hī/–] **112**–7
junior high... [jōōn/yər hī/–] **112**–6
middle... [mĭd/l–] **112**–6
parochial... [pə rō/kē əl–] **112**–3
private... [prī/vət–] **112**–2
trade... [trād/–] **112**–9
vocational... [vō kā/shə nəl–] **112**–9
School Registration Form [skōōl/ rĕj/ə strā/shən förm/] **4**
SCHOOLS, TYPES OF [tīps/ əv skōōlz/] **112**
SCHOOL SUBJECTS, MORE [mör/ skōōl/ sŭb/jĭkts] **121**
SCIENCE [sī/əns] **119**
science fiction story [sī/əns fĭk/shən stör/ē] **166**–12
scissors [sĭz/ərz] **23**–19, **73**–18
score [skör] **158**–1
scorpion [skör/pē ən] **132**–31
scrambled eggs [skrăm/bəld ĕgz/] **58**, **61**–1
scraper [skrā/pər] **151**–48
screen [skrēn] **2**–2, **144**–6, **152**–12, **165**–28
screen door [skrēn/ dör/] **38**–8
screwdriver [skrōō/drī/vər] **150**–25
Phillips... [fĭl/ĭps–] **150**–26
scrub [skrŭb] **46**–L
scrub brush [skrŭb/ brŭsh/] **47**–19
scuba [skōō/bə]
...diving [–dī/vĭng] **160**–12
...tank [–tăngk/] **155**–8
sculpture [skŭlp/chər] **152**–9
sea [sē(/–)]
...anemone [–ə nĕm/ə nē] **130**–21
...horse [–hörs/] **130**–23
...lion [–lī/ən] **131**–34
...urchin [–ür/chən] **130**–20
Sea animals [sē/ ăn/ə məlz] **130**
SEAFOOD [sē/fōōd/] **53**
seal [sēl] **131**–33
seam [sēm(/–)] **73**–11
...ripper [–rĭp/ər] **73**–19
Sea mammals [sē/ măm/əlz] **131**
search and rescue team [sürch/ ən rĕs/kyōō tēm/] **103**–17

seashell [sē′shĕl′] **155**–21
Seasons [sē′zənz] **19**
seat [sēt(′–)] **2**–E, **152**–11
...belt [–bĕlt′] **109**–36
seat [sēt] **62**–B
seaweed [sē′wēd′] **155** ✦
second [sĕk′ənd] **14, 16**–1
...floor [–flör′] **36**–2
secretary [sĕk′rə tër′ē] **139**–52, **142**–3
section [sĕk′shən] / [–sĕk′shən]
dairy... [dër′ē–] **54**–9
produce... [prō′dōōs–] **54**–11
security [sĭ kyŏŏr′ə tē] **111**–C
...gate [–gāt′] **36**–13
...guard [–gärd′] **97**–4
...system [–sĭs′təm] **36**–9
see [sē] **75**–A
seed [sēd] **129**–1
seedling [sēd′lĭng] **129**–2
seesaw [sē′sö′] **153**–16
See you [sē′ yə] **8**
Selective Service [sə lĕk′tĭv sür′vəs] **116**–F
sell [sĕl] **21**–B, **140**–H
semi [sĕm′ī] **106**–15
semicolon [sĕm′ē kō′lən] **113**–13
Senate [sĕn′ət] **116**–3
Senator [sĕn′ə tər] **116**–4
send [sĕnd] **96**–B
senior citizen [sēn′yər sĭt′ə zən] **22**–12
Senses [sĕn′səz] **75**
sentence [sĕn′tns] **113**–4
sentence the defendant [sĕn′tns dhə dĭ fĕn′dənt] **99**–F
September [sĕp tĕm′bər] **19**–33
serious [sĭr′ē əs] **167**–26
Serious Diseases [sĭr′ē əs dĭ zē′zəz] **79**
serve (sports) [sürv] **157**–N
serve on a jury [sürv′ än ə jŏŏr′ē, –ön–] **116**–G
server [sür′vər] **62**–4, **63**–6, **139**–53
serve the meal [sürv′ dhə mēl′] **62**–F
service elevator [sür′vəs ĕl′ə vā tər] **145** ✦
serviceman [sür′vəs măn′, –mən] **139**–54
servicewoman [sür′vəs wŏŏm′ən] **139**–54
serving dish [sür′vĭng dĭsh′] **41**–6
set [sĕt(′–)]
...hair [–hër′] **23**–C
...the table [–dhə tā′bəl] **62**–A
set of dishes [sĕt′ əv dĭsh′əz] **41**–2
seven [sĕv′ən] **14**
seventeen [sĕv′ən tēn′] **14**
seventeenth [sĕv′ən tēnth′] **14**
seventh [sĕv′ənth] **14**
seventy [sĕv′ən tē] **14**
sew [sō(′–)]
...by hand [–bī hănd′] **73**–A
...by machine [–bī mə shēn′] **73**–B
...clothes [–klōz′] **140**–L
SEWING AND ALTERATIONS [sō′ĭng ən öl′tə rā′shənz] **73**
sewing machine [sō′ĭng mə shēn′] **73**–10
sex [sĕks] **4**–12
shade [shād] **155**–11
shampoo [shăm pōō′] **76**–9
Shapes [shāps] **118**
share [shër] **6**–I
shark [shärk] **130**–7
shave [shāv] **77**–M

shaving cream [shā′vĭng krēm′] **77**–27
shears [shïrz] **39**–15
sheep [shēp] **133**–7
sheet [shēt] **44**–13, 14
shelf [shĕlf] **40**–8
Shellfish [shĕl′fĭsh′] **53**
shelter [shĕl′tər] **34**–10
shingles [shĭng′gəlz] **149**–19
shin guards [shĭn′ gärdz′] **161**–13
ship [shĭp] **146**–C
shipping clerk [shĭp′ĭng klürk′] **146**–15
shirt [shürt] **64**–4, **65**–20
shock [shäk] **82**–C
shoe [shōō(′–)]
...department [–dĭ pärt′mənt] **68**–3
...store [–stör′] **92**–10
shoelace [shōō′lās′] **68**–14
SHOES AND ACCESSORIES [shōōz′ ən ĭk sĕs′ə rēz] **68**–69
shoot [shōōt] **156**–I
shop [shäp] **21**–A
shop [shäp] **121**–10
SHOPPING [shäp′ĭng] **21**
shopping [shäp′ĭng]
...basket [–băs′kət] **54**–7
...cart [–kärt′] **54**–3
...program [–prō′grăm] **167**–25
shore [shör] **117**–12
short [shört] **22**–18, **23**–1, **71**–35
shorten [shör′tn] **73**–D
short-sleeved [shört′slēvd′] **71**–30
shorts [shörts] **64**–13, **67**–3, 12
shortwave radio [shört′wāv′ rā′dē ō] **164**–5
shoulder [shōl′dər] **74**–10
...bag [–băg′] **69**–27
...harness [–här′nəs] **109**–37
...pads [–pădz′] **161**–21
shoulder-length [shōl′dər lĕngkth′] **23**–2
shout [showt] **169**–G
shovel [shŭv′əl] **39**–13, **149**–21
show (puppet) [shō] **152**–14
shower cap [show′ər kăp′] **76**–1
showerhead [show′ər hĕd′] **43**–10
shrimp [shrĭmp] **53**–24, **130**–19
shutter [shŭt′ər] **38**–18
sick [sĭk] **30**–14
side [sīd] **118**–22
sideburns [sīd′bürnz′] **23**–7
sideview mirror [sīd′vyōō′ mïr′ər] **108**–8
sidewalk [sīd′wök′] **91**–26
sight impaired [sīt′ ĭm përd′] **22**–26
sign [sīn(′–)]
...a rental agreement [–ə rĕn′təl ə grē′mənt] **35**–C
...your name [–yər nām′] **4**–D
sign [sīn] **91**–29
signature [sĭg′nə chər] **4**–18
Signs [sīnz] **107**
silk [sĭlk] **70**–15
silk scarves [sĭlk′ skärvz′] **68**–4
silver dollar [sĭl′vər däl′ər] **20**–6
simmer [sĭm′ər] **58**–R
sing [sĭng] **120**–B, **169**–I
single [sĭng′gəl]
...father [–fä′dhər] **25**–25
...mother [–mŭdh′ər] **25**–26
sink [sĭngk] **40**–6, **43**–22, **49**–17

sister [sĭs/tər] **24**–8, **25**–30, 32
sister-in-law [sĭs/tər ĭn lö/] **24**–15
sitcom [sĭt/käm/] **167**–18
sit down [sĭt/ down/] **2**–E
situation comedy [sĭch/ōō ā/shən käm/ə dē] **167**–18
six [sĭks] **14**
six-pack [sĭks/păk/] **56**–9
six-pack of soda [sĭks/păk/ əv sō/də] **56**–21
sixteen [sĭks/tēn/] **14**
sixteenth [sĭks/tēnth/] **14**
sixth [sĭksth] **14**
sixty [sĭks/tē] **14**
six-year-old [sĭks/yïr ōld/] **22**–4
Sizes [sī/zəz] **70**
skate [skāt] **157**–V
skateboarding [skāt/bör/dĭng] **159**–12
skating [skā/tĭng] **160**–4, 5
Skeleton [skĕl/ə tn] **75**
ski [skē] **157**–V
ski [skē(/–)]
...boots [–bōōts/] **161**–26
...cap [–kăp/] **66**–10
...mask [–măsk/] **66**–14
...poles [–pōlz/] **161**–25
skiing [skē/ĭng] **160**–1, 3, 7
skin [skĭn] **75**–51
skinless [skĭn/ləs] **52** ✦
skirt [skürt] **64**–10, **65**–25
skis [skēz] **161**–24
skull [skŭl] **75**–52
skunk [skŭngk] **134**–12
skyscraper [skī/skrā/pər] **88** ✦
slacks [slăks] **64**–8
sledding [slĕd/ĭng] **160**–6
sledgehammer [slĕj/hăm/ər] **149**–22
sleeping bag [slē/pĭng băg/] **154**–12
sleepy [slē/pē] **30**–3
sleeve [slēv] **73**–6
sleeveless [slēv/ləs] **71**–29
slice [slīs] **58**–O
slide [slīd] (science) **119**–5, (park) **153**–13
slides [slīdz] **165**–31
slide tray [slīd/ trā/] **165**–30
slim [slĭm] **22**–22
sling [slĭng] **80**–8
slippers [slĭp/ərz] **67**–6
slot [slät] **144**–19
slow [slō] **11**–4
small [smöl(/–)] **70**–2
...town [–town/] **34**–3
smell [smĕl] **75**–C
smog [smäg(/–), smög(/–)] **126**–10
...check [–chĕk/] **109**–57
smoggy [smä/gē, smö/–] **10**–14
smoke detector [smōk/ dĭ tĕk/tər] **37**–25, **45**–11
smoked turkey [smōkt/ tür/kē] **53**–4
snack foods [snăk/ fōōdz/] **55**–16
snail [snāl] **130**–24
snake [snāk] **131**–38, 39
sneeze [snēz] **78**–B
snorkeling [snör/kə lĭng] **160**–11
snowboard [snō/börd/] **161**–23
snowboarding [snō/bör/dĭng] **160**–2
snowing [snō/ĭng] **10**–9
snowstorm [snō/störm/] **10**–20

soap [sōp(/–)] **43**–23, **76**–2
...dish [–dĭsh/] **43**–24
...pads [–pădz/] **47**–5
soap opera [sōp/ äp/rə] **167**–21
soccer [säk/ər] **158**–12
...ball [–böl/] **161**–12
Social Security card [sō/shəl sĭ kyōōr/ə tē kärd/] **29**–5
Social Security number [sō/shəl sĭ kyōōr/ə tē nŭm/bər] **4**–15
socks [säks] **67**–15
soda [sō/də] **55**–52, **60**–4
sofa [sō/fə] **42**–19
soft [söft] **11**–6
softball [söft/böl/] **158**–10
Software [söft/wër/] **144**
solar [sō/lər]
...eclipse [–ĭ klĭps/] **127** ✦
...energy [–ĕn/ər jē] **126**–1
...system [–sĭs/təm] **127**
sole [sōl] (fish) **53**–21, (shoe) **68**–12
solid [säl/əd] **70**–6
Solids [säl/ədz] **118**
son [sŭn] **24**–22
son-in-law [sŭn/ĭn lö/] **24** ✦
sore throat [sör/ thrōt/] **78**–6
Sorry. [sär/ē, sör/ē] **8**
sort [sört] **72**–A
soup [sōōp(/–)] **54**–24
...bowl [–bōl/] **63**–18
...of the day [–əv dhə dā/] **61**–10
soupspoon [sōōp/spōōn/] **63**–29
sour cream [sow/ər krēm/] **54**–37
south [sowth] **107**, **123**, **124**
soybeans [soy/bēnz/] **148**–3
space [spās(/–)] **127**–22
...station [–stā/shən] **127**–18
spades [spādz] **163**–28
spaghetti [spə gĕt/ē] **54**–27
spare tire [spër/ tīr/] **109**–53
sparrow [spăr/ō] **132**–8
spatula [spăch/ə lə] **59**–19
speak [spēk] **140**–J
speaker [spē/kər] **36**–8
speakers [spē/kərz] **164**–11
specialist [spĕsh/ə lĭst] **86** ✦
speed [spēd(/–)] **144** ✦
...limit [–lĭm/ət] **107**–5
speedometer [spĭ däm/ə tər] **108**–20
spell [spĕl] **4**–A, **6**–E
sphere [sfïr] **118**–14
spices [spī/səz] **55**–46
spider [spī/dər] **132**–30
spinach [spĭn/ĭch] **51**–11
spinal column [spī/nəl käl/əm] **75**–54
spiral notebook [spī/rəl nōt/bŏŏk/] **3**–26
splint [splĭnt] **83**–11
split skirt [splĭt/ skürt/] **65**–25
sponge [spŭnj] **47**–24
spool of thread [spōōl/ əv thrĕd/] **73**–17
spoon [spōōn] **41**–23, **59**–9
SPORTS [spörts] **158**–160
sports [spörts(/–)]
...car [–kär/] **106**–6
...coat [–kōt/] **64**–6
...shirt [–shürt/] **65**–26
SPORTS EQUIPMENT [spörts/ ĭ kwĭp/mənt] **161**

Index

SPORTS VERBS [spörts/ vürbz/] **156–157**
sprained ankle [sprānd/ ăng/kəl] **78**–18
spray [sprā(/–)]
 …gun [–gŭn] **151**–19
 …starch [–stärch/] **72**–12
spring [sprĭng] **19**–37
sprinkler [sprĭng/klər] **39**–8
square [skwër] **118**–6
squash [skwäsh, skwösh] **51**–13
squeegee [skwē/jē] **47**–9
squid [skwĭd] **130**–10
squirrel [skwür/əl] **133**–21
stacking tray [stăk/ĭng trā/] **142**–5
stadium [stā/dē əm] **152**–26
stage [stāj] **32**–4
stain [stān] **70**–22
stairs [stërz] **37**–35, **105**–8, 9
stairway [stër/wā/] **37**–26
stall shower [stöl/ show/ər] **43** ✦
stamp [stămp(/–)] **96**–10
 …collection [–kə lĕk/shən] **162**–12
standard [stăn/dərd]
 …time [–tīm/] **17**–32
 …transmission [–trănz mĭsh/ən, –trăns–] **109**
stand trial [stănd/ trī/əl, –trīl/] **99**–D
stand up [stănd/ ŭp/] **2**–D
stand-up comedy [stănd/ŭp/ kăm/ə dē] **166**–5
staple [stā/pəl] **142**–G
staple [stā/pəl] **143**–29
stapler [stā/plər] **143**–28
star [stär] **127**–23
starfish [stär/fĭsh/] **130**–15
start [stärt(/–)] **157**–X
 …school [–skōōl/] **28**–B
starving [stär/vĭng] **30** ✦
state [stāt] **4**–8
station wagon [stā/shən wăg/ən] **106**–8
stay [stā] **101**–B
steak [stāk(/–)] **52**–2, **61**–13
 …knife [–nīf/] **63**–26
steam [stēm] **58**–I
steamer [stē/mər] **59**–4
steel-wool soap pads [stēl/wōōl/ sōp/ pădz/] **47**–5
steering wheel [stïr/ĭng wēl/] **108**–26
steers [stïrz] **148**–21
stem [stĕm] **129**–4
stepbrother [stĕp/brŭdh/ər] **25**–33
stepdaughter [stĕp/dö/tər] **25** ✦
stepfather [stĕp/fä/dhər] **25**–28
stepladder [stĕp/lăd/ər] **47**–7
stepmother [stĕp/mŭdh/ər] **25**–31
steps [stĕps] **38**–13, **48**–7
stepsister [stĕp/sĭs/tər] **25**–32
stereo system [stër/ē ō sĭs/təm] **42**–14
sterile pad [stër/əl păd/] **83**–4
stethoscope [stĕth/ə skōp/] **84**–8
stewing beef [stōō/ĭng bēf/] **52**–3
stick shift [stĭk/ shĭft/] **109**–48
stir [stür] **58**–E
stir-fry [stür/frī/] **58**–W
stitches [stĭch/əz] **83**–15
stock clerk [stäk/ klürk/] **139**–55
stockings [stäk/ĭngz] **67**–26
stomach [stŭm/ək] **75**–41
stomachache [stŭm/ək āk/] **78**–4

stop [stäp] **165**–F
stop [stäp] **107**–3
stopover [stäp/ō/vər] **111** ✦
stopped up [stäpt/ ŭp/] **49**–18
storage locker [stör/ĭj läk/ər] **36**–14
store [stör(/–)] / [–stör/]
 …owner [–ō/nər] **139**–56
 candy… [kăn/dē–] **92**–3
 card… [kärd/–] **92**–7
 convenience… [kən vēn/yəns–] **90**–3
 department… [dĭ pärt/mənt–] **93**–13
 electronics… [ĭ lĕk trän/ĭks–] **93**–18
 jewelry… [jōō/əl rē–] **92**–2
 music… [myōō/zĭk–] **92**–1
 pet… [pĕt/–] **92**–6
 shoe… [shōō/–] **92**–10
 toy… [toy/–] **92**–5
 video… [vĭd/ē ō–] **93**–15
storm [störm] **10**–16, 18, 20, 21
storm door [störm/ dör/] **38**–12
stove [stōv] **40**–18, **154**–16
stow [stō] **111**–H
straight [strāt(/–)]
 …hair [–hër/] **23**–9
 …line [–līn/] **118**–18
strainer [strā/nər] **59**–22
stranger [strān/jər] **101**–F
straw [strö] **60**–20
strawberries [strö/bĕr/ēz] **50**–17
straw hat [strö/ hăt/] **66**–23
stream [strēm] **117** ✦
street [strēt(/–)] **90**–9
 …vendor [–vĕn/dər] **91**–30
streetlight [strēt/līt/] **91**–23
strep throat [strĕp/ thrōt/] **79**–4
stretch [strĕch] **157**–Q
stretcher [strĕch/ər] **87**–28
string beans [strĭng/ bēnz/] **51**–25
string of pearls [strĭng/ əv pürlz/] **69**–30
Strings [strĭngz] **120**
striped [strīpt] **70**–7
stroller [strō/lər] **94**–2
stucco [stŭk/ō] **149**–14
student [stōōd/nt] **2**–3, **139**–57
STUDYING [stŭd/ē ĭng] **6–7**
stuffed animals [stŭft/ ăn/ə məlz] **45**–23
subcompact [sŭb/käm/păkt] **106**–1
subtraction [səb trăk/shən] **118**–2
suburbs [sŭb/ürbz] **34**–2
subway [sŭb/wā/] **104**–9
sugar [shōōg/ər] **55**–48, **60**–21
 …bowl [–bōl/] **41**–12
 …substitute [–sŭb/stə tōōt/] **60**–22
suit [sōōt] (clothing) **64**–2, (diving) **155**–7
summer [sŭm/ər] **19**–38
sun [sŭn] **127**–10
sunbather [sŭn/bā/dhər] **155**–17
sunblock [sŭn/bläk/] **155**–13
sunburn [sŭn/bürn/] **78**–14
Sunday [sŭn/dā, –dē] **18**–1
sunflower [sŭn/flow/ər] **129**–10
sunglasses [sŭn/glăs/əz] **66**–21
sunny [sŭn/ē] **10**–6
sunscreen [sŭn/skrēn/] **76**–6, **155**–13
superintendent [sōō/prĭn tĕn/dənt, sōō/pər ĭn–] **36**–12

supervise people [soō/pər vīz pē/pəl] **140**–K
supply cabinet [sə plī/ kăb/ə nət] **142**–13
Supreme Court [sə prēm/ kört/] **116**–8
surfboard [sürf/börd/] **155**–5
surfing [sür/fĭng] **160**–9
surgeon [sür/jən] **87**–30
surge protector [sürj/ prə tĕk/tər] **144**–10
surgical [sür/jĭ kəl]
...cap [–kăp/] **87**–31
...gown [–gown/] **87**–32
...nurse [–nürs/] **87**–29
surprised [sər prīzd/, sə–] **31**–31
suspect [sŭs/pĕkt] **99**–A
suspenders [sə spĕn/dərz] **68**–2
SUV (sports utility vehicle)
[ĕs/yoō/vē/] / [spörts/ yoō tĭl/ə tē vē/ĭ kəl] **106**–9
swallow [swäl/ō] **82**–J
swap meet [swäp/ mēt/] **152**–22
sweater [swĕt/ər]
cardigan... [kär/də gən–] **65**–27
crewneck... [kroō/nĕk/–] **71**–26
pullover... [poōl/ō/vər–] **64**–11
turtleneck... [tür/tl nĕk/–] **71**–28
V-neck... [vē/nĕk/–] **71**–27
sweatpants [swĕt/pănts/] **64**–15
sweatshirt [swĕt/shürt/] **64**–14
sweep [swēp] **46**–E
sweet peppers [swēt/ pĕp/ərz] **51**–7
swim [swĭm] **157**–T
swimming [swĭm/ĭng]
...pool [–poōl/] **37**–16
...trunks [–trŭngks/] **66**–22
swimsuit [swĭm/soōt/] **66**–26
swing [swĭng] **157**–O
swings [swĭngz] **153**–12
Swiss cheese [swĭs/ chēz/] **53**–11
swivel chair [swĭv/əl chër/] **143**–22
swollen [swō/lən] **78**–16
swordfish [sörd/fĭsh/] **130**–12
SYMPTOMS AND INJURIES [sĭmp/təmz ən ĭn/jə rēz] **78**
synagogue [sĭn/ə gäg/] **88**–9
synthetic materials [sĭn thĕt/ĭk mə tïr/ē əlz] **70**
syringe [sə rĭnj/] **84**–14
syrup [sïr/əp, sür/–] **61**–5
table [tā/bəl] / [–tā/bəl]
dining room... [dī/nĭng roōm/–] **41**–17
night... [nīt/–] **44**–21
picnic... [pĭk/nĭk–] **153**–8
tablecloth [tā/bəl klöth/] **41**–18
tablespoon [tā/bəl spoōn/] **57**–7
tablet [tăb/lət] **81**–25
table tennis [tā/bəl tĕn/əs] **159**–13
tackle [tăk/əl] **156**–M
taco [tä/kō] **60**–9
tail [tāl] **134**–22
taillight [tāl/līt/] **108**–14
tailor [tā/lər] **73**–9
take [tāk(/–)]
...a bath [–ə băth/] **76**–B
...a citizenship test [–ə sĭt/ə zən shĭp tĕst/] **116**–C
...a message [–ə mĕs/ĭj] **142**–A
...a nap [–ə năp/] **94**–L
...a picture [–ə pĭk/chər] **32**–D
...a seat [–ə sēt/] **2**–E
...a shower [–ə show/ər] **26**–C, **76**–A

...medicine [–mĕd/ə sən] **80**–F
...ownership [–ō/nər shĭp/] **35**–J
...the bus [–dhə bŭs/] **26**–H, **104** ✦
...the children to school [–dhə chĭl/drən tə skoōl/] **26**–G
...the order [–dhē ör/dər] **62**–E
...(your) temperature [–yər tĕm/prə chər] **85**–C
take care of [tāk/ kër/ əv] **140**–L
take in [tāk/ ĭn/] **73**–E
take off [tāk/ öf/] **111**–L
take out [tāk/ owt/] **2**–K, **46**–Q
take out (food) [tāk/ owt/] **62** ✦
talcum powder [tăl/kəm pow/dər] **76**–3
talk [tök] **2**–B, **7**–P, **35**–B, G, **141**–A, I
talk show [tök/ shō/] **167**–20
tall [töl] **22**–16
tambourine [tăm/bə rēn/] **120**–19
tangerines [tăn/jə rēnz/] **50**–13
tank top [tăngk/ tăp/] **67**–2
tape [tāp(/–)] **83**–5, **143**–39, 42
...deck [–dĕk/] **108**–30
...measure [–mĕzh/ər] **73**–13, **150**–22
target [tär/gət] **161**–8
tartar [tär/tər] **84**–17
taste [tāst] **75**–D
taxi [tăk/sē] **104**–18
...driver [–drī/vər] **104**–20
...license [–lī/səns] **104**–22
...stand [–stănd/] **104**–19
TB (tuberculosis) [tē/bē/] / [toō bür/kyə lō/səs] **79**–13
tea [tē] **60**–5, **61**–24
teach [tēch] **140** ✦
teacher [tē/chər] **2**–5, **5**–2, **139**–58
teakettle [tē/kĕt/l] **40**–17
team [tēm] **103**–17, **158**–3
TEAM SPORTS [tēm/ spörts/] **158**
teapot [tē/pät/] **41**–11
tear [tër] **70**–23
teaspoon [tē/spoōn/] **57**–6, **63**–28
technician [tĕk nĭsh/ən] **86**–8, 16
teddy bear [tĕd/ē bër/] **45**–10
teenagers [tē/nā/jərz] **22**–6
teeth [tēth] **74**–25, **77**–J, K, **85**–I
teething ring [tē/dhĭng rĭng/] **95**–30
telemarketer [tĕl/ə mär/kə tər] **139**–59
TELEPHONE [tĕl/ə fōn/] **9**
telephone [tĕl/ə fōn/] **9**–1, 15
...book [–boōk/] **9**–15
...card [–kärd/] **9**–10
...number [–nŭm/bər] **4**–11
telescope [tĕl/ə skōp/] **127**–21
television (TV) [tĕl/ə vĭzh/ən] **42**–26, **164**–6
...program [–prō/grăm] **166**–3
teller [tĕl/ər] **97**–1
Temperature (weather) [tĕm/prə chər] **10**
temperature (fever) [tĕm/prə chər] **78**–8
temperature gauge [tĕm/prə chər gāj/] **108**–23
ten [tĕn] **14**, **15**–7, **16**–6, **20**–9
tenant [tĕn/ənt] **37**–33
tennis [tĕn/əs] **159**–14
...court [–kört/] **153**–7
...racket [–răk/ət] **161**–2
...shoes [–shoōz/] **68**–22
tent [tĕnt] **154**–10
tenth [tĕnth] **14**
ten-year-old [tĕn/yïr ōld/] **22**–5

Index

termites [tür/mīts] **49**–22
terrified [tĕr/ə fīd/] **30** ✦
test tube [tĕst/ tōōb/] **119**–16
textbook [tĕkst/bōōk/, tĕks/–] **3**–22
thank [thăngk] **8**–H
Thanksgiving [thăngks gĭv/ĭng] **168**–15
Thank you [thăngk/ yōō] **8**
theater [thē/ə tər] / [thē/ə tər] **88**–10
   ...arts [–ärts/] **121**–12
   movie... [–mōō/vē–] **88**–11
thermometer [thər mäm/ə tər] **84**–15
thick book [thĭk/ bōōk/] **11**–7
thigh [thī] **74**–16
thighs [thīz] **52**–21
thimble [thĭm/bəl] **73**–20
thin [thĭn] **11**–8, **22**–22
third [thürd(/–)] **14**
   ...floor [–flör/] **36**–3
thirsty [thür/stē] **30**–2
thirteen [thür/tēn/] **14**
thirteenth [thür/tēnth/] **14**
thirteen-year-old [thür/tēn/yïr ōld/] **22**–7
thirty [thür/tē] **14**
this week [dhĭs/ wēk/] **18**–19
thorn [thörn] **129**–28
thousand [thow/zənd] **14**
thread [thrĕd] **73**–17
three [thrē(/–)] **14**
   ...times a week [–tīmz/ ə wēk/] **18**–24
three-fourths [thrē/förths/] **15**–5
three-piece suit [thrē/pēs/ sōōt/] **64**–1
throat [thrōt(/–)] **75**–36
   ...lozenges [–lăz/ən jəz] **81**–21
through [thrōō] **105**–11
throw [thrō] **156**–D
throw pillow [thrō/ pĭl/ō] **42**–20
throw up [thrō/ ŭp/] **78**–E
thumb [thŭm] **75**–56
thunderstorm [thŭn/dər störm/] **10**–16
Thursday [thürz/dā, –dē] **18**–5
tick [tĭk] **132**–28
ticket [tĭk/ət] **104**–14
tidal wave [tīd/l wāv/] **103**–15
tide [tīd] **155** ✦
tie [tī] **94**–I
tie [tī] (clothing) **69**–40, (sports) **158** ✦
ties [tīz] (clothing) **69**–10
tiger [tī/gər] **135**–37
tight [tīt] **71**–43
tights [tīts] **66**–11
tile [tīl] **43**–9
TIME [tīm] **16**–17
time clock [tīm/ kläk/] **146**–4
Time zones [tīm/ zōnz/] **17**
tire [tīr] **108**–10, **109**–53
tired [tīrd] **31**–33
tires [tīrz] **109**–59
title [tīt/l] **98**–21, **113**–3
toad [tōd] **130**–28
toast [tōst] **33, 61**–3
toaster [tō/stər] **40**–7
   ...oven [–ŭv/ən] **40**–15
today [tə dā/] **18**–15
toddler [täd/lər] **22**–3
toe [tō(/–)] **68**–15, **75**–63

...guard [–gärd/] **147**–21
toenail [tō/nāl/] **75**–64
toggle bolt [täg/əl bōlt/] **150**–33
toilet [toy/lət] **43**–17, **49**–18
   ...brush [–brŭsh/] **43**–16
   ...paper [–pā/pər] **43**–15
token [tō/kən] **104**–11
tomatoes [tə mā/tōz] **51**–23
tomorrow [tə mär/ō, –mör/ō] **18**–16
tongs [tängz, töngz] **59**–23, **119**–15
tongue [tŭng] **74**–26
too big [tōō/ bĭg/] **70**–21
TOOLS AND BUILDING SUPPLIES
   [tōōlz/ ən bĭl/dĭng sə plīz/] **150**–**151**
too small [tōō/ smöl/] **70**–20
toothache [tōōth/āk/] **78**–2
toothbrush [tōōth/brŭsh/] **43**–20, **77**–20
   ...holder [–hōl/dər] **43**–21
toothpaste [tōōth/pāst/] **77**–21
tornado [tör nā/dō] **103**–13
total [tōt/l] **21**–8, **118** ✦
tote bag [tōt/ băg/] **69**–29
touch [tŭch] **75**–E
towel [tow/əl] **43**–8, 12, 13
   ...rack [–răk/] **43**–8
townhouse [town/hows/] **34**–7
tow truck [tō/ trŭk/] **106**–13
toy [toy(/–)]
   ...chest [–chĕst/] **45**–24
   ...store [–stör/] **92**–5
toys [toyz] **46**–H, **94**–5
track [trăk] (athletic) **5**–11, (train) **104**–10
track and field [trăk/ ən fēld/] **159**–17
trackball [trăk/böl/] **144**–15
track lighting [trăk/ lī/tĭng] **42**–3
tractor [trăk/tər] **148**–9
   ...trailer [–trā/lər] **106**–15
trade school [trād/ skōōl/] **112**–9
traffic light [trăf/ĭk līt/] **90**–6
TRAFFIC SIGNS [trăf/ĭk sīnz/] **107**
tragedy [trăj/ə dē] **166**–11
trailer [trā/lər] **106**–17
train [trān(/–)] **104**–17
   ...station [–stā/shən] **104**–13
training pants [trā/nĭng pănts/] **95**–24
transcribe [trăn skrīb/] **142**–C
transcriber (medical) [trăn skrī/bər] **142**–4
transfer [trăns für/, trăns/fər] **97**–E
transfer [trăns/fər] **104**–6
translator [trănz/lā/tər, trăns/–] **138**–34
transmission [trănz mĭsh/ən, trăns–]
   automatic... [ö/tə măt/ĭk–] **109**
   standard... [stăn/dərd–] **109**
TRANSPORTATION, PUBLIC [pŭb/lĭk trăns/pər tā/shən] **104**
trash [trăsh(/–)]
   ...bags [–băgz/] **47**–12
   ...bin [–bĭn/] **37**–20
   ...chute [–shōōt/] **37**–24
travel [trăv/əl] **29**–N
travel [trăv/əl]
   ...agency [–ā/jən sē] **92**–9
   ...agent [–ā/jənt] **139**–60
traveler's check [trăv/lərz chĕk/] **20**–17
tray [trā(/–)] **41**–10, **62**–H, **63**–7
   ...table [–tā/bəl] **110**–16

treatment [trēt/mənt] **80** ✦
TREES AND PLANTS [trēz/ ən plănts/] **128**
trench coat [trĕnch/ kōt/] **66**–20
triangle [trī/ăng/gəl] **118**–7
tricycle [trī/sĭ kəl] **153**–9
trigonometry [trĭg/ə näm/ə trē] **118**–27
trim [trĭm] **39**–E
tripe [trīp] **52**–8
tripod [trī/päd] **165**–20
trombone [träm bōn/] **120**–12
trout [trowt] **53**–16
trowel [trow/əl] **39**–14, **149**–12
truck driver [trŭk/ drī/vər] **139**–61
TRUCKS [trŭks] **106**
trumpet [trŭm/pət] **120**–13
trunk [trŭngk] (car) **109**–49, (tree) **128**–4, (animal) **135**–47
T-shirt [tē/shürt/] **64**–12, **70**–16, **72**–15, 16, 17, 18
tuba [tōō/bə] **120**–14
tube [tōōb(/–)] **56**–12
…of toothpaste [–əv tōōth/pāst/] **56**–24
Tuesday [tōōz/dā, –dē] **18**–3
tulip [tōō/ləp] **129**–11
tuna [tōō/nə] **54**–25, **130**–9
tuner [tōō/nər] **164**–13
tunic [tōō/nĭk] **65**–22
tunnel [tŭn/əl] **105**–11
turbulence [tür/byə ləns] **111**–N
turkey [tür/kē] **52**–17, **53**–4, **168**–17
turn [türn(/–)]
…left [–lĕft/] **107**–C
…right [–rīt/] **107**–B
turn in [türn/ ĭn/] **113**–E
turnips [tür/nəps] **51**–14
turn signal [türn/ sĭg/nəl] **108**–4
turntable [türn/tā/bəl] **164**–12
turquoise [tür/koyz, –kwoyz] **12**–4
turtle [tür/tl] **131**–42
turtleneck [tür/tl nĕk/] **64**–7
…sweater [–swĕt/ər] **71**–28
tusk [tŭsk] **135**–48
tuxedo [tŭk sē/dō] **65**–28
TV (television) [tē/vē/] **42**–26, **164**–6
…antenna [–ăn tĕn/ə] **38**–22
tweezers [twē/zərz] **83**–2
twelfth [twĕlfth] **14**
twelve [twĕlv] **14**
twentieth [twĕn/tē əth] **14**
twenty [twĕn/tē] **14**, **16**–8, 9, **20**–10
twenty-five after one [twĕn/tē fīv/ ăf/tər wŭn/] **16**–9
twenty-five to two [twĕn/tē fīv/ tə tōō/] **16**–11
twenty percent [twĕn/tē pər sĕnt/] **15**–8
twenty to two [twĕn/tē tə tōō/] **16**–12
twice a week [twīs/ ə wēk/] **18**–23
twig [twĭg] **128**–1
two [tōō] **14**
two-story house [tōō/stör/ē hows/] **38** ✦
type [tīp] **140**–M, **142**–D
Types of entertainment [tīps/ əv ĕn/tər tān/mənt] **166**
Types of material [tīps/ əv mə tïr/ē əl] **70**
Types of math [tīps/ əv măth/] **118**
TYPES OF SCHOOLS [tīps/ əv skōōlz/] **112**
Types of stories [tīps/ əv stör/ēz] **166**
Types of TV programs [tīps/ əv tē/vē/ prō/grămz] **167**
typewriter [tīp/rī/tər] **142**–2
…cartridge [–kär/trĭj] **143**–31

ugly [ŭg/lē] **11**–22
umbrella [ŭm brĕl/ə] **66**–16, **155**–9
umpire [ŭm/pīr] **158** ✦
uncle [ŭng/kəl] **24**–11
uncomfortable [ŭn kŭmf/tə bəl, –tər–] **30**–8
under [ŭn/dər] **13**–9, **105**–1
underexposed [ŭn/dər ĭk spōzd/] **165**–35
underline [ŭn/dər līn/] **7**–V
underpants [ŭn/dər pănts/] **67**–17
undershirt [ŭn/dər shürt/] **67**–10
uniform [yōō/nə förm/] **65**–17, **161**–16
UNIVERSE [yōō/nə vürs/] **127**
university [yōō/nə vür/sə tē] **112**–10
unload [ŭn lōd/] **72**–E
unpack [ŭn păk/] **35**–E
unscented [ŭn sĕn/təd] **77** ✦
up [ŭp] **105**–9
upset [ŭp sĕt/] **31**–30
upstairs [ŭp/stërz/] **38** ✦
Uranus [yōōr/ə nəs, yōō rā/nəs] **127**–3
urban area [ür/bən ër/ē ə] **34**–1
use [yōōz(/–)] **140**–N
…deodorant [–dē ō/dər ənt] **76**–C
user's manual [yōō/zərz măn/yōō əl] **144**–22
U.S. GOVERNMENT AND CITIZENSHIP
[yōō/ĕs/ gŭv/ər mənt ən sĭt/ə zən shĭp/] **116**
U.S. HISTORY [yōō/ĕs/ hĭs/tə rē] **114**–**115**
Using a pay phone [yōō/zĭng ə pā/ fōn/] **9**
Using the ATM machine [yōō/zĭng dhē ā/tē/ĕm/ mə shēn/] **97**
U.S. MAIL [yōō/ĕs/ māl/] **96**
utilities [yōō tĭl/ə tēz] **35** ✦
U-turn OK (sign) [yōō/türn/ ō kā/] **107**–7
vacancy sign [vā/kən sē sīn/] **36**–11
vacation [vā kā/shən] **19**–46
vaccination [văk/sə nā/shən] **80** ✦
vacuum [văk/yōōm] **46**–I
vacuum cleaner [văk/yōōm klē/nər] **47**–13
…attachments [–ə tăch/mənts] **47**–14
…bag [–băg/] **47**–15
valedictorian [văl/ə dĭk tör/ē ən] **32**–8
Valentine's Day [văl/ən tīnz dā/] **168**–4
valet parking [văl/ā pär/kĭng] **145**–1
valley [văl/ē] **117**–18
van [văn] **106**–10, 14
vandalism [văn/də lĭz/əm] **100**–1
vase [vās, văz, väz] **41**–9
vault [völt] **97**–2
VCR (videocassette recorder)
[vē/sē/är/] / [vĭd/ē ō kə sĕt/ rĭ kör/dər] **164**–8
veal cutlets [vēl/ kŭt/ləts] **52**–6
vegetable [vĕj/tə bəl]
…casserole [–kăs/ə rōl/] **58**
…garden [–gär/dn] **148**–12
…peeler [–pē/lər] **59**–15
VEGETABLES [vĕj/tə bəlz] **51**
vegetables [vĕj/tə bəlz] **55**–43
vegetarian [vĕj/ə tër/ē ən] **52** ✦
vein [vān] **75**–44
vendor [vĕn/dər] **91**–30
Venus [vē/nəs] **127**–8
vest [vĕst] **65**–24, **66**–13
veterinarian [vĕt/ər ə nër/ē ən] **139**–62
Vice President [vīs/ prĕz/ə dənt] **116**–7
victim [vĭk/təm] **100** ✦
video [vĭd/ē ō]

Index

...camera [–kăm/rə] **165**–19
...game system [–gām/ sĭs/təm] **162**–1
...store [–stör/] **93**–15
videocassette [vĭd/ē ō kə sĕt/] **98**–13, **164**–8, 10
view [vyōō] **11**–21, 22
vine [vīn] **128**–22
vineyard [vĭn/yərd] **148**–14
violet [vī/ə lət, vī/lət] **129**–22
violin [vī/ə lĭn/] **120**–8
vise [vīs] **150**–21
visor [vī/zər] **147**–11
vital signs monitor [vīt/l sīnz/ män/ə tər] **87**–21
vitamins [vī/tə mənz] **81**–19
V-neck sweater [vē/nĕk/ swĕt/ər] **71**–27
vocational school [vō kā/shə nəl skōōl/] **112**–9
volcanic eruption [väl kăn/ĭk ĭ rŭp/shən] **103**–14
volleyball [väl/ē böl/] (sport) **158**–14, (equipment) **161**–3
Volume [väl/yəm, –yōōm] **57**
volunteer [väl/ən tïr/] **87**–19
vomit [väm/ət] **78**–E
vote [vōt] **116**–D
waffles [wä/fəlz, wö/–] **61**–4
waist [wāst] **74**–4
waistband [wāst/bănd/] **73**–3
wait [wāt] **90**–B
waiter [wā/tər] **62**–4
waiting room [wā/tĭng rōōm/] **84**–1
wait on customers [wāt/ än kŭs/tə mərz, –ön–] **140**–O
waitress [wā/trəs] **63**–6
wake up [wāk/ ŭp/] **26**–A
walk [wök] **101**–A, **156**–A
walker [wö/kər] **80**–5, **95**–12
wall [wöl(/–)] **42**–6, **48**–4
...unit [–yōō/nət] **42**–13
wallet [wä/lət, wö/–] **69**–26
wallpaper [wöl/pā/pər] **45**–5
walrus [wöl/rəs] **131**–32
War [wör] **114**
warehouse [wër/hows/] **146**–9
warm [wörm] **10**–2
warning label [wör/nĭng lā/bəl] **80**–15
wash [wäsh(/–), wösh(/–)]
...hair [–hër/] **76**–E
...the dishes [–dhə dĭsh/əz] **46**–M
...the windows [–dhə wĭn/dōz] **46**–D
washcloth [wäsh/klöth/, wösh/–] **43**–14
washer [wä/shər, wö/–] **72**–3, **150**–32
wasp [wäsp, wösp] **132**–18
wastebasket [wāst/băs/kət] **43**–25, **46**–F
watch [wäch, wöch] **69**–34
watch TV [wäch/ tē/vē/, wöch/–] **27**–5
water [wö/tər] **39**–B
water [wö/tər] **117**, **155**–1
...fountain [–fown/tn] **153**–11
...glass [–glăs/] **63**–19
...pollution [–pə lōō/shən] **126**–12
...polo [–pō/lō] **158**–15
watercolor [wö/tər kŭl/ər] **163**–25
waterfall [wä/tər föl/] **117**–2
watering can [wö/tər ĭng kăn/] **39**–17
watermelons [wö/tər mĕl/ənz] **50**–24
waterskiing [wö/tər skē/ĭng] **160**–7
WATER SPORTS [wö/tər spörts/] **160**
wave [wāv] **155**–6
wavy [wā/vē] **23**–10

Ways to pay [wāz/ tə pā/] **20**
WEATHER [wĕdh/ər] **10**
Wednesday [wĕnz/dā, –dē] **18**–4
weed [wēd] **39**–A
week [wēk] **18**–11
weekdays [wēk/dāz/] **18**–12
weekend [wēk/ĕnd/] **18**–13
weigh [wā] **57**–B
weight [wāt] **22**–21, **57**
weightlifting [wāt/lĭf/tĭng] **159**–15
weights [wāts] **161**–19
WEIGHTS AND MEASURES [wāts/ ən mĕzh/ərz] **57**
welder [wĕl/dər] **139**–63
well [wĕl] **30**–15
west [wĕst] **107, 123, 124**
western [wĕs/tərn] **166**–9
wet [wĕt(/–)] **72**–17
...mop [–mäp/] **47**–16
...suit [–sōōt/] **155**–7
whale [wāl] **131**–29
wheat [wēt(/–)] **148**–2
...bread [–brĕd/] **53**–2
wheelbarrow [wēl/băr/ō] **39**–16
wheelchair [wēl/chër/] **80**–6
whisk [wĭsk] **59**–21
whiskers [wĭs/kərz] **134**–18
white [wīt(/–)] **12**–14
...bread [–brĕd/] **53**–1
White House [wīt/ hows/] **116**–5
whole [hōl(/–)] **15**–6
...salmon [–săm/ən] **53**–18
wide [wīd] **71**–44
widow [wĭd/ō] **29** ✦
widower [wĭd/ō ər] **29** ✦
width [wĭdth, wĭtth] **15**–17
wife [wīf] **24**–20, **25** ✦
wild animals [wīld/ ăn/ə məlz] **133** ✦
willow [wĭl/ō] **128**–14
win [wĭn] **158** ✦
wind [wĭnd] **126**–2
windbreaker [wĭnd/brā/kər] **66**–24
window [wĭn/dō] **38**–17, **42**–17
...pane [–pān/] **149**–15
...shade [–shād/] **44**–6
windshield [wĭnd/shēld/] **108**–2
...wipers [–wī/pərz] **108**–3
windy [wĭn/dē] **10**–10
wine glass [wīn/ glăs/] **63**–20
wing [wĭng] **132**–2
wings [wĭngz] **52**–20
winter [wĭn/tər] **19**–40
WINTER SPORTS AND WATER SPORTS
   [wĭn/tər spörts/ ən wö/tər spörts/] **160**
wipes [wīps] **95**–17
wipe the counter [wīp/ dhə kown/tər] **46**–O
wire [wīr(/–)] **151**–13
...stripper [–strĭp/ər] **151**–37
wish [wĭsh] **169**–J
withdraw cash [wĭdh drö/ kăsh/, wĭth–] **97**–D
witness [wĭt/nəs] **99**–11
wolf [wōŏlf] **134**–5
woman [wōŏm/ən] **22**–10
wood [wōŏd(/–)] **149**–17, **151**–18
...screw [–skrōō/] **150**–28
wooden spoon [wōŏd/n spōōn/] **59**–9

woodpecker [woŏd/pĕk/ər] **132**–9
Woodwinds [woŏd/wĭndz/] **120**
woodworking kit [woŏd/wûr/kĭng kĭt/] **162**–16
wool [woŏl(/–)] **70**–14
...scarf [–skärf/] **66**–4
work [wûrk/] **26**–K, **140**–P
workbook [wûrk/boŏk/] **3**–23
Work in a group [wûrk/ ĭn ə groŏp/] **6**
working [wûr/kĭng] **48**–1
work out [wûrk/ owt/] **157**–P
Work with a partner [wûrk/wĭdh/ ə pärt/nər, –wĭth/–] **6**
WORLD [wûrld] **124**–**125**
worm [wûrm] **130**–22
worried [wûr/ēd] **30**–13
wrap [răp] **169**–D
wrench [rĕnch] **109**–50, **151**–42, 43
wrestling [rĕs/lĭng] **159**–16
wrinkled [rĭng/kəld] **72**–19
wrist [rĭst] **69**–34, **75**–60
wristwatch [rĭst/wäch/, –wŏch/] **69**–34
write [rīt] **2**–G, **113**–A
writer [rī/tər] **139**–64
writing assignment [rī/tĭng ə sīn/mənt] **113**–1
wrong [rŏng(/–)]
...number [–nŭm/bər] **9** ✦
...way [–wā/] **107**–4
X-ray [ĕks/rā/]
...technician [–tĕk nĭsh/ən] **86**–8
xylophone [zī/lə fōn/] **120**–17
yams [yămz] **51**–22
YARD [yärd] **39**
yard [(–)yärd(/)]
front... [frŭnt/–] **38**–15
yard (measurement) [yärd] **15** ✦
yardstick [yärd/stĭk/] **151**–15
yarn [yärn] **163**–17
year [yïr] **4**–16, **18**–8
yellow [yĕl/ō] **12**–12
yesterday [yĕs/tər dā/, –dē] **18**–17
yield [yēld] **107** ✦
yogurt [yō/gərt] **54**–33, **60**–11
young [yŭng] **22**–13
zebra [zē/brə] **135**–34
zero [zïr/ō] **14**
ZIP code [zĭp/ kōd/] **4**–9
zipper [zĭp/ər] **73**–16
zoo [zoŏ] **152**–1
zookeeper [zoŏ/kē/pər] **152**–3
zoom lens [zoŏm/ lĕnz/] **165**–25
zucchini [zoŏ kē/nē] **51**–4

Geographical Index

Continents

Africa [ăf/rĭ kə] **125**–5
Antarctica [ănt ärk/tĭ kə, –är/tĭ–] **125**–7
Asia [ā/zhə] **125**–4
Australia [ö strāl/yə] **125**–6
Europe [yŏŏr/əp] **125**–3
North America [nörth/ ə mĕr/ə kə] **124**–1
South America [sowth/ ə mĕr/ə kə] **124**–2

Countries and other locations

Afghanistan [ăf găn/ə stăn/] **124–125**
Albania [ăl bā/nē ə] **124–125**
Algeria [ăl jĭr/ē ə] **124–125**125
American Samoa [ə mĕr/ə kən sə mō/ə] **124–125**
Andorra [ăn dör/ə] **124–125**
Angola [ăng gō/lə] **124–125**
Argentina [är/jən tē/nə] **124–125**
Armenia [är mē/nē ə] **124–125**
Australia [ö strāl/yə] **124–125**
Austria [ö/strē ə] **124–125**
Azerbaijan [ăz/ər bī jän/] **124–125**
Bahamas [bə hä/məz] **122–125**
Bahrain [bä rän/] **124–125**
Bangladesh [băng/glə dĕsh/, băng/–] **124–125**
Barbados [bär bā/dōs] **124–125**
Belarus [bē/lə rōōs/, byĕl/ə–] **124–125**
Belgium [bĕl/jəm] **124–125**
Belize [bə lēz/] **124–125**
Benin [bə nĭn/, –nēn/] **124–125**
Bermuda [bər myōō/də] **122–125**
Bhutan [bōō tän/] **124–125**
Bolivia [bə lĭv/ē ə] **124–125**
Borneo [bör/nē ō] **124–125**
Bosnia-Herzegovina [băz/nē ə hër/tsə gō vē/nə] **124–125**
Botswana [bät swä/nə] **124–125**
Brazil [brə zĭl/] **124–125**
Brunei [brōō nī/] **124–125**
Bulgaria [bŭl gër/ē ə] **124–125**
Burkina Faso [bər kē/nə fä/sō] **124–125**
Burundi [bōō rōōn/dē] **124–125**
Cambodia [kăm bō/dē ə] **124–125**
Cameroon [kăm/ə rōōn/] **124–125**
Canada [kăn/ə də] **122–125**
Cape Verde [kāp/ vürd/] **124–125**
Central African Republic [sĕn/trəl ăf/rĭ kən rĭ pŭb/lĭk] **124–125**
Chad [chăd] **124–125**
Chile [chĭl/ē] **124–125**
China [chī/nə] **124–125**
Colombia [kə lŭm/bē ə] **124–125**
Comoros [kăm/ə rōz] **124–125**
Congo [käng/gō] **124–125**
Costa Rica [kōs/tə rē/kə, käs/–] **122–125**
Croatia [krō ā/shə] **124–125**
Cuba [kyōō/bə] **122–125**
Cyprus [sī/prəs] **124–125**
Czech Republic [chĕk/ rĭ pŭb/lĭk] **124–125**
Democratic Republic of the Congo [dĕm/ə krăt/ĭk rĭ pŭb/lĭk əv dhə käng/gō] **124–125**
Denmark [dĕn/märk] **124–125**
Djibouti [jĭ bōō/tē] **124–125**
Dominica [däm/ə nē/kə] **124–125**
Dominican Republic [də mĭn/ĭ kən rĭ pŭb/lĭk] **122–125**
Ecuador [ĕk/wə dör/] **124–125**
Egypt [ē/jĭpt] **124–125**
El Salvador [ĕl săl/və dör/] **122–125**

Equatorial Guinea [ē/kwə tör/ē əl gĭn/ē, ĕk/wə–] **124–125**
Eritrea [ĕr/ə trē/ə] **124–125**
Estonia [ĕ stō/nē ə] **124–125**
Ethiopia [ē/thē ō/pē ə] **124–125**
Fiji [fē/jē] **124–125**
Finland [fĭn/lənd] **124–125**
France [frăns] **124–125**
French Guiana [frĕnch/ gē ăn/ə, –ä/nə] **124–125**
French Polynesia [frĕnch/ päl/ə nē/zhə] **124–125**
Gabon [gă bōn/] **124–125**
Georgia [jör/jə] **124–125**
Germany [jür/mə nē] **124–125**
Ghana [gä/nə] **124–125**
Greece [grēs] **124–125**
Greenland [grēn/lənd, –lănd/] **122–125**
Grenada [grə nā/də] **124–125**
Guatemala [gwä/tə mä/lə] **122–125**
Guinea [gĭn/ē] **124–125**
Guinea-Bissau [gĭn/ē bĭ sow/] **124–125**
Guyana [gī ăn/ə] **124–125**
Haiti [hā/tē] **122–125**
Honduras [hän dŏŏr/əs] **122–125**
Hong Kong [häng/ käng/] **124–125**
Hungary [hŭng/gə rē] **124–125**
Iceland [īs/lənd] **124–125**
India [ĭn/dē ə] **124–125**
Indonesia [ĭn/də nē/zhə] **124–125**
Iran [ĭ rän/, ĭ răn/] **124–125**
Iraq [ĭ räk/, ĭ răk/] **124–125**
Ireland [īr/lənd] **124–125**
Israel [ĭz/rē əl, –rā–] **124–125**
Italy [ĭt/l ē] **124–125**
Ivory Coast [īv/rē kōst/] **124–125**
Jamaica [jə mā/kə] **122–125**
Japan [jə păn/] **124–125**
Java [jä/və] **124–125**
Jordan [jör/dn] **124–125**
Kazakhstan [kä/zäk stän/] **124–125**
Kenya [kĕn/yə, kēn/–] **124–125**
Kiribati [kïr/ə băs/] **124–125**
Kuwait [kōō wāt/] **124–125**
Kyrgyzstan [kïr/gĭ stän/, –stän/] **124–125**
Laos [lows, lä/ōs] **124–125**
Latvia [lăt/vē ə] **124–125**
Lebanon [lĕb/ə nən, –nän/] **124–125**
Lesotho [lə sō/tō, –sōō/tōō] **124–125**
Liberia [lī bïr/ē ə] **124–125**
Libya [lĭb/ē ə] **124–125**
Liechtenstein [lĭk/tən stīn/] **124–125**
Lithuania [lĭth/ōō ā/nē ə] **124–125**
Luxembourg [lŭk/səm bürg/] **124–125**
Macedonia [măs/ə dō/nē ə] **124–125**
Madagascar [măd/ə găs/kər] **124–125**
Malawi [mə lä/wē] **124–125**
Malaysia [mə lā/zhə] **124–125**
Maldives [möl/dēvz, –dīvz] **124–125**
Mali [mä/lē] **124–125**
Malta [möl/tə] **124–125**
Marshall Islands [mär/shəl ī/ləndz] **124–125**
Mauritania [mör/ə tā/nē ə] **124–125**
Mauritius [mö rĭsh/əs] **124–125**
Mexico [mĕk/sĭ kō/] **122–125**
Micronesia [mī/krə nē/zhə] **124–125**
Moldova [mäl dō/və, möl–] **124–125**
Monaco [män/ə kō/] **124–125**

Mongolia [mäng gō**/**lē ə] **124–125**
Montenegro [män**/**tə nē**/**grō, –nē**/**–] **124–125**
Morocco [mə räk**/**ō] **124–125**
Mozambique [mō**/**zəm bēk**/**] **124–125**
Myanmar [myän**/**mär] **124–125**
Namibia [nə mĭb**/**ē ə] **124–125**
Nauru [nä ōō**/**rōō] **124–125**
Nepal [nə pöl**/**, –päl**/**] **124–125**
Netherlands [nĕdh**/**ər ləndz] **124–125**
New Guinea [nōō**/** gĭn**/**ē] **124–125**
New Zealand [nōō**/** zē**/**lənd] **124–125**
Nicaragua [nĭk**/**ə rä**/**gwə] **122–125**
Niger [nī**/**jər, nē zhër**/**] **124–125**
Nigeria [nī jïr**/**ē ə] **124–125**
North Korea [nörth**/** kə rē**/**ə] **124–125**
Norway [nör**/**wā] **124–125**
Oman [ō män**/**] **124–125**
Pakistan [păk**/**ə stăn**/**] **124–125**
Palau [pə low**/**] **124–125**
Panama [păn**/**ə mä**/**] **122–125**
Papua New Guinea [păp**/**yōō ə nōō**/** gĭn**/**ē] **124–125**
Paraguay [păr**/**ə gwī**/**, –gwä**/**] **124–125**
Peru [pə rōō**/**] **124–125**
Philippines [fĭl**/**ə pēnz**/**, fĭl**/**ə pēnz**/**] **124–125**
Poland [pō**/**lənd] **124–125**
Portugal [pör**/**chə gəl] **124–125**
Puerto Rico [pwër**/**tə rē**/**kō, pör**/**tə–] **122–125**
Qatar [kä**/**tär, kə tär**/**] **124–125**
Romania [rō mā**/**nē ə, rōō–] **124–125**
Russia [rŭsh**/**ə] **124–125**
Rwanda [rōō än**/**də] **124–125**
Saudi Arabia [sow**/**dē ə rä**/**bē ə, sö**/**dē–] **124–125**
Senegal [sĕn**/**ə göl**/**, –gäl**/**] **124–125**
Serbia [sür**/**bē ə] **124–125**
Seychelles [sā shĕlz**/**, –shĕl**/**] **124–125**
Sierra Leone [sē ĕr**/**ə lē ōn**/**, –lē ō**/**nē] **124–125**
Singapore [sĭng**/**ə pör**/**] **124–125**
Slovakia [slō vä**/**kē ə] **124–125**
Slovenia [slō vē**/**nē ə] **124–125**
Solomon Islands [säl**/**ə mən ī**/**ləndz] **124–125**
Somalia [sə mä**/**lē ə] **124–125**
South Africa [sowth**/** ăf**/**rĭ kə] **124–125**
South Korea [sowth**/** kə rē**/**ə] **124–125**
Spain [spān] **124–125**
Sri Lanka [srē**/** läng**/**kə, shrē**/**–] **124–125**
Sudan [sōō dăn**/**] **124–125**
Sumatra [sōō mä**/**trə] **124–125**
Suriname [sōŏr**/**ə nä**/**mə] **124–125**
Swaziland [swä**/**zē lănd**/**] **124–125**
Sweden [swēd**/**n] **124–125**
Switzerland [swĭt**/**sər lənd] **124–125**
Syria [sïr**/**ē ə] **124–125**
Tahiti [tə hē**/**tē] **124–125**
Taiwan [tī**/**wän**/**] **124–125**
Tajikistan [tä jĭk**/**ə stăn**/**, –stăn**/**] **124–125**
Tanzania [tăn**/**zə nē**/**ə] **124–125**
Tasmania [tăz mā**/**nē ə] **124–125**
Thailand [tī**/**lănd**/**, –lənd] **124–125**
The Gambia [dhə găm**/**bē ə] **124–125**
Togo [tō**/**gō] **124–125**
Tonga [täng**/**gə] **124–125**
Tunisia [tōō nē**/**zhə] **124–125**
Turkey [tür**/**kē] **124–125**
Turkmenistan [türk mĕn**/**ə stăn**/**, –stăn**/**] **124–125**
Uganda [yōō gän**/**də] **124–125**

Ukraine [yōō**/**krān, yōō krān**/**] **124–125**
United Arab Emirates [yōō nī**/**təd är**/**əb ĕm**/**ər əts] **124–125**
United Kingdom [yōō nī**/**təd kĭng**/**dəm] **124–125**
United States of America [yōō nī**/**təd stāts**/** əv ə mĕr**/**ə kə] **122–125**
Uruguay [yōŏr**/**ə gwī**/**, –gwä**/**] **124–125**
Uzbekistan [ōŏz bĕk**/**ə stän**/**, –stän**/**] **124–125**
Venezuela [vĕn**/**ə zwā**/**lə] **124–125**
Vietnam [vē**/**ĕt näm**/**, –năm**/**] **124–125**
Western Sahara [wĕs**/**tərn sə här**/**ə] **124–125**
Western Samoa [wĕs**/**tərn sə mō**/**ə] **124–125**
Yemen [yĕm**/**ən] **124–125**
Zambia [zăm**/**bē ə] **124–125**
Zimbabwe [zĭm bäb**/**wā] **124–125**

Bodies of water

Arabian Sea [ə rā**/**bē ən sē**/**] **124–125**
Arctic Ocean [ärk**/**tĭk ō**/**shən] **122–125**
Baffin Bay [băf**/**ən bā**/**] **122–125**
Baltic Sea [böl**/**tĭk sē**/**] **124–125**
Barents Sea [băr**/**ənts sē**/**] **124–125**
Beaufort Sea [bō**/**fərt sē**/**] **122–125**
Bering Sea [bër**/**ĭng sē**/**, bïr**/**–] **122–125**
Black Sea [blăk**/** sē**/**] **124–125**
Caribbean Sea [kăr**/**ə bē**/**ən sē**/**, kə rĭb**/**ē ən–] **122–125**
Caspian Sea [kăs**/**pē ən sē**/**] **124–125**
Coral Sea [kör**/**əl sē**/**] **124–125**
East China Sea [ēst**/** chī**/**nə sē**/**] **124–125**
Greenland Sea [grēn**/**lənd sē**/**, –lănd**/**–] **124–125**
Gulf of Alaska [gŭlf**/** əv ə lăs**/**kə] **122–125**
Gulf of California [gŭlf**/** əv kăl**/**ə förn**/**yə] **122–125**
Gulf of Honduras [gŭlf**/** əv hän dōŏr**/**əs] **122–125**
Gulf of Mexico [gŭlf**/** əv mĕk**/**sĭ kō**/**] **122–125**
Gulf of St. Lawrence [gŭlf**/** əv sānt**/** lör**/**əns, –lär**/**–] **122–125**
Hudson Bay [hŭd**/**sən bā**/**] **122–125**
Indian Ocean [ĭn**/**dē ən ō**/**shən] **124–125**
Labrador Sea [lăb**/**rə dör**/** sē**/**] **122–125**
Mediterranean Sea [mĕd**/**ə tə rā**/**nē ən sē**/**] **124–125**
North Atlantic Ocean [nörth**/** ət lăn**/**tĭk ō**/**shən] **122–125**
North Pacific Ocean [nörth**/** pə sĭf**/**ĭk ō**/**shən] **122–125**
North Sea [nörth**/** sē**/**] **124–125**
Norwegian Sea [nör wē**/**jən sē**/**] **124–125**
Persian Gulf [pür**/**zhən gŭlf**/**] **124–125**
Philippine Sea [fĭl**/**ə pēn**/** sē**/**] **124–125**
Red Sea [rĕd**/** sē**/**] **124–125**
Sea of Japan [sē**/** əv jə păn**/**] **124–125**
Sea of Okhotsk [sē**/** əv ō kätsk**/**] **124–125**
South Atlantic Ocean [sowth**/** ət lăn**/**tĭk ō**/**shən] **124–125**
South China Sea [sowth**/** chī**/**nə sē**/**] **124–125**
Southern Ocean [sŭdh**/**ərn ō**/**shən] **124–125**
South Pacific Ocean [sowth**/** pə sĭf**/**ĭk ō**/**shən] **124–125**

The United States of America

Capital: Washington, D.C. (District Of Columbia)
   [wä**/**shĭng tən dē**/**sē**/**, wö**/**–]

Regions of the United States

Mid-Atlantic States [mĭd**/**ət lăn**/**tĭk stāts**/**] **123–10**
Midwest [mĭd**/**wĕst**/**] **123–9**
New England [nōō**/** ĭng**/**glənd] **123–11**
Pacific States [pə sĭf**/**ĭk stāts**/**] **123–7**
Rocky Mountain States [räk**/**ē mown**/**tn stāts**/**] **123–8**
South [sowth] **123–13**
Southeast [sowth**/**ēst**/**] **123–13**
Southwest [sowth**/**wĕst**/**] **123–12**
West Coast [wĕst**/** kōst**/**] **123–7**

Geographical Index

States of the United States
Alabama [ăl/ə bàm/ə] **122–123**
Alaska [ə lăs/kə] **122–125**
Arizona [ăr/ə zō/nə] **122–123**
Arkansas [är/kən sö/] **122–123**
California [kăl/ə förn/yə] **122–123**
Colorado [kăl/ə răd/ō, –ra/dō] **122–123**
Connecticut [kə nĕt/ĭ kət] **122–123**
Delaware [dĕl/ə wër/] **122–123**
Florida [flör/ə də, flär/–] **122–123**
Georgia [jör/jə] **122–123**
Hawaii [hə wī/ē] **122–123**
Idaho [ī/də hō/] **122–123**
Illinois [ĭl/ə noy/] **122–123**
Indiana [ĭn/dē ăn/ə] **122–123**
Iowa [ī/ə wə] **122–123**
Kansas [kăn/zəs] **122–123**
Kentucky [kən tŭk/ē] **122–123**
Louisiana [lōō ē/zē ăn/ə] **122–123**
Maine [mān] **122–123**
Maryland [mër/ə lənd] **122–123**
Massachusetts [măs/ə chōō/səts] **122–123**
Michigan [mĭsh/ĭ gən] **122–123**
Minnesota [mĭn/ə sō/tə] **122–123**
Mississippi [mĭs/ə sĭp/ē] **122–123**
Missouri [mə zōōr/ē, –zōōr/ə] **122–123**
Montana [măn tăn/ə] **122–123**
Nebraska [nə brăs/kə] **122–123**
Nevada [nə văd/ə, –vä/də] **122–123**
New Hampshire [nōō/ hămp/shər] **122–123**
New Jersey [nōō/ jür/zē] **122–123**
New Mexico [nōō/ mĕk/sĭ kō/] **122–123**
New York [nōō/ yörk/] **122–123**
North Carolina [nörth/ kăr/ə lī/nə] **122–123**
North Dakota [nörth/ də kō/tə] **122–123**
Ohio [ō hī/ō] **122–123**
Oklahoma [ō/klə hō/mə] **122–123**
Oregon [ör/ĭ gən, –găn/, är/–] **122–123**
Pennsylvania [pĕn/səl vān/yə] **122–123**
Rhode Island [rōd/ ī/lənd] **122–123**
South Carolina [sowth/ kăr/ə lī/nə] **122–123**
South Dakota [sowth/ də kō/tə] **122–123**
Tennessee [tĕn/ə sē/] **122–123**
Texas [tĕk/səs] **122–123**
Utah [yōō/tö, –tä] **122–123**
Vermont [vər mänt/] **122–123**
Virginia [vər jĭn/yə] **122–123**
Washington [wä/shĭng tən, wö/–] **122–123**
West Virginia [wĕst/ vər jĭn/yə] **122–123**
Wisconsin [wĭs kän/sən] **122–123**
Wyoming [wī ō/mĭng] **122–123**

Canada
Capital: Ottawa [ät/ə wə]

Regions of Canada
Atlantic Provinces [ət lăn/tĭk prăv/ən səz] **123 – 6**
British Columbia [brĭt/ĭsh kə lŭm/bē ə] **123 – 2**
Northern Canada [nör/dhərn kăn/ə də] **123 – 1**
Ontario [än tër/ē ō/] **123 – 4**
Prairie Provinces [prë/ē prăv/ən səz] **123 – 3**
Quebec [kwĭ bĕk/] **123 – 5**

Provinces of Canada
Alberta [ăl bür/tə] **122–123**
British Columbia [brĭt/ĭsh kə lŭm/bē ə] **122–123**
Manitoba [măn/ə tō/bə] **122–123**

New Brunswick [nōō/ brŭnz/wĭk] **122–123**
Newfoundland [nōō/fən lənd] **122–123**
Northwest Territories [nörth/wĕst/ tĕr/ə tör/ēz] **122–123**
Nova Scotia [nō/və skō/shə] **122–123**
Ontario [än tër/ē ō/] **122–123**
Prince Edward Island [prĭns/ ĕd/wərd ī/lənd] **122–123**
Quebec [kwĭ bĕk/] **122–123**
Saskatchewan [sä skäch/ə wən, –wän/] **122–123**
Yukon Territory [yōō/kän tĕr/ə tör/ē] **122–123**

Mexico
Capital: Mexico (City) [mĕk/sĭ kō/ (sĭt/ē)]

Regions of Mexico
Chiapas Highlands [chē ä/pəs hī/ləndz] **123 – 18**
Gulf Coastal Plain [gŭlf/ kō/stəl plān/] **123 – 16**
Pacific Northwest [pə sĭf/ĭk nörth/wĕst] **123 – 14**
Plateau of Mexico [plă tō/ əv mĕk/sĭ kō/] **123 – 15**
Southern Uplands [sŭdh/ərn ŭp/ləndz] **123 – 17**
Yucatan Peninsula [yōō/kə tän/ pə nĭn/sə lə, yōō/kə tän/–] **123 – 19**

States of Mexico
Aguascalientes [ä/gwəs käl yĕn/täs] **122–123**
Baja California Norte [bä/hä kăl/ə förn/yə nör/tä] **122–123**
Baja California Sur [bä/hä kăl/ə förn/yə sōōr/] **122–123**
Campeche [käm pā/chä, käm pē/chē] **122–123**
Chiapas [chē ä/pəs] **122–123**
Chihuahua [chĭ wä/wä, –wə] **122–123**
Coahuila [kō/ə wē/lə] **122–123**
Colima [kə lē/mə] **122–123**
Distrito Federal [dĭ strē/tō fĕd/ə räl/] **122–123**
Durango [dōō răng/gō, –răng/–] **122–123**
Guanajuato [gwä/nə hwä/tō] **122–123**
Guerrero [gə rër/ō] **122–123**
Hidalgo [hĭ dăl/gō, ē dhäl/gō] **122–123**
Jalisco [hə lĭs/kō, –lēs/–] **122–123**
México [mĕk/sĭ kō/, mĕ/hē kō] **122–123**
Michoacán [mē/chō ä kän/] **122–123**
Morelos [mö rēl/ōs] **122–123**
Nayarit [nä/yə rēt/] **122–123**
Nuevo León [nwā/vō lā ōn/] **122–123**
Oaxaca [wə hä/kə, wä–] **122–123**
Puebla [pwĕb/lä] **122–123**
Querétaro [kə rĕt/ə rō/] **122–123**
Quintana Roo [kēn tä/nə rō/] **122–123**
San Luis Potosí [sän/ lōō ēs/ pō/tə sē/] **122–123**
Sinaloa [sē/nə lō/ə] **122–123**
Sonora [sə nör/ə] **122–123**
Tabasco [tə băs/kō] **122–123**
Tamaulipas [tä/mow lē/pəs] **122–123**
Tlaxcala [tlä skä/lə] **122–123**
Veracruz [vĕr/ə krōōz/, –krōōs/] **122–123**
Yucatán [yōō/kə tän/, –tän/] **122–123**
Zacatecas [zä/kə tā/kəs, sä/–] **122–123**

アーチェリー **159**–1
アーティチョーク **51**–20
アームストロング月面着陸 **115**
I 形鋼 **149**–3
あいさつをする **8**–A
アイシャドー **77**–34
アイスクリーム **55**–44
アイスクリーム屋 **93**–20
アイススケート **160**–4
アイススケート靴 **161**–9
アイスティー **60**–5
アイスホッケー **158**–13
間に **13**–10
アイデアを次々と出し合いリ
　ストにする **6**–K
アイフック **150**–35
アイライナー **77**–35
アイリス **129**–20
アイルランド人 **114**
アイロン **72**–13
アイロン台 **72**–14
アイロンのかかったシャツ **72**–20
合う項目を選ぶ **7**–X
青色 **12**–1
アオカケス **132**–7
青緑色 **12**–4
赤色 **12**–13
赤毛 **23**–14
赤砂糖1/4カップ **57**–8
明るい道を選ぶ **101**–B
赤ん坊 **22**–2
秋 **19**–39
空部屋の表示 **36**–11
アクション **166**–13
アクセル **109**–47
アクリル絵具 **162**–9
揚げる **58**–S
アコーディオン **120**–21
あご先 **74**–31
顎髭 **23**–6
朝 **17**–16
麻のジャケット **70**–17
アザラシ **131**–33
足 (くるぶしから下) **74**–7
脚 **74**–6
アジア **125**–4
足首 **75**–61
足首のねんざ **78**–18
足のつめ **75**–64
足場 **149**–4
味わう **75**–D
明日 **18**–16
預ける **94**–A
アスパラガス **51**–24
遊びに行く場所 **152**
遊び場 **36**–6
遊ぶ **94**–K
暖かい **10**–2
アダプタ **164**–17
頭 **74**–1
新しいアパートを探す **35**–A
新しい靴 **71**–32
暑い **10**–1, **30**–1
厚い本 **11**–7
厚手のジャケット **71**–41
宛先 **96**–8

アナウンサー **152**–27
穴を開ける **84**–21
兄 **24**–9
姉 **24**–8
アパート **34**–5, **36**–37
アパート番号 **4**–6
アパートを借りる **28**–I, **35**
アヒル **132**–13
アフターシェーブローション **77**–28
油 **55**–49
油1カップ **57**–2
油絵具 **163**–24
アフリカ **125**–5
アプリケーション **144**–21
あぶり焼きにする **58**–V
アボカド **50**–14
アポストロフィ **113**–11
雨靴 **66**–19
雨戸 **38**–12
雨樋 **38**–19
網戸 **38**–8
編み針 **163**–18
編み物をする **163**–F
雨 **10**–8
アメリカ合衆国の各地方 **123**
アメリカ国境を閉鎖 **114**
アメリカ史 **114**–**115**
アメリカ政府と市民権 **116**
アメリカ独立記念日 **168**–7
アメリカに5年以上住んでいる **116**–B
アメリカンインディアン **114**, **115**
アメリカンチーズ **53**–9
アメリカンライオン **134**–2
あやまる **8**–I
アラスカ時間 **17**–25
あり **49**–24
アリクイ **135**–24
アリゲーター **131**–36
歩く **156**–A
アルバム **165**–32
アルファベット **3**–30
アルファルファ **148**–5
アルマジロ **134**–8
アルミフォイル **55**–55
アルメニア人、南欧人及び東欧人 **115**
アレルギー **79**–8
アレルギー反応をおこす **82**–E
泡立器 **59**–21
暗証番号を押す **97**–B
安心して **30**–16
あんず **50**–7
安全靴 **147**–20
安全ピン **73**–24
アンテロープ **135**–35
案内係 **62**–1
案内所 **93**–22
案内板 **93**–19
胃 **75**–41
イーゼル **163**–21
家 **34**–6, **38**
家に帰る **27**–Q
家に住む害虫 **49**
家の修理 **48**–**49**
家の掃除をする **27**–N
家を買う **29**–O, **35**
家を飾り付けする **169**–C

家を見つける **35**
イカ **130**–10
いかだを漕ぐ **154**–4
行き止まり **107**–8
イグニション
　(エンジンの点火装置) **108**–25
池 **117**–21, **153**–6
生け垣 **39**–1
生け垣を刈込む **39**–E
石 **155**–24
医師 **137**–22
石壁 **149**–18
意識を失う **82**–B
医者 **84**–6, **137**–22
移住する **28**–C
衣装 **168**–13
いす **2**–7
イソギンチャク **130**–21
痛い **30**–12
板チョコ **55**–41
炒める **58**–W
一 **14**
いちご **50**–17
1時 **16**–4
1時間煮込む **58**–R
1時55分 **16**–15
1時5分 **16**–5
1時50分 **16**–14
1時35分 **16**–11
1時30分 **16**–10
1時15分 **16**–7
1時10分 **16**–6
一時停止する **165**–E
1時25分 **16**–9
1時20分 **16**–8
1時45分 **16**–13
1時40分 **16**–12
1ドル **20**–7
1ドル銀貨 **20**–6
一番 **14**
一万 **14**
一輪車 **39**–16
胃痛 **78**–4
1階 **36**–1
1缶のスープ **56**–15
一生の中の出来事 **28**–**29**
1セント **20**–1
一等賞 **152**–20
いっぱい入ったコップ **11**–9
一般的な疾患と子供がよくかかる病気 **79**
一方通行 **107**–6
1本のソーダ **56**–13
移動式電燈 **42**–3
移動バン **106**–14
糸くずを取り除く **72**–D
いとこ **24**–12
糸ぬき **73**–19
田舎 **34**–4
稲光り **10**–17
犬 **133**–11
衣服の説明 **70**–**71**
異母(父)兄弟 **25**–29, **25**–30
居間 **42**
移民 **114**
妹 **24**–8
イモムシ **132**–21

イモリ **130**–26
いやな **30**–9
イヤリング **69**–38
いり卵 **58, 61**–1
医療廃棄物用ゴミ箱 **86**–14
衣類 I **64**–65
衣類 II **66**
衣類 III **67**
イルカ **131**–30
色 **12**
岩 **155**–24
引火性 **147**–2
いんげん **51**–25
インコ **133**–15
印刷工 **138**–46
印刷屋 **91**–22
飲酒運転 **100**–3
飲酒運転をしない **101**–G
インスタントコーヒー **55**–51
インターコム **36**–8
インターネット普及 **115**
インチ **15**–13
インディアン排斥法 **114**
咽頭炎 **79**–4
インラインスケート **159**–9
インラインスケート靴 **161**–10
飲料 **55**–15
ヴァイオリン **120**–8
ウィンタースポーツとウォー
　タースポーツ **160**
ウィンドサーフィン **160**–10
ウインドブレーカー **66**–24
ウールのスカーフ **66**–4
ウールのセーター **70**–14
ウーンデッドニー戦い **115**
ウエイター **62**–4
ウエイトリフティング **159**–15
ウエイトレス **63**–6
ウェート **161**–19
ウエーブしている髪 **23**–10
植木 **42**–18
植木に水をやる **39**–B
植木鉢 **39**–18
ウエストバンド **73**–3
ウェットスーツ **155**–7
ヴェトナム戦争 **115**
上に **13**–6, **13**–8
植える **148**–A
ウォーターポロ **158**–15
ウォールユニット **42**–13
うがいをする **77**–L
受け皿 **63**–22
受付 **84**–2
受付係 **138**–47
受取る **96**–D
うさぎ **133**–13
牛の肩肉の薫製または塩漬け肉 **53**–6
後ろに **13**–3
薄い本 **11**–8
薄手のジャケット **71**–40
右折のみ **107**–9
歌をうたう **120**–B
内鍵 **37**–29
打ち身 **78**–12
宇宙 **127, 127**–22
宇宙ステーション **127**–18

宇宙飛行士 **127**–17
打つ **156**–G
美しい眺め **11**–21
腕 **74**–9
(腕) 時計 **69**–34
ウナギ **130**–5
ウニ **130**–20
乳母車 **95**–16
馬 **133**–4
馬に乗る **154**–9
生まれる **28**–A
海 **155**–1
海に住む哺乳類 **131**
海の生物、両生類、は虫類 **130**–**131**
裏庭 **38**–2
売上税 **21**–7
売る **21**–B
ウルシ **128**–25
うれしい **31**–32
うろこ **130**–3
上掛け **44**–11
上着 **66**–7, **66**–25
運転免許証 **29**–4
運動する **27**–W, **80**–D, **157**–P
運動靴 **68**–23
エアコン **108**–28
エアバッグ **108**–16
エイ **130**–6
映画 **152**–10, **166**–1
映画館 **88**–11
英作文 **113**
永住権カード **29**–3
HIV **79**–10
ATM/キャッシュディスペンサー **97**–3
ATMを使う **97**
栄養士 **87**–25
駅 **104**–13
液果 **128**–20
エクスクラメーションマーク **113**–8
餌をやる **148**–D
絵辞典 **3**–29
SF (サイエンスフィクション) **166**–12
エスカレーター **93**–21
枝 **128**–2
枝角 **134**–16
エチケット袋 **110**–15
X線技士 **86**–8
X線写真を撮る **85**–H
エネルギー源 **126**
エネルギーと環境 **126**
エネルギーを節約する **126**–C
エビ **130**–19
絵筆 **163**–23
絵本 **45**–17
えら **130**–2
襟 **73**–7
襟巻 **66**–4
エレベーター **37**–34
絵を描く **6**–M, **163**–E
絵を指す **2**–F
円 **118**–5
宴会サービス係 **33**–12
演劇 **121**–12
演算 **118**
エンジニア **137**–23
円周 **118**–15

エンジン **109**–41
円錐 **118**–11
演壇 **32**–5
円柱 **118**–12
延長コード **151**–14
エンドウまめ **51**–19
煙突 **38**–21
円の部位 **118**
鉛筆 **3**–20
鉛筆削り **3**–13
鉛筆をしまう **2**–L
鉛筆をとり出す **2**–K
尾 **134**–22
甥 **24**–18
オイルゲージ **108**–19
応急処置の手引き書 **83**–7
応急手当 **83**
横断歩道 **90**–8, **107**–10
横断幕 **33**–15
おう吐 **78**–E
OHP **2**–4
大枝 **128**–3
大型車 **106**–4
大型手さげ袋 **69**–29
オーガナイザー **143**–30
オオカミ **134**–5
大きい手 **11**–2
大きすぎる **70**–21
オーク **128**–18
オーケストラ **120**–1
大皿 **41**–3, **41**–6
オーストラリア **125**–6
大たつまき **103**–13
大津波 **103**–15
オートバイ **91**–19
オーバーオール **65**–21
大ハンマー **149**–22
大吹雪 **103**–11
オーブン **40**–20
オープンカー **106**–5
オーブンクリーナー **47**–3
オーブンで焼く **58**–U
オーブントースター **40**–15
オーブンを掃除する **46**–C
オーボエ **120**–5
丘 **117**–16
置物 (像) **162**–10
お客様を席に案内する **62**–B
お客に給仕する **140**–O
起きる **26**–B
屋外観覧席 **5**–10
屋上 **36**–5
奥行き **15**–15
贈り物 **33**–18
贈り物を包む **169**–D
送る **96**–B
贈る **21**–D
怒って **31**–29
伯父 **24**–11
叔父 **24**–11
押し入れ **44**–4
押込み **100**–6
押しピン **143**–43
おしゃぶり **95**–29
おしろい **77**–39
雄の子牛 **148**–21

汚染 **126**
遅い **17**–23
お惣菜と魚介類 **53**
お互いに話し合う **7**–P
おたふくかぜ **79**–7
おたま、しゃく **59**–7
落ち着いた **30**–10
落ち葉を集める **39**–F
オックスフォードシューズ **68**–20
夫 **24**–19
おつり **21**–9
弟 **24**–9
男 **4**–13
男の片親 **25**–26
大人 **22**–9
踊る **33**–J
驚いて **31**–31
お腹がいっぱい **30**–6
お腹がすいた **30**–5
おの **150**–3
伯母 **24**–10
叔母 **24**–10
オヒョウ **53**–20
オフィス **142**–143
オフィスビル **89**–24
オフィスマネージャー **143**–25
オペラ **166**–8
お弁当を作る **26**–F
溺れる **82**–I
お盆を運ぶ **62**–H
おまる **86**–13, **95**–10
おむつ交換台 **45**–12, **95**–9
おむつピン **95**–22
おむつ用バケツ **95**–23
おむつを替える **94**–E
重い箱 **11**–13
重さ **57**
重さと計量ハ **57**
面白い本 **167**–27
おもちゃ **94**–5
おもちゃの家 **45**–14
おもちゃ箱 **45**–24
おもちゃ屋 **92**–5
おもちゃをしまう **46**–H
おもり **161**–19
親 **94**–1
親指 **75**–56
お湯 **43**–5
泳ぐ **157**–T
オランウータン **135**–40
オルガン **120**–22
オレンジ **50**–10
オレンジ色 **12**–6
おろしがね **59**–2
お笑い芸 **166**–5
音楽 **120**
音楽家 **138**–41
温室 **152**–5
温水ボイラー (湯沸器)
　が故障している **48**–1
オンタリオ **123**–4
温度計 **108**–23
雄鶏 **133**–6
女 **4**–14
女の片親 **25**–24
オンラインカタログ **98**–9
カ (蚊) **132**–23

ガ (蛾) **132**–22
ガーゼ **83**–6
ガーターヘビ **131**–39
ガーターベルト **67**–19
カーディガン **65**–27
カーテン **42**–16, **44**–5
カート **91**–31
カード **168**–5
カード式索引 **98**–10
カードショップ **92**–7
カートリッジ **162**–2
ガードル **67**–18
カートン **56**–4
カーニバル **152**–16
カーネーション **129**–18
カーペット **42**–27
カーペットに掃除器をかける **46**–I
カーラー **23**–31
ガーリックブレッド **61**–16
海王星 **127**–2
絵画 **42**–7, **152**–8
貝殻 **155**–21
海岸 **155**
会議室 **145**–19
会計士 **136**–1
外国語 **121**–8
会社を出る **26**–M
海水パンツ **66**–22
階段 **37**–26, **37**–35, **38**–13
階段が壊れている **48**–7
階段を上に **105**–9
階段を下に **105**–8
害虫駆除業者 **49**–21
懐中電灯 **151**–39
回転椅子 **143**–22
回転式カードファイル **143**–17
街灯 **91**–23
解答用紙の答えに印を付ける **7**–T
買値を伝える **35**–H
外被 **134**–19
解剖器具 **119**–7
買物 **21**
〜の買物をする **21**–A
海洋 **117**–6
海洋動物 **130**
カイロプラクティックに行く **81**–H
会話を終える **8**–C
会話を始める **8**–B
下院 **116**–1
下院議員 **116**–2
下院女性議員 **116**–2
買う **21**–C
ガウン **32**–2, **67**–5
カウンセラー **5**–16
カウンセラー室 **5**–15
カエデ **128**–13
カエル **130**–25
顔 **74**
画架 **163**–21
画家 **138**–43
化学 **119**–2
科学 **119**
かかと **68**–13, **75**–62
鏡 **43**–18, **44**–1
カキ **53**–27
かぎ **150**–34
鍵 **37**–31, **109**–34

鍵が壊れている **48**–6
(かぎ) つめ **132**–4
かぎつめのある足 **134**–20
垣根 **38**–3
かぎ針編み **163**–20
かき混ぜる **58**–E
鍵屋 **48**–11
学習 **6**–7
角錐 **118**–13
学生 **2**–3, **139**–57
家具のつやだし **47**–18
家具のほこりをはらう **46**–A
革命戦争 **115**
家具屋 **88**–13
隠れる **169**–E
家具を配置する **35**–K
家具をみがく **46**–K
掛け算 **118**–3
掛け布団 **45**–2
囲い **148**–19
囲い柵 **148**–17
傘 **66**–16
火災 **102**–7
飾り **168**–19
過酸化水素 **83**–8
火山の噴火 **103**–14
家事 **46**
貸金庫 **97**–13
貸し出しカウンター **98**–16
加湿器 **80**–2
菓子屋 **92**–3
カジュアルな服 **71**–37
果樹園 **148**–16
ガスペダル **109**–47
ガスメーター **48**–14
風邪 **79**–1
火星 **127**–6
家政学 **121**–9
家政婦 **138**–33
風がある **10**–10
カセットテープ **98**–12
カセットプレーヤー **3**–11
カセットレコーダー **164**–3
風邪の錠剤 **81**–17
河川 **117**–3
家族 **24**–25
ガソリンスタンド **88**–12
ガソリンスタンド従業員 **137**–28
肩 **74**–10
固い椅子 **11**–5
肩までの髪 **23**–2
塊 **56**–10
花壇の草むしりをする **39**–A
家畜 **148**–13
家畜とげっ歯動物 **133**
ガチョウ **132**–14
楽器店 **92**–1
楽器を演奏する **120**–A
学校 **89**–27, **5**
学校で **26**–J
学校登録用の用紙 **4**
学校の種類 **112**
合衆国アラスカを買収 **115**
合衆国憲法 **115**
かど **107**–1
カトリック系の学校 **112**–3
角を曲がって **105**–10

悲しい **31**–20
悲しい本 **167**–28
カナダの各地方 **123**
カナダ北部 **123**–1
金槌 **150**–1
金物屋 **88**–14
カニ **130**–16
蟹 **53**–22
カヌーを漕ぐ **154**–3
カバ **135**–43
鞄はなるべく体の近くでもつ **101**–C
花瓶 **41**–9
かぶ **51**–14
カフェイン抜きのコーヒー **61**–23
カフェテリア **5**–4
株価暴落 **114**
カフス **73**–15
カプセル **81**–27
カブトムシ **132**–19
壁 **42**–6
壁紙 **45**–5
壁取付棚 **42**–13
壁にひびが入っている **48**–4
かぼちゃの提灯 **168**–11
髪 **74**–19
髪型の特徴 **23**
紙製品 **55**–14
かみそり **77**–25
かみそりの刃 **77**–26
髪止めピン **76**–18
雷をともなった嵐 **10**–16
紙袋 **55**–22
紙吹雪 **168**–3
紙ヤスリ **151**–50
髪用クリップ **76**–17
髪を洗う **76**–E
髪を乾かす **76**–H
髪を切る **23**–A
髪をすすぐ **76**–F
髪をセットする **23**–C
髪を染める **23**–D
髪をとかす **76**–G
髪を分ける **23**–4
ガム **55**–42
カムコーダー **165**–21
カメ **131**–42
カメラケース **165**–27
仮面 **168**–12
画面 **152**–12
カモ **132**–13
かも肉 **52**–18
カモノハシ **135**–46
火曜日 **18**–3
柄 **70**
ガラガラ **95**–31
ガラガラヘビ **131**–38
辛子 **60**–24
ガラスクリーナー **47**–8
体 **74**–75
体と歯の診断 **85**
身体を洗うタオル **43**–14
空のコップ **11**–10
刈込み用植木ばさみ **39**–15
カリフォルニアで金を発見 **115**
カリフラワー **51**–16
軽い箱 **11**–14

カルーセル **110**–18
カルテ **87**–20
カレイ **130**–13
カレンダー **18**–19
かわいい **22**–24
乾いた Tシャツ **72**–18
為替 **20**–16
皮のジャケット **66**–3
皮のブーツ **70**–18
缶 **56**–3
巻 **56**–11
ガン **132**–14
眼科医 **86**–7
カンガルー **135**–44
観客 **32**–10
缶切り **59**–1
韓国人 **115**
看護婦 **84**–10, **138**–42
観察する **119**–B
鉗子、ピンセット **119**–8
監視 **99**–3
監視員 **155**–18
元日 **168**–1
監視塔 **155**–20
患者 **84**–3
感謝祭 **168**–15
患者を補助する **140**–B
感情 **30**–31
勘定係 **55**–19
勘定台 **60**–13
環状のおしゃぶり **95**–30
勘定を支払う **62**–I
管制塔 **110**–7
肝臓 **75**–39
乾燥機 **72**–4
乾燥機から洗濯物を取り出す **72**–E
乾燥機用のシート **72**–5
観測所 **127**–19
カンタロープ **50**–15
簡単な問題 **11**–23
感嘆符 **113**–8
缶詰類 **54**–4
かんな **151**–52
(缶の) スープ **54**–24
乾杯する **33**–I
干ばつ **103**–10
看板 **91**–29
乾物類の計量 **57**
丸薬 **81**–26
管理人 **36**–12, **138**–35
管理人と話す **35**–B
聞いたことを確認する **8**–E
キーボード **144**–7
キーホルダー **69**–43
黄色 **12**–12
気温 **10**
機械オペレータ **138**–37
幾何学 **118**–26
気が転倒して **31**–30
機器を修理する **140**–G
キク **129**–19
聴く **75**–B
喜劇 **166**–10
危険な状況 **147**–8
危険廃棄物 **126**–9
危険物質 **147**–7

岸 **117**–12
技術工作 **121**–10
傷口を縫う **83**–15
キスする **33**–F
傷ついた **30**–17
着せ替え人形 **163**–30
規則正しい **87**–18
北アメリカ **124**–1
北アメリカと中央アメリカ **122**–**123**
きついズボン **71**–43
キックする **156**–L
喫茶店のメニュー **61**
キッチンタイマー **59**–18
キツツキ **132**–9
キツネ **134**–15
軌道 **127**–11
木ねじ **150**–28
記念日 **19**–42
技能 **140**
木のスプーン **59**–9
木の部分 **128**
牙 **135**–48
木ばさみ **39**–12
義父 **24**–14, **25**–28
気分が良い **30**–15
気分が悪い **30**–14
義母 **24**–13, **25**–31
気泡マット **154**–13
気持ちがいい **30**–7
客 **145**–11
客 (ゲスト) を招待する **169**–B
客室 **145**–10
客室乗務員 **110**–13
キャセロール皿 **59**–11
脚立 **47**–7
キャッシャー **136**–14
キャッシュカード **97**–9
キャッシュカードを挿入する **97**–A
キャッシュカードを抜き取る **97**–F
キャッチする **156**–E
キャッチャーマスク **161**–15
キャップ **66**–6
キャベツ **51**–2
キャミソール **67**–21
キャラクター人形 **163**–31
キャンディ **168**–14
キャンパー **106**–11
キャンバス **163**–22
キャンプする **154**–1
キャンプファイア **154**–11
キャンプ用コンロ **154**–16
九 **14**
キューバ人 **115**
休暇 **19**–46
球技場 **153**–1
救急医療士 **87**–26
救急の病状 **82**
救急箱 **83**–1
救急病院 **87**
救急用の医療腕輪 **83**–14
球根 **129**–9
給士 **62**–4, **63**–6
給仕人 **139**–53
九十 **14**
救助員 **155**–18
球場 **152**–26

求職 **141**
求人掲示板を見る **141**–B
求人掲示を探す **141**–C
求人広告欄で探す **141**–D
球体 **118**–14
牛肉 **52**
牛乳1クオート **57**–4
九番 **14**
救命胴衣 **154**–14
救命道具 **155**–19
きゅうり **51**–12
給料についてたずねる **141**–K
今日 **18**–15
教会 **88**–6
胸郭 **75**–53
教科書 **3**–22
競技場 **152**–26
競技場 **5**–12
教区学校 **112**–3
教師 **5**–2, **139**–58
教室 **2**–3, **5**–1
教室で学ぶ **7**
矯正器 **84**–24
競争する **157**–Y
興味深い本 **167**–30
曲線 **118**–19
霧が出ている **10**–11
切り傷 **78**–13
きり先 **150**–23
義理の兄弟 **24**–16, **25**–33
義理の姉妹 **24**–15, **25**–32
キリン **135**–33
きれいなTシャツ **72**–16
木を植える **39**–D
銀河系 **127**–26
緊急サービス (911) **9**–9
緊急事態と自然災害 **102**–103
金魚 **133**–16
キング牧師暗殺 **115**
銀行 **88**–3, **97**
銀行の窓口係 **97**–1
金庫室 **97**–2
金星 **127**–8
緊張して **30**–11
筋肉 **75**–48
金髪 **23**–16
勤務時間についてたずねる **141**–F
金曜日 **18**–6
空気清浄器 **80**–4
空気ドリル **149**–9
空港 **110**
空欄を埋める **7**–R
9月 **19**–33
茎 **129**–4
釘 **150**–29
釘をうつ **149**–D
腐った **50**–30
鎖 **69**–31
クシ **23**–22
櫛 **76**–13
クジャク **132**–15
くしゃみ **78**–B
クジラ **131**–29
くずかご **43**–25
くずかごを空にする **46**–F
薬のラベル **80**–14

薬を過量にとる **82**–K
薬を飲む **80**–F
管継手 **151**–17
果物 **50**
果物ナイフ **59**–16
口 **74**–22
クチナシ **129**–16
くちばし **132**–1
口髭 **23**–5
唇 **74**–30
口紅 **77**–37
靴売り場 **68**–3
クッキー **54**–31
クッキー 1箱 **56**–20
クッキーシート **59**–27
靴下 **67**–15
クッション **42**–20
靴底 **68**–12
靴とアクセサリー **68**–69
靴ひも **68**–14
靴紐をむすぶ **94**–I
靴屋 **92**–10
くつろぐ **27**–U
句読法 **113**
首 **74**–2
クマ **134**–11
熊手 **39**–11
組立工 **136**–6
組立ライン **146**–8
クモ **132**–30
曇り **10**–7
クラクション **108**–24
クラゲ **130**–14
グラス **41**–26
クラッチ **109**–45
クラブ **163**–26
グラフィックアーティスト **137**–29
クラリネット **120**–4
クリアテープ **143**–39
グリーティングカード **96**–4
クリーム入れ **41**–13
クリスマス **168**–18
クリスマスツリー **168**–20
クリップ **143**–44
クリップボード **143**–26
くり抜き機 **150**–12
グリル **58**–T
グリルチーズサンドイッチ **61**–8
グループで学習する **6**
車椅子 **80**–6
車で通勤する **26**–I
車とトラック **106**
車の運転を習う **28**–E
車の部品とメンテナンス **108**–109
車用安全椅子 **95**–13
車を運転する **90**–C
車を販売する **140**–H
グレープフルーツ **50**–9
クレーン **149**–7
クレジットカード **20**–15
クレヨン **45**–21
クレンザー **47**–23
黒色 **12**–15
グローブ **161**–17
グローブボックス **108**–33
黒髪 **23**–15

クロコダイル **131**–37
クロスカントリースキー **160**–3
クロッカス **129**–25
軍人 **139**–54
軍隊に入る **28**–F
郡の農産物・家畜品評会 **152**–19
経営管理アシスタント **136**–3
経済学 **121**–6
警察官 **99**–1, **138**–44
警察署 **89**–19
警察に犯罪を通報する **101**–H
計算機 **142**–8
掲示板 **3**–14
芸術家 **136**–5
携帯テレビ **164**–7
携帯電話 **9**–13
毛糸 **163**–17
鶏肉 **52**–16
鶏肉を切る **58**–M
鶏肉を茹でる **58**–P
競馬 **159**–18
警備員 **97**–4
警備ゲート **36**–13
警備保障システム **36**–9
刑務所に入る **99**–G
計量値を換算する **57**–C
経歴を話す **141**–I
刑を宣告する **99**–F
ケーキ **54**–32, **61**–19
ケーキミックス **55**–47
ケーキ用焼き型 **59**–26
ゲート **110**–5
ゲートで搭乗手続きをする **111**–D
ケーブル **144**–16
ゲーム **152**–18
ゲームショー **167**–23
ゲームをする **162**–B
外科医 **87**–30
毛皮 **134**–19
ケガをする **82**–A
劇場 **88**–10
消印 **96**–9
消しゴム **3**–21
化粧しっくい **149**–14
化粧台 **44**–2
化粧をする **77**–P
ゲスト **33**–14
ゲストスピーカー **32**–9
けた **149**–3
ケチャップ **60**–23
血圧計 **84**–12
血圧をはかる **85**–B
血液検査 **86**–17
血液をとる **85**–G
結核 **79**–13
結果を記録する **119**–C
結婚 **25**–23
結婚証明書 **29**–8
結婚する **28**–L
げっ歯動物 **133**
月曜日 **18**–2
毛ぬき **83**–2
ケネディ暗殺 **115**
ケベック **123**–5
毛虫 **132**–21
煙探知器 **37**–25, **45**–11

県 **4**–8
検眼検査士 **81**–34
玄関で応対する **169**–F
玄関のドア **38**–11
現金 **20**–13
現金を引き出す **97**–D
弦月 **127**–15
検査技師 **86** 16
検察官 **99**–10
原子 **119**–17
拳銃 **100**–9
原子力エネルギー **126**–8
建設工事 **149**
建築家 **136**–4
現場労働者 **149**–1
顕微鏡 **119**–4
権利章典 **115**
権利と責務 **116**
五 **14**
コアラ **135**–45
子犬 **133**–12
故意の破壊行為 **100**–1
恋をして **30**–19
恋をする **28**–K
コイン収集 **162**–13
コインランドリー **90**–1
高圧危険 **147**–1
公園 **88**–8
公園と運動場 **153**
郊外 **34**–2
甲殻類 **53**
硬貨を入れる **9**–C
交換手 **9**–7
公共の安全 **101**
公共の交通機関 **104**
抗菌性軟膏 **83**–9
航空会社の係員 **110**–2
航空会社のターミナル **110**–1
航空券を買う **111**–A
口腔内洗浄剤 **77**–23
航空便 **96**–13
合計 **21**–8
工芸技術 **121**–10
高血圧 **79**–15
高校 **112**–7
工作をする **162**–D
交差点 **90**–91
講師 **139**–58
格子柄 **70**–9
公式 **119**–19
子牛の肉 **52**–6
公衆衛生員 **139**–51
公衆電話 **9**–11, **91**–21
公衆電話の使用 **9**
工場 **146**
工場所有者 **146**–2
工場労働者 **146**–6
香辛料 **55**–46
香水 **76**–5
洪水 **103**–16
高層ビル **89**–25
紅茶 **61**–24
校長 **5**–14
校長室 **5**–13
交通事故 **102**–2
交通信号 **90**–6

講堂 **5**–3
強盗 **100**–5
公認准看護婦 **87**–24
合板 **149**–16
抗ヒステミンのクリーム **83**–10
後部席 **109**–38
興奮して **31**–23
公民権運動 **115**
コウモリ **134**–7
公立学校 **112**–1
港湾労働者 **137**–21
小枝 **128**–1
小エビ **53**–24
コーチ **158**–2
コート **66**–2
コードレス電話 **9**–12
コーヒー **61**–22
コーヒー (紅茶) カップ **63**–21
コーヒーショップ **88**–2
コーヒー茶碗 **41**–27
コーヒーテーブル **42**–23
コーヒーメーカー **40**–11
コーラス **121**–3
氷が張っている **10**–13
ゴールインする **157**–Z
コールスロー **53**–14
コオロギ **132**–24
コーンビーフ **53**–8
戸外のレクリエーション **154**
小型車 **106**–2
小型トラック **106**–7
5月 **19**–29
小切手帳 **97**–7
ごきぶり **49**–25
顧客 **62**–5
呼吸ができない **82**–N
呼吸数・脈拍を示すモニター **87**–21
国際電話 **9**–6
国際連合 **114**
黒板 **2**–1
黒板消し **3**–17
黒板に書く **2**–G
黒板を消す **2**–H
午後 **17**–18
凍えそうに寒い **10**–5
ココナッツ **50**–22
腰 **74**–5
五十 **14**
50ドル **20**–11
50セント **20**–5
50パーセント **15**–9
コショウ入れ **41**–15
個人競技 **159**
個人用小切手 **20**–14
小銭入れ **69**–25
5セント **20**–2
答えを確認する **7**–Y
答えを丸で囲む **7**–S
ごちそう **168**–16
骨格 **75**
コック **137**–17
骨折する **82**–P
小包 **96**–5
小包郵便 **96**–14
骨盤 **75**–55
こて **76**–15, **149**–12

固定装具 **81**–31
コテージチーズ 1パック **56**–17
5通りの鶏肉調理法 **58**
言葉に下線を引く **7**–V
言葉を言う **6**–C
言葉を書き写す **6**–F
言葉をくりかえす **6**–D
言葉を調べる **6**–A
言葉を正しい順に並べる **7**–W
言葉をつづる **6**–E
言葉を読む **6**–B
子供 **22**–1
子供が生まれる **29**–M
子供の世話をする **140**–L
子供番組 **167**–24
子供部屋 **45**
子供用安全シート **109**–39
子供を学校に連れていく **26**–G
子供を迎えに行く **27**–O
5ドル **20**–8
子猫 **133**–10
小ねじ **150**–27
この車はオイルが必要です **109**–55
この車はガソリンが必要です **109**–54
この車はスモッグ検査が必要
　です **109**–57
このタイヤは空気が必要です **109**–59
このバッテリは再充電が必要
　です **109**–58
このラジエーターはクーラントが
　必要です **109**–56
五番 **14**
コピー機 **142**–14
コピー屋 **91**–22
コピーをとる **142**–E
子羊肉の厚切り **52**–15
子羊の足 **52**–14
子羊のすね肉 **52**–13
子羊の肉 **52**
こぶ **135**–51
コブラ **131**–40
ごみ入れ **37**–20, **39**–3
ごみ収集車 **91**–27
ごみ袋 **47**–12
ごみを出す **46**–Q
ゴム印 **143**–40
小麦 **148**–2
小麦粉 **55**–45
小麦粉1カップ **57**–10
小麦パン **53**–2
ゴム製手袋 **87**–33
ゴムぞうきん **47**–9
ゴム手袋 **47**–4, **147**–17
ゴム糊 **143**–38
ゴムマット **43**–3
米 **54**–28, **148**–1
子守 **136**–12
コヨーテ **134**–3
娯楽 **166**–167
娯楽の種類 **166**
ゴリラ **135**–30
ゴルフ **159**–7
ゴルフクラブ **161**–1
コロン **76**–5, **113**–12
怖い **31**–24
壊れたファスナー **70**–24

紺色 **12**–2
コンクリート **149**–10
コンサート **166**–6
今週 **18**–19
コンセント **44**–20, **151**–41
コンタクトレンズ **81**–36
コンディショナー **76**–10
コンビニエンスストアー **90**–3
コンピューター **3**–15, **144**
コンピューターサイエンス **121**–4
コンピューターで仕事をする **140**–P
コンピューター普及 **115**
コンピュータープログラマー **136**–16
コンピューターワークステーション **143**–21
梱包係 **146**–13
梱包用テープ **143**–42
コンマ **113**–10
混乱して **31**–27
サージ保安器 **144**–10
サーフィン **160**–9
サーブする **157**–N
サーフボード **155**–5
サイ **135**–29
菜園 **148**–12
サイクリスト **153**–3
サイクリング **159**–4
最高裁判所 **116**–8
最高裁判所判事 **116**–10
在庫管理事務員 **139**–55
さいころ **162**–4
再婚 **25**–27
祭日 **19**–44
サイズ **70**
再生する **165**–B
再生利用する **126**–A
採草地、牧草地 **117**–20
裁断機 **143**–15
サイドテーブル **42**–21
サイドブレーキ **109**–44
サイドミラー **108**–8
裁判官 **99**–6
裁判所 **89**–18
裁判を受ける **99**–D
財布 **69**–26
財布を守る **101**–D
裁縫師 **137**–27
裁縫とサイズ直し／\ **73**
材木 **149**–17, **151**–18
採用される **141**–L
材料を測定する **57**–A
材料を混ぜ合わせる **58**–K
サインする **4**–D
魚 **53**
魚釣りをする **154**–5
魚捕り網 **154**–17
魚の部位 **130**
魚のフライ **61**–17
砂丘 **117**–5
昨日 **18**–17
サクソフォーン **120**–7
作文 **113**–2
作物 **148**
サクランボ **50**–16
サソリ **132**–31
作家 **139**–64

サッカー **158**–12
サッカーボール **161**–12
雑誌 **98**–7
雑誌入れ **42**–22
殺人 **100**–8
砂糖 **55**–48, **60**–21
砂糖入れ **41**–12
砂糖大さじ1杯 **57**–7
砂糖代替品 **60**–22
砂漠 **117**–4
寂しい **30**–18
サボテン **128**–21
寒い **10**–4, **30**–4
寒気 **78**–9
サメ **130**–7
皿 **41**–24
皿洗い機 **40**–4
サラダドレッシング **60**–18
サラダバー **60**–16
サラダフォーク **63**–24
サラダ用の皿 **63**–17
皿拭き用タオル **47**–22
サラミ **53**–5
皿を洗う **46**–M
皿を拭く **46**–N
サランラップ **55**–54
サル **135**–27
ざる **59**–22
サワークリーム **54**–37
騒がしい子供 **11**–11
三 **14**
産科医 **86**–1
3階 **36**–3
三角形 **118**–7
三角法 **118**–27
3月 **19**–27
三脚 **165**–20
サングラス **66**–21
三十 **14**
35ミリカメラ **165**–24
サンショウウオ **130**–27
酸性雨 **126**–11
酸素マスク **110**–14
残高 **97**–11
サンタフェにスペイン人 **114**
サンダル **68**–24
山地時間 **17**–27
山頂 **117**–14
三番 **14**
350度のオーブンで45分焼く **58**–L
3分の1 **15**–3
山脈 **117**–15
三輪車 **153**–9
四 **14**
市 **4**–7
幸せな **31**–32
C型クランプ **150**–6
飼育者 **148**–15
シーソー **153**–16
シーツを換える **46**–P
CD (コンパクトディスク) **98**–14
CD プレーヤー **164**–14
CD ROM ディスク **144**–2
シートベルト **109**–36
シートベルト (腰) **109**–37
シートベルトを締める **111**–I

ジーパン **64**–5
CPU (中央処理装置) **144**–1
ジーンズ **64**–5
シェード **44**–18
シェービングクリーム **77**–27
ジェットコースター **152**–15
シェフ **63**–11
シェフのサラダ **61**–9
ジェル **76**–11
塩入れ **41**–14
塩小さじ1杯 **57**–6
シカ **134**–14
歯科 **84**
歯科医 **84**–18
市外局番 **4**–10
歯科衛生士 **84**–16
視覚障害のある **22**–26
歯科助手 **84**–19, **137**–19
4月 **19**–28
時間 **16**–3, **16**–17
四季 **19**
資金を振替える **97**–E
茂み **39**–20
試験管 **119**–16
時刻表 **104**–3
自己紹介 **4**
自己紹介する **8**–D
仕事と職業 **136**–139
指示に従う **7**
磁石 **119**–21
刺繍 **163**–19
四十 **14**
司書 **98**–1
辞書 **3**–28
司書デスク **98**–2
辞書を使う **6**
静かな子供 **11**–12
歯石 **84**–17
自然ドキュメンタリー **167**–22
舌 **74**–26
下あご **74**–23
下着 **67**–10
仕出し屋 **33**–12
下に **13**–7, **13**–9
シタビラメ **53**–21
七 **14**
7月 **19**–31
七十 **14**
七番 **14**
七面鳥 **168**–17
七面鳥の薫製 **53**–4
七面鳥の肉 **52**–17
シチュー鍋 **59**–25
シチュー用牛肉 **52**–3
疾患と症状 **79**
実験をする **119**–A
湿疹 **78**–10
室内の鉢植え植物 **129**–29
質問する **6**–G
質問に答える **6**–H
自転車 **153**–4
自転車競技用半ズボン **67**–3
自転車道 **153**–2
自転車に乗る **91**–E
自動車運転教習 **121**–5
自動車修理工 **136**–7

自動車販売店 **88**–4
市内通話 **9**–4
死ぬ **29**–R
芝居 **166**–2
芝刈り機 **39**–22
芝生 **39**–21
芝生を刈る **39**–C
支払方法 **20**
シフトレバー **109**–48
紙幣 **20**
島 **117**–8
シマウマ **135**–34
縞模様 **70**–7
シマリス **133**–20
しみ **70**–22
市民権獲得証明書 **29**–6
市民権申請の必要条件 **116**
市民権の試験を受ける **116**–C
市民権を得る **28**–H
事務室 **5**–17
氏名 **4**–1
しもやけになる **82**–G
社会保障番号 **4**–15
社会保障番号証 **29**–5
じゃがいも **51**–21
市役所 **89**–17
蛇口 **43**–6
蛇口から水漏れがする **49**–16
釈放される **99**–H
借家人 **37**–33
ジャケット **66**–7
車庫 **38**–6
車庫の戸 **38**–7
車掌 **104**–16
写真 **44**–7
写真店 **90**–4
写真を撮る **32**–D
ジャスミン **129**–21
シャツ **64**–4, **64**–10
ジャッキ **109**–51
ジャックチーズ **53**–12
シャッター **38**–18
シャベル **39**–13, **149**–21
車輪つき担架 **87**–28
シャワーキャップ **76**–1
シャワーヘッド **43**–10
シャワーを浴びる **26**–C, **76**–A
ジャングルジム **153**–14
ジャンパーケーブル **109**–52
ジャンパースカート **65**–18
シャンプー **76**–9
ジャンプスーツ **65**–16
ジャンプする **156**–J
週 **18**–11
十 **14**
10ドル **20**–9
獣医 **139**–62
十一 **14**
11月 **19**–35
週 1度 **18**–22
十一番 **14**
十億 **14**
収穫する **148**–B
10月 **19**–34
重機械を操作する **140**–F
19歳の少女 **22**–8

住居 **34**
住居侵入 **100**–6
十九 **14**
十九番 **14**
十五 **14**
十五番 **14**
十三 **14**
13歳の少年 **22**–7
週 3度 **18**–24
十三番 **14**
十七 **14**
十七番 **14**
住所 **4**–5
就職する **28**–G
修正液 **143**–33
10代の少年少女 **22**–6
住宅ローンを払う **35**–L
じゅうたん **44**–23
シュートする **156**–I
柔軟仕上げ剤 **72**–6
十二 **14**
十二か月 **19**
12月 **19**–36
週 2度 **18**–23
十二番 **14**
十八 **14**
十八番 **14**
18歳に達している **116**–A
十番 **14**
週末 **18**–13
十万 **14**
重油流出 **126**–15
十四 **14**
十四番 **14**
修理工 **138**–48
修理人 **48**–10
十六 **14**
十六番 **14**
祝祭日 **168**
祝日 **19**–43
熟していない **50**–28
熟している **50**–29
宿題をする **27**–T
手術看護婦 **87**–29
手術室 **87**
手術台 **87**–34
手術帽 **87**–31
手術用ガウン **87**–32
出荷係 **146**–15
出荷する **146**–C
出血する **82**–M
10才の少女 **22**–5
出生証明書 **29**–1
出生地 **4**–17
10セント **20**–3
出廷する **99**–C
10パーセント **15**–7
出発 **111**–L
授乳する **94**–D
シュノーケル **160**–11
主婦 **137**–32
趣味とゲーム **162**–163
樹木と植物 **128**
シュレッダー **143**–24
受話器 **9**–2
受話器を取る **9**–A

巡回見世物 **152**–16
準小型車 **106**–1
順番 **14**
ジョイスティック **144**–9
小 **70**–2
上院 **116**–3
上院議員 **116**–4
消火器 **147**–22
消火栓 **91**–28
小学校 **112**–5
定規 **3**–27
乗客 **104**–7, **110**–23
衝撃を受ける **82**–C
証拠 **99**–9
正午 **17**–17
症状と重い病気 **79**
症状とけが **78**
消毒剤 **95**–19
小児科医 **86**–4
小児用の食事椅子 **95**–7
商品 **152**–24
消防士 **102**–8, **137**–24
消防車 **102**–9
消防署 **88**–1
静脈 **75**–44
じょうろ **39**–17
小惑星帯 **127**–12
ショーケース **69**–7
ショートパンツ **64**–13
ジョギングする **156**–B
職員 **5**–18
職業教育 **121**–2
職業訓練校 **112**–9
食後のテーブルを片づける人 **63**–9
食事客 **62**–5
食餌を変える **80**–C
食卓 **41**–17
食堂 **5**–4, **41**, **62**–2
食堂の椅子 **41**–16
職場の安全対策 **147**
食品を計量する **57**–B
植物園 **152**–4
初稿を書く **113**–A
女子選挙権実現 **114**
女性 **22**–10
食器一式 **41**–2
食器だな **41**–1
食器用洗剤 **47**–21
食器用の部屋 **63**–12
食器を洗う人 **63**–13
ショッピングカート **54**–3
ショッピングかご **54**–7
ショッピング番組 **167**–25
ショッピングモール **92**–93
処方薬 **80**–11, **80**–13
署名 **4**–18, **98**–21
書類トレー **142**–5
書類を照合する **142**–F
書類をファイルする **142**–H
ショルダーバッグ **69**–27
ショルダーパッド **161**–21
シラカバ **128**–8
知らない人にドアを開けない **101**–F
尻 **74**–12
ジリス **133**–19
私立学校 **112**–2

資料整理係 **142**–12
視力検査表 **84**–11
シルクのスカーフ **68**–4
シルクのスカーフ **70**–15
歯列矯正医 **84**–23
白あり **49**–22
白色 **12**–14
シロップ **61**–5
白パン **53**–1
しわだらけのシャツ **72**–19
心音を聴く **85**–D
神経 **75**–50
新月 **127**–13
人口 **114**
人口呼吸 **83**–16
信号を待つ **90**–B
申告書 **110**–22
診察室 **84**–9
診察台 **84**–13
診察用ガウン **86**–15
寝室 **44**
伸縮性のある包帯 **83**–12
針状葉 **128**–12
(紳士用) 仕立て屋 **73**–9
新鮮な魚 **53**–29
心臓 **75**–38
腎臓 **75**–45
心臓専門医 **86**–3
心臓病 **79**–14
心臓発作をおこす **82**–D
身体障害者 **22**–25
身体障害者用の駐車スペース **107**–14
進入禁止 **107**–4
心配して **30**–13
心肺蘇生法 **83**–17
審判員 **158**–6
新聞 **98**–8
新聞雑誌店 **90**–11
新聞紙をリサイクルする **46**–B
新聞を読む **27**–V
診療所 **84**
森林 **117**–11
巣 **132**–3
スイカ **50**–24
水球 **158**–15
スイギュウ **134**–6
水彩絵具 **163**–25
水質汚染 **126**–12
水準儀 **150**–24
水上スキー **160**–7
水上を横切って **105**–3
スイスチーズ **53**–11
水星 **127**–9
彗星 **127**–25
垂線 **118**–20
スイセン **129**–26
膵臓 **75**–46
スイッチ **44**–19
水筒 **154**–24
水道管が凍結している **49**–19
水分を補給する **80**–B
水曜日 **18**–4
水力発電 **126**–5
スウィングする **157**–O
スウェットシャツ **64**–14
スウェットパンツ **64**–15
数学 **118**

数字 **3**–31, 14
数学の種類 **118**
数字と度量法 **14**–15
スーツ **64**–2
スーパー **54**–55, 89–20
スーパーに行く **26**–L
スープ皿 **63**–18
スープスプーン **63**–29
ズームレンズ **165**–25
スカートなどの裾 **73**–1
頭蓋骨 **75**–52
スカンク **134**–12
スキー **161**–24
スキー靴 **161**–26
スキーストック **161**–25
スキーマスク **66**–14
スキーをする **157**–U
スキャナー **144**–13
スキューバダイビング **160**–12
スクリーン **2**–2, 144–6, 165–28
スクワッシュ **51**–13
図形 **118**
スケートボード **159**–12
スケートをする **157**–V
スケジュール管理帳 **143**–27
スコア **158**–1
スコットランド人、アイルランド人、
　ドイツ人 **115**
スコップ **39**–14
頭上の収納用スペース **110**–10
涼しい **10**–3
スズメ **132**–8
スズメバチ **132**–18
スタートする **157**–X
スタンプ台 **143**–41
頭痛 **78**–1
ズッキーニ **51**–4
ステーキ **61**–13
ステーキナイフ **63**–26
ステーキ用肉 **52**–2
ステージ **32**–4
ステーションワゴン **106**–8
すてきな **22**–23
ステレオ **42**–14
ストーリーの種類 **166**
ストッキング **67**–26
ストロー **60**–20
砂 **155**–23
スナック菓子 **55**–16
砂の城 **155**–10
砂場 **153**–15
すね当て **161**–13
スノーボード **160**–2, 161–23
スパゲッティ **54**–27
スパッツ **65**–23
スパナ **151**–43
スピーカー **36**–8, 164–11
スピーチをする **32**–E
スプーン **41**–23
スプリンクラー **39**–8
スプレーガン **151**–19
スプレー糊 **72**–12
スペード **163**–28
すべり台 **153**–13
スポイト **119**–14
スポーツカー **106**–6
スポーツ関連の動詞 **156**–157

スポーツコート **64**–6
スポーツシャツ **65**–26
スポーツユーティリティー車 **106**–9
スポーツ用品 **161**
スポンジ **47**–24
ズボン下 **67**–11
ズボンつり **68**–2
スミレ **129**–22
スモッグ **126**–10
スモッグが出ている **10**–14
スライド **119**–5, 165–31
スライドトレー **165**–30
スラックス **64**–8
スリット入りスカート **65**–25
スリッパ **67**–6
スリップ **67**–22
スロット **144**–19
座る **2**–E
寸法 **15**
寸法をはかる **149**–C
姓 **4**–4
星雲 **127**–26
青果売り場 **54**–11
税関 **110**–20
税関検査官 **110**–21
整形外科医 **81**–28
制限速度 **107**–5
星座 **127**–24
制酸薬 **81**–18
精神科医 **86**–6
成人学校 **112**–8
清掃カート **145**–14
清掃係 **145**–15
製造する **146**–B
盛装用ドレス **71**–36
生年月日 **4**–16
製氷器 **145**–18
制服 **65**–17
西部劇 **166**–9
生物学 **119**–1
生物学的危険 **147**–5
性別 **4**–12
正方形 **118**–6
正方形の部位 **118**
整理された押し入れ **11**–15
セイウチ **131**–32
セイヨウヒイラギ **128**–19
セーター **64**–11
セーリング **160**–8
セール価格 **21**–3
世界 **124**–125
背が高い **22**–16
背が低い **22**–18
せき **78**–A
席 **152**–11
石炭 **126**–4
脊柱 **75**–54
せき止めのシロップ **81**–20
席につく **2**–E
石油 **126**–6
セキュリティーチェックを受ける **111**–C
席を見つける **111**–G
セコイア **128**–7
絶縁テープ **151**–38
設計士 **146**–3
設計する **146**–A
石鹸 **43**–23, 76–2

石鹸付金属たわし **47**–5
石鹸箱 **43**–24
節約 **126**
背中 **74**–11
セミコロン **113**–13
セミトレーラー **106**–15
ゼロ **14**
零 **14**
セロリ **51**–9
世話をする **94**–C
千 **14**
線 **118**
千一 **14**
洗剤を加える **72**–B
選手 **158**–5
先週 **18**–18
潜水用タンク **155**–8
先生 **2**–5, **5**–2
先生と話す **2**–B
喘息 **79**–11
洗濯かご **72**–2
洗濯機 **72**–3
洗濯機に入れる **72**–C
洗濯ばさみ **72**–10
洗濯物 **72**–1
洗濯物かご **43**–1
洗濯物を仕分ける **72**–A
洗濯物をたたむ **72**–F
洗濯用洗剤 **72**–7
洗濯をする **72**
センチ **15**–12
前置詞 **13**
選抜徴兵に登録する **116**–F
1812戦争 **114**
全部 **15**–6
前部席 **109**–35
洗面台 **43**–22
洗面台があふれている **49**–17
専門学校 **112**–9
線路 **104**–10
ゾウ **135**–42
ぞうきん **47**–6
倉庫 **146**–9
走行距離計 **108**–21
総合大学 **112**–10
捜索救助隊 **103**–17
掃除、洗濯の用具 **47**
掃除機 **47**–13
掃除機の中の袋 **47**–15
掃除機の付属品 **47**–14
操縦士 **110**–12
操縦室 **110**–11
装飾の多いブラウス **71**–39
添え木 **83**–11
ソーサー **63**–22
ソーセージ **52**–12, **61**–2
ソーダ **60**–4
速度計 **108**–20
側面 **118**–22
素材のタイプ **70**
卒業 **32**–33
卒業学年 **32**–1
卒業証書 **32**–7
卒業証明書 **29**–2
卒業する **28**–D
卒業する **32**–A

卒業生 **32**–6
卒業生代表 **32**–8
袖 **73**–6
そで口 **73**–15
袖なしシャツ **71**–29
その他の科目 **121**
祖父 **24**–3
ソファー **42**–19
ソフトウェア **144**
ソフトボール **158**–10
祖父母 **24**–1
祖母 **24**–2
空の旅 **111**
そり遊び **160**–6
タートルネック **64**–7
タートルネックのセーター **71**–28
ターンテーブル **110**–18, **164**–12
大 **70**–4
題 **113**–3
ダイアモンド **163**–27
体育 **121**–11
体育館 **5**–9
第一胃と第二胃の食用部分 **52**–8
第一次世界大戦 **114**
体温計 **84**–15
対角線 **118**–23
大学卒業証書 **29**–7
大学に行く **28**–J
大学寮 **34**–9
大気汚染 **126**–10
大恐慌 **114**
大峡谷 **117**–17
〜の代金を払う **21**–C
大工 **136**–13, **48**–12
退屈な **31**–26
退屈な本 **167**–29
台車 **146**–11
体重計 **43**–26, **84**–7
体臭防止剤 **76**–4
体臭防止剤を使う **76**–C
大豆 **148**–3
代数学 **118**–25
大西洋時間 **17**–30
大西洋諸州 **123**–6
体操 **159**–8
大腿部 **74**–16
タイツ **66**–11
大統領 **116**–6
台所 **40**
台所用品 **59**
体内 **75**
第二言語としての英語 **121**–7
第二次世界大戦 **114**
第二次世界大戦避難民の移民 **114**
ダイニングテーブル **41**–17
堆肥の山 **39**–10
ダイビングマスク **155**–3
タイプライター **142**–2
タイプライターカートリッジ **143**–31
タイプを打つ **140**–M
太平洋時間 **17**–26
太平洋諸州 **123**–7
太平洋北西部 **123**–14
ダイム **20**–3
タイムレコーダー **146**–4
タイヤ **108**–10

ダイヤルを回す **9**–D
太陽 **127**–10
太陽エネルギー **126**–1
大陸 **124**
大陸横断鉄道 **115**
タイル **43**–9
ダウンジャケット **66**–15
タウンハウス **34**–7
ダウンヒルスキー **160**–1
ダウンベスト **66**–13
楕円形 **118**–9
タオルかけ **43**–8
倒れる **82**–O
高いヒール **71**–47
高い指輪 **11**–19
高さ **15**–14
滝 **117**–2
抱き合う **33**–G
タキシード **65**–28
抱く **94**–B
タクシー **104**–18, **106**–16
タクシー許可証 **104**–22
タクシーの運転手 **104**–20
タクシーの外へ **105**–5
タクシーの中へ **105**–4
タクシー乗り場 **104**–19
託児所 **94**–95
託児所職員 **94**–3
卓上カレンダー **142**–6
宅配の配達人 **138**–38
タコ **130**–4
タコス **60**–9
足し算 **118**–1
ダストラッフル **44**–22
立つ **2**–D
卓球 **159**–13
タックルする **156**–M
ダッシュボード **108**–17
タツノオトシゴ **130**–23
たてがみ **135**–49
たな **40**–8
谷 **117**–18
ダニ **132**–28
タヌキ **134**–13
種 **129**–1
だぶだぶのズボン **71**–42
卵 **54**–34
卵 1パック **56**–16
卵 3個を割る **58**–A
卵の泡立器 **59**–20
たまねぎ **51**–28
玉葱を炒める **58**–H
玉葱を切る **58**–G
多目的ナイフ **154**–20
タラ **130**–8
タルカムパウダー **76**–3
たわし **47**–19
タンクトップ **67**–2
炭酸飲料 **55**–52
誕生日 **19**–41
たんす (箪笥) **45**–8
ダンスフロアー **33**–16
男性 **22**–11
男性用スポーツサポーター **67**–14
団体競技 **158**
断熱材 **149**–13

胆のう **75**–40
短髪 **23**–1
短波ラジオ **164**–5
タンバリン **120**–19
ダンプカー **106**–12
暖房炉が故障している **49**–15
段落 **113**–5
暖炉 **42**–9
暖炉棚 **42**–8
暖炉のスクリーン **42**–11
小さい手 **11**–1
小さい町 **34**–3
小さすぎる **70**–20
チーズ **54**–38
チーズ1オンス **57**–11
チーズバーガー **60**–3
チーズをおろす **58**–J
チーム **158**–3
チェーン **150**–36
チェス **162**–6
チェダーチーズ **53**–10
チェッカー **162**–5
チェック柄 **70**–11
チェリークレーン
　（移動式クレーン）**149**–5
チェロ **120**–9
チェロキー族の「涙の道」虐殺 **114**
地下鉄 **104**–9
地球 **127**–7
地球儀 **3**–9
チキンスープ **58**
畜牛 **148**–21
畜舎 **148**–17
地震 **102**–5
地図 **3**–12
地図帳 **98**–3
父 **24**–6
乳をしぼる **148**–C
チップを置く **62**–J
地熱エネルギー **126**–7
乳房 **74**–14
地方 **34**–4
茶色 **12**–11
茶色髪 **23**–17
着陸 **111**–O
チャパス高地 **123**–18
中 **70**–3
注意書き **80**–15
注意深い **147**–24
中央アメリカ人 **115**
中央時間 **17**–28
中型車 **106**–3
中学校 **112**–6
中近東人 **115**
中国人、スカンジナビア人 **115**
注射器 **84**–14
駐車禁止 **107**–12
駐車場 **36**–15, **89**–26, **90**–5
駐車する **91**–D
駐車メーター **91**–18
注射をうつ **80**–E
中西部 **123**–9
中大西洋諸州 **123**–10
チューナー **164**–13
中年の **22**–14
チューバ **120**–14

チューブ **56**–12
注文品取揃え係 **146**–10
注文を受ける **62**–E
チューリップ **129**–11
チュニック **65**–22
チョウ **132**–20
腸 **75**–42
聴覚訓練士 **81**–32
長距離電話 **9**–5
調合乳 **95**–25
彫刻 **152**–9
朝食を食べる **26**–E
聴診器 **84**–8
朝鮮戦争 **115**
蝶ネクタイ **69**–40
腸の寄生虫 **79**–16
長髪 **23**–3
長方形 **118**–8
調理済みの鶏肉 **52**–25
調理台 **40**–22
調理台を拭く **46**–O
調理場 **63**–10
チョーク **3**–16
直線 **118**–18
直毛 **23**–9
著者 **98**–22
チョッキ **65**–24
直径 **118**–17
散らかった押し入れ **11**–16
地理 **117**
ちりとり **47**–11
賃貸契約に署名する **35**–C
鎮痛剤 **81**–16
チンパンジー **135**–28
通貨 **20**
通学路 **107**–13
通勤する **26**–I
通訳 **138**–34
通路 **54**–5
つえ **80**–7
使い捨ておむつ **95**–20
月 **4**–16, **18**–9, **19**–25
月々の貸借表 **97**–10
机 **2**–6
ツタウルシ **128**–25
つち **150**–2
ツナ（缶）**54**–25
角 **118**–24, **134**–21
つばさ **132**–2
つぼみ **129**–6
つま先 **68**–15, **75**–63
爪先保護 **147**–21
積み木 **45**–15
つめ **75**–58
つめきり **77**–29
詰め物 **84**–22
つめやすり **77**–30
つめを切る **77**–N
つめを磨く **77**–O
釣竿 **154**–18
つり包帯 **80**–8
つるはし **149**–20
手 **74**–8
手洗い **5**–8
ティーシャツ **64**–12
ティースプーン **63**–28

ティーポット **41**–11
定価 **21**–2
定期刊行物セクション **98**–6
デイジー **129**–14
停止して取り出す **165**–F
ディスク **144**–5
ディスクドライブ **144**–3
停電している **48**–2
ディナー皿 **63**–15
ディナーフォーク **63**–25
低木 **39**–20
廷吏 **99**–13
テープ **83**–5
テープデッキ **108**–30
テーブル **110**–16
テーブルクロス **41**–18
テーブルをかたづける **62**–G
テーブルを整える **62**–A
テープを聞く **2**–C
デオドラント **76**–4
手紙 **96**–2
手紙をタイプする **142**–D
手紙をファックスする **142**–B
でき上がるまで調理する **58**–F
手首 **75**–60
デザート用のトレー **63**–7
手提げランプ **154**–22
手仕事をする **140**–D
手錠 **99**–2
デスク **142**–1
デスクジョッキー/DJ **33**–17
デスクパッド **142**–7
デッキ **38**–16
テディベア **45**–10
手で縫う **73**–A
テニス **159**–14
テニス靴 **68**–22
テニスコート **153**–7
テニスラケット **161**–2
手荷物受取所 **110**–17
手荷物運搬カート **145**–6
手荷物運搬人 **110**–19
手のひら **75**–59
手羽 **52**–20
デパート **93**–13
手拭 **43**–13
手袋 **66**–5
手持ち削岩機 **149**–9
テラス **39**–6
テラス用家具 **39**–5
テレビ **42**–26, **164**–6
テレビのアンテナ **38**–22
テレビの普及 **115**
テレビ番組 **166**–3
テレビ番組の種類 **167**
テレビを見る **27**–S
テレフォンカード **9**–10
テレマーケッター **139**–59
手をあげる **2**–A
電化製品と写真 **164**–165
天気 **10**
電気鉛筆削り **142**–9
電気かみそり **77**–24
電気缶切り **40**–14
電気ショックを受ける **82**–F
電気ドリル **150**–8

電気ミキサー **40**–25
電気屋 **48**–9, **93**–18
電球 **42**–4
電球 (エジソン) **115**
電源 **144**–4
伝言を受ける **142**–A
伝言を残す **9**–E
展示会 **152**–21
電子キーボード **120**–20
電車 **104**–17
電車の模型 **163**–32
店主 **139**–56
天井 **42**–5
天井扇風機 **41**–4
電子レンジ **40**–13
デンタルフロス **77**–22
電池 **151**–40
店長 **54**–8
点滴 **87**–27
テント **154**–10
電燈 **41**–5
テントウムシ **132**–27
天然ガス **126**–3
天王星 **127**–3
天板 **59**–13
天板棚 **59**–14
天秤 **119**–11
天文学者 **127**–20
天文台 **127**–19
展覧会 **152**–21
電話 **9**, **9**–1
電話 (ベル) **115**
電話線 **9**–3
電話帳 **9**–15
電話番号 **4**–11
電話番号案内 (411) **9**–8
電話をかけて情報を集める **141**–E
電話を切る **9**–F
ドアに鍵をかける **101**–E
ドアのチェーン **37**–28
ドアノブ **37**–30
ドアマン **36**–10, **145**–2
トイレ、風呂場 **43**
トイレットトレーニングパンツ **95**–24
トイレットブラシ **43**–16
トイレットペーパー **43**–15
胴 **74**–4
唐辛子 **51**–8
道具と建築用材 **150–151**
動作の前置詞 **105**
当座預金口座番号 **97**–8
搭乗口 **110**–6
搭乗券を受け取る **111**–E
搭乗する **111**–F
搭乗手続カウンター **110**–3
胴体 **135**–47
到着 **111**–O
東南アジア人 **115**
糖尿病 **79**–9
投票する **116**–D
東部時間 **17**–29
動物 **152**–2
動物園 **152**–1
動物園職員 **152**–3
動脈 **75**–43
とうもろこし **51**–27

トウモロコシ **148**–4
等量 **15**
動力式サンダー **150**–9
登録看護婦 **87**–22
トークショー **167**–20
トークン (代用硬貨) **104**–11
トースター **40**–7
トースト **61**–3
ドーナッツ **60**–15
ドーナツ型スライド映写機 **165**–29
ドーナツ屋 **91**–20
都会 **34**–1
トカゲ **131**–41
特小 **70**–1
特大 **70**–5
毒物を飲む **82**–J
独立宣言 **115**
トグルボルト **150**–33
とげ **129**–28
時計 **3**–10
時計付きラジオ **164**–1
床屋 **88**–15
年 **4**–16, **18**–8
都市 **34**–1
土砂崩れ **102**–6
図書館 **89**–28, **98**
図書館員 **98**–17
図書館カード **98**–19
図書館の本 **98**–20
年をとった **22**–15図書館 **5**–6
土星 **127**–4
戸棚 **40**–1, **43**–19
取っ手 **37**–30
トド **131**–34
隣近所 **37**–22
飛び込む **157**–S
トマト **51**–23
止まれ **107**–3
友達と歩く **101**–A
友達にお礼を言う **8**–H
友達を紹介する **8**–F
友達をほめる **8**–G
土曜日 **18**–7
トラ **135**–37
ドライ壁 **149**–18
ドライクリーニング店 **91**–24
ドライブウエイ **38**–5
ドライブスルー用の窓 **90**–13
ドライヤー **23**–20, **76**–16
トラクター **148**–9
トラック **5**–11
トラック運転手 **139**–61
トラックボール **144**–15
トラックを運転する **140**–E
トラッシュシュート **37**–24
トラベラーズチェック **20**–17
ドラム **120**–18
トランク **109**–49
トランプをする **163**–H
トランペット **120**–13
取り替える **21**–G
鳥、昆虫、蛛形類 **132**
鳥の部位 **132**
ドリブルする **156**–K
度量法 **15**
トルネード **103**–13

奴隷 **115**
奴隷制廃止 **115**
トレーナー **64**–14
トレーラー **106**–17
トレーラートラック **106**–15
ドレス **73**–1
ドレッサー **44**–2
トレンチコート **66**–20
トロンボーン **120**–12
トング **59**–23
トンネルをぬけて **105**–11
名 **4**–2
ナースステーション **87**
内科専門医 **86**–2
ナイトテーブル **44**–21
ナイトライト **45**–3
ナイフ **41**–22, **63**–27
ナイロンストッキング **70**–19
苗木 **129**–2
長いスカート **71**–34
長くする **73**–C
長靴 **66**–19
長さ **15**–16
流し台 **40**–6
長袖シャツ **71**–31
中に **13**–5
中庭 **37**–18
泣く **32**–C
投げる **156**–D
なし **50**–6
なす **51**–18
ナチョス **60**–10
夏 **19**–38
夏時間 **17**–33
ナッツ **50**–23
ナット (留めねじ) **150**–31
ナツメヤシの実 **50**–25
ナプキン **41**–19, **63**–23
鍋 **40**–16, **59**–6
なべつかみ **59**–29
名前を活字体で書く **4**–C
名前をつづる **4**–A
生ごみ処理機 **40**–5
鯰 (なまず) **53**–17
生の鶏肉 **52**–24
波 **155**–6
納屋 **148**–11
なわとびの縄 **153**–5
南極大陸 **125**–7
軟こう **81**–24
南西部 **123**–12
難聴の **22**–27
南東部 **123**–13
ナンバープレート **108**–15
南部 **123**–13
南部台地 **123**–17
南北戦争 **115**
二 **14**
臭いをかぐ **75**–C
2階 **36**–2
2月 **19**–26
肉切り用ナイフ **59**–12
肉と鳥肉売り場 **54**–2
肉屋 **136**–11
肉類 **52**
西海岸 **123**–7

2時 5分前 **16**–15
2時 15分前 **16**–13
2時 10分前 **16**–14
2時 25分前 **16**–11
2時 20分前 **16**–12
二十 **14**
二十一 **14**
25セント **20**–4
20ドル **20**–10
二重鍋 **59**–8
二十二 **14**
二十番 **14**
20パーセント **15**–8
二段ベッド **45**–1
日常会話 **8**
日常生活 **26**–27
日曜日 **18**–1
ニッケル **20**–2
日光浴をしている人 **155**–17
ニットシャツ **65**–20
荷積みドック **146**–16
二番 **14**
2分の１ **15**–4
日本人 **115**
日本人収容 **114**
荷物を預ける **111**–B
荷物を受け取る **111**–P
荷物を解く **35**–E
ニューイングランド地方 **123**–11
入学する **28**–B
乳牛 **133**–3
入植者 **114**
入植者及び自由黒人 **115**
ニュース **167**–17
乳製品売り場 **54**–9
ニューファウンドランド時間 **17**–31
ニレ **128**–17
庭 **39**
庭師 **137**–26, **152**–6
(鶏の) 砂嚢 **52**–23
鶏の骨付脚肉 **52**–22
人形 **45**–18
人形劇 **152**–14
人形作りキット **162**–15
人参 **51**–3
妊娠している **22**–19
人参の皮をむく **58**–N
人参をうす切りにする **58**–O
にんにく **51**–29
ニンニク圧搾器 **59**–10
妊婦服 **65**–19
ぬいぐるみ **45**–23
縫い目 **73**–11
布おむつ **95**–21
ぬりえ **45**–20
濡れたTシャツ **72**–17
ぬれモップ **47**–16
根 **128**–5, **129**–3
願い事をする **169**–J
ネールサロン **91**–25
ねぎ **51**–17
ネクタイ **69**–10
猫 **133**–9
ねじまわし **150**–25
ねずみ **49**–27
ネズミ **133**–18

ネズミイルカ **131**–31
値段 **21**–6
熱 **78**–8
ネックレス **69**–9
熱帯雨林 **117**–1
熱波 **10**–15
熱をはかる **85**–C
寝袋 **154**–12
値札 **21**–1
寝間着 **67**–9
眠い **30**–3
眠る **27**–Y
練歯みがき1つ **56**–24
寝る **27**–X
粘土 **162**–14
燃料計 **108**–22
燃料タンク **108**–12
燃料噴射装置 **109**–40
年齢、体の特徴 **22**
脳 **75**–35
農園労働者 **148**–8
脳がん **79**–12
農耕機具 **148**–10
農耕と牧畜 **148**
農場 **34**–13
農場主 **148**–15
農場の動物 **133**
農場労働者 **148**–20
納税する **116**–E
農薬汚染 **126**–14
ノート **3**–24
ノートパッド **143**–36
のこぎり **150**–4
のぞき穴 **37**–27
喉 **75**–36
のど飴 **81**–21
のどが渇いた **30**–2
のどがつまる **82**–L
のどの炎症 **78**–6
喉を見る **85**–E
伸ばす **157**–Q
のみ **49**–23, **151**–51
のみの市 **152**–22
飲む **60**–B
のり **162**–8
糊 **143**–37
乗り換え **104**–6
乗り物 **152**–17
乗る **157**–W
刃 **150**–11
葉 **128**–6, **129**–5
歯 **74**–25
バーコード **21**–4
バージニアで最初のアフリカ人
　奴隷売買 **114**
バージニアでの最初のインディ
　アン居留地 **114**
バージニアに最初のイギリス人 **114**
パーセント **15**
パーティー **169**
パーティを計画する **169**–A
ハート **163**–29, **168**–6
ハードウェア **144**
ハードディスクドライブ **144**–20
パートナーを手伝う **6**–J
バーナー **40**–19

バーベキュー **58**–T
バーベキューグリル **39**–7
パーマをかける **23**–B
パール (の鎖) **69**–30
肺 **75**–37
パイ **61**–21
灰色 **12**–5
ハイウエイへ **105**–6
ハイウエイを出る **105**–7
ハイエナ **135**–31
配管工 **49**–20
ハイキング (登山用) ブーツ **68**–21
ハイキングをする **154**–6
歯医者 **137**–20
陪審員 **99**–8
陪審員をつとめる **116**–G
排水口 **43**–4
ハイソックス **67**–25
歯痛 **78**–2
配達証明郵便 **96**–11
配達する **96**–C
配達人 **137**–18
ハイチ島人 **115**
パイナップル **50**–2
ハイヒール **68**–17
ハイビスカス **129**–12
パイプ **151**–16
パイプレンチ **151**–42
ハイムリッヒ法 **83**–18
売薬 **80**–12
俳優 **136**–2
パイ用焼き型 **59**–28
パイロット **110**–12
バインダー **3**–24
ハエ **132**–29
ハガキ **96**–3
ハガキに宛名を書く **96**–A
吐き気がする **78**–D
歯茎 **74**–24
拍手する **32**–B
白髪 **23**–13
爆発 **102**–4
はげ **23**–12
バケツ **47**–20, **155**–22
箱 **56**–6
はさみ **23**–19
はさみ (1丁) **73**–18
はしか **79**–5
はしご **149**–2
橋の上 **105**–2
橋の下 **105**–1
パジャマ **67**–4
走る **156**–C
バス **90**–15, **104**–4, **120**–10
バス、スズキ **130**–11
バスーン **120**–6
恥ずかしい **31**–25
バスケット **42**–2
バスケットボール **158**–8, **161**–4
バスケットボールコート **158**–7
パスする **156**–H
パスタ **61**–15
バスタオル **43**–12
パスタサラダ **53**–15
バス停 **104**–1
バス停留所 **91**–16

バスに乗って学校に行く **26**–H
バスの運転手 **104**–8
パスポート **29**–9
バスマット **43**–27
パズル **45**–22
バスローブ **67**–8
パセリ **51**–10
旗 **168**–9
バター **54**–36
パターン **73**–8
はたき **47**–1
畑 **148**–7
働く **26**–K
八 **14**
8月 **19**–32
八十 **14**
ハチドリ **132**–11
八番 **14**
8分の1 **15**–1
は虫類 **131**
ハツカダイコン **51**–5
ハツカネズミ **49**–26, **133**–17
バックサポーター **147**–16
バックパック **69**–28, **154**–15
バックパックを背負って歩く **154**–7
バックホー **149**–8
バックミラー **108**–1
パッケージ **56**–8
発信音を聞く **9**–B
バッタ **132**–25
発着便表示モニター **110**–4
バッテリー **109**–43
バッテリーチャージャー **165**–23
バッテリーパック **165**–22
パッド **45**–7
初の音声映画 **114**
初の原爆投下 **114**
「ハッピーバースディ」を歌う **169**–I
初飛行 **114**
ハト **132**–16
花 **39**–19, **129**, **129**–7
鼻 **74**–21
花柄 **70**–12
鼻血 **78**–17
鼻づまり **78**–7
バナナ **50**–3
鼻のスプレー **81**–23
花火 **168**–8
花びら **129**–8
ハナミズキ **128**–16
花屋 **92**–12, **137**–25
歯に穴を開ける **85**–K
歯にフロスをかける **77**–K
羽 **132**–5
歯のクリーニングを行う **85**–I
母 **24**–5
幅 **15**–17
パパイヤ **50**–20
幅を詰める **73**–E
幅を広げる **73**–F
ハブキャップ **108**–9
歯ブラシ **43**–20, **77**–20
歯ブラシ立て **43**–21
ハマグリ **53**–38
浜辺 **117**–10
歯磨粉 **77**–21

ハム **52**–9
早い **17**–22
早送りする **165**–C
速く運転する人 **11**–3
腹 **74**–3
バラ **129**–15
針 **73**–22, **134**–23
針金 **151**–13
ハリケーン **103**–12
針治療を受ける **81**–G
針山 **73**–15
春 **19**–37
バルコニー **37**–17
晴れ **10**–6
バレー **166**–7
パレード **168**–2
バレーパーキング **145**–1
バレーボール **158**–14, **161**–3
腫れた指 **78**–16
バレンタインデー **168**–4
ハロウィーン **168**–10
ハワイ・アリューシャン時間 **17**–24
歯を抜く **85**–M
歯を磨く **77**–J
パン **54**–6, **54**–29, **55**–13
パン1個 **56**–22
ハンガー **72**–11
ハンカチ **69**–42
ハンガリー人 **115**
半径 **118**–16
判決をくだす **99**–E
犯罪 **100**
盤上ゲーム **162**–3
帆船 **155**–4
ばんそうこう **83**–3
半袖シャツ **71**–30
パンダ **135**–41
パンツ **67**–17
パンティーストッキング **67**–27
半島 **117**–7
ハンドタオル **43**–13
パンとバター用の皿 **63**–16
ハンドバック **69**–6
ハンドル **108**–26
バンパー **108**–7
ハンバーガー **60**–1
販売員 **68**–1, **139**–50
パンプス **68**–16
半分 **15**–4
ハンモック **39**–2
パン屋 **89**–16, **136**–8
パン用のバスケット **63**–8
火 **42**–10
日 **4**–16, **18**–10
ピアス **69**–37
ピアノ **120**–16
ビーカー **119**–13
ビーズ **69**–32
ヒーター **108**–29
ビーチタオル **155**–15
ビーチチェアー **155**–14
ビーチパラソル **155**–9
ヒーティングパッド
　(電気毛布など) **80**–3
ビート **51**–6
ビーバー **134**–9

ピーマン **51**–7
日陰 **155**–12
ヒキガエル **130**–28
引き算 **118**–2
引き出し **40**–23, **44**–3
(ビキニ型)パンティー **67**–16
挽肉 **52**–4
低いヒール **71**–46
ピクニック **153**–D
ピクニックテーブル **153**–8
ピクニックをする **153**–D
ひげ **134**–18
悲劇 **166**–11
髭を剃る **77**–M
飛行機 **110**–9
飛行機事故 **102**–3
被告側の弁護士 **99**–4
被告人 **99**–5
膝 **74**–17
ピザ **60**–7
膝丈ソックス **67**–24
肘 **74**–15
ひじかけ椅子 **42**–24
ビジネスウーマン **136**–10
ビジネスマン **136**–10
秘書 **136**–3, **139**–52, **142**–3
非常口 **36**–7, **37**–23
非常口を確認する **111**–J
非常時のガイドを見る **111**–K
微積分学 **118**–28
ひたい **74**–20
ビタミン剤 **81**–19
左側に **13**–1
左にまがる **107**–C
「びっくりー」と叫ぶ **169**–G
日付 **18**–14
引越し業者 **138**–40
引っ越しする **29**–P, **35**–D
羊 **133**–7
ひづめ **134**–17
ビデオカメラ **165**–19
ビデオゲーム機 **162**–1
ビデオテープ **98**–13, **164**–10
ビデオ屋 **93**–15
尾灯 **108**–14
ヒトデ **130**–15
1箱のシリアル **56**–18
1瓶のジャム **56**–14
1袋の小麦粉 **56**–19
1巻の糸 **73**–17
一人分の食器 **63**–14
人を管理する **140**–K
避難所 **34**–10
ヒヒ **135**–32
備品キャビネット **142**–13
皮膚 **75**–51
ヒマワリ **129**–10
百 **14**
百一 **14**
100ドル **20**–12
100パーセント **15**–11
180パーセント **15**–10
百万 **14**
日焼け **78**–14
日焼け止め **76**–6, **155**–13
日焼け止めをぬる **76**–D

百科事典 **98**–18
ヒューズの箱 **48**–13
ピューマ **135**–39
ビュッフェ **33**–13
ヒョウ **135**–25, **135**–39
雹 **10**–19
秒 **16**–1
病院 **86**–87, **88**–7
病院の職員 **86**
病院のベッド **86**–11
標識 **107**
病室 **86**
標準時 **17**–32
標的 **161**–8
氷嚢 **83**–13
雹の大降り **10**–18
漂白剤 **72**–8
平鍋 **40**–24
ピラフ **61**–18
ヒラメ **130**–13
ピリオド **113**–6
ビリヤード **159**–2
昼寝する **94**–L
ひれ **130**–1, **155**–2
瓶 **56**–2, **73**–14
ピンク **12**–10
ピンセット **83**–2
瓶の返却口 **54**–1
ピンぼけ **165**–33
ピンポン **159**–13
ファーストフード **60**
ファーストフードレストラン **90**–14
ファイルキャビネット **142**–10
ファイルホルダー **142**–11
ファクシミリ **143**–23
ファスナー **73**–16
ファン **158**–4
ファンデーション **77**–40
フィードバックを受ける **113**–C
フィールド **5**–12
フィギュアスケート **160**–5
VCR/ビデオテープレコーダー **164**–8
フィッテッドシーツ **44**–14
Vネックのセーター **71**–27
フィリピン人 **115**
フィルム **165**–26
ブーケ、花束 **129**–27
ブース **60**–19, **152**–23
封筒 **96**–1, **143**–20, **143**–32
フード付き上着 **66**–8
フードプロセッサー **40**–26
風力 **126**–2
プール **37**–16, **145**–16
プールサービス **145**–17
フェリー **104**–23
プエルトリコ人 **114**
フェンシング **159**–5
フォーク **41**–21
フォークリフト **146**–14
フォード第一号車 **114**
フォトボールヘルメット **161**–20
不快な **30**–8
不快な眺め **11**–22
深さ **15**–15
ふき取りペーパー **95**–17
布巾 **47**–22

副大統領 **116**–7
服にアイロンをかける **72**–G
ふくらはぎ **74**–18
福利厚生についてたずねる **141**–J
袋 **56**–7, **135**–50
フクロウ **132**–6
袋詰め係 **55**–21
フクロネズミ **134**–4
服を着せる **94**–J
服を着る **26**–D
服を縫う **140**–I
服をハンガーにかける **72**–H
腐食性 **147**–4
(婦人用) 仕立て屋 **73**–2
付箋紙 **143**–34
蓋 **59**–24
ブタ **133**–8
豚肉 **52**
豚肉の厚切り **52**–10
二人で学習する **6**
二人用ソファー **42**–25
普段着 **71**–37
縁石 **90**–10
不注意な **147**–23
普通預金口座番号 **97**–6
フック **150**–34
フットボール **158**–11, **161**–22
物理学 **119**–3
太いネクタイ **71**–44
埠頭 **155**–16
ぶどう **50**–1
武道 **159**–10
ブドウ園 **148**–14
不動産業者と話す **35**–G
舞踏場 **145**–20
ブドウの木 **128**–22
太っている **22**–20
フナクイムシ **130**–22
部品 **146**–7
部品を組み立てる **140**–A
吹雪 **10**–20
不法の薬物 **100**–4
不満な **31**–28
踏切 **107**–11
冬 **19**–40
プライオリティメール **96**–12
フライ返し **59**–19
フライドポテト **60**–2
フライパン **59**–5
フライパンに油をひく **58**–C
フライパンに卵を流し込む **58**–D
ブラインド **44**–6
ブラウス **64**–9
プラグ **164**–18
ブラシ **23**–18, **76**–14
ブラジャー **67**–20
ブラシをかける **76**–I
プラスチック保存容器 **59**–3
プラスのねじまわし **150**–26
フラットシーツ **44**–13
プラットホーム **104**–15
プラム **50**–8
ブランコ **153**–12
ブランコを押す **153**–B
プランジャー **151**–44

フランス、スペイン、イギリスの探検家 **114**
ブリーチ **72**–8
ブリーフ型ショーツ **67**–13
フリスビー **159**–6, **161**–27
プリズム **119**–20
フリッパー **155**–2
ブリティッシュコロンビア **123**–2
プリン **61**–20
プリンタ **144**–12
プリント柄 **70**–10
古い靴 **71**–33
フルート **120**–3
ブルーベリー **50**–19
プルーン **50**–26
ブルドーザー **149**–6
ブレーキペダル **109**–46
ブレーキライト **108**–13
プレーリー諸州 **123**–3
プレーリードッグ **133**–22
ブレスレット **69**–35
プレゼントを開ける **169**–L
触れる **75**–E
フレンチ・インディアン戦争 **115**
フレンチホルン **120**–15
フロアランプ **42**–15
ブロイラー **40**–21
ブローアー **39**–4
フローズンヨーグルト **60**–11
ブローチ **69**–36
プログラム **144**–21
ブロック **107**–2
ブロッコリー **51**–15
ブロッコリーを蒸す **58**–I
フロッピー **144**–5
風呂にはいる **76**–B
フロント **145**–8
フロント係 **145**–9
フロントグラス **108**–2
分 **16**–2
文 **113**–4
分子 **119**–18
噴水 **92**–11
噴水式水飲み場 **153**–11
分数 **15**
ブンゼンバーナー **119**–9
文を書き取り用に口述する **6**–N
ヘアースプレー **76**–12
ヘアネット **147**–18
平均身長 **22**–17
平均体重 **22**–21
平行線 **118**–21
米国郵便 **96**
平日 **18**–12
米西戦争 **115**
米墨戦争 **114**
平野 **117**–19
ベークドポテト **61**–14
ベーコン **52**–11, **61**–7
ベージュ **12**–9
ベースボールカード **162**–11
ペーズリー柄 **70**–13
ペーパータオル **40**–2
ペーパータオル1巻 **56**–23
ベスト **65**–24
ペチコート **67**–23

ベッド **44**–8
ペット **133**
ベッドカバー **44**–11
ベッドサイドテーブル **44**–21
ペットショップ **92**–6
ベッドで安静にする **80**–A
ベッドテーブル **86**–9
ベッド調整 **86**–12
ペットフード **54**–10
ヘッドボード **44**–15
ペットボトル水 **55**–53
ヘッドホン **164**–16
ヘッドホンステレオ **164**–15
ヘッドライト **108**–5
ベッド枠 **44**–27
ベッドを整える **46**–G
別の言語を話す **140**–J
ペトリ皿 **119**–6
ペニー **20**–1
ベニヤ板 **149**–16
ベビーカー **94**–2
ベビーキャリヤー **95**–14
ベビーサークル **95**–11
ベビーシッター **136**–12
ベビーパウダー **95**–18
ベビーバックパック **95**–15
ベビーフード **95**–28
ベビーベッド **45**–6
ベビーモニター **45**–9
ベリー **128**–20
ヘリコプター **110**–8
ベルキャプテン **145**–4
ヘルスクラブ **89**–21
ヘルスケア **80**–81
ベルト **69**–11
ベルトコンベヤー **146**–12
ベルトのバックル **69**–41
ヘルメット **147**–19
ペン **3**–18
便器 **43**–17, **86**–13
ペンキ **151**–20
ペンキ入れ **151**–45
便器が詰まっている **49**–18
ペンキはけ **151**–47
ペンキローラー **151**–46
ペンキを塗る **149**–A
ペンギン **132**–12
弁護士 **138**–36
弁護士を雇う **99**–B
変速装置 **108**–27
ベンチ **153**–10
ベンチ **5**–5
ペンチ **150**–7
返品する **21**–F
保安帽 **147**–19
保育園、幼稚園 **112**–4
ポイズンオーク
　(触れるとかぶれる) **128**–23
ポイズンスマク
　(触れるとかぶれる) **128**–24
ポインセチア **129**–23
望遠鏡 **127**–21
防寒用耳あて **66**–12
ほうき **47**–10
冒険もの **166**–13
方向 **107**

暴行 **100**–7
膀胱 **75**–47
方向指示灯 **108**–4, **108**–18
方向と交通標識 **107**
防護ゴーグル **147**–9
防護バイザー **147**–11
防護ベスト **147**–15
防護耳おおい **147**–14
防護めがね **147**–10
帽子 **32**–3, **66**–1, **68**–5
放射性 **147**–6
放射線医 **86**–5
放射能 **126**–13
宝石店 **92**–2
宝石類 **69**–8
法廷 **99**–7
法廷記者 **99**–12
防毒マスク **147**–12
棒によじ登る **153**–C
法律 **99**
法律家 **138**–36
法律に従う **116**–H
暴力団乱暴行為 **100**–2
ほうれんそう **51**–11
ホース **39**–9
ポーチの電灯 **38**–9
ポート **144**–17
ボートを漕ぐ **154**–2
ほお紅 **77**–36
ホームシックにかかった **31**–21
ホームヘルパー **137**–31
ボーリング **159**–3
ボーリングのボール **161**–5
ボール **41**–25, **45**–16, **59**–31
(ボールを) 投げる **156**–F
北欧人が開拓した大西洋沿
　岸の植民地 **114**
牧場 **34**–12
牧場主 **148**–22
牧場労働者 **148**–22
ポケット **73**–4
ポケットベル **9**–16
保険請求用紙 **84**–5
歩行器 **80**–5, **95**–12
歩行者 **90**–7
誇りに思って **31**–22
ほこり払いモップ **47**–17
星 **127**–23
干し草 **148**–18
保持する **21**–E
細い **22**–22
細いネクタイ **71**–45
ホタテ貝 **53**–25
ホタテガイ **130**–18
ボタン **73**–21
ボタンホール **73**–12
ホチキス **143**–28
ホチキスでとめる **142**–G
ホチキスの針 **143**–29
補聴器 **81**–33
ホック **73**–23
ボックス型ショーツ **67**–12
ボックススプリング **44**–26
ホッケースティック **161**–11
ホットケーキ **61**–6
ホットドッグ **60**–6

ほつれ **70**–23
ボディーローション **76**–7
ポテトサラダ **53**–13
ポテトチップ **55**–40
ホテル **88**–5, **145**
歩道 **91**–26
ボトル **56**–1
ほ乳びん **95**–26
(ほ乳びんの) 乳首 **95**–27
哺乳類 **134**–135
骨 **75**–49
骨付のあばら肉 **52**–5
ボビーピン **76**–19
ホラー **166**–14
ボランティア **87**–19
ポリ袋 **55**–23
ボルト **150**–30
ホワイトハウス **116**–5
盆 **41**–10
本日のスープ **61**–10
本棚 **3**–8, **42**–1
ポンチョ **66**–18
ボンネット **108**–6
本部 **146**–1
本屋 **92**–4
翻訳家 **138**–34
本を一緒に使う **6**–I
本を閉じる **2**–J
本を開く **2**–I
マーガリン **54**–39
マイクロカセットトランス
　クライバー **142**–4
マイクロフィルム **98**–5
マイクロフィルム読み取り機 **98**–4
マイクロホン **164**–4
迷子 **102**–1
毎日 **18**–21
マウス **144**–8
マウンテンバイクに乗る **154**–8
前髪 **23**–8
前に **13**–4
前庭 **38**–15
前道 **38**–14
曲がり角 **91**–17
まき **42**–12
巻貝 **130**–24
巻き戻しする **165**–D
巻毛 **23**–11
巻き尺 **73**–13, **150**–22
マグカップ **41**–28
枕 **44**–9
枕カバー **44**–10
マグロ **130**–9
曲げる **157**–R
孫が生まれる **29**–Q
マザーボード **144**–18
マジック (ペン) **3**–19
まじめな本 **167**–26
鱒 (ます) **53**–16
麻酔専門医 **87**–35
麻酔をうつ **85**–J
マスカラ **77**–38
マスキングテープ **151**–49
マタニティ用品店 **93**–17
街 **88**–89
待合室 **84**–1

間違いを正す 7–Z
マツ **128**–10
松傘 **128**–11
まつげ **74**–34
マッシュポテト **61**–11
マッシュルーム **51**–26
まっすぐ行く **107**–A
マッチ **154**–21
マットレス **44**–25
まつば杖 **80**–1
まつぼっくり **128**–11
窓 **38**–17, **42**–17
窓ガラス **149**–15
窓が割れている **48**–5
間取り **38**–1
窓を洗う **46**–D
まな板 **40**–27
マニキュア液 **77**–31
マニキュアおとし **77**–32
まねをする **163**–G
マフィン **60**–14
まぶた **74**–33
マフラー **108**–11
豆 (の缶) **54**–26
眉毛 **74**–32
眉墨 **77**–33
真夜中 **17**–21
マヨネーズ **60**–25
マリーゴールド **129**–13
丸首のセーター **71**–26
丸のこ **150**–10
漫画 **167**–19
満月 **127**–16
マンゴ **50**–21
万力 **150**–21
三日月 **127**–14
みかん **50**–13
幹 **128**–4
ミキサー **40**–12
右側に **13**–2
右にまがる **107**–B
短いスカート **71**–35
短くする **73**–D
ミシン **73**–10
ミシンで縫う **73**–B
水 **43**–7, **155**–1
水1オンス **57**–1
水色 **12**–3
湖 **117**–13
ミズーリ妥協 **114**
水着 **66**–26
水切りかご **40**–3
水きり器 **59**–17
水玉模様 **70**–8
ミステリー **166**–15
水ぶくれ **78**–15
水ぼうそう **79**–6
水を入れるコップ **63**–19
水を節約する **126**–B
水を注ぐ **62**–C
みだしなみ **76**–77
道 **90**–9
道を渡る **90**–A
三つ揃え **64**–1
ミツバチ **132**–26
緑色 **12**–8

ミドルネーム **4**–3
ミトン **66**–9
南アメリカ **124**–2
ミニバン **106**–10
(ミニ) ブラインド **43**–11
耳 **74**–28
耳が聞こえない **22**–27
耳栓 **147**–13
耳の痛み **78**–3
耳の感染 **79**–3
ミュージシャン **138**–41
見る **75**–A
ミルク **54**–35
ミルクシェイク **60**–12
(Min と Luの) 孫 **24**–7
ムース **134**–1
ムール貝 **53**–26
迎えに行く **94**–G
麦わら帽子 **66**–23
無菌ガーゼ **83**–4
蒸し暑い **10**–12
蒸し器 **59**–4
虫さされ **78**–11
無地の緑 **70**–6
無地のブラウス **71**–38
虫歯 **84**–20
虫歯を埋める **85**–L
虫避けスプレー **154**–23
難しい問題 **11**–24
息子 **24**–22
娘 **24**–21
胸 **74**–13
胸肉 **52**–19
ムラサキイガイ **130**–17
紫色 **12**–7
目 **74**–27
姪 **24**–17
冥王星 **127**–1
メーター **104**–21
メカジキ **130**–12
眼鏡 **81**–35
眼鏡店 **92**–8
目が見えない **22**–26
メキシコ高原 **123**–15
メキシコ人 **114**
メキシコの各地方 **123**
目薬 **81**–22
メッセージ **138**–38
メッセンジャー **145**–5
メディアセクション **98**–11
メニュー **62**–3
メニューで注文をする **62**–D
目の検査を行う **85**–F
めまいがする **78**–C
目盛付シリンダー **119**–10
メロドラマ **167**–21
メロン **50**–15
目を覚ます **26**–A
面接に行く **141**–H
雌鶏 **133**–5
綿のティーシャツ **70**–16
麺棒 **59**–30
モイスチャライザー **76**–8
申込書に記入する **141**–G
毛布 **44**–12, **67**–7
毛布を頼む **111**–M

モーテル **89**–22
モービルホーム **34**–8
目撃者 **99**–11
木星 **127**–5
木曜日 **18**–5
モクレン属の花木 **128**–9
模型を組み立てる **162**–C
文字を線で消す **7**–U
モスク **89**–23
持ち込み荷物をしまう **111**–H
持ち主となる **35**–J
木琴 **120**–17
木工キット **162**–16
モデム **144**–11
モデル **138**–39
モデルキット **162**–7
モニター **144**–6
物置 **36**–14
物語を読む **94**–F
もの差し **151**–15
物の描写 **11**
物干し綱 **72**–9
ものを集める **162**–A
モビール **45**–4
もみあげ **23**–7
もも **50**–5
もも肉 **52**–21
モルモット **133**–14
問題 **70**
矢 **161**–7
夜会服 **65**–29
やかん **40**–17
ヤギ **133**–1
焼菓子製品 **54**–6
焼菓子の材料 **55**–13
野球 **158**–9
ヤギュウ **134**–6
野球の試合 **152**–25
野球のバット **161**–14
野球のボール **161**–18
野球帽 **66**–6, **66**–27
薬剤師 **80**–10
約束 **19**–45
薬品用トレイ **87**–23
薬味 **60**–26
火傷をする **82**–H
野菜 **51**
野菜サラダ **60**–8
野菜のオーブン焼 **58**
野菜の皮剥き器 **59**–15
野菜を加える **58**–Q
ヤシ **128**–15
安い指輪 **11**–20
やせた **22**–22
屋台 **91**–30
家賃を払う **35**–F
薬局 **80**–9, **90**–2
やっとこ **150**–7
ヤナギ **128**–14
家主 **37**–32
屋根 **38**–20
屋根板 **149**–19
屋根から雨漏りがする **48**–3
屋根の修理屋 **48**–8
破れ **70**–23
ヤマアラシ **134**–10

ヤムイモ **51**–22
柔らかい椅子 **11**–6
遊園地 **152**–13
夕方 **17**–19
ユーザーマニュアル **144**–22
有罪を宣告する **99**–14
夕食を食べる **27**–R
夕食を作る **27**–P
友人に相談する **141**–A
郵送する **96**–B
郵送用パッケージ **143**–32
UターンOK **107**–7
有毒 **147**–3
郵便受け **37**–36, **38**–4
郵便局 **89**–29
郵便局員 **138**–45
郵便集配人 **96**–6
郵便ポスト **90**–12
郵便番号 **4**–9
郵便料金 **96**–10
郵便料金メーター **143**–16
床 **44**–24
ユカタン半島 **123**–19
床を掃く **46**–E
床をみがく **46**–L
床をモップでふく **46**–J
雪 **10**–9
行方不明のボタン **70**–25
ユダヤ教会 **88**–9
ゆっくり運転する人 **11**–4
ユニフォーム **161**–16
指 **75**–57
指ぬき **73**–20
指輪 **69**–39
弓 **161**–6
弓のこ **150**–5
揺らす **94**–H
ユリ **129**–24
ゆりかご **45**–19
ゆるい **71**–42
揺れを感じる **111**–N
良い犬 **11**–17
容器 **56**–5
容疑者を逮捕する **99**–A
容器とパッケージ食品 **56**
要件を書き写す **142**–C
幼児 **22**–3
用紙に記入する **4**–B
幼児用整理棚 **94**–4
用紙を集める **7**–Q
用紙を配る **7**–O
溶接工 **139**–63
腰痛 **78**–5
曜日 **18**
用務員 **138**–35
ヨーグルト **54**–33
ヨーグルト1パイント **57**–3
ヨーロッパ **125**–3
ヨーロッパコマドリ **132**–17
預金する **97**–C
預金伝票 **97**–12
翌日配達郵便 **96**–15
浴槽 **43**–2
よく混ぜる **58**–B
汚れたおむつ入れ **45**–13
汚れたTシャツ **72**–15

よだれ掛け **95**–8
ヨット **155**–4
予備タイヤ **109**–53
呼び出しボタン **86**–10
呼び鈴 **38**–10
予約 **19**–45
予約をとる **85**–A
夜 **17**–20
4階 **36**–4
四番 **14**
4分の1 **15**–2
4分の3 **15**–5
ライオン **135**–36
来週 **18**–20
ライター **108**–32, **139**–64
ライム **50**–12
ライ麦パン **53**–3
ライン管理者 **146**–5
ラクダ **135**–38
ラグレンチ **109**–50
ラケットボール **159**–11
ラジエーター **109**–42
ラジオ **108**–31
ラジオ時計 **44**–16
ラジオ番組 **166**–4
ラジカセ **164**–2
ラズベリー **50**–18
らせんノート **3**–26
ラッコ **131**–35
ラップトップ **144**–14
ラブシート **42**–25
ラベル **143**–35
ラマ **135**–26
ラン **129**–17
ランチョンマット **41**–20
ランプ **44**–17
ランプの笠 **44**–18
リーガルパッド **143**–18
理学療法士 **81**–30
陸上競技 **159**–17
リサイクル品入れ **47**–2
リス **133**–21
リストについて話し合う **6**–L
立方体 **118**–10
リポーター **139**–49
リモコン (リモートコントロール) **164**–9
流感 **79**–2
料金 **104**–5
料金カード **104**–12
漁師 **136**–15
領収書 **21**–5
両親 **24**–4
両生類 **130**
料理 **58**
料理する **140**–C
料理を出す **62**–F
旅行案内業者 **139**–60
旅行者小切手 **20**–17
旅行社社員 **139**–60
旅行する **29**–N
旅行代理店 **92**–9
離陸 **111**–L
リンカーン暗殺 **115**
りんご **50**–4
りんごジュース **55**–50
りんごジュース1ガロン **57**–5

ルイジアナを購入 **114**
ルーズリーフ **3**–25
ルート **104**–2
ルームサービス **145**–12
留守番電話 **9**–14
るつぼばさみ **119**–15
冷戦 **114**
冷蔵庫 **40**–9
冷凍庫 **40**–10
冷凍食品 **55**–12
冷凍の魚 **53**–30
冷凍野菜 **55**–43
冷房 **37**–19
レインコート **66**–17
レーズン **50**–27
レーズン1/2カップ **57**–9
レオタード **67**–1
歴史的及び政治的出来事 **114**
レギンズ **65**–23
レコード **98**–15
レジ **55**–18
レシート **21**–5
レジ係 **136**–14
レジ係 **55**–19
レジ台 **55**–17
レジを使う **140**–N
レストラン **62**–63
レストラン街 **93**–14
レスリング **159**–16
レターヘッド紙 **143**–19
レタス **51**–1
レタス **60**–17
列 **55**–20
レッカー車 **106**–13
レバー **52**–7
レフリー **158**–6
レポートの課題 **113**–1
レポートを書き直す **113**–D
レポートを提出する **113**–E
レポートを編集する **113**–B
レモン **50**–11
恋愛もの **166**–16
煉瓦 **149**–11
れんが積み職人 **136**–9
れんがを積む **149**–B
レンジ **40**–18
連続ホームコメディ **167**–18
レンチ **151**–43
連邦最高裁判所長官 **116**–9
廊下 **145**–13
老人 **22**–12
老人ホーム **34**–11
ろうそく **41**–7
ろうそく立て **41**–8
ロウソクに灯をともす **169**–H
ロウソクを吹き消す **169**–K
ろうと **119**–12
ローストチキン **61**–12
ローストビーフ **52**–1, **53**–7
ローストビーフ1ポンド **57**–12
ロープ **154**–19
ローファー **68**–19
ローマ数字 **14**
ロールパン **54**–30
ローンを受ける **35**–I
六 **14**

録音する **165**–A
6月 **19**–30
6才の少年 **22**–4
六十 **14**
六番 **14**
ロケット **69**–33
露光過度の **165**–34
露光不足の **165**–35
路地 **37**–21
ロシア人 **115**
ロッカー **5**–7
ロッキー山脈諸州 **123**–8
ロッキングチェア **94**–6
ロックバンド **120**–2
6本入りのソーダ1パック **56**–21
6本入りのパック **56**–9
ロバ **133**–2
ロビー **145**–3
ロブスター **53**–23
ロングドレス **65**–29
論文 **113**–2
ワークブック **3**–23
ワイパー **108**–3
ワイヤーストリッパー **151**–37
ワイングラス **63**–20
若い **22**–13
惑星 **127**
輪ゴム **143**–45
ワゴンを引っ張る **153**–A
ワシ **132**–10
ワシントン初代大統領 **115**
綿 **148**–6
ワッシャー **150**–32
ワッフル **61**–4
ワニ **131**–36
ワニ **131**–37
笑う **33**–H
割り算 **118**–4
悪い犬 **11**–18
湾 **117**–9
湾岸戦争 **115**
湾岸平野 **123**–16
ワンピース **64**–3